# Blockchain, IoT, and AI Technologies for Supply Chain Management

## Apply Emerging Technologies to Address and Improve Supply Chain Management

Dr. Veena Grover
Dr. B. Balamurugan Balusamy
Dr. Mariofanna Milanova
Dr. A. Yovan Felix

## Blockchain, IoT, and AI Technologies for Supply Chain Management: Apply Emerging Technologies to Address and Improve Supply Chain Management

Dr. Veena Grover
Noida Institute of Engineering and Technology
Faridabad, Haryana, India

Dr. Mariofanna Milanova
Little Rock, AR, USA

Dr. B. Balamurugan Balusamy
Campus Housing, Tower 7
Shiv Nadar University, Flat 754
Tensil Dadri, Uttar Pradesh, India

Dr. A. Yovan Felix
Chennai, Tamil Nadu, India

ISBN-13 (pbk): 979-8-8688-0314-7
https://doi.org/10.1007/979-8-8688-0315-4

ISBN-13 (electronic): 979-8-8688-0315-4

Managing Director, Apress Media LLC: Welmoed Spahr
Acquisitions Editor: Spandana Chatterjee
Development Editor: James Markham
Editorial Assistant: Kripa Joseph
Copy Editor: Mary Behr

Cover designed by eStudioCalamar

Cover image designed by Freepik (www.freepik.com)

Distributed to the book trade worldwide by Springer Science+Business Media New York, 1 New York Plaza, Suite 4600, New York, NY 10004-1562, USA. Phone 1-800-SPRINGER, fax (201) 348-4505, e-mail orders-ny@springer-sbm.com, or visit www.springeronline.com. Apress Media, LLC is a California LLC and the sole member (owner) is Springer Science + Business Media Finance Inc (SSBM Finance Inc). SSBM Finance Inc is a **Delaware** corporation.

For information on translations, please e-mail booktranslations@springernature.com; for reprint, paperback, or audio rights, please e-mail bookpermissions@springernature.com.

Apress titles may be purchased in bulk for academic, corporate, or promotional use. eBook versions and licenses are also available for most titles. For more information, reference our Print and eBook Bulk Sales web page at www.apress.com/bulk-sales.

Any source code or other supplementary material referenced by the author in this book is available to readers on GitHub. For more detailed information, please visit www.apress.com/gp/services/source-code.

If disposing of this product, please recycle the paper

# Table of Contents

# About the Authors

**Dr. Veena Grover** is a Professor in Department of Management at Noida Institute of Engineering & Technology, Greater Noida, India. Her interests include micro finance, sustainability, macro economic variables, supply chain management, and innovation strategy. She has published multiple articles in various journals and presented papers at various conferences. She serves as an Editor of *International Journal of Advanced Trends in Technology, Management & Applied Science* and a reviewer of *International Journal of Applied Behavioural Economics* (IJABE) ISSN: 2160-9802|EISSN: 2160-9810|DOI: 10.4018/IJABE.

**Dr. Balamurugan Balusamy** is currently working as Associate Dean–Student Engagement in Shiv Nadar University, India. He has 15 years of experience in the field of computer science. His areas of interest are Internet of Things, big data, and networking. He has published more than 150 papers and 100 books and contributed multiple book chapters.

**Dr. Mariofanna Milanova** is a Professor in Computer Science at the University of Arkansas at Little Rock, USA. She has 30 years of experience in the field of artificial intelligence. Dr. Milanova has extensive academic experience at various academic and research organizations worldwide. Dr. Milanova is an IEEE Senior Member, Fulbright U.S. Scholar, and NVIDIA Deep Learning Institute University Ambassador. Dr. Milanova's work is supported by NSF, NIH, DARPA, DoD, Homeland Security, and NATO as well as Nokia Bell Lab, NJ, USA and NOKIA, Finland. She has published more than 130 publications, over 53 journal papers, 35 book chapters, and numerous conference papers. She also has two patents.

## ABOUT THE AUTHORS

**Dr. A. Yovan Felix** has mentored students in the project areas of big data, deep learning, and data mining. He has published technical papers in national and international journals. He has over 17 years of experience and expertise in data analytics, smart prediction systems, and deep learning algorithms. He has also coordinated several events at national and international levels.

# About the Technical Reviewer

**Atonu Ghosh** is a Ph.D. research scholar at the Indian Institute of Technology Kharagpur, West Bengal, India. He holds a B.Tech. and an M.Tech. in Computer Science and Engineering from Maulana Abul Kalam Azad University of Technology (MAKAUT), West Bengal, India. IoT, IIoT, and Edge Computing are his domains of research. Atonu has been building IoT solutions for over nine years now. He is an active reviewer for several journals. He welcomes you to connect with him through LinkedIn (https://www.linkedin.com/in/atonughoshcse/) and email (atonughosh@outlook.com).

# Introduction

The book will examine the synergistic possibilities of combining blockchain, IoT, and AI technologies in supply chain management. The current state of supply chain management involves several challenges, including lack of transparency, limited visibility into product movements, inefficient inventory management, and difficulty in tracking and tracing products. Blockchain, IoT, and AI are three emerging technologies that can potentially address some of these challenges and improve supply chain management.

This book will also address the difficulties and possibilities of integrating these technologies and offer helpful implementation advice. Case studies and actual instances of businesses implementing or experimenting with blockchain, IoT, and AI technology in their supply chains will be included in the book. It will provide helpful advice on implementation and highlight successful deployments, lessons learned, and the impact of these technologies on supply chain visibility, agility, sustainability, and customer experience. It will further elaborate the fundamental concepts of AI and ML algorithms and demonstrate how AI can process enormous volumes of supply chain data to produce actionable insights, improve inventory control, forecast demand, and increase forecasting precision.

The book will serve as a comprehensive guide for supply chain professionals, researchers, and technology enthusiasts interested in understanding the potential of blockchain, IoT, and AI technologies in revolutionizing supply chain management practices.

# What You Will Learn

- You will explore the evolving landscape of technology, potential advancements, and how Blockchain, IoT, and AI can shape the future of supply chains.

- You will gain insight into upcoming developments and prepare for changing dynamics in the industry.

- You will learn the intricate details of blockchain, IoT, and AI technologies in real-life scenarios.

- You will explore the convergence of blockchain, IoT, and AI technologies to improve supply chain operations.

# Who Is This Book For

This book is for industry professionals working in the domain of supply chain management including supply chain managers, logistics managers, procurement officers, and operations managers. It's also for academics, research scholars, and university students at the graduate and post-graduate levels who are interested in understanding how these technologies can enhance efficiency, transparency, and optimization in supply chains.

# CHAPTER 1

# Supply Chain Management Strategy and Practices: Traditional vs. Advanced

*Dr. Veena Grover[1], Professor, School of Management, NIET, Greater Noida, India.*

*Ms. Mahima Dogra[2], Assistant Professor, School of Management, NIET, Greater Noida, India.*

*Ms. Divya Sahu[3], Assistant Professor, School of Management, NIET, Greater Noida, India.*

*Dr. Manju Nandal[4], Assistant Professor, Department of Management, Chandigarh University, Mohali, India.*

*Dr. Abhijit Gnaguly[5], Professor, Westford University College, Sharjah, UAE.*

© The Editor(s) (if applicable) and The Author(s),
under exclusive license to APress Media, LLC, part of Springer Nature 2024
Dr. V. Grover et al. (eds.), *Blockchain, IoT, and AI Technologies for Supply Chain Management*,
https://doi.org/10.1007/979-8-8688-0315-4_1

When an abundance of articles and books on the subject emerged in the mid-1990s, the term "supply chain management" (SCM) gained popularity. SCM involves the centralized coordination of the flow of goods and services to and from a business. It encompasses the entirety of the processes required to convert raw materials and components into finalized products. Companies may save costs and deliver items to customers faster and more efficiently by optimizing the supply chain. A well-managed supply chain can assist in avoiding costly product recalls, lawsuits, and negative press by ensuring quality control, selecting reliable suppliers, maintaining transparency, complying with regulations, managing risks, fostering communication, and continuously improving processes. SCM's five most important phases are planning, sourcing, production, distribution, and returns. A supply chain manager is responsible for regulating and reducing expenses as well as avoiding supply shortages.

While traditional supply chains focus on the accessibility, transportation, and cost of physical assets, contemporary supply chains prioritize the administration of data, services, and products packaged as integrated solutions. Contemporary supply chain management systems extend beyond the mere tracking of the location and timing of product deliveries. They play a pivotal role in influencing product and service quality, pricing, customer experience, and, ultimately, the overall profitability of a business. In 2017, a standard supply chain processed 50 times more data than it did just five years earlier. Despite this surge in data, only about a quarter of it has been thoroughly analyzed. As a result, crucial and time-sensitive information such as weather conditions, unexpected labor shortages, political unrest, and sudden spikes in demand might go unexplored, posing potential risks to the supply chain efficiency. Modern supply networks are curated by analytical professionals and data scientists and take advantage of large volumes of data created by the chain process. Future supply chain leaders and the ERP systems they run will almost certainly focus on maximizing the usefulness of this data by analyzing it in real time with minimal latency.

In contrast to supply chain management, a supply chain refers to a network of companies collaborating to transport materials in a directional manner. It represents a collective of organizations intricately connected through upstream and downstream flows of products, services, funds, or information, extending from a source to a client. The administration of such a chain is known as supply chain management (La Londe, B. and Masters, J. M., 2023). Supply chain professionals play pivotal roles in shaping and overseeing supply chain operations. Their responsibilities extend to determining whether a company produces a product or service internally (insourcing) or outsources it to another entity. They orchestrate manufacturing processes across multiple providers, ensuring seamless production and transportation with minimal challenges related to quality control and inventory. The ultimate aim of a well-designed and efficiently managed product supply chain is to achieve the production of goods at the most economical cost possible. Such a well-structured supply network can be viewed as a competitive advantage for a company, as highlighted by Enver Yücesan (2007) and David Blanchard (2007). Companies engage in ongoing efforts to enhance the efficiency and cost-effectiveness of their supply chains, making SCM a continuous and vital undertaking.

SCM aims to centrally control or link a product's manufacturing, shipment, and distribution. Companies can reduce superfluous expenses and unnecessary stages in the supply chain, allowing them to deliver items to customers faster. Achieving this involves exercising more stringent control over internal inventories, internal manufacturing, distribution, sales, and vendor stocks. SCM operates on the principle that nearly every product entering the market is the outcome of collaborative efforts from various organizations within a supply chain. Although supply networks have existed for centuries, most businesses have only recently seen them as a value-add. The following five important components of SCM are commonly referred to by experts and practitioners:

- **Planning:** Develop strategies and oversee the allocation of resources to meet the product or service demand of a company. Establish metrics to assess the efficiency, effectiveness, customer value, and alignment with the organizational goals of the formed supply chain.

- **Sourcing:** Select suppliers to provide the items and services required to manufacture the product. Then, create systems for monitoring and managing supplier relationships. Ordering, receiving, and maintaining inventory and authorizing supplier payments are all critical operations.

- **Manufacturing:** Organize the actions required to accept raw materials, make the product, test for quality, package for shipping, and deliver on time.

- **Logistics and delivery:** Customer orders must be coordinated, delivery must be scheduled, cargo must be dispatched, customers must be invoiced, and payments must be received.

- **Returns:** Establish a system or framework to handle the return of damaged, surplus, or unwanted goods. SCM holds considerable importance in achieving various corporate objectives. For instance, exerting control over manufacturing processes can enhance product quality, mitigate the risk of recalls and legal issues, and contribute to the development of a robust consumer brand. Similarly, managing shipping methods can enhance customer service by averting costly shortages or instances of excess inventory. In essence, SCM provides organizations with multiple avenues to boost profit margins, particularly pertinent for large-scale and global businesses. Within the production cycle, efficient SCM solutions result in reduced costs, waste, and time. The adoption of a just-in-time supply chain, where retail sales automatically trigger replenishment requests to manufacturers, has become an industry standard. This facilitates rapid replenishment of retail shelves, keeping pace with product sales. An additional strategy to enhance this process involves analyzing data from supply chain partners to identify areas for improvement.

# The Concept of SCM

SCM involves overseeing the movement of goods and services to and from a company, encompassing the entire process from converting raw materials and components into finished products to delivering them to the end customer. A well-executed SCM process enables a company to optimize its operations, minimize waste, enhance customer value, and gain a competitive edge in the market. SCM encompasses a comprehensive framework that includes procurement, operations management, logistics, and marketing channels. These elements collectively contribute to the transformation of raw materials into finished products, which are then delivered to end customers (Kozlenkova, Irina; et al., 2015; Ghiani, Gianpaolo; Laporte, Gilbert; Musmanno, Roberto., 2004). A more specific definition of SCM is "the design, planning, execution, control, and monitoring of supply chain activities with the goal of creating net value, building a competitive infrastructure, leveraging global logistics, synchronizing supply with demand, and measuring global performance."

SCM is a pivotal facet of business operations, entailing the orchestration and integration of diverse activities, processes, and stakeholders throughout the entire supply chain. This encompasses activities ranging from the procurement of raw materials to the ultimate delivery of finished products to end consumers. The primary goal of SCM is to optimize the overall efficiency, effectiveness, and responsiveness of the supply chain to meet customer demands while minimizing costs. The following is a list of additional key concepts:

- **Supply chain components**

  - **Upstream:** Involves activities such as sourcing, procurement, and inbound logistics

  - **Internal operations:** Encompasses the processes related to manufacturing, assembly, and quality control

  - **Downstream:** Encompasses distribution, outbound logistics, marketing, sales, and customer service

- **Supplier relationship management:**

  - Fostering strong relationships with suppliers is crucial for a smooth and efficient supply chain.

  - Collaboration, communication, and trust-building are essential elements of SRM.

- **Demand planning and forecasting:**

  - Accurate demand forecasting helps organizations anticipate customer needs and align production and distribution accordingly.

  - Advanced analytics and data-driven insights play a significant role in demand planning.

- **Inventory management:**

  - Balancing the costs of holding inventory against the costs of stockouts is crucial.

  - Just-in-time (JIT) and economic order quantity (EOQ) are common inventory management strategies.

- **Logistics and transportation:**

  - Efficient transportation and logistics ensure timely delivery of products.

  - Mode selection, route optimization, and carrier selection are key considerations.

- **Information flow:**

  - Real-time information sharing is essential for effective decision making.

  - Technologies like enterprise resource planning (ERP) and advanced analytics enhance information flow.

- **Risk management:**

  - Identifying and mitigating risks throughout the supply chain is crucial.

  - External factors like natural disasters, geopolitical events, and supply chain disruptions can impact operations.

- **Sustainability:**

  - Consideration of environmental and social factors in supply chain operations

  - Green and sustainable practices are becoming increasingly important.

- **Globalization and outsourcing:**

  - Many organizations operate on a global scale, necessitating the management of complex international supply chains.

  - Outsourcing certain processes can lead to cost efficiencies but requires careful oversight.

- **Continuous improvement:**

  - Regular evaluation of supply chain performance and implementation of process improvements

  - Lean and Six Sigma principles are often applied for continuous improvement.

Effective SCM can contribute to increased customer satisfaction, reduced costs, improved product quality, and enhanced overall competitiveness in the market. The dynamic nature of markets and technologies requires supply chain professionals to stay adaptable and responsive to changes to maintain a competitive edge.

# Traditional SCM

Conventional SCM pertains to the traditional practices and methodologies historically utilized by businesses to oversee the movement of goods and services from their origin to the point of consumption. While there

have been advancements in technology and methodologies, many
organizations still operate with some aspects of traditional SCM. Here are
key features of traditional SCM: linear and sequential, silos and functional
departments, forecast-driven planning, bulky inventory, long lead times,
manual processes, limited visibility, risk management challenges, limited
use of technology, and less emphasis on collaboration.

Traditional SCM often follows a linear and sequential process where
each stage in the supply chain is viewed as a distinct and separate
function. It typically starts with procurement of raw materials, followed
by manufacturing, distribution, and finally, reaching the end customer.
Each stage of the supply chain is often treated as a separate functional unit,
and departments may operate in isolation. Siloed communication can
lead to inefficiencies and a lack of coordination across different functions.
Forecasting is a crucial element in traditional SCM where companies rely
on historical data and predictions to plan production and distribution.
The focus is on producing large quantities to meet anticipated demand.
Traditional SCM tends to involve holding larger inventories as a buffer
to meet potential demand fluctuations. Warehousing is a significant
aspect of this approach, with large storage spaces used to stockpile
goods. Due to the sequential nature of traditional SCM, lead times can
be long, particularly when sourcing materials from different suppliers
or when relying on a make-to-order production model (an approach
where product is not built until confirmed order for product is received).
Manual processes, paperwork, and human intervention are common in
traditional SCM, leading to potential errors and delays. This can include
manual order processing, inventory tracking, and communication.
Limited real-time visibility into the entire supply chain is a characteristic
of traditional SCM. Companies may lack the tools and technologies to
monitor and respond quickly to changes or disruptions. Traditional
SCM may face challenges in effectively identifying and managing risks,
especially in a global and dynamic business environment. Issues such as

supply chain disruptions or unforeseen demand changes can be harder
to navigate. While some technology is used, it may be limited compared
to more modern approaches. Enterprise resource planning systems may
be in place, but they may not be as integrated or advanced as in more
contemporary supply chain practices. Collaboration between different
partners in the supply chain may be less emphasized in traditional
SCM. Limited information sharing and collaboration with suppliers and
distributors can hinder overall efficiency.

It is worth noting that while traditional SCM has certain limitations,
many organizations are evolving towards more modern and agile supply
chain practices, leveraging advanced technologies, data analytics, and
collaborative platforms to enhance efficiency and responsiveness.
This evolution is often driven by the need to adapt to changing market
dynamics, customer expectations, and global challenges. For a comparison
of traditional supply chain, consider the former as a relatively static entity.
Conventional supply chains operate reactively, relying on guidelines
derived from past transactions. They often rely on isolated systems,
functioning independently with limited data sharing. These supply chains
encompass processes that guide a product from the procurement of raw
materials through production to the final delivery to the end customer. As
a result, the following are the essential components of traditional supply
chains: acquisition of raw materials, manufacturing of raw materials by
converting it to finished products, shipping and distribution, sales, and
consumption.

Traditional supply chains and SCM are solely concerned with
manufacturing and distribution, not with consumer needs. They are also
not optimized and lack the "intelligence" to detect problems along the
value chain as fast as possible. Even when an issue has been recognized,
projecting its likely consequences and determining a solution can take
a significant amount of time and effort. This causes production to be
delayed, introduces errors, and extends time-to-market, all of which can
impact consumer happiness and corporate revenues.

# Advanced SCM

Advanced SCM represents the modern and innovative approaches
that leverage cutting-edge technologies, data analytics, and strategic
methodologies to enhance the efficiency, agility, and overall performance
of supply chain processes. Advanced SCM is a complete and sophisticated
strategy to managing a product's or service's whole lifetime, from raw
material acquisition to final product delivery to the end consumer. This
notion entails leveraging sophisticated technology, data analytics, and
strategic techniques to improve efficiency, save costs, increase customer
happiness, and boost overall competitiveness. Here are some key concepts
and features associated with advanced SCM:

- **End-to-end visibility:** Comprehensive visibility across
  the entire supply chain is a hallmark of advanced
  SCM. Real-time tracking of inventory, shipments, and
  production processes allows for quick responses to
  changes and disruptions.

- **Predictive analytics and forecasting:** Advanced SCM
  utilizes sophisticated predictive analytics models
  to forecast demand more accurately. Predictive
  capabilities help in optimizing inventory levels,
  production schedules, and distribution strategies.

- **Demand-driven planning:** Moving away from
  traditional forecast-driven planning, advanced SCM
  focuses on demand-driven strategies. It emphasizes
  a more dynamic and responsive approach to
  align production and distribution with actual
  customer demand.

- **Collaborative supply chain networks:** Collaboration is a key element, involving seamless communication and coordination between suppliers, manufacturers, distributors, and other partners. Cloud-based platforms facilitate real-time collaboration and information sharing.

- **Agile and flexible supply chains:** Advanced SCM prioritizes flexibility and agility to adapt quickly to changes in demand, supply, or market conditions. Quick responses to disruptions and the ability to reconfigure supply chain processes are critical.

- **E-commerce integration:** With the rise of e-commerce, advanced SCM integrates seamlessly with online sales channels. Order fulfilment, inventory management, and last-mile delivery are optimized for e-commerce demands.

- **Sustainable and ethical practices:** There is an increased focus on sustainability and ethical sourcing in advanced SCM. Companies strive to incorporate environmentally friendly practices and ensure ethical treatment throughout the supply chain.

- **Blockchain for transparency:** Blockchain technology is employed for enhanced transparency and traceability. It helps in tracking the origin of products, ensuring authenticity, and reducing the risk of counterfeiting.

- **Robotic process automation (RPA):** RPA is used to automate routine and repetitive tasks in supply chain operations, such as order processing, invoicing, and data entry. This reduces errors, improves speed, and frees up human resources for more strategic tasks.

- **Customer-centric approach:** Advanced SCM places
  a strong emphasis on meeting customer expectations
  by offering personalized experiences and fast, reliable
  service. Customization and quick response to changing
  customer preferences are prioritized.

- **Continuous improvement and learning:** Continuous
  improvement methodologies, such as Six Sigma and
  lean, are applied to optimize processes continually.
  Learning from data and adapting strategies based on
  insights are integral to advanced SCM.

The adoption of advanced SCM practices is driven by the need for
businesses to stay competitive, responsive, and resilient in a rapidly
changing global market. By embracing innovation and leveraging
advanced technologies, companies can build more adaptive and efficient
supply chains that contribute to overall business success. In summary,
advanced SCM is a holistic and dynamic approach to creating efficient,
adaptable, and customer-centric supply chains that blend sophisticated
technologies, data-driven decision making, and collaborative practices.
This approach is critical for organizations seeking to survive in today's
quickly changing and competitive global business landscape.

# Transitioning from Traditional to Advanced SCM

Transitioning from traditional SCM to advanced SCM involves a strategic
and systematic approach. This transformation is driven by the need
to enhance efficiency, agility, and responsiveness to changing market
dynamics. Traditional SCM is a reactive process that follows rules based on
previous transactions. It is typically based on isolated systems that operate
in silos with little or no data sharing. Digital SCM, on the other hand, is a

dynamic and integrated process that optimizes the supply chain ecosystem
by leveraging sophisticated technologies such as artificial intelligence,
machine learning, and the Internet of Things. Organizations must invest in
solid and dependable SCM systems, procedures, and people to make the
shift from traditional to digital SCM. Digital SCM empowers organizations
to diminish time-to-market, cut costs, enhance product and service
quality, mitigate the risk of recalls and legal issues, elevate customer
experience and satisfaction, fortify brand reputation, and enhance
relationships with all stakeholders, including third parties and customers.
To summarize, organizations must shift from traditional to advanced SCM
to streamline their supply chains and fulfil their major business objectives.

SCM involves a collaborative network of processes, systems, and
entities working together to transform a concept into a finished product
that is ready for the customer. This network encompasses functions
such as procurement, inventory control, manufacturing, distribution,
logistics, shipping, vendor and distributor management, and information
technology. When executed proficiently, SCM unifies materials, product
development, finance, facilities, technology, third-party collaborations,
and customer interactions into a seamless, centralized system. A
successfully implemented SCM strategy enables organizations to elevate
the quality of products and services, mitigate risks associated with
recalls and legal matters, enhance customer experience and satisfaction,
bolster brand reputation, and cultivate improved relationships with all
stakeholders, including third-party entities and customers.

Organizations are moving from traditional supply chains to digital
supply chains as technology progresses and profit constraints increase.
While each has benefits and drawbacks, the advantages of digital SCM
continue to improve and expand. Traditional supply networks are reactive,
with rules based on previous transactions. They typically rely on stand-
alone systems that operate in silos with little or no data sharing. These

supply chains involve processes that take a product from raw material purchase to production and delivery to the ultimate client. Thus, typical supply chains' major aspects include raw material acquisition, raw material to production, manufacturing, distribution and shipping, sales, and consumption.

Traditional supply chains and SCM are solely concerned with manufacturing and distribution, not with consumer needs. They are also not optimized and lack the "intelligence" to detect problems along the value chain as fast as possible. Even when an issue has been recognized, projecting its likely consequences and determining a solution can take a significant amount of time and effort. This causes production to be delayed, introduces errors, and extends time-to-market, all of which can impact consumer happiness and corporate revenues. Other significant shortcomings of traditional supply networks include:

- Lack of visibility and transparency

- Inability to respond to changes in real time

- Inability to manage risk effectively

- Inability to optimize inventory levels

- Inability to collaborate with suppliers and partners

On the other hand, digital supply chains are proactive, data-driven, and agile. They use cutting-edge technologies like the Internet of Things (IoT), artificial intelligence (AI), machine learning (ML), blockchain, and cloud computing to build a more connected, intelligent, and responsive supply chain ecosystem.

A corporation can, for example, utilize IoT sensors to track the position and condition of goods in transit; AI and ML algorithms to estimate demand and optimize inventory levels; blockchain to secure transactions and decrease fraud; and cloud computing to share data and communicate with partners. As a result, the organization can cut

expenses, improve efficiency, improve the client experience, and acquire
a competitive advantage. Organizations can systematically transition from
traditional to advanced SCM, improving overall efficiency, responsiveness,
and competitiveness in the marketplace. Continuous monitoring and
adaptation to emerging technologies and market trends will be crucial for
sustaining success in the evolving business landscape.

# Aligning Supply Chain Objectives with Business Strategy: Business Environment Perspective

The supply chain plays a vital role in meeting customer demands,
optimizing costs, and enhancing overall efficiency. From a business
environment perspective, several key considerations should be taken into
account to ensure a seamless alignment between supply chain objectives
and business strategy:

- **Customer focus**

  - **Understanding customer needs:** The supply chain
    should be aligned to meet the specific needs and
    expectations of customers. This requires a thorough
    understanding of customer preferences, market
    trends, and evolving demands.

  - **Responsive supply chain:** Develop a supply
    chain that is agile and responsive to changes in
    customer demand. This may involve implementing
    technologies like demand forecasting, real-time
    inventory management, and flexible manufacturing
    processes.

- **Cost optimization**

  - **Efficient operations:** Aligning supply chain objectives with cost optimization involves streamlining operations, reducing waste, and improving overall efficiency. This may include implementing lean manufacturing principles (an approach where the focus is on minimizing waste while simultaneously maximizing productivity), optimizing transportation routes, and minimizing excess inventory.

  - **Strategic sourcing:** Evaluate and select suppliers strategically to ensure the best value for money. This may involve considering factors such as cost, quality, reliability, and sustainability.

- **Innovation and technology**

  - **Adopting technology:** Leverage technology to enhance supply chain visibility, traceability, and communication. Technologies such as RFID, IoT, and advanced analytics can provide real-time insights, improving decision making and overall efficiency.

  - **Continuous improvement:** Foster a culture of continuous improvement within the supply chain by encouraging innovation and staying abreast of technological advancements.

- **Risk management**

  - **Identifying and mitigating risk:** Understand and assess potential risks to the supply chain, such as geopolitical issues, natural disasters, or supply chain disruptions. Develop contingency plans to mitigate these risks and ensure business continuity.

  - **Diversification:** Consider diversifying suppliers and sourcing from multiple regions to reduce the impact of geopolitical or economic disruptions.

- **Environmental and social responsibility**

  - **Sustainable practices:** Align supply chain practices with corporate social responsibility (CSR) goals. Implement sustainable and ethical sourcing practices, reduce carbon footprint.

  - **Compliance with regulations:** Stay compliant with environmental regulations and standards relevant to the industry. This can involve adopting environmentally friendly practices and ensuring that suppliers adhere to similar standards.

- **Flexibility and scalability**

  - **Scalable operations:** Design the supply chain to be scalable and thus capable of handling fluctuations in demand and accommodating business growth.

  - **Flexibility in logistics:** Have a flexible logistics network that can adapt to changes in market conditions, enabling the company to respond quickly to unforeseen events.

# Supply Chain Design: Traditional vs. Advanced

Supply chain design has evolved significantly over the years with the advent of technology and changing business dynamics. Here's a comparison between traditional and advanced supply chain designs.

## Traditional Supply Chain Design

- **Linear and sequential**
  - **Characteristics:** Traditional supply chains are often linear and sequential, with distinct stages from procurement to manufacturing to distribution.
  - **Challenges:** This design may lead to delays and inefficiencies as each stage operates somewhat independently.
- **Forecast-driven**
  - **Planning approach:** Traditional supply chains rely heavily on forecast-driven planning where decisions are based on predictions rather than real-time data.
  - **Issues:** This approach can result in overstocking or stockouts if forecasts are inaccurate.
- **Batch processing**
  - **Production model:** Traditional supply chains often use batch processing, producing goods in large quantities to achieve economies of scale.
  - **Drawbacks:** This can lead to excess inventory and longer lead times.

- **Single-tier relationships**

    - **Supplier and customer relations:** Relationships
      with suppliers and customers are typically
      transactional and focused on a single tier in the
      supply chain.

# Advanced Supply Chain Design

- **Agile and responsive**

    - **Characteristics:** Advanced supply chains are
      designed to be agile and responsive, capable
      of adapting quickly to changes in demand or
      disruptions.

    - **Dynamic planning**. Real-time data and dynamic
      planning allow for more accurate and flexible
      decision-making.

- **Demand-driven**

    - **Planning approach:** Advanced supply chains often
      adopt a demand-driven approach where decisions
      are based on actual customer demand rather than
      forecasts.

    - **Benefits:** This reduces the risk of overstocking and
      stockouts, leading to better inventory management.

- **Lean and flexible**

    - **Production model:** Lean principles are applied,
      focusing on reducing waste and producing in
      smaller, more flexible batches.

- **Benefits:** This minimizes excess inventory and allows for quicker responses to changes in market demand.

- **Technology integration**

  - **Information flow:** Advanced supply chains leverage technology for seamless information flow, providing real-time visibility into every stage of the supply chain.

  - **Data analytics:** Advanced analytics enable better decision-making and predictive capabilities.

- **Collaborative relationships**

  - **Supplier and customer relations:** Advanced supply chains emphasize collaborative relationships with suppliers and customers, promoting information sharing and joint planning.

  - **Supply chain networks:** Companies often operate within broader supply chain networks where collaboration extends beyond immediate suppliers and customers.

- **Risk mitigation**

  - **Proactive approach:** Advanced supply chains are proactive in identifying and mitigating risks, whether they be related to geopolitical issues, natural disasters, or other disruptions.

  - **Resilience:** The design incorporates resilience strategies to ensure business continuity in the face of unforeseen events.

# Technology and Automation in Supply Chain Operations

Technology and automation play crucial roles in enhancing efficiency, accuracy, and overall performance in supply chain operations. These advancements have the potential to transform traditional supply chain processes, making them more streamlined, responsive, and cost-effective. Technology and automation significantly influence supply chain operations in several key aspects. Some key aspects are as follows:

- **Inventory management:** RFID (radio-frequency identification) technology enables real-time tracking of inventory throughout the supply chain. This helps in reducing errors, minimizing stockouts, and optimizing inventory levels. Automated barcode scanning systems enhance accuracy in inventory management, reduce manual errors, and improve the speed of order fulfilment.

- **Warehouse automation:** AGVs (automated guided vehicles) are used for material movement within warehouses, reducing the need for manual labour and improving efficiency. AS/RS (automated storage and retrieval systems) automate the storage and retrieval of goods, optimizing space utilization and minimizing human intervention. Robotics in warehouses automate tasks such as picking, packing, and sorting, leading to faster order fulfilment and reduced labor costs.

- **Supply chain visibility:** IoT devices offer up-to-the-minute information on the whereabouts, condition, and status of goods during transit, enabling proactive decision-making and minimizing the likelihood of disruptions. Meanwhile, blockchain technology

22

improves transparency and traceability within
the supply chain, mitigating the risk of fraud and
guaranteeing the authenticity of products.

- **Transportation management:** Automated systems
  optimize transportation routes, reducing fuel costs
  and improving delivery times. The use of autonomous
  trucks and drones is being explored to further automate
  and optimize the transportation of goods.

- **Collaboration and communication:** Cloud-based
  platforms facilitate real-time collaboration and data
  sharing among different stakeholders in the supply chain.
  Tools like enterprise resource planning (ERP) systems
  and SCM software enable seamless communication and
  coordination across the supply chain.

Implementing these technologies requires strategic planning,
investment, and a commitment to adapt to the evolving landscape of
supply chain operations. Companies that successfully integrate technology
and automation into their supply chains can gain a competitive edge by
improving efficiency, reducing costs, and meeting the increasing demands
of the modern market.

# Inventory Management: Traditional vs. Advanced Approaches

Inventory management is a crucial aspect of business operations,
ensuring that a company maintains optimal levels of stock to meet
customer demand while minimizing holding costs. Over time, inventory
management approaches have evolved from traditional methods to more
advanced and sophisticated techniques. Here's a comparison of traditional
and advanced inventory management approaches.

# Traditional Inventory Management

- **Manual tracking**

  - **Traditional approach:** Manual tracking of inventory is done using paper-based systems or simple spreadsheets.

  - **Characteristics:** It's labor-intensive, prone to errors, and offers limited scalability.

- **Periodic reordering:**

  - **Traditional approach:** Reordering is done at fixed intervals, often based on historical sales data or arbitrary timelines.

  - **Characteristics:** Risk of stockouts or excess inventory, lack of real-time responsiveness to demand fluctuations

- **Safety stock**

  - **Traditional approach:** Maintaining a buffer of safety stock to account for uncertainties in demand or supply

  - **Characteristics:** Inefficient use of capital, may lead to overstocking

- **Forecasting**

  - **Traditional approach:** Relying on historical sales data and basic forecasting methods

  - **Characteristics:** Limited accuracy, especially in dynamic markets with changing trends

# Advanced Inventory Management

- **Automation**

    - **Advanced approach:** Leveraging technology and software for real-time tracking, reducing manual errors

    - **Characteristics:** Improved accuracy, efficiency, and scalability

- **Just-in-Time**

    - **Advanced approach:** Ordering and receiving inventory just in time to meet customer demand, minimizing holding costs

    - **Characteristics:** Reduces holding costs, minimizes excess inventory, requires precise demand forecasting

- **ABC analysis**

    - **Advanced approach:** Classifying inventory into categories (A, B, C) based on value and managing each category differently

    - **Characteristics:** Prioritizes high-value items, optimizing resource allocation

- **Demand forecasting with analytics:**

    - **Advanced approach:** Using advanced analytics, machine learning, and statistical models for more accurate demand forecasting

    - **Characteristics:** Better prediction of future demand, improved inventory planning

- **RFID and barcoding**

    - **Advanced approach:** Implementing RFID or barcoding for efficient and accurate tracking of inventory

    - **Characteristics:** Real-time visibility, reduced risk of errors, enhanced traceability

- **Integration with ERP Systems**

    - **Advanced approach:** Integrating inventory management with ERP systems for seamless coordination across departments

    - **Characteristics:** Streamlined processes, improved communication, better decision-making

- **Dynamic reordering**

    - **Advanced approach:** Using dynamic algorithms that consider real-time demand, lead times, and other factors for optimized reordering

    - **Characteristics:** Minimizes stockouts, reduces excess inventory, adapts to changing market conditions

In summary, while traditional inventory management methods may still be applicable in certain scenarios, advanced approaches leverage technology, data analytics, and collaboration to optimize inventory levels, reduce costs, and enhance overall efficiency. The choice between traditional and advanced methods depends on factors like the nature of the business, industry dynamics, and the level of technological infrastructure in place. Many businesses today opt for a combination of both, integrating modern technologies into existing systems for a more balanced and effective approach to inventory management.

# Transportation and Distribution: Evolution and Efficiency

The evolution of transportation and distribution systems has been a critical aspect of global economic development. Over the years, advancements in technology, infrastructure, and logistics practices have significantly improved the efficiency of transporting goods from manufacturers to consumers.

## Evolution of Transportation

- **Pre-Industrial Revolution**: Reliance on manual labour and animal power for transportation, limited trade, and commerce.

- **Industrial Revolution**: Introduction of steam engines and railways, revolutionizing land transportation. Growth of seafaring with steamships. Faster and more efficient movement of goods.

- **20th century**: Widespread use of automobiles and trucks for road transportation. The aviation industry takes off, providing faster air transport. Containerization revolutionizes maritime shipping.

- **Late 20th century to present**: Emphasis on intermodal transportation, integrating multiple modes (road, rail, air, sea) for seamless cargo movement. Adoption of advanced technologies such as GPS, RFID, and telematics for better tracking and coordination.

# Evolution of Distribution

- **Localized distribution**: Small, localized markets with limited distribution networks. Goods produced and consumed within a limited geographic area.

- **Regional distribution**: Expansion of distribution networks to cover larger regions. Improved transportation infrastructure supports broader market reach.

- **National and international distribution**: Growth of distribution networks to cover entire nations and, eventually, global markets. International trade facilitated by advancements in shipping and air transport.

- **E-Commerce and digitalization**: The rise of e-commerce transforms distribution channels. Direct-to-consumer models become more prevalent. Digital platforms and online marketplaces reshape the retail landscape

# Efficiency Improvements

- **Technological advancements**

  - **Evolution**: From steam engines to electric vehicles, technology has played a crucial role in improving transportation efficiency.

  - **Efficiency gains**: GPS for route optimization, telematics for real-time tracking, and data analytics for demand forecasting

- **Intermodal transportation**

  - **Evolution**: Integration of various modes of transportation (road, rail, air, sea) for more efficient cargo movement

  - **Efficiency gains**: Faster transit times, reduced costs, and increased flexibility

- **Containerization**

  - **Evolution**: Standardized containers for shipping, simplifying loading and unloading processes

  - **Efficiency gains**: Faster turnaround times at ports, reduced cargo handling costs, and increased security

- **Lean supply chain practices**

  - **Evolution**: Adoption of lean principles to eliminate waste and streamline processes in distribution

  - **Efficiency gains**: Reduced lead times, lower inventory costs, and improved overall supply chain responsiveness

- **Automation and robotics**

  - **Evolution**: Increasing use of automation in warehouses and distribution centers

  - **Efficiency gains**: Improved order accuracy, faster order fulfilment, and reduced labor costs

- **Data analytics and IoT**

  - **Evolution**: Utilization of data analytics and the IoT for real-time monitoring and decision-making

  - **Efficiency gains**: Better demand forecasting, route optimization, and overall supply chain visibility

- **Sustainability initiatives**

  - **Evolution**: Growing emphasis on sustainable practices in transportation and distribution

  - **Efficiency gains**: Reduced environmental impact and cost savings through energy-efficient practices

# Resilience and Risk Management in Modern Supply Chain: Safeguarding the Global Flow

Resilience and risk management are fundamental pillars of contemporary supply chain strategies, particularly within the context of a highly interconnected and globalized business environment. The intricate nature of supply chain networks, coupled with the unpredictability of external factors, underscores the need for proactive measures to safeguard the seamless flow of goods worldwide. As a response to these challenges, companies are adopting comprehensive approaches to enhance both the resilience and risk management capabilities of their supply chains.

To bolster resilience, organizations are diversifying their supplier base, avoiding overreliance on a single source or geographic region. This strategy aims to minimize vulnerability to disruptions by spreading risks across multiple suppliers. Simultaneously, there is a focus on optimizing inventory levels, incorporating real-time tracking systems, and cultivating collaborative relationships throughout the supply chain. These measures contribute to increased flexibility and agility, enabling rapid adjustments to unforeseen circumstances and improving overall responsiveness to market dynamics.

In tandem with resilience, effective risk management practices are essential for navigating the complexities of the modern supply chain landscape. Businesses conduct thorough risk assessments that encompass a spectrum of factors, including geopolitical considerations, regulatory changes, financial stability of suppliers, and cybersecurity threats. Continuous monitoring and evaluation ensure that risk management strategies remain adaptive to evolving conditions.

The integration of resilience and risk management is evident in strategies such as scenario planning, where organizations develop contingency plans for various potential disruptions. This proactive approach enables swift decision-making and the implementation of alternative strategies when unforeseen events occur. Additionally, the importance of collaboration cannot be overstated, as strong relationships with suppliers, distributors, and other partners facilitate coordinated responses to disruptions and collaborative problem-solving.

The realization that supply chain disruptions can have far-reaching consequences has led to a paradigm shift in the approach to risk management. Rather than treating disruptions as isolated events, businesses are adopting a holistic and continuous improvement mindset. Regular testing through simulations and scenario analyses involves creating hypothetical situations or using historical data to stimulate potential disruptions or crises within an organization's operations or supply chain. By doing so, organizations can identify vulnerabilities, weaknesses, and gaps in their contingency plans. Through these exercises, they can refine and optimize their response strategies, ensuring they are better prepared to effectively manage and mitigate risks when real-world events occur.

In conclusion, the safeguarding of the global flow of goods in the modern supply chain requires a multifaceted approach that combines resilience and risk management. By diversifying suppliers, embracing technological innovations, fostering collaboration, and implementing proactive risk mitigation strategies, businesses can build robust and adaptable supply chains capable of withstanding and recovering from disruptions in an ever-evolving global landscape.

# Lean Operations in Supply Chain: Optimizing Efficiency and Minimizing Waste

Lean operations in the supply chain refer to the application of lean principles to enhance efficiency, minimize waste, and optimize processes throughout the entire value chain. Originating from manufacturing, the concept of lean has been widely adopted across various industries, emphasizing the elimination of non-value-added activities and the continuous pursuit of operational excellence. In the context of the supply chain, lean practices aim to streamline processes, reduce lead times, and enhance overall responsiveness to customer demand. At the core of lean operations in the supply chain are several key principles:

- **Waste elimination**

    - **Focus**: Identify and eliminate activities that do not add value to the end product or service.

    - **Impact**: Reduces unnecessary costs, enhances efficiency, and accelerates processes

- **Continuous improvement (Kaizen):**

    - **Focus**: Encourage a culture of continuous improvement and incremental changes.

- **Impact:** Drives ongoing enhancements in processes, leading to increased efficiency over time

- **Pull systems (Just-in-Time)**

  - **Focus:** Align production and distribution with actual customer demand.

  - **Impact:** Minimizes inventory holding costs, reduces lead times, and enhances responsiveness to market fluctuations

- **Standardization**

  - **Focus:** Establish standard operating procedures and processes.

  - **Impact:** Improves consistency, reduces errors, and facilitates easier identification of opportunities for improvement

- **Flexibility and Adaptability**

  - **Focus:** Build flexibility into operations to respond rapidly to changes in demand or disruptions.

  - **Impact:** Enhances the ability to adapt to dynamic market conditions and unforeseen challenges

- **Value stream mapping**

  - **Focus:** Visualize and analyze the entire value stream to identify areas for improvement.

  - **Impact:** Provides insights into process flow, enabling targeted interventions to eliminate waste and inefficiencies

- **Cross-functional collaboration**

  - **Focus**: Encourage collaboration among different departments within the supply chain.

  - **Impact**: Improves communication, breaks down silos, and enhances overall coordination

- **Supplier and customer collaboration**

  - **Focus**: Collaborate closely with suppliers and customers to streamline the entire value chain.

  - **Impact**: Reduces lead times, enhances communication, and fosters a more integrated and responsive supply chain

Lean operations in the supply chain are applied across various functional areas:

- **Procurement and sourcing**: Streamlining supplier relationships, reducing lead times, and optimizing order quantities to minimize excess inventory

- **Production and manufacturing**: Implementing JIT production, reducing setup times, and improving production flow to minimize downtime and overproduction

- **Inventory management**: Adopting pull systems, optimizing safety stock levels, and leveraging demand forecasting to minimize excess inventory holding costs

- **Distribution and logistics**: Optimizing transportation routes, reducing lead times, and enhancing the efficiency of distribution centers to minimize handling costs

- **Information flow and technology:** Implementing
  advanced technologies such as RFID and real-time
  tracking to improve visibility and information flow
  across the supply chain

- **Customer service:** Focusing on customer demand
  to ensure that products are delivered promptly and
  meeting customer expectations without excess
  inventory

The benefits of implementing lean operations in the supply chain
include cost reduction, improved customer satisfaction, increased agility,
and better utilization of resources. However, it's essential to note that the
successful implementation of lean principles requires a cultural shift,
ongoing commitment to continuous improvement, and collaboration
across all stakeholders in the supply chain.

# Sustainability and Corporate Social Responsibility in SCM

Sustainability and corporate social responsibility have become integral
components of modern SCM. As global awareness of environmental and
social issues increases, businesses are recognizing the importance of
integrating sustainable and socially responsible practices into their supply
chain operations. The market for tools promoting socially responsible
supply chains is set to grow significantly in the next five years. There
is an increasing demand for tools that extend beyond conventional
social compliance audits. These tools are expected to offer real-time
transparency into the practices of supply chain actors. Additionally,
there is a rising interest in digital programs that facilitate ethical sourcing
from suppliers, along with mechanisms for addressing grievances from
workers, enabling employers or buyers to respond promptly when issues

are identified. Companies can defend their long-term profitability and earn a social license to operate by implementing socially responsible supply chain practices. While consumer sentiment contributes to this shift, existing global regulations are already in effect to ensure companies adhere to socially responsible supply chain practices. In 2011, the United Nations Human Rights Council endorsed the United Nations Guiding Principles on Business and Human Rights (UNGPs), outlining expectations for the operation of nations and corporations in three crucial areas: the state's obligation to protect human rights, corporate responsibility to uphold human rights, and providing remedies for victims of business-related abuses. According to the UNGPs, companies are obligated to safeguard human rights across their entire value chain, encompassing both manufacturing and outsourced supplier chains. Embracing new socially responsible supply chain tools is imperative for corporations due to various factors including public opinion, investment pressures, and compliance with global regulations. Here are key aspects of sustainability and CSR in SCM: environmental sustainability, ethical sourcing, supply chain transparency, social responsibility, life cycle assessments, regulatory compliance, risk management, supplier collaboration, continuous improvement, circular economy practices, collaboration with stakeholders, innovation, and technology.

- **Green logistics:** Adopting eco-friendly practices in transportation, warehousing, and distribution to reduce carbon emissions and minimize environmental impact

- **Energy efficiency**: Implementing energy-efficient technologies and practices in manufacturing and transportation

- **Waste reduction**: Minimizing waste through recycling, reusing materials, and adopting circular economy principles

- **Fair labor practices**: Ensuring fair wages, safe working conditions, and ethical treatment of workers throughout the supply chain

- **Ethical sourcing of raw materials**: Sourcing materials from suppliers who adhere to ethical and responsible practices, especially in industries like mining and agriculture

- **Traceability:** Providing transparency into the origin and journey of products through the supply chain using technologies like blockchain

- **Communication**: Openly communicating about sustainability initiatives and performance with stakeholders, including customers and investors

- **Product lifecycle analysis:** Assessing the environmental impact of products from raw material extraction to end-of-life disposal

- **Designing for sustainability:** Integrating sustainability considerations into product design to minimize environmental impact

- **Adherence to standards:** Complying with environmental and social regulations and certifications, such as ISO 14001 (Environmental Management System) and Fair Trade certifications

- **Legal and ethical compliance**: Ensuring compliance with labor laws and ethical standards in all aspects of the supply chain

- **Identifying and mitigating risks**: Identifying potential environmental, social, and ethical risks in the supply chain and implementing strategies to mitigate these risks

- **Resilience planning**: Developing contingency plans to address disruptions caused by environmental or social issues

- **Sustainable procurement**: Collaborating with suppliers to ensure they adhere to sustainable and ethical practices

- **Supplier audits**: Conducting regular audits to assess and verify the sustainability and CSR practices of suppliers

- **Continuous learning**: Learning from successes and challenges to continuously improve and adapt strategies

- **Product recycling**: Designing products for easier recycling and encouraging the return of products for recycling at the end of their life

- **Reusing and refurbishing**: Exploring opportunities to reuse and refurbish products to extend their lifecycle

- **Engaging customers and investors**: Involving customers and investors in sustainability initiatives and sharing progress

- **Industry collaboration**: Collaborating with industry peers and stakeholders to drive collective sustainability efforts

- **Adopting sustainable technologies**: Integrating innovative and sustainable technologies into supply chain operations

- **Digitalization for efficiency**: Using digital technologies for efficiency gains, reduced waste, and enhanced sustainability

Incorporating sustainability and CSR into SCM is not only a moral imperative but also a strategic business decision. Organizations that prioritize sustainability are more likely to build stronger relationships with customers, attract environmentally and socially conscious investors, and ensure long-term viability in an increasingly conscious global marketplace.

# Future Trends of SCM

The supply chain industry is always changing, with new trends and technology developing daily. Organizations must keep up with the newest trends to remain competitive and increase the efficiency, effectiveness, and resilience of supply chain operations. These developments are already having an impact on the supply chain business and will continue in the future. The future of the supply chain will likely be shaped by a combination of technological advancements, sustainability imperatives, and the need for increased resilience in the face of unforeseen disruptions. Organizations that embrace these trends and proactively adapt their supply chain strategies are likely to gain a competitive advantage in the evolving business landscape.

SCM forecasting entails anticipating trends based on the present business climate, technology improvements, and changing consumer wants. While forecasting with 100% accuracy is difficult, numerous trends are predicted to affect the future of SCM. SCM is an exciting and continuously changing field. The following sections provide some of the most disruptive developments shaping the industry.

# Blockchain Technology

Blockchain technology is being utilized in SCM to safeguard financial transactions and contracts. Smart contracts streamline processes by autonomously triggering predetermined actions on a computer network when specific conditions are validated. These actions include disbursing funds to pertinent parties, recording sourced materials or ingredients, issuing certificates or tickets, and producing signatures. This efficiency reduces the supply chain's complexity by reducing the reliance on direct communications between contracted parties, eliminating the necessity for intermediaries. Increased blockchain adoption will increase job opportunities while altering established roles. *Immutability* means that blockchain technology creates a tamper-proof ledger where once data is recorded, it cannot be altered or deleted without consensus from the network participants. This ensures the integrity and authenticity of data throughout the supply chain, reducing the risk of fraud, counterfeiting, and data manipulation. *Traceability* means that blockchain enables the transparent tracking of products and components at every stage of supply chain. Each transaction or movement is recorded and time-stamped, allowing for a complete audit trail from the source to the end consumer. This enhances visibility, accountability, and trust among stakeholders.

# Artificial Intelligence and Automation

The usage of AI and automation in the supply chain business is becoming more prevalent, with the goal of streamlining and optimizing the supply chain process by automating dull and repetitive operations. This includes warehouse management system automation, eProcurement, and big data analytics. The circular supply chain is a closed-loop system that strives to reduce waste and maximize resource utilization. It entails creating items that can be easily disassembled and recycled, utilizing less raw resources and reusing or repurposing products. The Covid-19

epidemic has underlined the necessity of risk management and resiliency
in SCM. Companies are increasingly concentrating their efforts on
developing more robust supply chains that can survive interruptions

## Increased Sustainability

Sustainability is quickly becoming a primary focal area for SCM.
Companies want to lower their carbon footprint, eliminate waste, and
encourage ethical and sustainable supply chain practices.

## Agility

Future supply chains must be far more dynamic, able to forecast, prepare
for, and respond to fast changing demand as well as a constantly shifting
product and channel mix. In short, supply chains must become more agile.

## Data Protection and Privacy

A greater emphasis has been placed on developing strong cybersecurity
measures to protect critical supply chain data from cyber threats. Data
protection policies and standards must be followed to safeguard the
security and privacy of supply chain information.

## E-commerce Integration
## and Last-Mile Optimization

E-commerce expansion is increasing demand for effective last-mile
delivery and fulfilment solutions. Drone deliveries and self-driving
vehicles are being investigated for speedier and more cost-effective last-
mile logistics.

# Conclusion

The evolution of SCM from traditional to advanced approaches underscores a transformative journey driven by technological advancements, strategic realignment, and growing emphasis on efficiency, resilience, and sustainability.

Traditional SCM models, while effective in their time, are gradually being replaced by advanced SCM paradigms that leverage technology, data analytics, and automation to streamline operations, enhance visibility, and mitigate risks. This transition requires organizations to align their supply chain objectives with broader business strategies, considering the dynamic nature of the global business environment.

The design of supply chains has evolved significantly, with advanced approaches emphasizing flexibility, agility, and scalability to adapt to changing market dynamics and consumer preferences. Technology and automation play pivotal roles in optimizing supply chain operations, driving efficiency gains, and enhancing customer satisfaction.

Inventory management and transportation have also undergone notable transformations, with advanced approaches focusing in lean principles, JIT inventory strategies, and efficient distribution networks to minimize costs and maximize responsiveness.

Resilience and risk management have become paramount in modern supply chains, necessitating proactive measures to safeguard against disruptions and ensure continuity of operations amidst uncertainties.

Moreover, sustainability and corporate social responsibility have emerged as key imperatives, compelling organizations to adopt environmentally friendly practices, ethical sourcing, and social accountability throughout their supply chains.

Looking ahead, the future of SCM promises continued innovation and evolution, driven by emerging technologies like artificial intelligence, blockchain, and the Internet of Things. The ongoing digitization and integration of supply chain processes are expected to further optimize efficiency, enhance transparency, and foster collaboration across global networks.

In essence, the journey from traditional to advanced supply chain management reflects a strategic imperative for organizations to embrace change, leverage technology, and cultivate sustainable practices to thrive in an increasingly complex and interconnected global marketplace.

# CHAPTER 2

# Convergence of IoT, Artificial Intelligence and Blockchain Approaches for Supply Chain Management

*Vinolyn Vijaykumar, Assistant Professor, Department of Computer Applications, Alpha Arts and Science College, Chennai, India,* *vinolynvijay@gmail.com.*

*Mercy P, Assistant Professor & Head, Department of B. Voc. Software Development, Holy Cross College (Autonomous), Tiruchirappalli, India,* *mercycs@hcctrichy.ac.in.*

*Lucia Agnes Beena T, Assistant Professor, Department of Information Technology, St. Joseph's College, Tiruchirappalli, India,* *jerbeena@gmail.com.*

Dr. V. Grover et al. (eds.), *Blockchain, IoT, and AI Technologies for Supply Chain Management,*
https://doi.org/10.1007/979-8-8688-0315-4_2

*Leena H M, Dean, School of Mathematical Computation Sciences and Assistant Professor, Department of Computer Applications, Holy Cross College (Autonomous), Tiruchirappalli, India,* `leenacshcc@gmail.com.`

*Charles Savarimuthu, Senior Lecturer, IT Department, University of Technology and Applied Sciences - Al Mussanah, Muladdah, Mussanah, South Batina, Sultanate of Oman,* `charlessavarimuthu1973@gmail.com.`

In a world driven by an unwavering pursuit of efficiency, transparency, and innovation, supply chain management (SCM) emerges as a pivotal arena where the intersection of cutting-edge technologies and enduring principles reshapes the very landscape of commerce. This chapter initiates an exploration into the core of this transformation, wherein the fusion of the Internet of Things, blockchain, and artificial intelligence converges to create a new paradigm for supply chain management. At its core, supply chain management encapsulates the intricate dance of demand and supply orchestration. It navigates the complex web of procurement, production, distribution, and all the touchpoints in between. It shoulders the burden of meeting consumer expectations and responding to market dynamics. In this era, the success or failure of businesses hinges upon their capacity to navigate the labyrinth of global trade, operate with efficiency, and deliver quality products punctually. Supply chain management has transcended mere operational functions; it now embodies the essence of competitive advantage. In recent times, there has been an increasing focus on the application of advanced digital technologies such as the IoT, AI, and blockchain to improve SCM. These technologies have the potential to revolutionize the way supply chains are managed, making them more efficient, transparent, and resilient [1].

The opening section of this chapter delves into the foundational principles of supply chain management. It explores the core components, processes, and challenges that have defined supply chain operations for decades. It acknowledges the evolving market landscape and the obstacles that businesses confront in their pursuit of optimization. As the business world evolves, so does the approach to supply chain management. The integration of blockchain, IoT, and AI emerges as the fulcrum upon which supply chains find a renewed equilibrium. These technologies, once disparate, now converge to usher in a new era of innovation. Blockchain introduces trust and transparency into transactions, IoT extends the reach of logistics, and AI amplifies the cognitive capabilities of decision-makers. Together, they pave the way for a supply chain that is not just adaptive but predictive, not just efficient but intelligent.

Subsequent sections delve into the individual and collective roles of these technologies in supply chain management. They unveil how blockchain assures transparency and traceability, how IoT introduces real-time monitoring and data collection, and how AI empowers data-driven decision-making. These threads intertwine to weave a tapestry of augmented supply chain visibility and resilience [2].

# SCM's Transformation

Supply chain management is amid a profound transformation, catalyzed by the seamless integration of blockchain, IoT, and AI technologies. At its core, this transformation aims to address longstanding challenges that have plagued conventional supply chain practices. Firstly, blockchain, with its immutable ledger and smart contract capabilities, emerges as the linchpin for establishing trust and transparency within supply chains. It provides a tamper-proof mechanism for recording transactions, ensuring the authenticity of products and transactions. Secondly, IoT plays the role of an omnipresent sentinel by facilitating real-time data collection through sensors and connected devices. This constant influx of data equips supply chain stakeholders with invaluable insights into inventory levels, conditions, and precise locations, ultimately enhancing decision-making processes. Finally, AI, the harbinger of predictive analytics and machine learning, empowers supply chains with data-driven intelligence. AI algorithms enable proactive demand forecasting, precise inventory optimization, and predictive maintenance, resulting in operational efficiency and cost reduction.

Real-world case studies from various industries offer compelling evidence of the transformative potential of these integrated technologies. From ensuring the authenticity of luxury goods through blockchain to tracking the temperature and condition of perishable goods with IoT sensors and using AI for precise demand prediction, these examples vividly illustrate the impact of the technological synergy on supply chain operations. They showcase how integrated technologies have the power to revolutionize supply chains, providing real-time tracking, automating decision-making processes, and fortifying security measures. This technological triad of blockchain, IoT, and AI is ushering in a new era of resilience, efficiency, and transparency in supply chain management. Its transformative potential is nothing short of revolutionary. As supply chain stakeholders embark on this journey of discovery and innovation, they are poised to reshape the very foundations of modern supply chain practices, redefining how goods and services move through the global economy.

# Artificial Intelligence

AI can be used to improve SCM in several ways. For example, AI can be used to

- Forecast demand more accurately

- Optimize inventory levels

- Automate tasks such as order fulfilment and transportation scheduling

- Detect and prevent fraud

- Provide insights into customer behavior

# Blockchain

Blockchain serves as a decentralized ledger technology capable of
generating secure and immutable transaction records. This makes it ideal
for tracking the movement of goods and services through a supply chain.

Blockchain offers several avenues for enhancing supply chain
management:

- Offer immediate insight into the whereabouts and
  condition of products

- Make payments between supply chain partners more
  secure and efficient

- Reduce fraud and counterfeiting

- Improve compliance with regulatory requirements

# The Internet of Things

The Internet of Things is an ensemble of tangible gadgets that are linked
to the World Wide Web and can gather and exchange data. IoT devices can
monitor the flow of commodities and services, monitor environmental
conditions, and collect data on product usage.

IoT provides numerous opportunities for enhancing supply chain
management, such as

- Providing real-time data on the location and condition
  of goods

- Automating tasks such as inventory management and
  quality control

- Enabling predictive maintenance and preventive measures

- Improving collaboration between supply chain partners

However, the journey toward a technologically fortified supply chain is not without challenges of technical and operational natures. As the path unfolds, it becomes essential to comprehend and address these challenges, endeavoring to bridge gaps and foster a synergy befitting the modern era. This chapter embarks on a voyage through the contemporary supply chain landscape, a landscape where innovation harmonizes with tradition to craft a new narrative. As the exploration navigates the realms of blockchain, IoT, and AI, it uncovers not only the potential for transformation but also the associated responsibilities. The voyage offers insights into the challenges and opportunities that lie ahead, with supply chain management poised as a harbinger of progress. The next section propels the narrative forward, depicting the fundamentals of supply chain management and laying the groundwork for a deeper exploration of the integration of blockchain, IoT, and AI and the boundless potential they harbor for the world of supply chains.

# Mastering the Supply Chain Foundations

The supply chain is an integrated system of businesses, resources, processes, and technology used in the production and delivery of goods and services to end consumers. It includes each phase of the manufacturing process from raw material purchase to final product delivery to customers. A supply chain aims to optimize efficiency, reduce costs, and ensure the timely and efficient movement of goods or services while meeting customer demands and expectations. It plays a crucial role in the global economy, impacting businesses' competitiveness and the overall satisfaction of consumers.

The process of organizing, carrying out, and managing the movement
of goods and amenities from the spot of origin to the site of consumption
is known as supply chain management, or SCM. A complicated network
of manufacturers, distributors, retailers, and suppliers is involved, as
depicted in the Figure 2-1. SCM stands at the crossroads of commerce,
where goods and services find their way from producers to consumers,
navigating a complex web of processes, intermediaries, and geographic
distances. Essentially, SCM includes the planning, executing, controlling,
and tracking of the supply chain operations with the goals of generating
net value, constructing a competitive infrastructure, utilizing global
logistics, coordinating supply and demand, and assessing performance on
a worldwide scale.

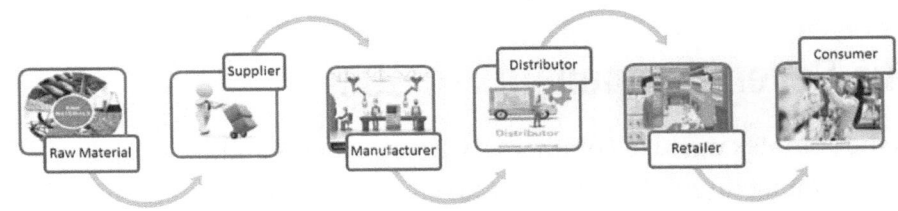

***Figure 2-1.*** *Navigating the dynamics of supply chain operations*

## The Significance of Supply Chain Management

In today's globalized and highly competitive corporate scenario SCM
is critical. SCM is the backbone of efficient operations, cost control,
and customer satisfaction for organizations. It enables companies to
streamline their processes, reduce waste, and optimize resources, resulting
in significant cost savings. Additionally, SCM facilitates the timely delivery
of products or services to end customers, enhancing customer satisfaction
and loyalty. Moreover, it plays a pivotal role in risk mitigation, helping
businesses adapt to unforeseen challenges and disruptions. In essence,
SCM is the key player of operational excellence, cost-effectiveness, and
resilience in the ever-evolving world of commerce [3].

Effective SCM can help businesses to do the following:

- Reduce inventory levels and improve transportation efficiency, which can lead to lower costs.

- Make sure that customers can access products whenever and wherever they choose, as this can increase customer satisfaction and loyalty.

- Reduce waste and pollution, and use sustainable practices, which can help businesses meet environmental regulations.

- Respond to disruptions quickly and effectively, minimizing the impact on customers and profitability.

# The Seven Components of SCM

In the complex world of commerce, where products and services flow from manufacturers to consumers, an effective supply chain is the lifeblood of success. SCM is a multidimensional strategy that hinges on the orchestration of several vital components, each playing a unique and indispensable role in ensuring the efficient, cost-effective, and timely delivery of goods and services. These seven components that serve as the building blocks of SCM, depicted in Figure 2-2, collectively shape the way businesses operate and interact in the global marketplace [4].

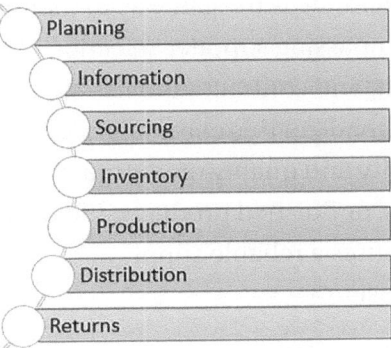

***Figure 2-2.*** *Components of supply chain management*

1. **Planning:** At the heart of any supply chain lies
   meticulous planning. This component encompasses
   the strategic vision and the blueprint for the entire
   supply chain. It involves setting objectives, defining
   strategies, and implementing tactics to create a
   supply chain that is both flexible and responsive.
   Planning is the compass that guides the allocation
   of resources, demand forecasting, and performance
   measurement.

2. **Information:** The information component is the
   nervous system of the supply chain, delivering real-
   time data to all stakeholders. Leveraging technology,
   it enables the collection, analysis, and sharing of
   information critical to the decision-making process.
   From inventory levels to supplier performance,
   timely and accurate data is the linchpin for efficient
   coordination among supply chain partners.

3. **Sourcing**: Sourcing is the gateway to the supply chain, encompassing supplier selection, procurement, and contract establishment. The choices made in this component dictate the availability and quality of raw materials, components, or finished products. Effective sourcing ensures a reliable supply at optimized costs.

4. **Inventory**: Inventory management is the art of maintaining just the right number of products at various points within the supply chain. Achieving this balance between product availability and cost containment is vital. This component involves inventory control strategies that help minimize storage expenses while ensuring products are on hand to meet demand.

5. **Production**: The production component revolves around the efficient manufacturing or assembly of products. It encompasses production planning, scheduling, quality control, and process optimization. Effectiveness in production ensures products are manufactured on time and meet rigorous quality standards.

6. **Distribution**: The distribution component is responsible for the seamless movement of products from the production facility to the eager hands of end customers. Transportation, warehousing, order fulfilment, and delivery are integral aspects. Effective distribution ensures the timely, cost-effective delivery of products, satisfying customer expectations.

7. **Returns**: Managing returns, repairs, recycling, or
   disposal is the essence of the returns component. It
   involves defining return policies, handling reverse
   logistics, and minimizing return-related costs.
   Proficiency in returns management can enhance
   customer satisfaction and operational costs

These seven components are the pillars on which SCM stands. They
work in unison, each serving its unique function while interacting with the
others. Successful supply chain management requires a holistic approach,
where these components collaborate to meet customer demands
efficiently, reduce costs, and increase competitiveness in the ever-evolving
landscape of global commerce. In the chapters that follow, we delve
deeper into each of these components, uncovering their intricacies and
their role in shaping the modern supply chain.

# Empowering with Blockchain

Blockchains are digital ledgers working in a distributed environment in a
decentralized manner. The transactions move from one block to another
without the interference of any central or a trusted authority. Nodes are
the participants or the devices used in the blockchain technology. The
decentralization concept of the blockchain technology enables the nodes
to hold the actual data that is processed in the transaction. A historical
record is maintained by adding the consequent transaction to form a
chain, Hence blockchain eliminates hacking through its decentralized
and immutable nature. The block of transactions is verified by consensus
mechanism and on success can form a chain of blocks. A simple
modification in the data is known to all the participants or nodes of the
blockchain network. The inability to modify the transactions in the blocks
often provides a way to have more trustworthy participants without relying
on a central authority. The blockchain technology evolves by bringing the
management solutions for different kinds of global industries [5].

# How Does Blockchain Work?

The blockchain technology works in a distributed fashion without any central authority like a bank, corporation, or governmental organization. The nodes and users in the network receive the blocks that comprise the public ledger that contains the transactions. The dispersed transaction is verified making the technology trustworthy and transparent. Once a block is tampered evident then another block can be added to the chain (with the previous one) thus forming the blockchains. A block contains the information like hash value of the previous block, timestamp, nonce, transaction details, and such. The transactions are validated and the transaction history is easily traceable. These transactions are available in the network and they are time stamped, irreversible, immutable, and connected to the previous block. This makes the blockchain technology as a trusted one. Many real-world use cases like smart contracts, identity management, cryptocurrencies, and supply chain management use the blockchain technology and are becoming the next innovation [6].

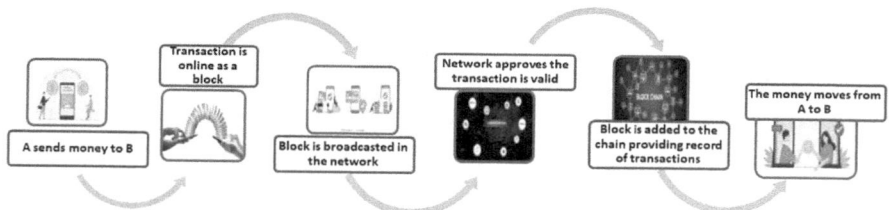

***Figure 2-3.*** *Transaction process using blockchain technology*

Figure 2-3 shows the flow of transaction through various stages when A wants to send money to B. The blockchain becomes more secured, trusted, and tamper-free by applying the most important mechanism called consensus. Once the block is validated and is encrypted using hash values, a new block is created. By applying the consensus algorithm, the decision is made to add a new block to the existing one [7].

# Enhancement of Supply Chain Performance Through Blockchain

It is proved that blockchain has improved the transaction journey. The two main goals of supply chains, increased efficiency and lowering costs are expected to bring using blockchain technology. Blockchain reduces the impacts of disruptions and eliminates intermediaries. Since it improves transparency of the entire process, it automates data analysis tasks and assists in monitoring an item's status during the process.

Additionally, the use of signatures in transactions improves security, which in turn secures transparency. The four characteristics of blockchain-based supply chains are traceability, reliability, coordinated transactions, and cost effectiveness [8].

## Traceability

Traceability in blockchain for the supply chain refers to the ability to track and trace the movement of products and related data throughout the supply chain network. By recording transactions on a decentralized ledger, blockchain ensures transparency and immutability, allowing stakeholders to verify the origin, authenticity, and journey of goods from production to consumption. This enhances accountability, reduces the risk of fraud or counterfeit products, and enables better quality control and compliance with regulations.

## Reliability

Since blockchain is a decentralized system and it reduces the risk of forged products being distributed, many of the industries like the food industry and the pharmaceuticals industry make use of this feature of blockchain technology to manage their inventory. The participants of the blockchain can verify all the information. Thus, tracking the shipment process and managing cargo history makes the product a trustworthy one. Thus, the blockchain based supply chain is becoming more popular.

# Coordinated Transactions

The smart contract process of blockchain technology reduces the preparation of unnecessary and complex documents. Thus, the contract procedure of supply chains to be established between the seller and the buyer is simplified on account of blockchain technology.

# Cost-Effectiveness

The authors emphasize the substantial cost-effectiveness provided by blockchain technology in SCM in their study [9] [10]. By providing a decentralized and immutable ledger system, blockchain enhances transparency and trust among supply chain partners, thereby reducing the need for intermediaries and the associated costs. The elimination of manual record-keeping processes and the prevention of fraud through tamper-proof data ensure efficiency gains and cost savings throughout the supply chain. Additionally, smart contracts enable automated execution of agreements, streamlining processes further and reducing administrative expenses. Through real-world applications, the paper demonstrates how blockchain technology optimizes costs in SCM, making it a promising solution for enhancing operational efficiency and financial performance within supply chains.

# Revolutionizing with Internet of Things

The Internet of Things is considered the most powerful and efficient
automation in Industry 4.0. IoT changes the SCM process, improving
overall efficiency and production. IoT is a worldwide network that provides
each interconnected object on the network a unique identity. It allows for
communication not only between objects but also between humans and other
things. Smart device and technology integration in supply chain management
creates new chances for businesses to become competitive, save money,
provide excellent customer service, and improve response accuracy by
allowing businesses to operate devices, analyze data, and automate processes.

## The Impact of IoT on SCM

Automation and computerization advancements contribute to Industry
3.0. It is the digitization era that combines computerized systems and
robotics to increase manufacturing while decreasing manual labor. While
Industry 3.0 technologies are broadly acknowledged, there is still need for
additional optimization and integration of supply chain process. Industry
4.0 enables digital transformation that improves connection and data-
driven intelligence, which can be accomplished by integrating IoT in SCM
processes [11]. IoT in SCM brings major changes in entire supply chain
processes and business model.

IoT-based technologies are becoming increasingly valuable due to
the extensive availability of the broadband Internet, the manufacture
of devices with Wi-Fi capabilities and the lower cost of connectivity
and technology [13]. IoT device deployment in SCM processes such as
production, transportation, and distribution hubs improve visibility and
data collection. Significant supply chain difficulties include an increase in
product demand, personnel shortages, a lack of crucial components and
raw materials, and so on. With the help of IoT device management in SCM,
one may gain meaningful insights into the operational status of any firm.

# Layered Architecture of IoT

IoT is typically divided into three basic layers: perception, network, and application. However, the IoT system needs have five distinct kinds of layered architecture to connect RFID-IoT to business or organizational models. The perception, network, middleware, application, and business layers comprise the five-layered architecture shown in Figure 2-4. [14].

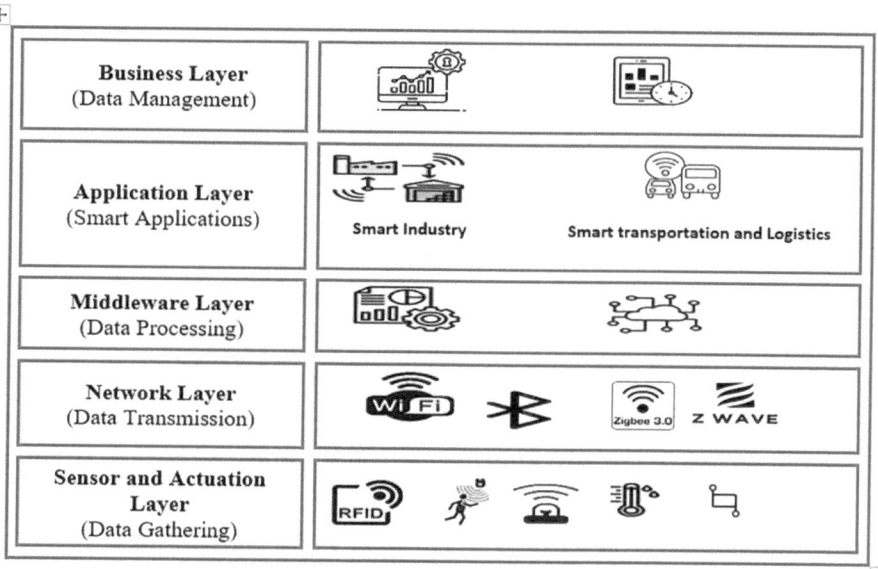

***Figure 2-4.*** *Five-layered IoT architecture for SCM*

Each layer has the following functions:

- **Sensors and actuation layer**: It is also called as perception layer. IoT Sensors such as accelerometers, humidity sensors, pressure sensor, proximity sensors, MEMs sensors, temperature sensors, and gyroscopes are used to gather data regarding the conditions of the goods. The integration of RFID tags with global positioning tags (GPT) can be used to detect the conditions of goods both in transit and in warehouses.

- **Network layer**: The communication protocols are used to transmit the data obtained from the IoT sensors to the middleware layer for data processing.

- **Middleware layer**: The data provided by the network layer are collected, stored, and processed using cloud computing services.

- **Application layer**: This layer provides a platform for clients to communicate with a physical device to access the allocated data. In SCM systems, information gathered is processed and visualized.

- **Business layer**: Business or management decisions can be modified or enhanced based on the information obtained from the smart systems.

# Features of IoT-Based SCM

When IoT is used in supply chain management, it becomes smarter and has the following features [15]:

- Real-time tracking and monitoring of goods and assets

- Predictive analytics for demand forecasting and maintenance optimization

- Condition monitoring to ensure product quality and safety

- Automation and optimization of processes in warehouses and transportation

- Supply chain visibility and transparency to track the movement of goods

- Improved collaboration and communication among supply chain partners through real-time data sharing

# Issues in Supply Chain Management

The supply chain management has following major issues [16]:

- **Globalization challenge**: The supply chain is complicated when suppliers are in multiple geographic regions.

- **Fast changing markets**: Due to rapidly changing nature of markets, firms must constantly forecast demand for new items.

- **Quality and compliance**: Enterprises must follow regulatory standards in the production, packaging, managing, and delivery of their products.

- **Inventory management**: Companies must maintain adequate supplies to satisfy every customer and client demand.

- **Managing suppliers**: Another aspect is identifying vendors who deliver consistent and dependable service at a reasonable price.

- **Managing safety and quality**: The interrelated nature of supply chains intensifies concerns about the quality of goods produced in other nations.

- **Rising transportation cost**: Increased fuel prices have an immediate effect on transportation expenses. Higher fuel costs increase the number of surcharges imposed to freight rates.

- **Redundant business processes**: Supply chain businesses are experiencing demand to discover innovative approach to plan, arrange, and supply services, as well as improve firm processes such as delivery density, production capacity utilization, cost-efficiency, and dealing with competition. Logistics businesses should employ current changes in business processes to remove inconsistencies to supply services that improve operational efficiency.

- **Changing customer expectation**: Managing consumer expectations and developing long-term customer relationships are critical in logistics. SCM companies are facing pressure to provide an exceptional and unique client experience while saving both money and time.

- **Inventory control and visibility**: Every logistics firm wants to always know the conditions of goods. Every business should gain visibility and control over inventory. Inadequate inventory management leads to insufficient, incorrect, and delayed delivery.

# Role of IoT in SCM

The Internet of Things has applications at each phase of supply chain management [17][18].

- **IoT in shipment tracking**: IoT devices are interconnected and attached to the products or storage containers by supply chain managers. The GPS satellites receive location data provided by IoT devices. This facilitates monitoring of products and shipments. They receive notification when the shipment begins to travel in the wrong direction or stops in an unapproved area. Managers' prompt actions help prevent delays or destruction of products.

- **IoT in monitoring storage conditions**: IoT sensors are used to monitor environmental factors. The environment of the warehouse in which items are stored can be detected by using various sensors. Supply chain managers regulate the environmental thresholds within warehouses and shipment based on the state of the climate. This aids in the reduction or elimination of decaying perishable commodities.

- **IoT in goods arrival estimation**: The IoT facilitates the effective processing of goods and decreases its management times. Supply chain managers monitor the speed at which containers move and the degree of congestion that slows down container movement to forecast the arrival time of the goods.

- **IoT in emergency planning and risk mitigation**: Shipment delays should be tracked down by supply chain managers. It can be accomplished by analyzing prior shipment data acquired by IoT devices. This could involve weather conditions, congestion, possible incidents, and other information. They can also reduce hazards by developing flexible strategies with other paths. As a result, traffic delays can be avoided by rerouting their shipment via a different scheduled route.

- **IoT in locating goods in storage**: Warehouse operations can be enhanced by using IoT technology. Inventory management and product identification in warehouse is simplified using RFID tagging. The enhanced IoT automation process increases the productivity and provides better employee safety.

When integrated with AI, IoT may completely automate
the management of warehouses, requiring minimal
or no supervision from humans. The product location
and its movement within the warehouse can be tracked
with IoT device using Bluetooth low energy beacons
and RFID.

- **IoT in administrative tasks:** The real-time monitoring
  abilities of IoT enable supply chain managers to
  initiate administrative responsibilities such as forward
  shipping requests, quality assessments, and payouts.
  The implementation of IoT-based technologies could
  enhance logistics across the supply chain, resulting in
  positive interactions between supplier and customer.
  The real-time data monitoring abilities of an IoT system
  can aid in the prevention of accidental shutdowns.

- **IoT in increasing customer satisfaction on SCM:** SCM
  companies are looking to enhance customer service
  by receiving feedback from customers through smart
  phones. Customers' feedback on products exchanged
  via smart phones can be instantly forwarded to the
  manufacturer, allowing businesses to provide effective
  customer care.

# Benefits of IoT in SCM

The IoT is changing complicated supply chains into interconnected
networks. IoT device data helps to simplify the processes throughout the
supply chain and take rapid corrections to reduce or prevent losses.

Some key benefits include the following:

- **Enhanced visibility**: IoT enables real-time tracking and monitoring of goods, assets, and vehicles throughout the supply chain, providing stakeholders with better visibility into the location, condition, and status of products.

- **Improved efficiency**: IoT sensors and devices automate manual processes such as inventory management, asset tracking, and order fulfillment, reducing the need for human intervention and streamlining operations.

- **Predictive maintenance**: IoT-enabled sensors collect data on equipment and machinery performance, allowing for predictive maintenance to be implemented. This helps in identifying and addressing potential issues before they lead to costly downtime or disruptions in the supply chain.

- **Optimal resource utilization**: IoT data analytics provide insights into resource utilization, enabling companies to optimize inventory levels, warehouse space, and transportation routes, leading to cost savings and improved efficiency.

- **Better decision making**: With access to real-time data and analytics, decision-makers can make informed decisions quickly, such as adjusting production schedules, rerouting shipments, or managing inventory levels, to respond to changing market conditions or disruptions in the supply chain.

- **Enhanced customer experience**: IoT facilitates end-
  to-end visibility and transparency in the supply chain,
  allowing companies to provide accurate tracking
  information to customers, reduce delivery times, and
  ensure product quality and safety, thereby enhancing
  the overall customer experience.

The benefits of IoT in SCM are shown in Figure 2-5 [8].

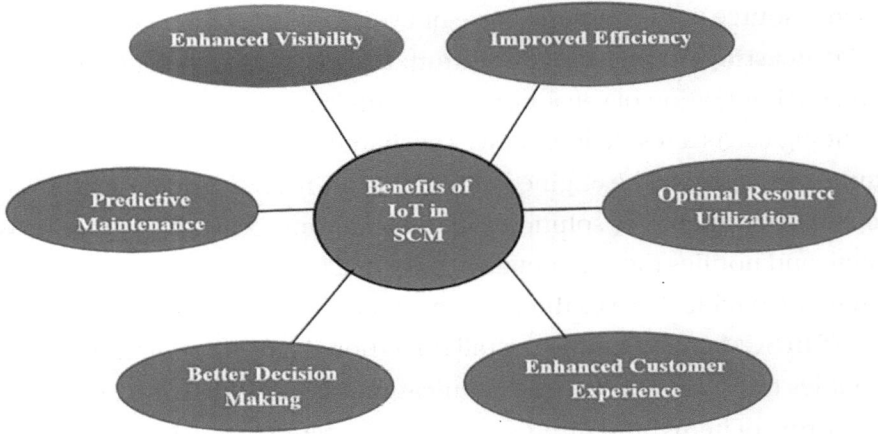

***Figure 2-5.*** *Benefits of IoT in supply chain management*

# IoT Use Cases in Supply Chains

**Smart warehouse**: A smart warehouse integrates computers and other
equipment to carry out daily operations such as rack shifting, packaging,
and more. These tasks were previously been done by humans. Amazon
now employs robots to complete jobs that involve moving quickly
and carrying huge objects. The warehouse floors are imprinted with
quick response (QR) code that helps the robot in navigation. Humans
collaborate with the robots but concentrate on activities that require

skill and problem-solving. IoT automation enables Amazon to store fifty percent more goods and retrieve it three times faster that leads to lowered supply cost.

**Remote container management (RCM)**: The current locations, humidity, and temperature of the refrigerated containers are tracked by the RCM system. It displays the current state of the power connection both inside and outside the ship while in transit. RCM is used by Maersk, a leading Danish shipping and logistics company. The RCM system helps to lessen resource waste and minimize or avoid spoiling of perishable cargo.

**Forecasting maintenance solution**: Equipment can be optimized using the integration of sensors, artificial intelligence, and data science technologies. As a result, it enhances availability and decreases basic maintenance costs. The engine plant of Volvo Group in France uses a predictive maintenance solution called Fluid Monitoring. It monitors the engine and notifies the maintenance personal before the occurrence of fault in the engine. It saves them an enormous amount of funds and effort.

IoT in SCM enhances the overall operational efficiency of industry. It enables more transparent communication, simplifies the tracking and monitoring of items, and improves planning accuracy. Businesses have started realizing the potential benefits of increased visibility and supply chain maturation that are provided by the Internet of Things.

# AI: The Cognitive Catalyst

SCM plays an essential role in contemporary business activities, covering the planning, execution, and optimization of product delivery. AI has the capability to revolutionize different facets of business procedures. It can be employed for tasks such as analyzing data, forecasting demand, improving transportation routes, and identifying inefficiencies within the supply chain. These uses can lead to enhanced adaptability to changes in demand, shortened lead times, and reduced costs. This section delves

into the utilization of AI in supply chain management. The goal is to fill
the existing research gap regarding AI's influence on SCM performance.
This involves identifying AI techniques that can enhance SCM, exploring
SCM subfields with significant AI potential, and assessing the impact of
AI applications on SCM performance. AI can be integrated into various
aspects of SCM, such as predicting demand, managing inventory,
enhancing relationships with suppliers, optimizing logistics and routes,
and automating warehouse processes.

# Demand Prediction

Forecasting demand plays a crucial role in enhancing the efficiency
and responsiveness of supply chain operations, serving as a foundation
for planning and procurement processes. Manufacturers, retailers, and
distributors increasingly recognize the significance of improving demand
forecasting methods. Various techniques, including AI-based, statistical,
and hybrid methods blending statistical and AI models, are employed
to forecast demand [19]. While statistical methods offer accuracy, they
face challenges in dealing with the growing dimensions and volume of
data, often falling short of the requirements of manufacturing companies.
The inclusion of AI in SCM has spurred the creation of pioneering
methodologies. These approaches combine conventional time series
prediction with machine learning techniques or utilize artificial neural
networks to enhance and refine the demand prediction process. Machine
learning (ML), a subset of AI, employs self-learning algorithms to
enhance results based on past data, making it particularly effective with
large and noisy datasets such as historical demand data. ML enables
businesses to adjust to shifts in market conditions and quickly react to
changes in customer demand. Implementing AI in demand forecasting
not only enhances the efficiency of supply chain operations but also
helps organizations optimize inventory levels, minimize costs, and meet
customer demands more effectively.

Organizations strive to maintain a balance between demand and supply, making accurate forecasting crucial for their supply chain and manufacturing operations. AI also detects trends and patterns, assisting in crafting efficient strategies for retail and manufacturing. For example, companies leverage AI to maintain precise stock levels, reduce waste, and procure in-demand items according to precise sales trends, ensuring product availability and averting potential lost sales.

The analysis of numerous publications reveals a distinct pattern in the widespread adoption of deep learning techniques, particularly the prevalent use of long short-term memory (LSTM), multi-layer perceptron (MLP), and artificial neural networks (ANN), all falling under the domain of deep learning [19]. Regarding data handling, techniques like clustering and reducing dimensions are utilized to improve data accuracy, particularly for the purpose of forecasting demand. Moreover, incorporating additional factors like weather conditions, location, and events typically enhances the precision of demand forecasts. This analysis also underscores a noticeable gap in the application of AI methods, particularly in the context of big data, involving extensive variables and substantial data volumes. Hybrid methods emerge as promising solutions to address these challenges.

The UK's National Grid employs Google's DeepMind platform to effectively forecast fluctuations in demand and supply, accounting for factors such as weather-related variables with high precision. ML approaches incorporate past sales data and real-time information, such as advertising campaigns, prices, and local weather forecasts. German online retailer Otto has successfully reduced 90% of their inventory by relying on AI forecasts, eliminating the need for human intervention. Additionally, AI is employed in research and development departments to assess the market potential of prototypes swiftly, leading to more efficient designs and reduced waste in the manufacturing process [20].

# Inventory Management

Modern successful retail businesses have embraced advanced real-time
inventory management systems that seamlessly integrate both online and
in-store transactions. These systems proactively prevent lost sales caused
by out-of-stock items and minimize non-value-adding inventory, freeing
up working capital. Additionally, these businesses experience lower
instances of shrinkage and spoilage in their inventory. However, many
traditional inventory management systems still rely on outdated demand
forecasting algorithms. These algorithms lack specificity to different sales
channels and struggle to comprehend online shopping patterns. They
are biased towards in-store shopping, leading to less accurate predictions
for digital platforms. As a result, consumers frequently face frustration
due to incomplete deliveries, with stockout rates averaging around 8%
for retailers and ecommerce businesses. Since the onset of the COVID-19
pandemic in 2020, these rates have surged by 250%. Simultaneously,
consumers increasingly desire omnichannel shopping experiences,
including online browsing, and purchasing with the option for in-store
pickup. Over the past few years, Google searches containing phrases like
"open now near me" have seen consistent annual growth of 400% [21].

The solution lies in the development of inventory optimization
capabilities utilizing ML, AI, and data science. Platforms utilizing these
technologies autonomously transform demand forecasting and inventory
management, effectively eliminating issues related to both stock shortages
and overstocking. In today's scenario, demand forecasting and inventory
optimization tools need to have features like being powered by AI,
operating autonomously, providing real-time data, demonstrating proven
accuracy, and being tailored to specific sales channels. These tools need
to comprehend signals from both in-store and online demands. Accurate
forecasts are imperative for each product, store, date, and time, and
they must factor in variables such as pricing, promotions, assortment,
seasonality, events, holidays, and weather.

Implementing effective autonomous demand forecasting facilitates the creation of a real-time perpetual inventory system. Such a system can support commitments to customers in real time and can be efficiently monitored and scaled. Despite challenges faced by many business-to-consumer (B2C) companies in maintaining real-time inventory due to lax receiving, inventory, and POS scanning practices, AI-powered autonomous inventory solutions offer an appealing alternative. They enable auto-detection and proactive prevention of inventory scarcity problems, resolving potential stockouts faster than manual perpetual inventory systems. Hypersonix Profit OS [21] offers sophisticated AI features for enhancing inventory and profit optimization for retail and e-commerce businesses. Through real-time monitoring of various factors and extensive continuous simulation capabilities, Hypersonix simplifies daily operations and protects businesses from unforeseen disruptions.

# Supplier Relationship

Effective procurement strategies rely heavily on SRM, with supplier selection being a critical component directly influencing procurement efficiency. AI, especially machine learning, is revolutionizing this process. Machine learning models significantly streamline supplier selection. For example, machine learning-powered automatic pricing engines play a crucial role. These algorithms analyze diverse data sources, offering valuable insights into pricing trends, historical purchase data, and competitive pricing strategies. By utilizing these insights, AI-driven solutions can suggest optimal prices for new products, detect competitor price changes, and assist organizations in making well-informed supplier selection decisions. This enables procurement professionals to secure products at the best prices while minimizing risks. In SRM, AI and machine learning act as essential assets, facilitating effective supplier selection and aligning supplier relationships with the organization's strategic objectives. Simultaneously, they optimize expenses and reduce potential risks [22].

Proactive supplier risk management powered by AI acts as a safeguard against unexpected disruptions. By utilizing machine learning models trained on historical data, such as past procurement issues like fraud or theft involving external suppliers, organizations can create a procurement risk score. This score, derived from attributes akin to past incident data, enables the early identification of high-risk suppliers. Methods like decision trees and random forests are employed to construct these risk scores. The outcome is a sturdy risk assessment system, enabling procurement experts to take pre-emptive measures, strengthening supplier relationships and providing protection against potential future incidents.

Fueled by machine learning, supplier performance monitoring systems constantly gather and analyze up-to-the-minute data from various sources. They offer a complete overview of supplier performance, monitoring essential metrics in line with an organization's objectives, such as on-time delivery, quality, defect rate, cost savings, and efficiency. In cases of deviations from predetermined standards, these AI systems promptly send alerts and notifications, empowering procurement experts to take prompt, data-driven measures. This instantaneous approach guarantees that supplier relationships stay in harmony with strategic goals, thereby improving the dependability and effectiveness of the supply chain.

Pricing engines driven by AI consider ever-changing market dynamics, seasonal variations, and consumer behavior trends. This comprehensive method allows them to suggest pricing tactics that are not only competitive but also adaptable. By providing guidance on optimal pricing models, these AI-based engines enable organizations to make informed procurement choices. They guarantee the procurement of goods and services at favorable prices, thereby improving cost efficiency and strengthening competitiveness in the market.

AI assists organizations in classifying suppliers based on criteria such as ownership and certifications, encouraging supplier diversity including businesses owned by minorities, women, or Indigenous individuals.

Additionally, AI evaluates supplier contributions to environmental,
social, and governance (ESG) objectives, considering factors like
carbon emissions and ethical labor standards. This data-driven method
allows organizations to make well-informed choices aligned with their
sustainability goals. Furthermore, AI aids in mitigating risks by identifying
potential disruptions linked to supplier dependencies. This proactive
strategy ensures continuous business operations while promoting ethical
and eco-friendly procurement practices.

# Logistics Optimization

SCM functions as a network linking suppliers, manufacturers, customers,
and other businesses in transactional relationships. Its main goal is
to secure efficient inventory control and prompt product delivery,
seeking to optimize company earnings and tackle the intricate hurdles
presented by the extensive market environment. Recognizing the
necessity of standardizing logistics systems, the Korean government
initiated the National Logistics Standardization Plan, focusing on six core
areas: unloading, storage, packaging, transportation, information, and
infrastructure. Still, due to separate standardization efforts by various
government agencies and functions, there has been a lack of mutual
connectivity and consistency across these areas. Anticipated rapid
technological progress is set to increase interconnections, introducing
more diversity and fluctuations in demand. As a result, advanced SCM
systems need to be highly adaptable to swiftly accommodate these
changes in the business environment.

Lately, the supply chain management field has shifted towards
Smart SCM, an innovative business model that prioritizes automation,
independence, and interconnectedness across the complete supply
chain. This transformation has been facilitated by the Fourth Industrial
Revolution (4IR) and its associated technologies, including AI and the IoT
[23]. This innovative solution aims to enhance the visibility, safety, and

efficiency of the supply chain encompassing manufacturers and suppliers while adhering to logistics standards. The objective was to integrate AI and IoT technologies into the industry, developing a technology capable of managing SCM processes effectively.

The Automated Ordering System (AOS) is an online platform that exchanges up-to-the-minute product information, encompassing production schedules, ordering, delivery logistics, quality assessments, and inventory details, among vendor companies. Additionally, an Automated Inventory Management System, relying on IoT sensors, automates incoming and outgoing inventory processes. An Adequate Inventory Calculation System analyses defective product patterns using AI, enabling the development of a safety stock ordering algorithm. The AOS, drawing data from interconnected SCM systems, ensures timely delivery and efficient inventory management for vendor companies. AI is employed to analyze defective product patterns, inform the safety stock ordering algorithm, and advance the overall system's capabilities.

Organizations employing AI to enhance their logistics operations include Echo Global Logistics Company in Illinois, HAVI Company in Illinois, C3 Company in California, Symbiotic Company in Massachusetts, TTEC Company in Colorado, Uptake Company in Illinois, Coyote Logistics Company in Illinois, Zebra Technologies Company in Illinois, Epicor Software Company in Texas, Live Person Company in New York, ASPENTECH Company in Massachusetts, Data Art Company in New York, and Infor Company in New York [24].

# Warehouse Automation

The progress in technology, changes in business processes, and the need to adapt warehouse operations due to increasing orders and their complexities, coupled with a shortage of management skills, have led to the emergence of smart warehouses. Warehousing is vital in managing supply chains and logistics, highlighting the necessity of intelligent warehousing for successful organizational management. AI application in warehouse operations enhances logistics, management, and coordination functions.

Pandian [25] proposed the integration of AI to create a smart environment for automated logistics. Automation in warehouse logistics, employing technologies like the IoT, AI, sensor networks, and cloud computing can enhance customer satisfaction by preventing incorrect order placement and improving efficiency in handling goods. Magnetic sensors track the total goods unloaded, RFID tags identify the type of goods, and barcodes ensure product variety. Robots, equipped with sensors, tag readers, and barcode scanners, use this information to autonomously load goods into appropriate racks. Sensors on the racks communicate the stock count via Wi-Fi to monitoring systems and the Thingspeak Cloud [26]. When a customer places an order, they receive an order number. Robots, guided by AI algorithms incorporating data mining and deep learning, locate the ordered items based on barcodes and their locations in the warehouse. Ant colony optimization finds the most efficient route to the items while robots utilize computer vision and machine learning to navigate safely, preventing collisions by employing a visual dual camera system for distance measurement among themselves. Robots update picked items and remaining stock counts through Wi-Fi to monitoring devices, production units, and the cloud, providing real-time stock information for customers and production planning.

The decision-making algorithms, based on deep learning and decision trees as well as path planning and data collection, are programmed using Python. Control devices gather data from various monitoring and executive devices for training. Deep learning algorithms analyze this data to enable informed decision-making in robot operations. The integration of AI, IoT, and cloud computing streamlines procurement and dispatch processes in warehouses, significantly reducing manual efforts and time consumption.

AI plays a commendable role in supply chain management, positively impacting various areas such as predicting demand, managing inventory, enhancing relationships with suppliers, optimizing logistics and routes, and automating warehouse processes. It holds promise for improving SCM performance, fostering greater agility and efficiency by boosting responsiveness, adaptability, minimizing inefficiencies, and improving teamwork and customer contentment. Nevertheless, integrating AI into SCM demands substantial expertise and resources. Moreover, ethical issues related to data security and privacy need attention. Consequently, companies must carefully evaluate feasibility and potential risks before incorporating AI into their SCM workflows.

# Fusion of Technologies

In the dynamic realm of SCM, where efficiency, adaptability, and transparency take precedence, a new era of transformation is emerging. The amalgamation of AI, blockchain, and the IoT heralds a convergence that not only enhances existing SCM models but also unifies them under a new paradigm. This convergence has the power to streamline operations, enhance visibility, and facilitate real-time decision-making, aligning with various SCM models and adapting to the ever-evolving demands of the modern supply chain landscape. This journey invites exploration into the synergy between these technologies and SCM models, where traditional models evolve to meet the dynamic challenges of today's business environment [27].

# Unifying Supply Chain Models

SCM represents a multifaceted discipline encompassing a variety of models, each finely tuned to cater to distinct organizational needs and objectives. Within the SCM domain, six distinct models have emerged, serving as strategic frameworks that guide businesses in streamlining the flow of goods, services, information, and resources throughout their supply chains [28]. The six models are listed in the Figure 2-6.

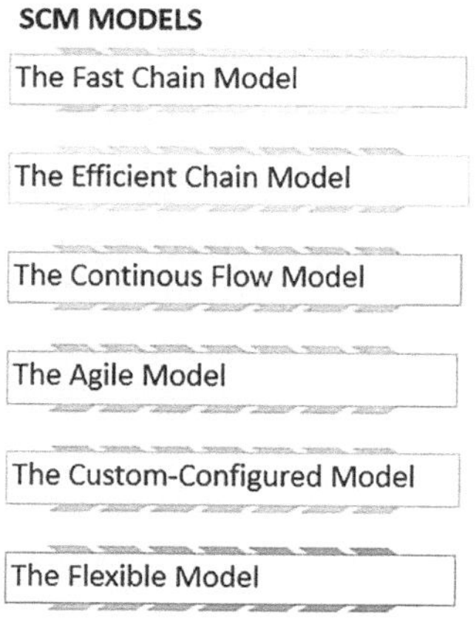

**SCM MODELS**

The Fast Chain Model

The Efficient Chain Model

The Continous Flow Model

The Agile Model

The Custom-Configured Model

The Flexible Model

***Figure 2-6.*** *Models of supply chain management*

These models epitomize adaptability and versatility, offering organizations the means to customize their supply chain strategies to achieve peak efficiency. In this exploration, the focus shifts to these six SCM models, unveiling their unique attributes, advantages, and practical applications. Whether a company's quest involves swiftness, efficiency, personalization, agility, seamless flow, or adaptability within its supply chain operations, a corresponding model exists to meet these precise demands. Comprehending the nuances and distinctions of these SCM models is foundational to the optimization of supply chain processes and the effective navigation of the intricate modern business landscape [29].

- The Fast Chain Model focuses on minimizing lead times and increasing the speed of product delivery. The convergence of AI, IoT, and blockchain enhances the Fast Chain Model by providing real-time insights into supply chain operations. AI enables quick

decision-making based on data analysis, while IoT
sensors ensure the fast tracking of products and assets.
Blockchain secures and records transactions for end-
to-end visibility, promoting speed and transparency.

- The Effective Chain Model emphasizes optimizing
  supply chain processes to maximize efficiency and
  resource utilization. AI, IoT, and blockchain make the
  Effective Chain Model more efficient and effective.
  AI optimizes processes by predicting demand and
  enabling data-driven decision-making. IoT provides
  real-time data for monitoring and control, while
  blockchain ensures the effectiveness of transactions
  through secure and transparent recording.

- The Continuous Flow Model seeks to maintain a
  steady and uninterrupted flow of goods and services
  through the supply chain. The Continuous Flow
  Model benefits from the convergence of AI, IoT, and
  blockchain by facilitating seamless and continuous
  operations. AI can predict and manage bottlenecks,
  while IoT sensors ensure the continuous monitoring of
  critical parameters. Blockchain records transactions to
  maintain a transparent and uninterrupted flow.

- The Agile Model prioritizes adaptability and
  responsiveness to changes in market conditions
  and customer demands. The Agile Model is further
  empowered by AI, IoT, and blockchain. AI helps in
  adapting to changing market conditions by providing
  insights and predictive analytics. IoT offers real-time
  visibility into supply chain dynamics, while blockchain
  ensures the integrity and transparency of agile
  decisions.

- The Custom-Configured Model prioritizes adapting goods and services to suit the needs of specific customers. Custom-Configured SCM is enriched by AI, IoT, and blockchain, enabling tailor-made solutions. AI supports customization by analyzing data for personalized demand forecasting. IoT sensors provide real-time data for configuring products, and blockchain secures the record of customization details.

- The Flexible Model is characterized by its ability to adapt to changing circumstances and market conditions. The Flexible Model benefits from the convergence of AI, IoT, and blockchain by enabling adaptability to changing circumstances. AI assists in dynamic decision-making, IoT ensures flexibility through real-time data monitoring, and blockchain provides the trust and security required for flexible supply chain changes.

# Transforming Industries with the Convergence of AI, IoT, and Blockchain

In the era of digital transformation, where innovation takes center stage in shaping progress, the convergence of three technological juggernauts—AI, the IoT, and blockchain—emerges as a pivotal force reshaping industries across the spectrum. This convergence is not just a mere amalgamation of technologies; it signifies a seismic shift in the operational landscape of businesses spanning diverse sectors. From healthcare to finance, manufacturing to supply chain management, the fusion of AI, IoT, and blockchain catalyzes a profound transformation. This journey embarks on an exploration to unveil the real-world impact of this technological convergence in a myriad of industries. These innovative tools are rewriting

the rulebook on data collection, information processing, and transaction
security, unlocking unprecedented levels of efficiency, transparency, and
integrity. The examples presented within these pages stand as a testament
to the transformative potential of the AI-IoT-blockchain trifecta, where
organizations are not merely adapting to the digital age but flourishing
within it [30] [31].

- **Food safety and traceability**: Walmart, one of the
  world's largest retailers, has integrated blockchain,
  IoT sensors, and AI for real-time monitoring of food
  products. IoT sensors track temperature and humidity
  during transportation, and this data is recorded on
  a blockchain. If the temperature exceeds predefined
  thresholds, AI triggers alerts and corrective actions.
  This convergence ensures that food products remain
  within safe temperature ranges throughout the supply
  chain. In case of deviations, the blockchain records
  the incident, providing end-to-end traceability. This
  integration enhances food safety and transparency,
  and in the event of a food safety issue, the source can
  be quickly identified and recalled, reducing the risk of
  foodborne illnesses [32].

- **Predictive maintenance in manufacturing**: Rolls-
  Royce, a leading aerospace manufacturer, employs
  IoT sensors on aircraft engines to monitor their
  performance. These sensors collect vast amounts of
  data on engine health, including temperature, pressure,
  and vibration. AI algorithms analyze this data in real
  time, predicting when maintenance is required based
  on deviations from standard performance. The result
  is predictive maintenance, which minimizes aircraft

downtime and reduces maintenance costs. Blockchain
can be integrated into this system to securely record
and verify maintenance actions, ensuring the integrity
and traceability of maintenance records [33].

- **Pharmaceutical supply chain**: IBM, in collaboration
  with pharmaceutical companies and supply chain
  partners, has developed a blockchain network
  to enhance transparency and traceability in the
  pharmaceutical supply chain (PSC). This PSC prevents
  counterfeit drugs through various measures such as
  implementing serialization and track-and-
  trace systems, utilizing tamper-evident packaging,
  conducting regular audits and inspections of suppliers,
  leveraging blockchain technology for transparent and
  immutable records, and collaborating with regulatory
  authorities and law enforcement agencies to enforce
  strict regulations and penalties against counterfeiters.
  These efforts ensure the authenticity and safety
  of pharmaceutical products from manufacturing
  to distribution, safeguarding public health and
  maintaining trust in the supply chain [34].

- **Energy management**: Power Ledger, an energy
  company, integrates blockchain and IoT to enable peer-
  to-peer energy trading. IoT sensors measure energy
  production and consumption in real time. Blockchain
  records and verifies these transactions, ensuring that
  energy trading is transparent and secure. AI can be
  integrated to predict energy demand and optimize
  energy distribution. This convergence not only enables
  individuals to buy and sell excess energy directly to one
  another but also contributes to more efficient energy
  consumption and reduced energy costs [35].

- **Cross-border trade and finance**: JPMorgan uses blockchain to enhance cross-border payments and correspondent banking. The network records payment data securely on a blockchain, providing real-time visibility and transparency to member banks. IoT and AI can be further integrated to track and predict the movement of goods related to these payments, enhancing the synchronization of financial and logistics processes. This convergence streamlines cross-border trade and finance by reducing the time and costs associated with international transactions [36].

The exploration of the assimilation of the IoT, AI, and blockchain reveals a profound synergy that transcends industry boundaries. This synergy redefines standards of efficiency, transparency, and innovation. Embracing the transformative power of this integration is essential as it promises a future where businesses operate with unparalleled precision and trust. The convergence of AI's predictive capabilities, IoT's real-time data, and blockchain's unassailable security paves the way for organizations to not only meet the challenges of the digital age but excel within it. This synergy is the architectural design for a more secure, efficient, and accountable global business landscape.

# Addressing Challenges and Charting the Future

The convergence of blockchain, IoT, and AI is an emerging technological phenomenon that changes the way we interact with our environment. This convergence is reshaping numerous industries, enabling new levels of intelligence, productivity, and safety, from self-driving cars to smart homes. The convergence of blockchain, IoT, and AI offers a number of challenges for supply chain management, including technical complexity and connectivity, unclear regulations and compliance, and organizational and cultural transformation. The integration of blockchain and IoT technologies is still overshadowed by technical problems with scalability, performance, and interoperability.

The challenges of blockchain technology in SCM are the following [37]:

- **Inadequate guidelines**: Implementing blockchain technology requires the formation of innovative organizational principles to reproduce shifting roles, accountabilities, and skill.

- **Minimal interaction**: The use of blockchain in SCM is hindered by inadequate interaction among SC stakeholders.

- **Data confidentiality and security**: The unauthorized access and publication of confidential information can occur as a consequence of cyberattacks.

- **Absence of cutting-edge technologies**: Lack of standardized instruments, procedures, and evaluation criteria results in complicated implementation of blockchain technology.

The challenges of IoT in SCM are the following [38]:

- **Scalability and interoperability**: The challenge of scaling IoT across the supply chain emerges from the requirement for highly specialized and highly customized solutions. Creating significant links between devices and opening up processes to promote accessibility and reusing are difficult tasks.

- **Poor security of IoT devices**: Large security systems are vulnerable to risk from improperly deployed IoT devices. IoT devices that have been compromised bring threats to workforces and businesses that go beyond the usual issues regarding data breaches.

- **Low privacy level**: IoT devices have the potential to collect private data about its owners. Data should be securely transferred and to prevent unauthorized interactions to the system are essential features of an IoT system.

- **Energy consumption**: The use of smart gadgets is expected to expand rapidly, increasing the requirement for energy. It is not simple to meet demand even with upgraded batteries and renewable energy sources like solar and wind.

- **Large volume of data generation**: Massive amounts of data are produced by all IoT systems, and these volumes need to be moved, stored, and processed. It is necessary to move and store millions of terabytes of data, and the traditional approaches for these tasks are not very beneficial in this context.

The challenges of AI in SCM are the following [39]:

- **Lack of big, clean data**: AI requires good data for all its computational process. Machine learning requires enormous amounts of reliable data to train algorithms and to create for predictive.

- **Short-sighted optimization**: The long-term impacts of a decision are sometimes overlooked in supply chains since they involve numerous partners and interconnected systems. So continuous optimization is preferable to occasional refinement of any AI process.

- **Geopolitical barriers**: Geopolitical tensions introduce noise into the fundamental information, which could affect the flow of data required to train the AI, which creates an unpredictable future regarding the stabilization of the conditions.

The common challenges found in the integration of blockchain, IoT, and AI are the following:

- **High cost of investment**: An organization must make a significant financial investment in implementing the new infrastructure blockchain, IoT, and AI technologies to streamline their SCM processes for gathering and analyzing information for efficient business operations.

- **Talent barrier**: Inadequate proficiency with the technology could lead to a delay in the process of resolving any abnormal situations that could occur in the digitalized supply chain management process.

- **Trust management**: Despite the fact that blockchain technology can enhance safety and confidentiality of data, concerns remain over the potential misuse of personal information and rights to privacy.

## Futuristic of SCM

AI, IoT, and blockchain are three technologies that can be integrated in
different ways. The integration of blockchain, IoT, and AI is revolutionizing
our lifestyles and workplaces. The convergence of technologies greatly
helpful to the SCM industry in which IoT makes precise data monitoring
possible, blockchain offers the auditability and transparency, and AI gives
the necessary intelligence to improve overall functioning. Successful
industrial advancement can be obtained through optimum use of
technologies in which blockchain supports AI in distributing resources,
scaling up data, and building a transparent and reliable data market
for industry. 5G networks will enable industries to handle enormous
numbers of devices and connections used for SCM. The adoption of
modern robotics in SCM provides benefits such as increased efficiency,
strengthen productivity, improved fulfilment processes and boost
customer satisfaction [40]. Robotics suppliers can operate their equipment
and incorporate it into workflows from a secure distance instead of relying
human interaction. Leveraging technology like blockchain, IoT, and AI
and robotic process automation will help to maintain the supply chains
flexible, adaptable, and scalable. Hence, it will be more crucial than ever
for businesses to monitor their operations in an agile manner so they can
adapt to changes in the marketplace.

## Conclusion

The emergence of blockchain, AI, and the IoT in the never-ending growth
of global trade stands as a transformative force, redefining the very essence
of supply chain management. This chapter has delved into the intricate
tapestry of these technologies and their converging impact on the world
of supply chains, unravelling a narrative of innovation, adaptability, and
efficiency. As the final curtain descends on this exploration, it is essential

to reflect upon the transformative potential and the responsibilities these technologies carry in reshaping the modern supply chain landscape. The journey commenced with an understanding of the fundamentals of supply chain management, recognizing its enduring significance in the global marketplace. It laid bare the intricate dance of demand and supply, emphasizing that SCM is not merely an operational function but a pivotal driver of competitiveness. This served as the springboard for the integration of blockchain, IoT, and AI, an evolution that signifies the convergence of the conventional and the cutting-edge.

Blockchain has emerged as the defender of supply chain transparency and trust, improving transaction veracity, and ensuring product traceability at every stage. IoT extends its reach, bringing the power of real-time data and the insights of smart sensors to the forefront. Meanwhile, AI lends its cognitive prowess, empowering decision-makers with predictive analytics, demand forecasting, and optimization tools. Yet, this journey is not without its challenges. The complexities of integration, concerns of data security, and the need for cross-sector standardization underscored the hurdles that must be surmounted. Supply chain practitioners must navigate these obstacles with wisdom and resilience.

As the curtain falls, it is evident that the transformative potential of integrating blockchain, IoT, and AI in SCM is not a mere hypothetical; it is a present reality. These technologies have demonstrated their ability to enhance visibility, reduce inefficiencies, and, crucially, provide the agility necessary to adapt to the demands of the contemporary market. The future beckons with new horizons for SCM, where technology plays an even greater role. The path forward involves addressing the challenges and staying attuned to the evolving trends. Security and privacy concerns demand attention, and the exploration of emerging technologies will continue to shape the landscape.

The merger of blockchain, IoT, and AI in supply chain management is a voyage of endless possibilities. As the final chapter unfolds, the underlying theme remains unchanged: the transformation of SCM is not a matter of "if" but "when." Those who seize the potential of these technologies and navigate the challenges with wisdom are poised to lead in the era of next-generation supply chains, where innovation and tradition converge, creating a narrative that adapts to the dynamics of the future. The journey continues, and the supply chain landscape evolves.

# CHAPTER 3

# Exploring the Potential of Blockchain in Transforming Supply Chain Financing

*M. Lawanyashri, Student, School of Computer Science Engineering and Information Systems, Vellore Institute of Technology, Vellore, India.*

*K.Santhi, School of Computer Science Engineering and Information Systems, Vellore Institute of Technology, Vellore, India. Corresponding author. ksanthi@vit.ac.in.*

*Saurya Raj Pandey, School of Computer Science Engineering and Information Systems, Vellore Institute of Technology, Vellore, India.*

*Balamurugan Balusamy, Shiv Nadar University, Noida, Uttar Pradesh, India.*

This chapter explores the transformative potential of blockchain
technology in revolutionizing supply chain finance (SCF). Through
a framework integrating service-dominant logic and social exchange
theory, we analyze the roles of key participants, their motivations, and
the resources and practices employed to create value for all stakeholders.
We delve deeper into the specific mechanisms through which buyers,
suppliers, financial institutions, and platform providers benefit from
blockchain-driven SCF solutions. By analyzing value creation across
financial, operational, risk management, sustainability, and social impact
dimensions, we demonstrate the tangible benefits of this technology.
Furthermore, we showcase real-world examples through case studies
and explore emerging applications such as decentralized trade finance,
data-driven insights, and tokenization of assets. These advancements
unlock new possibilities and underscore the transformative potential of
blockchain in shaping a more efficient, transparent, and sustainable future
for global supply chains.

# The Emergence of Blockchain

The intricate web of global supply chains fuels the modern economy, each
strand playing a vital role in delivering goods and services worldwide.
Financing the flow of products within these chains has traditionally been
riddled with inefficiencies and burdened by paper-based documentation,
manual reconciliation, and opaque information flows. However, the
emergence of blockchain technology has ignited a transformative spark,
offering a revolutionary approach to revolutionizing it and unlocking
immense value creation potential for all stakeholders involved. The supply
chain in financial sectors leverages various opportunities such as going
digital with tech such as cloud computing, blockchain, AI, and IoT to
streamline processes, increase visibility into data, and enable real-time
coordination between stakeholders. Automating repetitive tasks can cut

costs, boost efficiency, and minimize errors too. Using data analytics and predictive modeling is key for gaining valuable insights into supply chain performance, forecasting demand, managing risks and making smart decisions. It helps in optimizing the business operations by enhancing the collaborative factors within the supply chain. Blockchain pays a vital role in protecting the transactions carried out in financial sectors. It helps create a supply chain that facilitates access to funds and optimizes the cash flow more effectively by the management of a business process to meet operational needs. The vulnerabilities that exist in financial transactions can be easily mitigated by blockchain with extended supply chains. It also provides reliable relationships among suppliers and buyers to improve the financial stability. This comprehensive exploration delves into the world of blockchain-driven SCF, unveiling the multifaceted mechanisms through which it fosters value creation across the entire supply chain ecosystem. By meticulously examining the roles of key participants, their underlying motivations, and the resources and practices employed, we unravel intricate pathways, leading to enhanced financial performance and a more resilient and sustainable supply chain.

# Unveiling the Conceptual Framework

To effectively understand the value-creation process within blockchain-driven SCF, we adopt a conceptual framework that integrates service-dominant logic and social exchange theory. The supply chain in financial sectors needs collaboration between stakeholders and the implementation of regulatory standards. The need for blockchain creates great impact and potential benefits for increased transparency, efficiency, and security. This framework recognizes the intrinsic interdependence of value creation, acknowledging that each participant contributes resources and engages in practices that ultimately benefit themselves and their partners in the ecosystem.

# Key Participants and Their Driving Forces

Within the vibrant landscape of blockchain-driven SCF, several key players orchestrate the value creation process. They are the following:

- **Buyers (core companies)**: Driven by the desire to optimize working capital management, foster stronger supplier relationships, and enhance supply chain transparency

- **Suppliers (SMEs)**: Seeking faster and cheaper access to financing and to improve cash flow and mitigate payment risks

- **Financial institutions**: Striving to expand their reach into the burgeoning SCF market, offer novel financing solutions, and reduce operational costs

- **Platform providers**: Serving as the facilitators that connect various participants, manage the intricate blockchain network, and provide innovative SCF solutions

# Resources and Practices: The Building Blocks of Value Creation

Blockchain technology forms the bedrock upon which value creation in SCF is built. Its inherent features, such as immutability, transparency, and distributed ledger technology, facilitate efficient and secure data sharing, automate manual processes, and eliminate the need for costly intermediaries.

The value creation practices within blockchain-driven SCF encompass a range of activities, including

- **Data sharing**: Real-time visibility into transactions and inventory levels across the supply chain is achieved through secure data sharing across the platform.

- **Automated invoice processing**: Manual invoice processing tasks are eliminated through automation, streamlining the process, and reducing operational costs

- **Smart contracts**: Self-executing contracts govern the financial agreements between participants, ensuring automatic and transparent execution of payments based on predefined terms

- **Trade finance solutions**: Blockchain-based platforms facilitate innovative trade finance solutions such as dynamic discounting and reverse factoring, improving access to financing for both suppliers and buyers.

# Value Creation Mechanisms: Unraveling the Pathways to Success

The interplay of resources and practices within the blockchain-driven SCF ecosystem paves the way for a cascading effect of value creation benefits for all participants:

- **For buyers**

  - **Improved working capital management**: By automating invoice processing and utilizing dynamic discounting, buyers can optimize their cash flow by extending payment terms while still allowing suppliers to get paid early at a discounted rate. This improves the buyer's working capital position.

- **Enhanced supply chain transparency**: SCF platforms provide real-time visibility into transactions, outstanding invoices, and inventory levels across the entire supply chain. This transparency helps buyers manage their operations and supplier relationships more effectively.

- **Strengthened supplier relationships**: By facilitating faster payments to suppliers through early payment discounts or third-party financing, buyers can improve relationships with their suppliers, fostering trust and collaboration.

- **For suppliers**

  - **Faster and cheaper financing**: SCF solutions like dynamic discounting and reverse factoring provide suppliers with access to affordable financing by allowing them to get paid earlier by financiers at a discounted rate, improving their cash flow.

  - **Improved cash flow**: Instead of waiting extended periods for payments from buyers, suppliers can get paid much faster, improving their liquidity and cash flow position.

  - **Mitigated payment risks**: With SCF, payments are secure and automated, eliminating the risk of non-payment or delayed payments from buyers, which can be detrimental to suppliers' operations.

- **For Financial institutions**

  - **Expanded reach**: By offering SCF solutions, financial institutions can access new clients and opportunities within the growing SCF market, expanding their customer base and revenue streams.

  - **Reduced operational costs**: SCF platforms automate many manual processes and streamline workflows, leading to cost savings for financial institutions through increased efficiency.

  - **New revenue streams**: Providing innovative SCF solutions like invoice financing, dynamic discounting, and reverse factoring creates new revenue opportunities for financial institutions.

- **For platform providers**

  - **Scalable and secure platform**: SCF platform providers offer scalable and secure platforms capable of handling large volumes of transactions while ensuring data security and compliance.

  - **Subscription-based revenue model**: Platform providers can generate continuous revenue through subscription-based pricing models, where participants pay for access to the SCF platform and its features.

  - **Data-driven insights**: By aggregating and analyzing data from SCF transactions, platform providers can gain valuable insights, enabling them to develop additional services and solutions tailored to their clients' needs.

# Beyond the Horizon: Challenges and Future Opportunities

While blockchain-driven SCF holds immense potential for transforming the financial landscape of supply chains, challenges remain on the path to widespread adoption. These challenges include the following:

- **Technology infrastructure development**: The need for further development of robust and scalable blockchain infrastructure to accommodate increasing demands of the blockchain technology adaptation and usage across various industries and application which includes scalability, performance optimization, interoperability and governance and regulatory compliance

- **Regulatory landscape**: Uncertainty and evolving regulations surrounding blockchain technology across different jurisdictions

- **Standardization and interoperability**: Lack of standardization across platforms, hindering interoperability and seamless integration

# Addressing Challenges and Seizing Opportunities

Overcoming the hurdles that stand between blockchain-driven SCF and widespread adoption necessitates a collaborative effort from all stakeholders involved. Here are some key strategies for navigating these challenges:

1. **Technology infrastructure development**

   2. **Public-private partnerships**: When government bodies join hands with tech innovators and major players in the industry, they can significantly boost the development of durable, scalable blockchain networks. Picture this scenario: a national government collaborates with top blockchain developers and major names in finance to create a set of shared guidelines. These guidelines ensure that disparate blockchain systems can interact without a hitch. Such collective effort across the board helps dodge the pitfalls of a fragmented approach and paves the way for blockchain technology to be embraced on a broad scale.

   3. **Open-source platforms**: Encouraging the development of open-source blockchain platforms can accelerate innovation and drive down development costs.

   4. **Standardized data protocols**: Establishing standardized data protocols will ensure seamless data exchange and interoperability across platforms.

2. **Regulatory landscape**

   5. **Industry-led advocacy**: Collaborative efforts from industry associations and stakeholders can influence policymakers to develop clear and supportive regulations for blockchain technology.

6. **Regulatory sandboxes**: Implementing regulatory sandboxes can provide a safe environment for testing and piloting blockchain-based SCF solutions without undue regulatory burden.

7. **International cooperation**: Harmonizing regulations across different jurisdictions will facilitate cross-border transactions and global adoption.

3. **Standardization and interoperability**

8. **Industry-wide standards**: Establishing industry-wide standards for data formats, APIs, and smart contracts will ensure seamless integration and interoperability between different platforms.

9. **Interoperability frameworks**: Developing open-source interoperability frameworks will facilitate data exchange and communication between incompatible systems.

10. **Collaboration with existing standards bodies**: Collaborating with existing standards bodies like GS1 and UN/CEFACT can leverage existing standards and accelerate the development of SCF-specific standards.

# Future Frontiers: Emerging Trends and Potential Applications

Blockchain-driven SCF offers a transformative opportunity to revolutionize the way we finance and manage supply chains. By addressing current challenges and embracing emerging technologies, this powerful technology has the potential to unlock a new era of efficiency, transparency, and resilience for the global economy. As we move forward, continued collaboration between all stakeholders involved will be crucial in realizing the full potential of this technology and shaping a more sustainable and prosperous future for all. Beyond addressing current challenges, the future of blockchain-driven SCF holds exciting potential fueled by emerging trends and novel applications:

- **Artificial intelligence and machine learning**: AI-powered data analysis can provide predictive insights into supplier performance, enabling risk mitigation and financing decisions. ML algorithms can automate invoice processing and fraud detection, further streamlining the SCF process.

- **Decentralized finance (DeFi)**: DeFi protocols can provide alternative financing sources for both buyers and suppliers, particularly in underserved markets. DeFi-powered solutions can enable peer-to-peer lending and invoice trading, facilitating access to capital and reducing reliance on traditional financial institutions.

- **Internet of Things (IoT) and Sensor Data**: Real-time
  data from sensors embedded in goods and logistics
  systems can be integrated with blockchain platforms,
  providing enhanced transparency and traceability
  throughout the supply chain. IoT-enabled solutions can
  automate payment triggers based on specific events,
  such as goods delivery or quality verification.

- **Sustainability and carbon footprint tracking**:
  Blockchain-enabled platforms can track and verify the
  environmental impact of goods and services, enabling
  sustainable supply chain practices. Carbon footprint
  data can be incorporated into financing decisions,
  incentivizing sustainable business practices.

- **Cross-border trade finance**: Blockchain-based
  solutions can streamline cross-border trade finance
  processes, reducing costs and transaction times. Trade
  finance platforms can facilitate collaboration between
  banks and financial institutions across different
  jurisdictions.

# Expanding the Conversation: A Deeper Dive into Value Creation

While the previous sections have provided a comprehensive overview
of value creation in blockchain-driven SCF, it's crucial to delve deeper
into specific aspects to fully grasp the transformative potential of this
technology. Dissecting value creation across the supply chain means
understanding the specific value creation mechanisms for each participant
in the blockchain-driven SCF ecosystem. Let's explore how each
participant benefits from this innovative approach:

For buyers, blockchain brings a range of advantages like better management of working capital. It does this by offering features such as dynamic discounting, automated invoice handling, and the chance to grab early payment discounts. Additionally, it enhances transparency in the supply chain, simplifying product tracking and inventory management. It also cultivates better relationships with suppliers by guaranteeing prompt payments, facilitating smoother communication, and reducing payment-related risks.

As for suppliers, blockchain speeds up access to financing options that are both faster and cheaper. Think of solutions like reverse factoring and streamlined trade finance, which lessen the reliance on traditional bank loans. This means that you will get your money quicker, pay fewer fees, and have a better idea of when payments will come in. Plus, with blockchain tech, you can reduce the risk of fraud happening, resolve disputes automatically, and see transactions more clearly.

Financial institutions also benefit from blockchain by expanding their market reach and tapping into previously underserved segments. They achieve this while making operations more efficient through automation and smart contracts. This means lower costs and fresh revenue streams through platform and transaction fees, as well as data monetization opportunities.

For platform providers, blockchain offers a way to build scalable and secure platforms that leverage distributed ledger technology and robust data security measures. It also enables them to adopt subscription-based revenue models through platform fees.

In general, implementing blockchain technology in supply chain finance can bring advantages to everyone involved. It boosts efficiency, transparency, security, and improves access to financing, ultimately strengthening the entire supply chain network.

# Measuring and Quantifying Value Creation: Beyond Qualitative Analysis

To illustrate the transformative power of blockchain-driven SCF in action, let's delve into two insightful case studies: Walmart and Maersk.

## Walmart Leads the Charge

Global retail giant Walmart implemented a blockchain-based platform called Food Trust to track the origin and journey of food products across its vast supply chain. This system significantly improved transparency and traceability, enabling Walmart to identify and address food safety issues faster and more efficiently. Additionally, the platform facilitated faster payments to suppliers, strengthening supplier relationships and improving overall supply chain agility.

## Maersk Streamlines Global Shipping

Leading container shipping company Maersk partnered with several industry players to develop a blockchain-based platform called TradeLens. This platform provides real-time visibility into the movement of cargo around the world, streamlining logistics processes and reducing administrative costs. TradeLens also facilitates trade finance by enabling financial institutions to securely access and verify trade data, leading to faster and more efficient financing solutions.

These case studies demonstrate how blockchain-driven SCF can be successfully implemented to address real-world challenges and create tangible benefits across the supply chain ecosystem.

# Emerging Applications: Exploring the Frontiers of Innovation Quantifying

Beyond the current applications, blockchain technology holds immense potential for driving further innovation in SCF. Here are some promising emerging applications:

- **Decentralized trade finance**: Blockchain can facilitate peer-to-peer trade finance, eliminating the need for intermediaries and reducing transaction costs. This can provide underserved businesses, particularly SMEs, with greater access to affordable financing options.

- **Supply chain management platforms**: Blockchain-based platforms can be developed to manage the entire supply chain lifecycle, from procurement and production to logistics and delivery. This can improve efficiency, transparency, and collaboration throughout the supply chain.

- **Data-driven insights**: The vast data generated within blockchain-based SCF platforms can be analyzed to generate valuable insights into supply chain performance. This data can be used to optimize processes, identify risks, and make informed decisions.

- **Tokenization of assets**: Blockchain allows for the tokenization of physical assets, such as inventory and receivables. This can unlock additional financing opportunities and facilitate trade finance transactions.

- **Carbon footprint tracking**: Blockchain-based platforms can track the carbon footprint of goods throughout the supply chain, enabling businesses to reduce their environmental impact and promote sustainable practices.

105

These emerging applications represent the exciting future of
blockchain-driven SCF and demonstrate its potential to revolutionize the
way we manage and finance global supply chains. The exploration of value
creation in blockchain-driven SCF reveals its transformative potential
for stakeholders across the supply chain landscape. By embracing this
technology and exploring its diverse applications, we collectively unlock a
future of enhanced efficiency, transparency, resilience, and sustainability.
The time for action is now. Let's collaborate and leverage the power of
blockchain to drive a more prosperous and sustainable future for all.

# Conclusion

Quantifying the value creation of blockchain-driven SCF is essential
for understanding its true potential and driving its adoption. By using a
combination of financial, operational, risk management, sustainability,
and social impact metrics, stakeholders can assess the tangible benefits
and make informed decisions about implementing this transformative
technology. As the technology continues to evolve and mature, the
development of robust and standardized metrics will be crucial in
accurately measuring its impact and shaping a more efficient, transparent,
and sustainable future for global supply chains.

# CHAPTER 4

# Artificial Intelligence Applications for Demand Forecasting and Optimization

*Dr. Veena Grover, Professor, Noida Institute of Engineering and Technology, Greater Noida, India.* veena.grovere@gmail.com.

*Purnima Pal, Research Scholar, Kamla Nehru Institute of Technology, Sultanpur, India.* purnima22pal@gmail.com.

*Vidhi Bishnoi, Assistant Professor, Kiet Group of Institutions, Ghaziabad, India.* vidhibishnoi@gmail.com.

*Dr. Nassir Ul Haq Wani, Director and Associate Professor, Department of Research and Development, Kardan University, Kabul, Afghanistan.* nassirtciba786@gmail.com.

The rise of bike sharing systems in the continually evolving landscape of city mobility has emerged as an effective and sustainable remedy for addressing the challenges caused by the traffic environment and congestion concerns. With the increasing popularity of bike sharing systems, intelligent data-driven methods for optimizing their functioning are in demand. This chapter discovers the relevance of artificial intelligence (AI) in the specific spheres of demand forecasting and optimization within the context of predicting bike sharing usage. The collaboration between bike sharing and AI systems holds the potential for significant transformations in enhancing operational efficiency, user experience, and overall sustainability. Through the employment of sophisticated algorithms, machine learning models, and predictive analytics, this chapter investigates how AI methodologies can offer appreciated insights into forecast demand patterns, user behavior, and the allocation of resources within bike sharing networks. The exploration investigates the complexities of demand forecasting by utilizing external factors and historical usage data to develop robust models capable of precisely predicting future demand. The incorporation of AI in this domain allows operators to predict the peak usage periods and facilitate upbeat planning to meet fluctuating demand in real time.

Additionally, this chapter investigates optimization, where AI-driven algorithms play an essential role in planning routes, managing resource allocation, and overseeing fleet management. By analyzing the capabilities of artificial intelligence, bike sharing operators can dynamically adjust the distribution of their taskforces, ensuring an optimal balance of bikes across various stations to minimize downtime and enhance user satisfaction. The convergence of bike sharing forecasting and AI usage represents both technological advancement and strategic progression for creating more intelligent and responsive transportation systems. Through the presentation of real-world case studies and practical examples, this chapter illuminates the transformative potential of AI in reshaping bike-sharing operations, contributing ultimately to the development of more sustainable and efficient solutions for urban mobility. As we navigate the particulars of this dynamic intersection between bike sharing and artificial intelligence, we encourage readers to anticipate the possibilities that lie forward in influencing the future of urban transportation.

Bike-sharing systems (BSSs), also known as bike hire or bike rental, have become a widely sustainable and adopted solution for urban transportation in contemporary times. This advanced approach enables an individual to rent a bike on a pay-per-use basis for a short duration, presenting an environmentally friendly and convenient substitute to conventional transportation methods [1]. Bike-sharing systems improve promote diverse transportation options, offer access to urban areas, and contribute to sustainable mobility. Many cities worldwide are adopting these shared modes to address the growing challenges of urban mobility expansion, air pollution, and shifts in behaviors and mobility patterns, particularly diminished by the new pandemic crisis [2]. The global reception of bike-sharing schemes has been overwhelmingly positive. These services provide shared bikes to individuals on a short, temporary basis, either at a minimal rate or free of charge. Bike-sharing systems enable users to borrow and return bikes at distinct stations within the same network. The increasing popularity of bike sharing is part of broader proposals to improve the environmental impact of transportation activities and modes of transportation. The significant impacts of bike sharing include fostering a larger cycling community, boosting transportation usage, reducing greenhouse gas emissions, alleviating traffic congestion, and promoting public health [3].

The BSS in South Korea is designed to be accessible to all residents in various cities [4]. Unlike traditional renting, users can borrow a bike from one system station and return it to another, enhancing mobility and serving many users. Membership in a bike sharing program provides users with access to a city-wide bike fleet at minimal or no cost. Numerous bike-sharing systems operate automatically using either smart cards or mobile phones.

Although the advancement of bike sharing was sluggish in the beginning, the implementation of advanced tracking methods for bicycles after 1960 significantly contributed to the widespread adoption of bike sharing systems across continents. South Korea has embraced this trend, transforming into a nation of two-wheel enthusiasts. The increasing user base underscores the need to predict the number of rental bikes required for the system to operate consistently. This study uses machine learning and data mining algorithms to forecast the necessary quantity of rental bikes on an hourly basis.

Numerous bike-sharing enterprises operate globally. Some of the most prominent ones are Santander Cycles, Nextbike Ofo, Vélib, Lime, Mobike, JCDecaux, Call a Bike, Citi Bike, and BikeMi. The global reach incorporates over 500,000 bikes distributed across more than 500
bike-sharing system [5]. Based on this extensive scale, accurately forecasting the demand for bicycles becomes important for several reasons. Initially, demand prediction aids bike-sharing companies in effectively managing their portfolio. By accurately predicting the need for bikes, these firms can ensure an adequate supply at each station, preventing consequences where users face a scarcity of available bikes, which could lead to disappointment and missed sales prospects. Furthermore, demand prediction contributes to functioning improvements. Understanding how bikes are utilized and identifying high-demand areas allows bike-sharing companies to optimize their operations. This optimization could adjust pricing strategies or involve relocating bikes from low-demand to high-
demand regions to align with fluctuations in demand.

Furthermore, demand prediction helps long-term planning for bike-sharing businesses. Learned decisions about station placement, expansion, and new services can be made based on accurate forecasting, enhancing overall strategic planning. Demand prediction is involved in pricing optimization. By understanding the demand for bikes at different times of the day, bike-sharing companies can adapt pricing to reflect the demand more accurately for their services. This fine-tuning can lead to increased profitability and sales.

However, a considerable challenge faced by bike-sharing systems is the
randomness of the number of rental bikes needed at any given moment.
The motivation behind this study is to develop methods for estimating the
required number of bikes in a bike-sharing system. Real-world data sets
from Konya and Washington, D.C. were employed to forecast the demand,
focusing on this inherent challenge in bike-sharing systems.

# Related Work

Various empirical investigations have utilized numerous predictive models
to forecast the demand in bike-sharing systems. These models commonly
incorporate various external factors, including weather conditions,
temporal details, and spatial information. A forecasting system intended
to predict BSS outcomes [6] is introduced; it depends on specific data
formats derived from both docked and dockless BSS. This section provides
a comprehensive review of various models utilized.

Krishna et al. [7] conducted a comparison of various machine learning
techniques including linear regression, polynomial regression, lasso
regression, ridge regression, AdaBoost, gradient boost, and XGBoost
within the domain of forecasting. Their findings indicated that boosting
algorithms outperformed other methods. Sathish Kumar et al. [8] proposed
a rule-based model for Seoul Bike, and this study utilized the same
model. The authors explored five different machine learning algorithms,
including KNN, classification and regression trees, CUBIST (a regression
model), regularized random forest, and conditional inference tree. Among
these algorithms, CUBIST demonstrated the most accurate forecasting
based on variance. A study by Nair & Miller-Hooks [9] developed a model
for determining optimal locations for bicycle docking stations. This
model employed a two-level stochastic dynamic program in which the
upper-level task involved strategically placing stations to enhance user
flow and the lower level focused on minimizing transportation costs
for each consumer by selecting transportation modes and travel routes

based on station locations. Each individual consumer resolved this issue independently. To tackle the widespread network of locations, a heuristic solution approach employing a genetic algorithm was devised, making use of historical data derived from bike-sharing in Washington, D.C. An investigation was conducted by Kim [10] to explore diverse climate conditions and temporal characteristics, examining attributes at both the station level and framework level. In the practical station-level analysis, a clustering approach was utilized by researchers to detect sets of stations sharing comparable characteristics. To account for the influence of humidity and temperature, they incorporated a temperature–humidity index and a variable indicating the presence of a heat wave. Furthermore, a system-level analysis was performed and specific variables applied significant effects at different times of the day. Particularly, factors such as temperature, whether it was a workday, and rainfall influenced the demand for rental bikes at definite times. The prediction of future bike availability at the stations was conducted by continuous-time Markov chains models with rates that varied over time, as proposed in the work by Feng et al. [11].

In a study conducted by Lee et al. [12], an RNN model integrated a dual attention mechanism specifically crafted to capture temporal and spatial instantaneously. This mechanism recognized and assigned weights to all location-related features within the time series data, thereby enhancing the model's ability to learn mutual correlations. This approach promotes the model's efficiency in handling variations in local conditions across different bike stations.

Gast et al. [13] proposed a probabilistic predictions from a time-inhomogeneous queuing model for evaluation the future availability of bikes in bike-sharing framework stations. Furthermore, the influence of calendar and weather events on the number of trips for all City Cycle stations in Brisbane was reflected using a Poisson model by Corcoran et al [14].

Lin et al. [15] proposed a stacking model for forecasting changes in public bicycle traffic flow based on real-world data. The models were trained using XGBoost to classify factors affecting public bicycle traffic flow. To strengthen the examination, the authors employed the K-Medoids algorithm to cluster bike stations. This elaborate method created a unique station correlation matrix based on the distances between stations.

Schuijbroek et al. [16] explored bike-sharing systems that have become widely popular and are installed in numerous cities globally. The primary objective was to maintain an optimal balance of bikes and available docks for users. In addressing this issue, the authors proposed an innovative heuristic approach that prioritized clustering over routing. This strategy addressed a clustering challenge of polynomial size by concurrently considering the feasibility of service levels and the approximate routing costs.

Li and Zheng [17] proposed a hierarchical consistency prediction model to forecast citywide bike usage in the upcoming period. The authors proposed an adaptive transition constraint clustering algorithm, an efficient similarity-based Gaussian process regressor, and a general least square formulation. The efficiency of their model was established through experiments by utilizing real-world data, showcasing its practical pertinency.

The prediction by Chen et al. [18] of return and rental demand in the next hour for the New York City Bike Dataset was accomplished using a bidirectional recurrent neural network architecture. The features incorporated in the model encompassed data related to bike-sharing systems, meteorological metrics, and information data. A comparative analysis was conducted against ordinary least-squares regression (OLSR), random forest (RF), and a feedforward neural network. Notably, the BI-RNN outperformed the other models on the test set, demonstrating superior results in terms of metrics such as MAE, RMSLE, RMSE, and MAPE.

Acheampong et al. [19] determined that participants perceived cycling as an uncomplicated activity. They conveyed confidence in their ability to control their performance and riding skills, a factor substantially impacting their cooperation to engage in cycling.

On a similar note, Kadri et al. [20] conducted a study emphasizing
that the primary objective of bike sharing systems should be to meet
customer demand while reducing operational costs. They underscored the
importance of anticipating future customer demand and bike availability
through data analysis and metrics. Kaplan et al. [21] and additional
studies have demonstrated that individuals residing in bicycle-friendly
environments exhibit a positive attitude towards cycling, a keen interest in
bicycle technology, adherence to good bicycle practices, and a heightened
perception of comfort associated with bicycles. These residents also
tend to adopt habits conducive to bicycle-friendly countries in terms of
their living environment, choice of transportation modes, and their past
experiences and interest in bicycle travel, influencing their inclination and
intention to use bicycles.

Having reviewed the various predictive models and methodologies
employed in forecasting bike-sharing system outcomes, the subsequent
section will delve into the description of datasets employed in this
predictive analysis.

# Dataset Description and Exploratory Data Analysis

In our research for forecasting and optimizing the demand of the bike
sharing, we employed datasets comprising the utilization log of the Capital
Bike Sharing (CBS) system in Washington, D.C., USA [22]. The dataset
encompassed counts of rental bikes on both an hourly and daily basis,
accompanied by relevant weather and seasonal data. Specifically, we
focused on an hourly dataset containing 17,379 instances and featuring
attributes like date, season, year, month, and weather details, as shown in
Table 4-1.

***Table 4-1.*** *Dataset Description*

| Feature | Description | Type |
|---------|-------------|------|
| Day | Day of month (1 to 31) | Categoric |
| Holiday | 0: non-holiday, 1: holiday | Categoric |
| Weathersit | 1. Clear, partly cloudy, or few clouds<br>2. Misty/cloudy, mist broken by clouds; mist and few clouds<br>3. Light snow, thunderstorm, scattered clouds, light rain, or light rain with scattered clouds<br>4. Thunderstorm, ice pellets, heavy rain, snow, mist, fog | Categoric |
| Weekday | Day of the week (0: Monday to 6: Sunday) | Categoric |
| Cnt | Count of total rental bikes | Categoric |
| Windspeed | Normalized wind speed value | Numeric |
| Hum | Normalized humidity value | Numeric |
| Workingday | 0: non-working day,1: working day | Categoric |
| Temp | Normalized temperature value in Celsius | Numeric |
| Yr | 0:2011, 1:2012 | Categoric |
| Mnth | Month (1 to 12) | Categoric |
| Season | 1. Spring<br>2. Summer<br>3. Fall<br>4. Winter | Categoric |
| Hr | Hour (1 to 12) | Categoric |
| Atemp | Normalized feeling temperature in Celsius | Numeric |

Moreover, we conducted an outlier analysis to detect any anomalies within the dataset. The outlier, in this context, denotes a data point that substantially diverges from the anticipated pattern within the data.

These aberrations can exert a notable influence on statistical analyses and modeling outcomes, which is potentially important to biased or deceptive decisions. Consequently, we conducted an outlier analysis on selected input variables, as shown in Figure 4-1.

In the realm of bike demand, outliers have the capacity to disrupt inherent patterns and trends. Through the identification and comprehension of outliers, we gained insights into the broader trends, discerning whether they signify substantial shifts in demand or are merely noise.

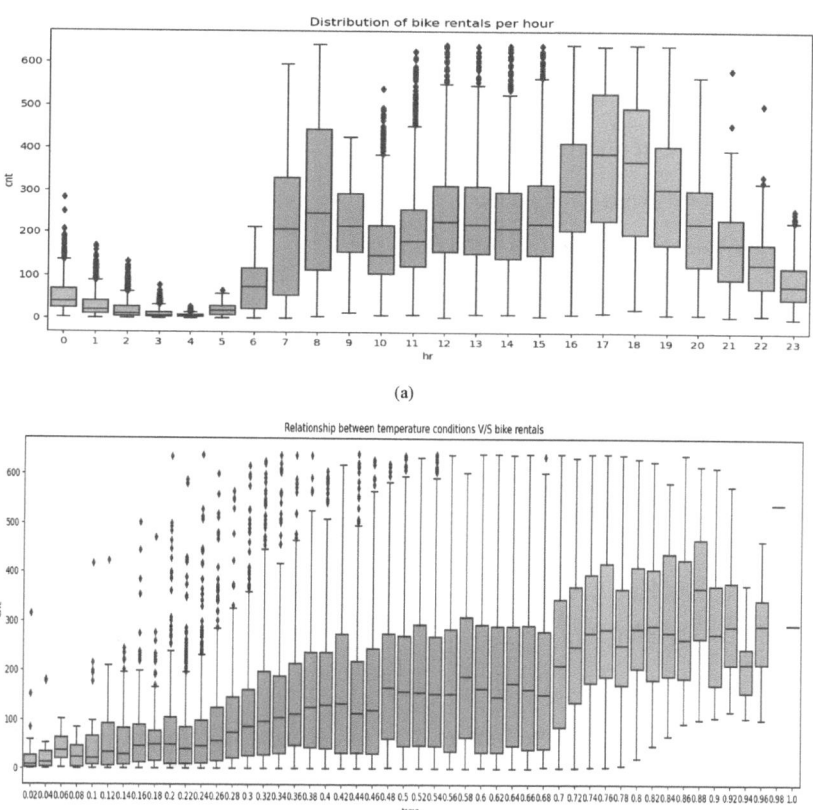

**Figure 4-1.**  *Outliers plot of the attributes of the dataset (a) bike rental per hour and (b) relationship between temperature conditions v/s bike rentals*

A heatmap serves as a graphical depiction enabling the exploration
of relationships and correlations within a dataset, offering an intuitive
means to comprehend underlying patterns and trends (Figure 4-2). In the
realm of bike-sharing data, this visualization becomes a potent tool for
illustrating the interconnectedness of various variables.

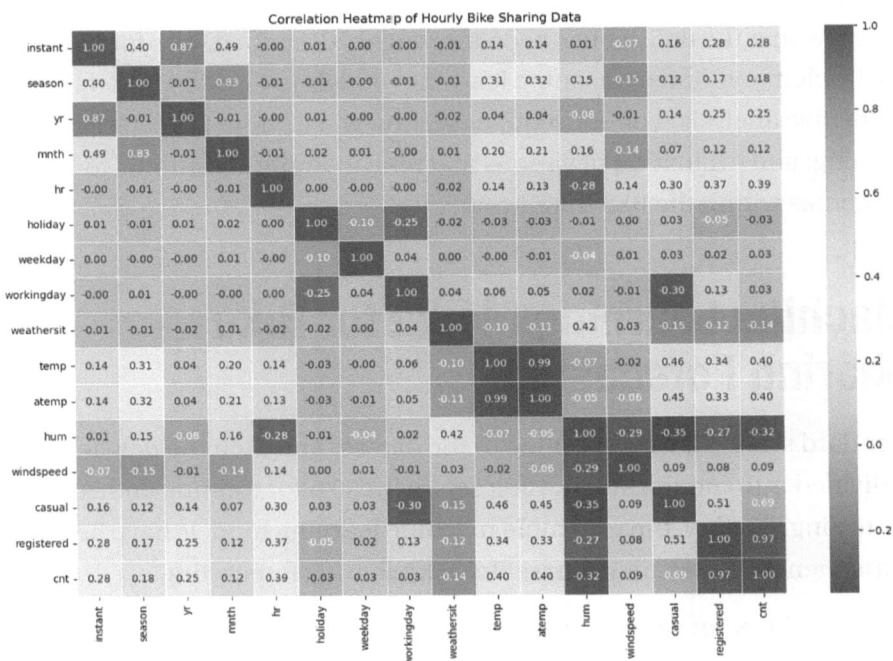

***Figure 4-2.***   *Heatmap of the hour bike sharing dataset*

For instance, one could generate a heatmap incorporating factors
like year, season, month, hour, weekday, holiday status, working day,
weather conditions, temperature, wind speed, humidity, as well as counts
such as casual riders, registered users, and total bike rentals. Utilizing a
color gradient to indicate the strength and direction of correlations, the
heatmap reveals valuable insights into the factors influencing patterns
in bike sharing. Intensified colors signify more pronounced positive or

negative correlations, enabling observers to discern relationships like the
association between the time of the day and the frequency of bike rentals,
or the impact of weather conditions on ridership. These visualizations play
an essential role in extracting important understandings from complex
bike-sharing datasets as shown in Figure 4-2, contributing to an improved
understanding of the dynamics shaping bike usage trends over time.

Now that the dataset has been thoroughly described, let's focus on
the implementation of machine learning models to leverage this data for
predictive analysis. The subsequent section will explore the selection,
training, and evaluation of various machine learning algorithms to forecast
outcomes within the BSS framework.

# Machine Learning Model for Bike Sharing Forecasting

Standard scaling is implemented to the dataset and then the dataset
is divided into training and testing sets, with 80% for training and 20%
for testing. Further, the ensemble machine learning models have been
implemented on training dataset for bike sharing forecasting.

- **Standard scaling:** Standard scaling is a preprocessing
  method in machine learning which is implemented
  to ensure a uniform scale for the numerical features
  within a dataset. This procedure involves adjusting
  each feature so that it reaches a mean of 0 and a
  standard deviation of 1[23].

$$Z = \frac{x - \mu}{\sigma} \tag{4.3.1}$$

where $\mu$, z, x, and $\sigma$ are the mean of the features value, the standardized value, the original value, and the standard deviation of the feature, respectively.

- **Random forest:** Random forest is a versatile and robust model for bike share forecasting, accurately handling the complexities involved in predicting bike demand. The random forest model captures complex relationships within the data, including holiday effects, temporal patterns, and weather conditions. The ensemble model random forest[24] works to resolve the issue of overfitting by providing flexibility in the presence of noisy or high-dimensional bike share data. The hyperparameter tuning requirement in the random forest model helps in adjusting parameters like the number of trees and depth and is a requirement for optimizing the model's performance.

- **Gradient boosting:** Gradient boosting is an ensemble learning technique. It was developed as a powerful tool for bike-sharing forecasting tasks. Its sequential construction of a decision tree as a weak learner enables the capturing of complex patterns and adjuncts in the dataset. It's particularly proficient at handling complex temporal relationships and the influence of features like special events and weather conditions in the framework of bike-sharing forecasting. Gradient boosting surpasses by iteratively correcting errors from previous weak learners, thus improving predictive accuracy. It often breaks traditional models by instantaneously minimizing both variance and bias.

119

- **Stacking:** A stacking model is employed for bike-sharing forecasting. It introduces an ensemble learning approach that incorporates the strengths of multiple week models to enhance forecasting accuracy. This technique involves combining forecasting from base models, including decision tree, random forest, and logistic regression, to create a meta-model that optimally combines their predicted errors. A stacking model is efficient in capturing a broad range of relationships and patterns in the bike share dataset, leading to more accurate and robust forecasting. The stacking process involves training multiple weak models on the same dataset and later using a meta-model to weigh their forecasting based on their individual performance.

# Performance Metrics

The following parameters were used to access the performance of the forecast model for the bike-sharing system:

- **RMSE:** The RMSE is the square root of the average of the squared differences between the predicted and actual values. RMSE demonstrates greater sensitivity to outliers, resulting in its superiority when the data lacks outlier cases.

- **R-squared ($R^2$) Error:** R2 evaluates the efficiency of independent variables in exposing the fluctuations observed in the dependent variable. The R-squared value ranges from 0 to 1.

- **MSE:** The MSE is the average of the squared differences between the predicted and observed values. It enforces a greater penalty for significant errors due to the squaring operation. Contrasting RMSE, MSE exhibits less sensitivity to outliers, proving it a more suitable alternative when the data contains outlier cases.

The subsequent section will delve the result and discussion of the machine learning models.

# Result and Discussion

The performance of the ensemble machine learning models for the BSS dataset for bike-sharing forecasting is summarized in Table 4-2.

*Table 4-2.* *Forecasting Error of Various Machine Learning Models*

| Model | MSE | RMSE | R² Score |
| --- | --- | --- | --- |
| Random forest | 3.0851 | 1.756 | 0.999 |
| Gradient boosting | 18.318 | 4.279 | 0.999 |
| Stacking | 0.003 | 0.0604 | 0.999 |

The outcomes derived from the predictive models for the BSS exhibit significant performance statistics. Specifically, the random forest model illustrates a root mean squared error (RMSE) of 1.756, a mean squared error (MSE) of 3.0851, and a remarkable R2 score of 0.999, revealing its robust predictive capacity for BSS. Similarly, the gradient boosting model displays worthy performance metrics by achieving an RMSE of 4.279, a MSE of 18.318, and an R2 score of 0.999, underscoring its effectiveness in capturing involved patterns within the data. The stacking model achieved a remarkably low MSE of 0.003 and an RMSE of 0.0604, along

with an $R^2$ score of 0.999. These findings highlight the accomplishment
of ensemble techniques, specifically stacking, in increasing predictive
accuracy, positioning them as valuable tools for bike-sharing forecasting.
The reduced RMSE and MSE values across all models indicate precise
forecasting, while the improved $R^2$ Scores signify robust model for the bike
sharing dataset.

# Conclusion

The bike-sharing system affects both society and the environment
significantly, initiating positive transformations in urban settings on a
global scale. From an environmental perspective, these systems play
an important role in reducing air pollution and carbon emissions. This
chapter significantly explores the application of AI in demand forecasting
and optimization, precisely focusing on utilizing bike-sharing data.
Ensemble machine learning techniques, including gradient boosting,
random forest, and stacking, are employed to improve the accuracy of
demand forecast. By utilizing these advanced models, the study not only
highlights their efficiency in capturing complex patterns within bike-
sharing datasets but also underscores their role in improving demand
forecasting processes. The comparative evaluation of random forest,
gradient boosting, and stacking yields valuable understandings into
their distinct strengths, providing a comprehensive understanding of
their relevance in the domain of bike-sharing prediction. The study's
outcomes influence the evolving body of intelligence on the practical use
of AI in optimizing demand forecasting, especially within the dynamic
domain of bike-sharing systems. The effective integration of these models
suggests promising prospects for their application in real-world scenarios,
promising improvements in the efficiency and accuracy of demand
forecast and optimization within the BSS sector.

# CHAPTER 5

# AI-Enabled Supply Chain Planning and Execution: A Pathway to Sustainability

*Vaishnavi Gadi, Pathik Govani, SVKM'S Narsee Monjee Institute of Management Studies, Mumbai-56, Maharashtra, India.*

*Dr. Veena Grover, Professor (School of Management), NIET, Greater Noida, India.*

*Dr. Balamurugan Balusamy, Associate Dean - SNIOE, Delhi NCR, India.*

Recently, supply chains and sustainability have dominated headlines in the world of business. The relationship between supply chain disruptions and climate change emphasizes the intricacy of supply chains, as well as their significance for achieving the sustainable development goals (SDGs) of the UN by 2030 (Ayan et al., 2022). These include promoting climate action, adequate employment and economic growth, and responsible

The original version of this chapter was revised. A correction to this chapter can be found at https://doi.org/110.1007/979-8-8688-0315-4_17

© The Editor(s) (if applicable) and The Author(s),
under exclusive license to APress Media, LLC, part of Springer Nature 2024,
corrected publication 2024
Dr. V. Grover et al. (eds.), *Blockchain, IoT, and AI Technologies for Supply Chain Management*,
https://doi.org/10.1007/979-8-8688-0315-4_5

consumption and production (SDGs 8, 12, and 13.) Nearly all 17 SDGs are touched by environmental, social, and governance (ESG) issues that are weaved throughout international supply chains. Many approaches have been put forth, but one that is much too frequently disregarded may be the most successful of them all: artificial intelligence (Tukker et al., 2010).

The next frontier in sustainability is supply chains. They are the main forces behind any organization's sustainability objectives. Supply chain executives are moving forward with sustainability in mind, protecting their access to resources and building resilience while also looking for new opportunities to explore and obstacles to conquer (Rae, 2022).

Essentially, the definition of supply chain sustainability is the incorporation of social, environmental, and corporate governance factors into the sourcing, production, and distribution of raw materials to the market (Ramos, 2022). Global sustainability implementation is influenced by two trends: global supply chain "greening" and technology like big data, AI, and digitization, which significantly impact business planning and supply chain operations (Sanders et al., 2019).

Supply network security, competitive pricing, sustainability, and interoperability may all be achieved by integrating AI and BCT (blockchain technology) to increase data collection, interoperability, and analysis capabilities throughout end-to-end operations. Big-box stores such as Walmart, Carrefour, and Alibaba have already begun using BCT to track down milk suppliers and agricultural items and to combat food fraud (Kshetri, 2018).

Within the realm of AI-enabled supply chain planning and execution, this chapter serves as an overview of sustainability in supply chain management. It elucidates the pivotal role sustainability plays in optimizing supply chains through the lens of artificial intelligence. Real-life case studies are dissected to highlight the symbiotic relationship between sustainability and various operational facets such as forecasting, inventory management, and customer support. The profound analysis of case studies featuring Country Delight and Mondelez not only underscores their challenges but also showcases how AI-driven strategies have catalyzed their journeys towards sustainable supply chain practices. This chapter serves as a testament to the transformative power of AI in fostering sustainability within supply chains, paving the way for a future where efficiency, ethics, and environmental responsibility harmoniously converge.

# Importance of Sustainability in Supply Chain Management

The production processes and supply chains have been strained by the ever-increasing demand for products and their consumption, which has had detrimental effects on society and the environment. Researchers and industry specialists have been compelled to focus on sustainable production and consumption issues within the framework of sustainable supply chain management (SSCM) due to the rising rates of pollution and environmental disasters brought on by industrial production (Rajeev et al., 2017).

The goal of supply chain sustainability is to reduce pollution, deforestation, ozone depletion, and global warming while maintaining standardized procedures. The main goals of supply chain management are efficiency, affordability, dependability, optimization, and ongoing development. Sustainable sourcing, production, packaging, and responsible distribution are all components of a sustainable supply chain. Corporate social responsibility initiatives ensure resource optimization and environmental friendliness by promoting green operations, cost savings, and long-term supply chain development. The most effective supply chain partnership tools utilize transformative technologies to consolidate procurement for all trading partners associated with an organization (*Supply Chain Sustainability: Importance, Roles & Best Practices | GEP*, n.d.).

The transportation sector is the main source of greenhouse gas emissions, according to the U.S. EPA (United States Environmental Protection Agency). It makes up a substantial 29% of all US emissions. Additionally, a sizeable portion of this 29% originates from the e-commerce industry (US EPA & OAR, 2022). The transportation sector contributes to nearly 25% of the total global greenhouse gas emissions (Date & Search, 2019). The rapid growth of e-commerce has made the integration of AI in supply chain management and logistics imperative. By optimizing operations and logistics, cutting waste, raising customer satisfaction, cutting prices, and improving efficiency, AI is revolutionizing the sector. Predictive analytics powered by AI can determine the best shipping routes, lowering the carbon footprint of transportation, and improving supply chain sustainability. The current state of supply chain management and e-commerce logistics is being altered by this change (Toorajipour et al., 2021).

Sustainable supply chains not only have a positive effect on the environment but also have a positive impact on business since they increase process efficiency and lower operating costs. Companies that want to create a sustainable supply chain must make sure that KPIs (key performance indicators) are modified, benchmarks are updated, and staff involvement and training are continuously improved (Villena and Gioia, 2020).

Rising product demand strains supply chains, harming society and the environment. SSCM aims to address these issues by focusing on reducing pollution, deforestation, and global warming. Key components include sustainable sourcing, production, packaging, and responsible distribution. The integration of AI in supply chain management is vital for optimizing logistics and reducing emissions, especially in e-commerce. Sustainable supply chains benefit the environment and business efficiency, requiring continuous improvement in KPIs, benchmarks, and staff training.

# Practical Applications of AI to Achieve Sustainable SCM

AI has an immensely transformative power across domains. Let's explore how AI-driven solutions revolutionize inventory control, logistics optimization, and ethical supplier collaboration for a greener, more efficient supply chain landscape.

## Inventory Optimization

A vital balancing act between preventing product shortages and reducing expenses related to excess inventory is inventory management (Waters, 2008).

Supply chain generative AI plays a critical role in preserving this equilibrium by analyzing past data, demand trends, and external factors to determine the ideal inventory levels. By using this technology, companies may avoid overstocking, cut down on excess inventory, and improve supply chain responsiveness. When taking into account demand changes, delivery timeframes, and transportation costs, generative AI models can determine the best distribution and storage techniques. Maximized operational efficiency and significant cost savings are the end results. Generative AI helps companies improve warehouse management by suggesting reorder points and safety stock levels, which reduces product shortages, minimizes excess inventory, and lowers holding costs (*Generative AI in Supply Chain | IBM*, n.d.).

## Logistics Optimization

Within supply chain logistics, AI revolutionizes sustainability through multifaceted optimizations. AI algorithms harness real-time data on traffic, weather, and road closures to streamline delivery routes, curbing fuel consumption and carbon emissions (Ahmed et al., 2021). Furthermore, AI aids in load consolidation, maximizing truck capacities to diminish the number of vehicles on roads, thus reducing the carbon footprint per transported unit. Energy efficiency in warehouses is bolstered by AI-driven systems that regulate lighting, heating, and cooling based on occupancy and external conditions, curtailing overall energy consumption (*8 Ways Artificial Intelligence Can Drive Decarbonization*, n.d.). Predictive maintenance empowered by AI ensures greener fleets through proactive vehicle repairs, enhancing efficiency and minimizing transportation emissions (Ivanova, 2022). Additionally, AI evaluates supplier sustainability criteria beyond cost and quality, enabling eco-conscious selections. Tools powered by AI monitor carbon footprints across the supply chain, allowing strategic reductions in environmental impact. By analyzing cost, time, and ecological factors, AI optimizes transportation modes, suggesting environmentally friendly options such as rail or sea freight. Leveraging AI-driven demand forecasting for precise inventory management, companies mitigate overproduction and waste, aligning production with actual demand to reduce environmental ramifications linked to excess inventory and disposal (Chen et al., 2023).

# Ethical Supplier Collaboration

Through AI-enabled systems, companies can collaborate with suppliers aligned not just with financial benchmarks but also ethical and environmental standards. AI evaluates supplier practices, certifications, and sustainability impact, fostering partnerships that prioritize eco-friendly practices and social responsibility. This collaboration facilitates the selection of suppliers committed to reducing carbon footprints and promoting ethical labor practices (Ali, 2018). By leveraging AI, companies engage in transparent, ethical collaborations, optimizing the supply chain for sustainability. Such initiatives not only enhance the ecological footprint but also foster efficiency by streamlining processes, reducing

waste, and promoting responsible sourcing practices. AI's role in ethical
supplier collaboration redefines the supply chain landscape by driving
collective efforts toward a greener, socially responsible, and more efficient
operational framework (Casandra Okogwu et al., 2023).

# Demand Forecasting

AI-powered demand forecasting epitomizes a revolutionary approach
in supply chain dynamics, leveraging advanced algorithms to execute
robust predictive analytics (*Role of Artificial Intelligence in Supply
Chain Analytics _ Marketing Analytics Companies _ Digital Analytics*,
n.d.). Employing machine learning models and neural networks,
businesses process multifaceted data sets comprising historical sales,
market variables, consumer behavior patterns, and real-time external
influences. This amalgamation of diverse data sources allows for the
development of sophisticated predictive models adept at anticipating
demand fluctuations with exceptional precision. Through recurrent neural
networks and deep learning frameworks, AI algorithms continuously
refine forecasts, optimizing inventory stocking levels and production
schedules (Perifanis and Kitsios, 2023). This not only minimizes the risk
of inventory imbalances but also fosters resource efficiency and waste
reduction. The adaptive nature of AI ensures a responsive system capable
of swiftly adapting to evolving market trends, thus fortifying supply chains
to proactively meet consumer demands while optimizing resources and
curbing environmental impact (Transmetrics, 2023).

# Chatbots for Customer Support

Chatbots are strategically deployed across multiple facets of SCM,
prominently in customer service and internal operations. Functioning
as a primary interface for customer inquiries, these AI-driven systems
adeptly handle order tracking, product information, and issue resolution,

freeing human resources for intricate tasks. Within SCM, chatbots streamline order processing by offering real-time updates on shipments, enhancing transparency in logistics. They efficiently manage inventory inquiries, providing insights into stock availability and specifications. Moreover, they facilitate seamless collaboration with suppliers, optimizing communication and expediting processes. Beyond external interactions, chatbots support internal SCM functions, aiding employees with HR-related queries and bolstering internal communication. Their data analytics prowess extracts valuable insights from customer interactions, refining strategies for an optimized supply chain. Constant learning cycles empower these chatbots, continually enhancing their capabilities and bolstering their pivotal role in ensuring efficiency, customer satisfaction, and operational excellence throughout the SCM landscape (*What Is the Role of Chatbots in Digitizing the Supply Chain_*, n.d.).

AI is revolutionizing supply chain management through inventory optimization, logistics, ethical supplier collaboration, demand forecasting, and customer support. AI-driven solutions balance inventory levels, reduce waste, and enhance operational efficiency. In logistics, AI optimizes routes and load consolidation for reduced emissions. AI also aids in selecting eco-friendly, ethical suppliers and predicts demand to minimize overproduction. Chatbots improve customer service and internal operations in supply chains. Overall, AI significantly boosts supply chain sustainability and efficiency.

# Integrating AI for End-to-End Supply Chain Resilience

In laying the groundwork for sustainable supply chains, companies must embrace long-term commitments while initiating immediate actions to drive meaningful change. EY's outlined strategies propose a comprehensive approach. Aligning supply chain sustainability with

organizational objectives, leveraging technological advancements
for enhanced visibility, and broadening ROI (return on investment)
assessments to encompass intangible impacts are pivotal. The shift from a
procurement-centric focus to embracing the entirety of the supply chain,
complemented by cross-functional collaboration, offers multifaceted
business opportunities. Moreover, leveraging available incentives and
grants underscores the financial viability of sustainability initiatives.
Trailblazing companies, accounting for a minority yet significantly
impactful group, prioritize transparency, extending their view into
deeper tiers of supply networks. Notably, their emphasis on public-facing
sustainability goals reflects a proactive stance toward societal expectations.
They demonstrate a nuanced approach, placing lesser emphasis on cost
savings while reaping financial gains, such as increased revenue and
anticipated share price escalation. As these trailblazers illuminate the way
forward, integrating AI technologies becomes crucial, enabling resilient
and transparent supply chains poised for sustainable growth (Rae, 2022).

# Models For Managing Supply Chains

BCG (Boston Consulting Group) has proposed three different operational
models for managing material flow in supply chains:

- **Siloed operating model:**

  - Described as having low performance due to siloed
    operations. This is due to the misalignment of
    objectives within the different compartmentalized
    departmental functioning (silos), inefficient
    resource allocation, and redundancy in efforts.
    This structural fragmentation impedes the flow
    of information across units, resulting in decision-
    making that is not fully informed by the collective

intelligence and resources of the organization,
thereby undermining synergistic potential and
leading to suboptimal outcomes.

- The material flow is segmented, with many breaks
  in the flow, indicating that the various stages of
  supply chain management are not well-integrated.

- Different departments or groups within the
  organization do not share information, resources,
  or processes with each other.

- **Hub-based operating model:**

  - It is said to put complexity on people's shoulders.

  - At the center is a "planning hub," which includes
    roles such as the demand planner, inventory
    planner, inbound planner, raw material planner,
    production scheduler, transport planner, and
    logistics planner.

  - This model implies a more centralized approach
    to planning, where different planning functions
    are coordinated through a central hub, potentially
    reducing silos but still relying heavily on human
    management and decision-making.

- **Flow-based, AI-driven operating model:**

  - It is characterized by end-to-end flows managed in
    a highly automated way.

  - The material flow is continuous and seamless,
    suggesting that AI and automation are used to
    optimize the supply chain and allow for a more
    integrated and efficient operation.

The concept illustrated in this study is the transformation of supply chain management from traditional, compartmentalized systems towards more integrated and automated solutions facilitated by AI. In the context of sustainability, using AI in supply chains can lead to more efficient use of resources, reduction of waste, and optimization of logistics and inventory, which all contribute to a more sustainable approach.

AI enables better demand forecasting, which can lead to fewer overproduced goods and less waste. It can also optimize routing and logistics for transportation, leading to reduced emissions. Inventory management becomes more accurate, reducing the need for excessive storage and minimizing the risk of products becoming obsolete. The transformation to AI-driven models can result in cost savings, improved customer satisfaction due to better service levels, and a reduced environmental footprint, all key components of sustainable supply chain management (Rodriguez Pepe et al., 2022).

BCG proposed three supply chain models: siloed (low performance, segmented flow), hub-based (centralized planning, human-dependent), and AI-driven flow-based (highly automated, seamless). Transition to AI-driven models enhances efficiency, reduces waste, and optimizes logistics, contributing to sustainable supply chain management with cost savings and reduced environmental impact.

# Planning and Execution of AI-Enabled Sustainable SCM

The strategic planning phase of supply chain management is foundational to its sustainable execution, and AI has become instrumental in enhancing this phase. AI-driven tools enable profound improvements in supplier selection processes by analyzing vast arrays of data on supplier performance, risk profiles, and sustainability practices. These tools not only predict potential delays and disruptions by learning from historical

patterns but also suggest corrective actions. Moreover, AI facilitates
a more nuanced approach to communication, ensuring alignment of
objectives and transparent sharing of information across the supply
chain. This is pivotal for executing a sustainable strategy as it ensures
that all stakeholders are informed and collaborative in their approach to
sustainability goals (Min, 2010).

The execution phase of a sustainable supply chain is replete with
challenges that AI is uniquely equipped to address. AI optimizes logistics
and transportation by determining the most efficient routes, thereby
reducing carbon emissions and energy consumption (Wang et al., 2016).
Real-time tracking of goods using AI not only ensures on-time delivery but
also helps in maintaining the integrity of sensitive products, contributing
to waste reduction (Srivastava, 2007). Furthermore, AI systems enhance
decision-making capabilities, processing real-time data to make informed,
sustainability-focused decisions. This is crucial in managing the return
networks of products, where AI can streamline the reverse logistics to
support recycling and remanufacturing, which is integral to a circular
economy (Govindan et al., 2020).

AI is pivotal in strategic planning for sustainable supply chains,
enhancing supplier selection and predicting disruptions. It optimizes
logistics, reduces emissions, and supports a circular economy through
informed, real-time decision-making.

# Metrics for the Evaluation of Sustainability in SCM

Metrics and accounting methods play a crucial role in quantifying
the sustainability of supply chain operations. The multi-dimensional
nature of sustainability requires comprehensive metrics that encompass
environmental, social, and economic aspects, collectively known as
the triple bottom line (Elkington, 1998). Environmental metrics often

include the measurement of carbon footprint, energy consumption, waste generation, and water usage, which are vital for assessing the ecological impact of supply chain activities (Hervani et al., 2005). Social metrics, on the other hand, evaluate the fair treatment of labor, community engagement, and consumer protection. Economic metrics focus on the long-term financial viability of sustainable practices. Life cycle assessment (LCA) is a systematic method used to assess the environmental aspects and potential impacts throughout a product's life cycle, from raw material acquisition through production, use, end-of-life treatment, recycling, and final disposal (ISO 14040/14044).

Accounting methods for sustainability in SCM have evolved to include the use of sustainability balanced scorecards and triple bottom line reporting, which facilitate the integration of sustainability into strategic management and reporting practices (Kaplan and Norton, 2005). These methods enable companies to not only track their performance against sustainability goals but also communicate this performance to stakeholders. Furthermore, activity-based costing (ABC) has been adapted to account for environmental costs, leading to more accurate costing models that reflect the true cost of environmental impacts in the supply chain (EPA, 1995). The Global Reporting Initiative (GRI) provides standards for sustainability reporting, which many companies adopt to enhance transparency and accountability in their supply chain operations (GRI, 2021).

# Mondelez Case – Net Zero 2050; The Role of Sustainable Sourcing

Mondelez's journey towards achieving net-zero greenhouse gas emissions by 2050 heavily relies on sustainable sourcing practices, the integration of AI, and a robust sustainable supply chain management strategy.

# Role of Sustainable Sourcing

Carbon footprint reduction, deforestation-free supply chains, and collaboration and innovation are three key factors in sustainable sourcing. Initiatives, like regenerative farming practices for cocoa, wheat, and dairy, are pivotal. Mondelez has launched the Harmony Wheat Sustainability program and the Cocoa Life program as part of its regenerative agriculture initiatives. These initiatives are integral to enhancing supply chain sustainability by targeting its environmental, social, and economic facets. Environmentally, they advocate for sustainable farming practices—such as biodiversity enhancement and pesticide reduction in wheat cultivation, alongside the diversification of cocoa farms through economic shade trees—that aim to preserve ecosystems and bolster resilience against agricultural threats. These efforts not only ensure the environmental integrity of the supply chain but also contribute to its social sustainability by improving livelihoods and community well-being among farmers. Economically, by investing in the sustainability of farming practices and communities, these programs help secure the long-term viability and reliability of agricultural supply chains, ensuring a stable supply of essential raw materials (*Regenerative, Sustainable Agriculture; Mondelez International, Inc*, n.d.).

These practices aim to reduce emissions, promote soil health, and enhance biodiversity. Commitments to no deforestation across primary commodities by 2025 ensure the preservation of ecosystems and contribute to mitigating climate change. Partnering with industry initiatives like the Cocoa Life and Forests Initiative showcases Mondelez's commitment to collaborative efforts aimed at implementing climate-smart practices, fostering innovation, and promoting sustainable landscapes.

# AI Integration

AI is employed to optimize farming techniques, fertilizer usage, and crop
rotation. The Harmony Academy platform and decision-making tools
utilize AI to encourage farmers to adopt regenerative practices, reduce
emissions, and enhance soil health. AI also helps in precision agriculture,
allowing for more efficient resource utilization, reduced waste, and
increased productivity, all contributing to lower environmental impact.

# Sustainable Supply Chain Management

Collaborating with suppliers on greenhouse gas reduction programs
in dairy showcases efforts to reduce emissions at the farm level. The
company's commitment involves improving sustainable sourcing, such
as advancing deforestation-free cocoa and wheat supply chains and
promoting regenerative agriculture practices. Specific actions include
training farmers in sustainable practices, distributing millions of trees,
implementing farm mapping, and promoting biodiversity. Additionally,
Mondelez is enhancing operational efficiencies by adopting renewable
energy, optimizing manufacturing processes, and improving logistics to
reduce emissions.

Aligning with SBTi protocols and transparently reporting progress
ensures accountability and drives continuous improvement in
sustainability practices. Mondelez plans to use its scale and influence
to drive technical advancements, public-private collaboration, and
investment. This includes incubating innovation in sustainable practices
throughout the supply chain.

Mondelez's Net Zero 2050 strategy heavily leans on sustainable
sourcing practices across its key commodities, integration of AI for
optimization and efficiency, and a sustainable supply chain management
plan. Through collaboration, innovation, and a commitment to
transparency, Mondelez aims not only to transform its own operations

but also to lead and inspire change within the industry towards a more
sustainable one (*Mondelez Net Zero 2050: The Role of Sustainable Sourcing,
Procurement Magazine*, n.d.).

# Country Delight Case: Using Tech to Build a Farm-To-Home Supply Chain of Milk

In India's traditional dairy market, Country Delight has emerged as a
pioneer, reshaping the industry landscape through its innovative fusion
of AI technology and sustainable supply chain practices. The company's
journey has been marked by transformative strides in ensuring high-
quality, farm-fresh dairy products reach consumers' doorsteps while
minimizing environmental impact.

## AI-Powered Operational Excellence

Country Delight employs advanced AI algorithms to analyze consumption
patterns and forecast demand accurately. This empowers the company to
optimize production, minimizing waste and ensuring resource efficiency.

Leveraging AI, the company designs optimized delivery routes,
reducing fuel consumption and carbon emissions while ensuring timely
and efficient deliveries, even in areas with infrastructural challenges.

Cutting-edge sensors and AI-powered monitoring systems conduct
real-time quality checks at various stages of the supply chain. This ensures
that only the freshest and highest-quality dairy products reach consumers,
reducing waste and upholding sustainability standards.

# Sustainable Supply Chain Practices

Country Delight's farm-to-table approach eliminates intermediaries and thus minimizes transportation and handling, thereby significantly reducing the carbon footprint associated with conventional supply chains.

Collaborating directly with local farmers not only ensures fresher products but also supports sustainable agricultural practices. This empowers local communities and fosters environmental sustainability.

Stringent quality control measures guarantee that only top-tier dairy products are delivered, minimizing waste and reinforcing the company's commitment to sustainability. Country Delight's operational framework integrates a direct-to-consumer delivery mechanism, which optimizes logistics and diminishes packaging redundancy, thereby reducing the environmental footprint associated with conventional retail distribution networks. The company's subscription model facilitates demand predictability, allowing for precise production forecasts, thereby preventing overproduction and subsequent waste. Furthermore, by building direct partnerships with agricultural producers and employing sustainable practices, the company enhances the efficiency of the supply chain, minimizing resource depletion and contributing to a reduction in food spoilage and waste, aligning with global sustainability objectives.

# Impact Amid Challenges and Growth

Country Delight's ownership of livestock ensured an uninterrupted supply chain during challenging times, sustaining operations and serving customers reliably. Through adherence to government guidelines and proactive stakeholder communication, the company not only survived but also thrived, navigating the pandemic with agility and resilience.

The company promotes market leadership through Innovation 's user-friendly website and mobile app, powered by AI. It offers seamless customer experiences, allowing for easy subscriptions, order

139

customization, and delivery tracking. It also features sustainable growth with technology. The convergence of AI-driven efficiencies and sustainable practices has catapulted Country Delight to the forefront of the dairy industry, establishing its position as a leader in delivering fresh, organic dairy products across India.

Country Delight's narrative is a testament to the transformative impact of merging cutting-edge AI technology with sustainable supply chain practices. Through innovation and a steadfast commitment to quality and sustainability, the company continues to set new benchmarks, revolutionizing the dairy market in India (*Country Delight Sucess Story: The Story of Country Delight's Farm-to-Table Delivery Model*, n.d.).

Sustainability in SCM requires metrics encompassing the triple bottom line: environmental, social, and economic. Environmental metrics measure ecological impact, social metrics assess fair labor and community engagement, and economic metrics gauge long-term financial sustainability. Life cycle assessment and methods like sustainability balanced scorecards and triple bottom line reporting track and communicate sustainability performance. AI is key in enhancing sustainable SCM, optimizing supplier selection, logistics, and decision-making. Mondelez and Country Delight exemplify this approach, integrating AI for sustainable sourcing, optimized logistics, and reduced environmental impact in their supply chains.

# Issues Using AI to Facilitate a Sustainable Supply Chain

There is a two-way interaction between AI and SSC, where AI acts as a pivotal element in mitigating various supply chain challenges and enabling sustainable operations.

The supply chain issues identified include the following:

- **Planning:** Challenges in forecasting and strategizing supply chain operations effectively.

- **Supplier selection:** Difficulty in choosing suppliers that meet criteria for cost, quality, sustainability, and reliability.

- **Delayed deliveries:** Problems caused by not receiving goods on time, affecting downstream processes.

- **Communication:** The need for improved coordination and information exchange between stakeholders.

- **Data availability/evaluation:** The importance of having accessible, reliable, and actionable data for decision-making.

- **Carbon emissions:** The environmental impact of supply chain activities.

- **Ineffective logistics/transportation:** Inefficiencies in the movement of goods that can lead to increased costs and environmental footprint.

- **Return network for products:** Managing the reverse flow of goods, whether for recycling, reuse, or disposal.

- **Information sharing:** Sharing data across the supply chain to improve transparency and coordination.

- **Decision-making:** The process of making informed and strategic decisions in supply chain management.

- Artificial intelligence techniques listed include machine learning, Bayesian networks, artificial neural networks, robotics, genetic algorithms, deep learning, fuzzy logic, and particle swarm optimization. These techniques can significantly enhance supply chain operations by providing advanced analytics, predictive insights, and autonomous decision-making capabilities.

For the above issues, AI-enabled operations promise the following:

- **Reduced carbon emissions:** Through optimization of logistics and resource use.

- **Real-time manufacturing:** Enabling adaptive production processes responsive to demand fluctuations.

- **On-time delivery:** Improved logistics planning to ensure timely deliveries.

- **Availability of data:** Ensuring data is collected and accessible for decision-making.

- **Effective information sharing:** Facilitating better communication throughout the supply chain.

- **Efficient remanufacturing:** Supporting circular economy initiatives by improving processes related to the reuse of materials and products.

- **Easy return of goods:** Streamlining reverse logistics.

- **Suitable supplier selection:** Leveraging AI to evaluate and choose suppliers that align with sustainability goals.

- **Demand forecast:** Enhancing the accuracy of demand predictions to reduce waste and inefficiencies.

- **Resilience under disruption:** Improving the supply chain's ability to respond to and recover from disruptions.

The sustainable supply chain components influenced by AI include the following:

- **Sustainable transportation:** Implementing greener transportation methods and optimizing routes.

- **Optimization in SC:** Streamlining operations to minimize waste and maximize efficiency.

- **Data analytics in SC:** Utilizing big data for insights that drive sustainability.

- **Proposed models for SSC:** Developing new models for sustainable supply chain management.

- **Remanufacturing in SC:** Supporting the return and reuse of products within the supply chain.

The model underscores the transformative impact of AI on sustainable supply chain management by fostering a data-driven, responsive, and environmentally conscious operational framework. The synergy between AI and SSC elements can lead to a more resilient, efficient, and sustainable supply chain ecosystem, capable of meeting modern demands and ecological considerations (Naz et al., 2022).

AI is pivotal in addressing challenges and enabling sustainable supply chain management. It enhances forecasting, supplier selection, on-time deliveries, data availability, and decision-making, leading to reduced carbon emissions, improved logistics, and support for a circular economy. AI fosters a resilient, efficient, and sustainable supply chain ecosystem.

# Conclusion

While predictions once indicated AI-powered automation as the forerunner of a supply chain revolution, the full transformation remains elusive. Despite substantial investments, companies grapple with the realization of AI-managed supply chains. A recent BCG and Aera Technology study uncovers the root cause—a misalignment in AI application. Rather than harnessing AI for recurring decision-making, most companies limit its use to analytics and predictions, missing the profound opportunity of AI's capacity to discern patterns in vast datasets, unobservable to humans.

To unleash AI's latent potential, a paradigm shift is imperative—an AI-powered learning system that pervades across functions, seamlessly making decisions based on comprehensive enterprise and external data. This system learns iteratively from outcomes, automating decisions instead of merely offering insights, thus relieving practitioners of the decision-making burden. Success demands not just technological prowess but also instilling trust in AI among personnel and introducing a novel operating model.

Despite this envisioned potential, fundamental supply chain issues persist, as evident in the analysis of KPIs from 2011 to 2020. Delivery performance declined, even with escalated inventory and staffing levels amid the COVID-19 onset, revealing the complexities that AI implementations strive to address.

Challenges to AI's successful integration in supply chains are multifaceted. Inherent complexities in supply chain management, comprising diverse functions and subfunctions, hinder holistic optimization. Organizational structures often prioritize isolated function optimization over end-to-end efficiency. These complexities compound due to high turnover, which disperses critical knowledge and impedes strategic problem-solving efforts. Moreover, technological hurdles persist, questioning the feasibility of comprehensive AI-driven learning systems and the acquisition of quality data for training.

Companies, constrained by misconceptions and overreliance on consensus decision-making, face impediments in deploying disruptive technology for supply chain enhancements. Addressing these multifaceted challenges necessitates a recalibration of approach, prioritizing learning systems, fostering talent retention, and embracing disruptive technology to propel AI's transformative potential within supply chains (Rodriguez Pepe et al., 2022).

AI's potential in revolutionizing supply chains is hindered by its underutilization for decision-making and a focus on analytics. Companies must shift to AI-driven learning systems for comprehensive decisions and overcome organizational, technological, and conceptual challenges to realize AI's full transformative potential.

# CHAPTER 6

# Leveraging IOT in Supply Chain Sustainability: A Provenance Perspective

*Dileep Kumar Murala, Department of Computer Science and Engineering, Faculty of Science and Technology (IcfaiTech), ICFAI Foundation for Higher Education, Hyderabad, Telangana, India.* `drdileepm@ifheindia.org`.

*Komali Siddamshetti, Department of Artificial Intelligence and Machine Learning, AVN Institute of Engineering and Technology, Hyderabad, Telangana, India,* `komaliguptha@gmail.com`.

*Dr. Mariofanna (Fanny) Milanova (IEEE Senior Member), 4NVIDIA Deep Learning Instructor, Fulbright Scholar, and Professor. Computer Science Department, University of Arkansas, Little Rock, AR 72204, USA.* `mgmilanova@ualr.edu`.

Dr. V. Grover et al. (eds.), *Blockchain, IoT, and AI Technologies for Supply Chain Management*, https://doi.org/10.1007/979-8-8688-0315-4_6

The global economy relies on logistics companies to help transfer
commodities and goods worldwide. However, logistics firms are feeling
the heat to cut costs and improve efficiency in light of the growing interest
in sustainability. One strategy for accomplishing this goal is to streamline
operations through the use of Internet of Things technologies and the
rationalization of supply chains. The goal of supply chain rationalization
is to reduce costs, maximize efficiency, and shorten the time for
commodities to transit from production to consumption. Technology,
data analytics, and careful preparation can help this process. An important
part of this process can be played by IoT technology. From manufacture
to delivery, data may be collected from the whole supply chain using IoT
sensors and devices. By conducting an analysis of these data, it is possible
to identify inefficiencies and bottlenecks within the supply chain. In order
to investigate the function that the Internet of Things plays and the impact
that it has on supply chain management (SCM), this study conducts a
comprehensive literature review. The article explores the definition of
IoT, the key technological components that facilitate IoT, and the diverse
procedures and applications of SCM. The existing literature is classified
using many approaches, including the technique utilized, the industry it
relates to, and the major emphasis on supply chain operations.

# Internet of Things

"IoT" is a term that can be used in many ways. Based on the study [8],
the main reason for this is that the phrase "IoT" is made up of just
two words: "internet" and "things." It looks like we have two main
ideas here. The first vision is more about the "internet" or network
part, while the second vision is more about the "things" part. In the
original conceptions of the IoT, the focus was on "things," specifically
radio frequency identification (RFID) tags that could send personal
information across a network [12]. Subsequently, more "things" such

as motors and sensors were introduced, which is how contemporary mobile gadgets are constructed. Listed below are a few definitions that represent the various ways in which individuals comprehend the IoT.

Things with real and virtual personalities that work in smart places and use smart interfaces to connect and talk to each other in social, environmental, and user settings. "Internet of Things" is an umbrella term for many different topics related to how the Internet and the Web are being brought into the real world by a large number of widely placed devices that can identify, sense, and/or act. The IoT imagines a world where digital and real things can be connected using the right kinds of information and communication technologies. This will make it possible for a whole new set of services and apps [13].

When sensing and acting devices are combined, they can communicate data across platforms by utilizing a single framework. This results in the creation of a shared operational picture, which in turn makes it feasible for new applications to be developed. Modern cloud computing and ubiquitous sensing make it easy to combine data analytics, information visualization, and large-scale sensing for a distributed network of smart objects (SOs) that collaborate but are not connected. Sensor objects are physical-digital objects that can perceive, act, process, store, and link to other devices [14]. SOs can feel, act on, store, and understand internal and external information when they are close to the outside world. They can also work together and share data with humans and computers. Both physical and digital "things" have distinct identities, attributes, and virtual personalities; they communicate with one another through intuitive user interfaces and maintain seamless internet connections. Physical or digital "things" can be part of this dynamic, worldwide network architecture that relies on open, compatible communication protocols [15].

It's a collection of infrastructures that connects devices that are already connected and gives you the ability to operate them, mine their data, and access the data that they generate. It is possible to define linked objects as those that possess a sensor and/or a motor that are capable of performing a certain task and communicating with other devices [16]. It is a component of an infrastructure that enables users or other systems to send, store, manage, and access data that they have created. How does the IoT relate to the management of supply chains? That is our objective. The collection of individuals, locations, and objects that collaborate to fulfill an order placed by a customer is referred to as a supply chain. Typical examples of these groupings include customers, distributors, wholesalers, and retailers, as well as suppliers and factories. The SCOR model (APICS 2015) identifies six distinct types of supply chain operations. These processes are as follows: planning, sourcing, making, sending, returning, and enabling. According to the author [18], the purpose of supply chain management is to "maximize the surplus," which is defined as the difference between the price that the customer pays and all of the costs that occur throughout the supply chain [17].

IoT greatly impacts supply chain management. It bridges the digital and physical worlds, enhancing operations, precision, and real-time data availability. By installing sensors on tangible resources, companies may monitor and manage their whereabouts, condition, and performance, easily integrating the collected data into their operational systems to gain useful insights. This IoT-enabled visibility enhances the process of fulfilling orders, reduces the impact of disruptions, and aids in managing risks related to inventories, delayed delivery, and product quality. For example, cars outfitted with sensors have the ability to monitor position and speed as well as issue maintenance notifications, hence minimizing transit delays. In the same way, interconnected sensors oversee the crucial temperature consistency required for perishable items, thereby reducing unnecessary loss. Furthermore, intelligent IoT sensors facilitate dynamic inventory management by actively notifying when shelves need restocking and predicting maintenance needs in advance.

Both SCM and information technology (IT) have been strongly dependent on one another for a considerable amount of time [6]. IT plays a crucial role in supporting supply chains in overcoming the challenges that are brought about by an environment that is constantly changing and a myriad of dangers that are present at different levels. Information technology's ability to connect various processes inside and, more significantly, externally with suppliers and customers has changed supply chains. Improvements in transmission, data collection, and communication have led to enhanced decision-making and supply chain performance. The expansion of the Internet of Things is having a significant impact on supply chain management, among other industries. Communications in the supply chain are being revolutionized by the IoT, which allows for two-way communication between objects and autonomous coordination of "things" in storage or transportation. These additional abilities will help with managing supply chain management concerns. An open, quick, and adaptable supply chain is possible with the use of the IoT [7]. When collected, processed, and translated properly, smart device data can provide priceless supply chain knowledge. This insight might highlight internal and external issues that need immediate attention. Responding quickly to these indications can boost supply chain efficiency to new heights. The problems have not been with a lack of information; rather, they have been with the technology that is meant to collect and understand enormous amounts of data, as well as the amount of time that is required to move from gathering data to doing something with it. The IoT will allow for more nimbleness and response to change. This is due to the fact that the Internet of Things will reduce the time it takes to go from collecting data to making a decision [8]. Smarter partner collaboration, remote supply chain administration, and access to more accurate data for better decision-making are all made possible by the IoT.

The implementation of the IoT in the supply chain offers significant opportunities for businesses of all sizes, including both large-scale manufacturers and small entrepreneurs. It has the ability to enhance responsiveness, improve customer experience, and reduce inefficiencies. Gartner's forecast of a thirty-fold surge in internet-connected devices indicates that supply chain operations will undergo a significant overhaul, enhancing productivity and enabling real-time decision-making. The IoT and the technologies that made it possible are described in this section. Additionally, we provide an IoT definition pertinent to SCM.

# A Look Back ...

The idea of interconnected gadgets was initially proposed in the early 1990s while working at the Auto-ID Center at MIT. The IoT was made possible as a result of this first step. Kevin Ashton, who is in charge of the Center, is credited with coming up with the name "IoT" in the year 1999 [1]. Ashton considered using RFID tags to track Procter & Gamble products in 1997. To read and identify items, RFID tags were utilized, and the information was transmitted remotely over a network. Previously, the first time that RFID tags were utilized in commercial settings was in 1980 [2]. A new idea evolved about using sensors and motors in a wireless sensor network (WSN) to detect, track, and monitor details. This could be used in traffic management and healthcare [3]. These networks enable the IoT with GPS, cell phones, social media, cloud computing, and data analytics.

Because of the Internet of Things, production in Europe, and particularly in Germany, has been able to build Industry 4.0. During the first three waves of the Industrial Revolution, mechanical power, mass manufacturing, and digitization were the driving forces behind progress. Currently, the time has come for Industry 4.0, which is also commonly referred to as the Fourth Industrial Revolution. Industry 4.0 is defined by the author [4] as the combination of information technology and industrial technology. The Internet of Things is merely a component of Industry 4.0. Cloud manufacturing and cyber–physical systems are also needed. A comprehensive production system (CPS) includes machines, storage systems, and production facilities that can communicate, act, and monitor each other [5]. According to the author [7], a CPS connects a production unit's virtual (computers) and real (machines) components via analog and digital hardware. The IoT lets us connect the CPS to sensors, motors, and other devices. IoT systems use cloud computing in other data centers. Cloud manufacturing was born from this in the Industry 4.0 [11].

# How We Define IoT

A group of physical objects that are digitally connected to enable them to detect, monitor, and interact with one another within an organization as well as with its supply chain is referred to as the IoT. This enables flexibility, visibility, tracking, and the sharing of information, which in turn makes the operations of planning, regulating, and coordinating the supply chain easier and more efficient. The four main points that make up our proposed definition are as follows: (i) All physical items in the supply chain must be digitally connected; (ii) Data storage, analysis, and sharing necessitate proactive connectivity; (iii) Organizations must connect with each other and the supply chain to cover all critical processes; (iv) The IoT will help supply chain management [19]. In Industry 4.0, the Industrial IoT resembles the IoT. CPS and the IoT enable Industry 4.0 in industrial robotics. The IoT underpins Industry 4.0, the fourth industrial revolution. In Industry 4.0, "things" may refer to intelligent machinery, products, and services like maintenance and logistics that use quality control [20]. In the following section, we will go over the specific benefits of IoT in supply chain management and logistics.

# Supply Chain Management and Logistics and the IoT

All aspects of supply chain management can benefit from the IoT. These instances are examined in the following sections.

## Locating Goods and Shipments in Real Time

IoT sensors attached to products or storage containers provide real-time tracking of the whereabouts of items and shipments, which is a huge benefit for supply chain management. IoT devices can send their locations to GPS satellites. The tracking of goods and shipments becomes much easier with this technology. In addition, managers are notified when shipments start heading in the wrong direction or come to a stop at an unauthorized location. This allows them to intervene promptly and prevent delays or loss of goods [21].

## Monitoring Storage Conditions

The IoT has several significant uses in the supply chain, but one of the most crucial is monitoring storage conditions. There would be a plethora of data included, including temps, light levels, pressure, humidity, and atmospheric exposure. Supply chain managers have an important role in ensuring that storage facilities, such as warehouses, comply with all applicable environmental requirements. As a result, less or no spoiling of perishable commodities will occur [22].

# Better Estimation of Arrival Time

The IoT improves the processing of goods and decreases their handling
times, leading to better arrival time estimation. Managers in the supply
chain can use it to more accurately predict when they will arrive. This is
accomplished by monitoring the shipment's progress and any traffic jams
that may be impeding its delivery [23].

# Improved Contingency Planning
# and Risk Mitigation

Supply chain managers can determine why shipments are running
behind schedule, which allows for better risk mitigation and improved
contingency planning. This is made possible by examining the information
about past shipments that are collected by IoT devices. Details would
cover things like weather, traffic, potential accidents, and more. Plus, by
making plans that are adaptable and include different pathways, they can
reduce the likelihood of negative outcomes. This allows them to redirect
shipments to preplanned alternate routes if they receive real-time alerts
indicating traffic delays [24].

# Locating Goods in Storage

The IoT has been a godsend for warehouses. IoT streamlines inventory
management and makes it easier to locate a particular product in a vast
warehouse. Improved productivity and worker safety are side effects of
the automated and streamlined procedures it provides. The integration
of IoT and AI allows for the complete automation of warehouse activities,
significantly reducing the need for human supervision. Items can be more
easily tagged with the use of IoT devices like RFID sensors and Bluetooth
Low Energy (BLE) beacons. It allows for the monitoring of the whereabouts
of items in certain aisles or their transit across the warehouse [25].

# Triggering Post-Arrival Administrative Tasks

With the use of IoT tracking, managers of supply chains can initiate
administrative tasks such as payment processing, quality checks, and
delivery requests in real time. The IoT has connected supply chains
like webs of commerce. Supply chain operations can be optimized and
losses reduced or eliminated by utilizing real-time data collected by IoT
devices. The following are a few ways in which logistics and supply chain
management can benefit from the IoT.

## Raised Profile

It permeates the entire supply chain, beginning with production and ending
with retail. IoT devices let raw material suppliers track the variables that
affect the availability of high-quality, on-time deliveries. For example, farms
can keep tabs on the well-being of their cattle, forestry on their logging
operations, and agriculture on the health of their crops. Similarly, merchants
are leveraging the power of IoT to improve the precision of goods pickup
and streamline material handling processes. By keeping tabs on customer
activity, they can optimize display and space utilization, and by following
products as they move across shelves, they can better manage inventory [26].

## Teams Work Together More Effectively

The data in complex value chains tends to get siloed. When groups in
the supply chain use different data and don't communicate effectively,
bottlenecks occur. This is particularly the case for businesses that are still
using antiquated systems that lack adequate tools for data analysis. With
the use of cloud computing and data analytics, IoT-based solutions may
unify all teams involved in the value chain by eliminating data silos. It
improves communication and cooperation amongst groups, which speeds
up problem-solving [27].

# Maximizing Asset Utilization

The IoT provides the connection that logistics and supply chain managers need to get the most out of their fleets. They can enhance delivery numbers through smarter route planning, faster asset identification, better asset efficiency monitoring, and operational fine-tuning. Additional procedures based on machine learning (ML) and AI aid in understanding the data supplied by IoT devices and doing predictive analytics. It paves the way for eco-friendlier operations, better fleet maintenance, freight management, and vehicle tracking. Hence, the IoT provides better asset utilization, less downtime, higher visibility, lower costs, and easier management [28].

# Improved Customer Experience

Managers can match the expectations of their end customers about the timeliness and quality of delivery when supply chains are operating well, which improves the customer experience. The upshot is an increase in revenue as a consequence of happier customers. They can also precisely predict when things will be delivered by tracking them in real-time. They can take action to fix delivery problems if they catch them early. To fulfill SLAs, they can additionally arrange for alternative delivery methods [29].

# Better Inventory Management

A key component of supply chain and warehouse management is inventory tracking and control, which can be improved with better inventory management. For improved administration and optimization, IoT devices track inventory levels and analyze them. Transportation and distribution businesses are part of the supply chain that benefits from the precise data provided by inventory monitoring systems enabled by the IoT. It aids in the efficient management of the supply chain by allowing them to monitor product availability, set order limits appropriately, and minimize unneeded shortages [22].

# Regulatory Compliance

A company must follow all applicable local laws and regulations to operate legally. When it comes to managing required paperwork and complying with regulations, the IoT assists firms in adhering to regulatory compliance and litigation prevention. Fast and reliable reports are generated by an IoT solution, which also provides a digital audit trail with precise timestamps [21].

# Process Automation

Automating the most tedious and complex paperwork chores is a breeze with smart logistics solutions. For instance, they can handle the carrier's bill of lading, which is used to confirm shipment receipt. Warehouse automation is another important benefit of IoT for supply chain management. It boosts precision and efficiency while reducing human effort and errors.

These are just a few benefits of how IoT technology is being applied in logistics and supply chain management to improve efficiency, visibility, and operational performance. The following section outlines the several use cases of IoT in logistics and supply chain.

# IoT Use Cases in Logistics and Supply Chain

Supply chain and logistics giants are integrating IoT into fundamental processes. Some significant business applications are discussed in the following sections.

# Smart Warehouse

Machines and computers perform routine tasks at a "smart warehouse,"
including labeling, rack shifting, and more. It had been done by others
before. Everything that involves moving quickly and carrying large objects
is handled by robots at Amazon. The warehouse floor is equipped with
QR tags that help the robots navigate more efficiently. Collaborating with
robots, humans excel at activities that demand precision and analytical
thinking. Because of the automation made possible by the IoT, Amazon
can store 50% more merchandise and retrieve it three times faster. There is
a 40% decrease in its fulfillment cost as well [11].

# Remote Container Management

Monitoring the whereabouts and internal conditions of refrigerated
containers is now possible with the use of RCM (remote container
management) technology. At any point during transit or when the vessel
is at sea, it displays the current state of the power connection. One of the
world's foremost shipping and logistics companies, Maersk, uses RCM to
keep perishable goods from spoiling and to cut down on resource waste.
To improve transportation planning and execution, it keeps an eye on
weather and other environmental factors [12].

# Predictive Maintenance Solution

Utilizing sensors, artificial intelligence, and data science, it aids in
optimizing equipment maintenance as a predictive maintenance solution.
This ensures the highest possible uptime with the lowest possible
maintenance expenditures. Fluid Monitoring is a predictive maintenance
solution used by Volvo Group at their engine factory in Lyon, France. At the
Group Truck Operations (GTO) facility, it keeps an eye on the five engine

test cells. Before any potential issue, the system notifies the maintenance
crew. That way, they don't have to stop the engine tests. It helps them save
both time and money [13].

These are just a few examples of how IoT technology is being applied
in logistics and supply chain management to improve efficiency, visibility,
and operational performance. The following section discusses several
applications of IoT in logistics and supply chain.

# IoT Applications in SCM

IoT' supply chain management apps are changing businesses'
transportation and operations strategies. IoT applications in supply chain
management are shown in Figure 6-1.

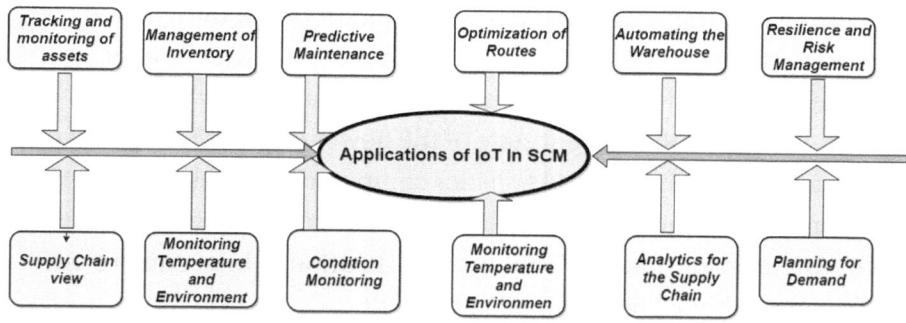

***Figure 6-1.*** *Applications of IoT in supply chain management*

IoT is mostly used in supply chain management for the following:

- **Tracking and monitoring of assets**: IoT sensors
  and global positioning system (GPS) trackers enable
  real-time monitoring and tracking of assets like
  vehicles, containers, and commodities. This improves
  transparency and accountability throughout the supply
  chain [14].

- **Management of inventory**: IoT devices installed in storage facilities and warehouses provide businesses with up-to-the-minute data on their inventory, allowing them to better manage stock levels, prevent shortages, and expedite order fulfillment.

- **Predictive maintenance**: Machine and tool health and performance data collected by IoT monitors enables predictive maintenance. By scheduling maintenance in advance, businesses may save repair costs and downtime [15].

- **Supply chain view**: The IoT provides a bird's-eye view of the entire supply chain, revealing the current status of products, any delays, and potential issues as they occur. Because of this candor, individuals are better able to make decisions and deal with danger.

- **Monitoring temperature and environment**: IoT sensors can monitor environmental conditions, including temperature and humidity, during the transportation or storage of perishable goods, such as food, medications, and other perishable commodities. This guarantees compliance with rules and the preservation of product quality.

- **Condition monitoring**: IoT devices can monitor the state of items throughout shipment. Products are protected from harm and ensured to function correctly by sensors that detect a wide range of environmental factors, including but not limited to shock, vibration, tilting, humidity, temperature, light intensity, pressure, and more [16].

- **Optimization of routes**: Businesses can discover
  the most efficient transportation plans and routes
  by combining data from the IoT with analytics and
  AI algorithms. This shortens delivery times, reduces
  transportation costs, and conserves gasoline.

- **Automating the warehouse**: By coordinating tasks
  and making optimal use of space, automation powered
  by the IoT streamlines warehouse work. Included in
  this category are the more efficient and error-proof
  automated selecting, packing, and sorting processes.

- **Monitoring temperature and environment**:
  Companies can monitor their suppliers' performance,
  ensure they meet delivery dates, and rate vendors using
  real-time data, all thanks to IoT data, and this improves
  supplier management [17].

- **Analytics for the supply chain**: Information gleaned
  from the IoT provides valuable insight into the current
  state and potential areas for improvement of the supply
  chain. Better decisions and more efficient company
  operations can be yours with the help of this data.

- **Resilience and risk management**: With the help of the
  IoT, businesses can anticipate and prevent supply chain
  risks and issues. Because of this, they can respond
  rapidly and ensure the supply chain is robust [18].

- **Planning for demand**: To make an accurate prediction
  of what consumers will want, demand planning models
  can be integrated with data collected from the IoT. This
  aids businesses in optimizing their work schedules and
  inventory levels, leading to cost and waste reduction.

- **Reporting on compliance and regulations**: The IoT
  facilitates real-time tracking, which aids companies
  in conforming to regulations, industry standards, and
  ethical sourcing criteria.

- **Management of the cold chain**: The IoT monitors
  humidity and temperature throughout shipment,
  protecting the cold chain in sectors such as food and
  medicine. In this way, the goods' quality and security
  are preserved. Customers are happier and more
  inclined to trust a company that can provide them with
  real-time tracking information and delivery updates,
  thanks to IoT-driven supply chain knowledge [19].

Multiple supply chain management use cases exist for the
IoT. Innovation and improvement will accelerate with the integration
of the IoT into supply chain management and the advancement of
technology.

# Using IoT to Control the Supply Chain

IoT in supply chain management aims to track and monitor. The system
helps warehouse and fleet managers track commodities and shipments.
Figure 6-2 describes controlling the supply chain using IoT.

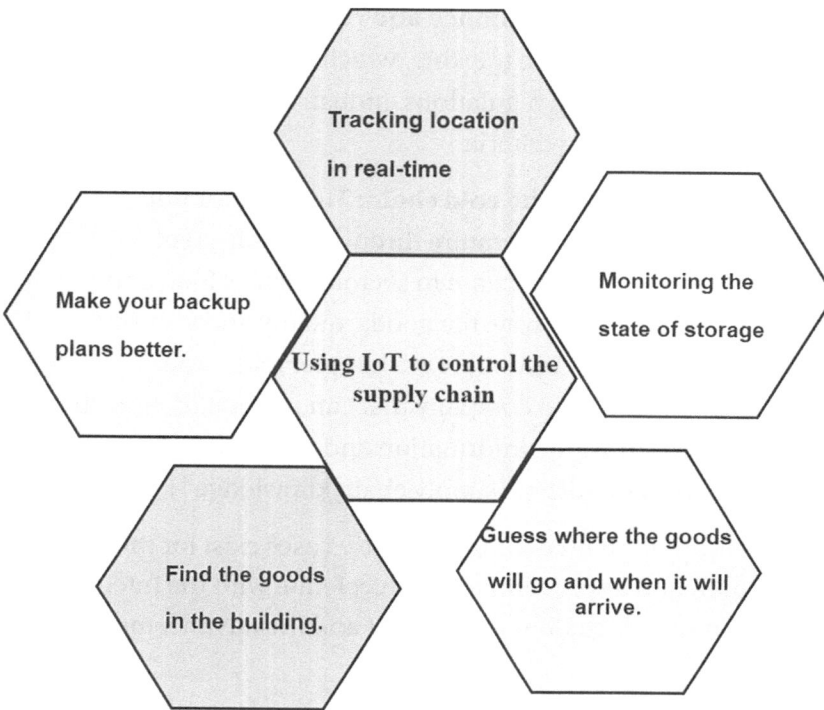

***Figure 6-2.*** *Controlling the supply chain using IoT*

IoT can be used for more than just managing assets, though. Here are some more reasons why IoT should be used in SCM:

- **Track your location in real time**: Managers can get data on the whereabouts and motion of products in real-time using the IoT. Ready goods and raw materials can be tracked and you will be alerted in the event of a product shipment error [5].

- **Monitor the state of storage**: By monitoring the status of shipments using environmental sensors, management can react swiftly to any changes. For example, a common IoT supply chain system

may automatically alter the product's status based
on collected data on environmental factors like
temperature, pressure, and humidity that could
jeopardize its integrity [7].

- **Know where the goods are going and when they
  will arrive**: Managers use IoT devices and data
  analytics systems to make better decisions and make
  more accurate predictions about when things will
  be delivered. Companies can keep an eye on goods
  while they're being shipped thanks to real-time
  tracking. They can also extrapolate when the goods
  will arrive and take steps to reduce the risks that come
  with delays.

- **Find the goods in the building**: One of the most
  important warehouse technology trends is the use of
  IoT-based supply chain management systems. There
  are many perks, such as making warehouse tasks more
  efficient, better-managing inventory, and making
  sure workers are safe. Real-time location trackers, for
  example, make it easy for workers on-site to find goods
  and quickly get to the right aisle for a certain item. In
  this case, the IoT makes it possible for performance
  and processes to be smooth in a way that would not be
  possible otherwise. Also, when IoT is paired with AI,
  it opens the door to fully automated warehouses that
  need little to no human supervision [11].

- **Make your backup plans better**: Using data analytics
  and the IoT, supply chain managers may plot routes
  that take inclement weather, traffic, and accidents into
  consideration. The data required to develop adaptable
  backup plans and detect delays can be collected using
  the IoT. Supply chain management is accelerated by
  the technology's real-time advice on risk reduction.

# Applications of IoT in the Management of Supply Chains

IoT has revolutionized supply chain management by providing real-time
visibility, tracking, and optimization of various processes. Here are some
applications of IoT in the management of supply chains.

## Keeping Track of Assets

In the past, industries that depend on a lot of assets, like manufacturing,
energy, and services, have had problems with late deliveries, theft, and
damaged or lost goods. Traditional ways of tracking assets, like tracking
numbers and bar codes, are being replaced by IoT devices and sensors.
This makes it possible to keep track of and handle goods through the
supply chain. IoT devices can find out where and when things are being
held up in transit, so backup plans and alternate routes can be made
to speed up the supply chain. They can also be used by businesses to
get detailed information like what temperature a product was stored at,
how long it was in travel, and when it was sold. IoT technology can give
companies this kind of data, which can help them focus on quality control,
making sure things happen on time and making better predictions. They

can keep an eye on deals and the movement of goods and assets between trade partners and organizations. With IoT asset tracking and tracing made possible by blockchain, you can keep a digital record of every step and keep business deals safe all along your supply chain [3].

# Forecasting and Planning for Inventory

A lot of producers and distributors are making business plans with old-fashioned forecasting methods. IoT sensors gather information about how products are used and bought, which lets companies switch from making predictions to planning based on real use. With the click of a button, you can keep track of your inventory, including items that are already on hand. This makes it easy to make important decisions. With all of this data, which goes into advanced analytics, trends and patterns can be found that help manufacturers make better plans and make sure brands sell as much as possible without oversaturating the market [7].

# Viewing in Real Time

Because so many people are involved in global supply lines, it's getting harder to see everything from beginning to end. Companies should be able to check and analyze data from all along the supply chain. They need to respond quickly when there are problems in the chain. IoT devices can keep track of the state of goods as they move through the supply chain and make sure that everyone in the chain can see the data at any time to see the status, get ready to ship, and complete transactions. IoT and blockchain technology can be used together to do all of these things. This data can also be mixed with data from outside sources, which lets businesses respond quickly to unplanned events in the supply chain, like a disruption in the supply chain or a sudden drop in customer demand [9].

# Finance for the Global Supply Chain

Cross-border transactions are a normal part of global supply chains. They take longer than expected because there are more people involved, foreign payments, local banking rules, and a lot of paperwork. Any problems, like having two or more bills, can make it take a long time to clear the payments. Together, IoT and blockchain could make it faster and easier for things to move across borders. This would lead to safer, faster, and cheaper transactions that don't involve fraud because they use a shared ledger that can't be changed. Companies can get rid of the need to reconcile papers between multiple parties when they use smart contracts powered by blockchain. They can keep track of the shipment's progress and follow the contract's payment terms once the package is delivered [12].

## Connected Fleets

The IoT can help handle fixed assets like machinery and equipment better. It can also help manage moving assets like cars, trucks, ships, and self-driving cars. Making sure that all of your vehicles shipping containers, delivery trucks from suppliers, and your delivery vans are linked up gives you a better view of the supply chain. This lets you cut down on transportation costs, make your vehicles more efficient, and improve customer service by making sure deliveries happen on time.

## Predictive Maintenance

IoT-enabled predictive maintenance uses sensor data to figure out how likely it is that machinery will break down or fail before it does. Preventive maintenance tries to lower the chance that a machine will break down by making sure it gets regular maintenance. With IoT-enabled predictive maintenance, businesses can find and fix potential problems before they happen by processing huge amounts of data and using complex

algorithms. This makes critical assets more productive. Companies can use
IoT sensors in their expensive machinery and equipment to make sure that
preventative and predictive repair is done on time. This way, companies
can avoid unplanned downtime that costs more [21].

## Compliance with Regulations

When moving goods in businesses with a lot of rules, like food and
medicine, they have to be kept in temperature ranges and delivered
at certain times. Manufacturers and distributors must be able to show
proof that they are following the rules. If they can't, high-value shipments
could be held up or taken by the authorities for inspection. An IoT and
blockchain-based framework can make sure that information is safe and
reliable and show proof of legal compliance. When IoT and blockchain are
used together, providers can set compliance conditions in a smart contract.
This makes sure that accurate information flows through the supply chain.

## Relationships with Vendors

For supply chain management to work, you and your suppliers need to
work together. IoT data lets businesses quickly change their business
strategies by letting them change their production plans and find vendors
that aren't doing their jobs well and are costing them money. It's possible
to look at how your suppliers handle your materials and how they handle
your finished product. When you sell better products, you build stronger
ties with your customers and keep more of them [22].

## Help for Customers

IoT devices and sensors can be added to your apps, collecting enough data
to completely change how field service, customer service, and end-user
training are done. For instance, you don't have to make a field worker call a

help desk every time a piece of equipment breaks. Instead, you can use IoT
apps and solutions that let the field worker figure out what's wrong and fix
it, often without help desk involvement. That can cut down on downtime
and the cost of customer service while making users more productive.
Firms can also get real-time information about how well and reliably their
assets work, which can be used to make their designs better.

# Blockchain Integration for Traceability

IoT data can be integrated with blockchain technology to create a secure
and immutable record of transactions and events across the supply chain.
This enhances traceability, transparency, and trust by providing a tamper-
proof audit trail of product movements, transactions, and compliance
certifications, reducing the risk of counterfeiting, fraud, and supply chain
disputes.

# Cold Chain Management

In industries such as food, pharmaceuticals, and chemicals, maintaining
the integrity of the cold chain is critical to preserving product quality and
safety. IoT sensors monitor temperature-controlled environments during
storage and transportation, ensuring that temperature-sensitive products
are maintained within specified temperature ranges to prevent spoilage or
degradation.

These applications exemplify the extensive advantages of IoT in supply
chain management, encompassing enhanced optimization, transparency,
adaptability, and environmental friendliness. The subsequent section
elucidates the challenges encountered in the application of IoT.

# Problems with IoT Implementation

There are many good things about using the IoT in supply chain management, but there are also some problems and things to think about. Taking care of the following problems is necessary to make sure that IoT technology is integrated well and quickly:

- **Data security and privacy**: IoT devices send and store a lot of private data, which means they could be attacked or have their data stolen. Making sure that this info is safe and private is very important [21].

- **Interoperability**: Some IoT platforms and devices may not work with each other, which can cause data silos and contact problems between devices.

- **Cost**: Putting IoT technology into use can have big up-front costs, especially for smaller companies.

- **Data overload**: IoT devices create huge amounts of data, which can be too much for some systems to handle and can make it hard to manage and analyze the data correctly.

- **Reliability and connectivity**: For data to be sent smoothly, IoT devices need to be able to connect to the Internet reliably. IoT devices can't always be monitored in real time if they can't join or if the network goes down.

- **Power management**: A lot of IoT devices are driven by batteries, and how long these batteries last has a direct effect on how well they work and how often they need to be maintained.

- **Scalability**: As a company grows, it needs to be able to handle and build IoT infrastructure that can grow with it.

- **Integration with current systems**: The IoT can be difficult to integrate with ERP or WMS systems [21].

- **Training and workforce readiness**: When companies adopt IoT, they need to train their employees on new technology and ways of doing things, which can be hard if employees don't know much about them or don't want to learn.

- **Compliance with regulations**: Using the IoT may require staff to follow certain rules and regulations about data safety, security, and the environment.

By dealing with these problems and taking the right things into account, companies can use IoT in their supply chain management in a way that makes it more effective, visible, and high-performing overall.

# Actions to Reduce Risks and the Best Ways to Deal with Problems

Businesses can lessen the problems that come with using IoT in supply chain management by following certain best practices and actions. These steps will help make sure that the IoT technology is integrated successfully and efficiently. Here are some possible steps that could help and best practices:

- **Data security and privacy**: Encrypt data before
  sending it and while it's being stored to keep others
  from getting to it without permission. Using multiple
  forms of login will make your device and system safer.
  Firmware and software should be updated often to fix
  security holes. Do full security check and risk studies to
  find any possible weak spots [27].

- **Interoperability**: Pick IoT gadgets and platforms that
  follow the rules and norms set by the industry. Spend
  your money on IoT options that can help devices talk to
  each other. Work together with partners and suppliers
  to agree on IoT implementation guidelines.

- **Cost**: To figure out the return on investment (ROI)
  of IoT implementation, do a thorough cost-benefit
  analysis. Look into ways to split costs with providers
  or other people in the supply chain. Think about
  implementing in stages to spread out costs and see how
  things go at first before going big.

- **Data overload**: Use advanced analytics tools and AI
  algorithms to handle big datasets and find insights
  within them. Use edge computing to take some of the
  work that central systems do handling data. Set up
  rules for managing data that will help you decide what
  data is most important and what data is not [29].

- **Reliability and connectivity**: To make sure IoT devices
  stay connected, use multiple, reliable network links. Set
  up backup ways to connect in case the network goes
  down for a short time. And before deploying them all
  over the world, make sure that IoT gadgets and network
  connections work well in real life [30].

- **Power management**: Make IoT gadgets use less power to make batteries last longer.

- Think about gadgets that use less energy and other power sources, like solar or kinetic energy.

- Set up a plan for maintenance and battery replacement to keep your gadget running.

- **Scalability**: Pick IoT solutions with adaptable and expandable building blocks to allow for future growth. Assess the IoT systems' capacity to deal with growing numbers of devices and data. Scalability should be planned from the start so that there aren't any big problems when the business grows.

- **Integration with current systems**: Give more weight to IoT options that can easily work with current supply chain management systems. Do thorough tests and sample projects to find early on any possible integration problems. Work with IT teams and suppliers to make sure that integration goes smoothly and that data is always the same. Give your workers a lot of training and workshops to help them get used to IoT technology. Make a change management plan to help employees accept and be excited about IoT usage. Make the interfaces and processes easy for people to use so that adoption is easier [24].

- **Regulatory compliance**: Keep up with the rules and regulations that apply to the application of IoT. Make sure that IoT solutions meet all the standards by working with the legal and compliance teams.

- Write down the steps you take to be compliant and keep the records for auditing reasons.

Businesses can get around problems and get the most out of IoT in supply chain management by using these best practices and actions that reduce risks. This will make things more visible, make things run more smoothly, and make businesses more competitive in the market.

# Future Directions

The IoT will play a bigger part in supply chain visibility as technology improves and more people use it. The IoT has changed how companies see their supply chains, which helps them run their businesses more efficiently and make customers happier. IoT has a lot of benefits, such as better tracking of assets, real-time inventory management, and upkeep that is planned ahead of time. To fully use the IoT in the supply chain, however, businesses must also deal with problems like data security and making sure that different systems can talk to each other. Supply chain management will certainly become more efficient and reliable as the IoT grows.

- **5G connectivity**: The introduction of 5G networks enables faster, more reliable communication between IoT devices, letting them be tracked in real time and share data on a scale that has never been seen before.

- **Edge computing**: Edge computing lowers delay and bandwidth use by processing data closer to where it comes from. This will make it easier to make decisions faster and improve the efficiency of supply chain management operations.

- **Blockchain integration**: Putting IoT and blockchain technology together can make the supply chain more open and easier to track. Smart contracts and decentralized ledgers keep records that can't be changed. This will cut down on scams and make sure that transactions are real.

# Conclusion

This research examined the IoT in SCM's current condition, difficulties, potential, and future horizons. You've seen how IoT has transformed supply chain operations by improving visibility, efficiency, and decision-making. It is clear that IoT devices, data analytics, blockchain, and edge computing are essential to supply chain agility, resilience, and sustainability. At the forefront of technological breakthroughs, IoT in supply chains has limitless possibilities. However, we must carefully address ethical, security, and privacy concerns while ensuring that all stakeholders can benefit from IoT. This article provides a roadmap for researchers, practitioners, and policymakers to use IoT to develop smarter, more responsive, and responsible supply chains for a dynamic and interconnected world. We will shape SCM's future with IoT via collaboration, creativity, and a dedication to ethics and sustainability. Organizations are adopting IoT to improve results. It opens doors to competitive advantage and sets the standard for sustainable supply chain practices. Industry 4.0 meets client need quickly. It boosts productivity and lets stakeholders make real-time decisions. It opens doors to new business models and production improvements.

# CHAPTER 7

# AI and Machine Learning in Supply Chain Optimization: Mapping the Territory

*R. Sethuraman, Associate Professor, Department of Computer Science and Engineering, School of Computing, Sathyabama Institute of Science and Technology, Chennai – 600 041. Tamil Nadu, India.*

*S. Murugan, Corresponding Author and Professor, Department of Computer Science and Engineering, School of Computing, Sathyabama Institute of Science and Technology, Chennai – 600 041. Tamil Nadu, India.* `murugan.cse@sathyabama.ac.in.`

*M. Saravanan, Associate Professor, Department of Computer Science and Engineering, School of Computing, Sathyabama Institute of Science and Technology, Chennai – 600 041. Tamil Nadu, India.*

Vishing attacks in financial transactions, the health care industry, and various other domains where sharing of credentials involved using interactive voice response are common. An interactive voice response system (IVR) is an automated mechanism in which the requestors/

callers are responded back with the solution to the raised query through
prerecorded messages. The objective of this research is to establish a
secured IVR system to ensure the traceability options from the customer
end through the telephone channels and this is achieved by establishing
a secured end-to-end smart contract between the supply chain product
traceability system and the customer. The developed model is secured and
fortified solution for collecting the information over the voice. Machine
learning techniques are applied for detecting the malicious IVR call flow
interactions before establishing the smart contract and are carried out
by analyzing the nature and type of call request queries raised in the
stages of supply chain process. A set of supply chain transactions-based
vocabulary is created in analyzing and evaluating the genuineness of the
IVR call flows by applying the machine learning algorithm. If the algorithm
detects the call flow request as a fake one, then the end user is notified and
the establishment of smart contract is blocked. If the algorithm identifies
that the call as a genuine one, then the smart contract of the block chain
technology is established and a set of secret tokens are exchanged between
the caller and the IVR system. If the exchange of tokens is successful,
then the interaction commences like business logic and functionalities
in supply chain scenarios. On successful completion of the transaction,
the life of the generated token is expired. The proposed methodology was
tested in the Ethereum platform and the results are promising. In the first
phase of the system in detecting the malicious IVR systems, the machine
learning algorithm's success rate was 88%. The generation of exchange
of tokens in the second phase of the secured transaction model was a
greater level of success at 98.78%. Even if the machine learning allowed the
malicious IVR call flow request to proceed to the smart contract, the level
of block at this phase was 96.23%.

# Blockchain and IVR Systems

The advent of blockchain technology has ushered in a new era of secure
and tamper-proof solutions for user authentication in IVR systems.
Traditional methods of authentication and authorization, like the
personal identification numbers (PINs) and passwords, have long been
plagued by vulnerabilities related to sharing, theft, and the limitations of
alphanumeric credentials. The chapter focuses on integrating blockchain
cryptography and smart contracts by redefining the user authentication
the authentication process by applying IVR systems in supply chain
management systems. Using this approach the challenges in the security
system are addressed. In this approach, the user authentication is
established by nonce keyword or random phrase exchange using the
asymmetric approach and the credentials are verified cryptographically
through the public key stored in the block chain system. The involvement
of the blockchain system reduces the disadvantage in the traditional
authentication approach. This approach also provides robust, secure and
anti-phishing in verifying the user identification process. Blockchain with
smart contracts enhances the security and privacy in the authentication
framework. Role-based authentication reduces the risk involved in
unauthorized access and data integrity, which enhances the security in
IVR-based systems.

Sensitive datasets/records such as health records, supply chain
management systems, and government documents can be made
highly secured when the IVR systems are integrated with blockchain
authenticated systems. The authorized individuals/roles alone are
permitted to access the confidential and secured data. The integration of
blockchain technology and smart contracts provides an enhancement in
the IVR systems that addresses security in the domains where the sensitive
data and data integrity is mandatory. This integration redefines IVR system
features in the near future.

IVR systems are commonly used in domains like online banking, customer service, appointment scheduling, and health care for establishing automated interacting with the callers through voice commands and responses. This is achieved using dial tones or language-specific voice recognition systems. Based on the input selection, the prerecorded/programmed voice response provides information to the callers. Due to this, the IVR systems automate user interactions and reduce human interventions in responding to the routine responses, which makes the system more reliable, efficient, quicker, and effective. However, this involves risk in the authentication process as sensitive information is shared knowingly or unknowingly with the genuine entities or the data is breached. Lack of authentication procedure leads to the access to personal information, financial data, or any other confidential data. When IVR is implemented with a secured system, the overall trustworthiness of system is enhanced. The robust user authentication process in the IVR systems is mandatory for protecting user data and maintaining system integrity.

# Enhanced Use Authentication Systems

The integration of blockchain and IVR systems by establishing the smart contract approach provides an enhanced use authentication system and the system cannot be tampered with. Digital agreements are established in the smart contract system between the user and the IVR system for secured transaction of information. Before establishing the connection between the user and the IVR system, the authentication is established using the smart contract in a secured manner at both the ends. Role-based access permission is established using the smart contract system, which reduces the risk of loss of data integrity. The private and public keys are exchanged using the blockchain and smart contract system using digital IDs. Using this digital ID the user authentication is verified in a secured manner and as of now, it is highly secured and cannot be compromised. So, when the IVR is used or other systems, the users can verify this secure phone book to confirm the individual. This adds a strong layer of security, ensuring that only the right people can use IVR services and access private information. Cryptographic verification with private keys is like having a special, secret key that only the owner of the key possesses. When the user wants to prove the identity in IVR or other systems, the key is used to create a unique, unforgeable "digital signature." It's a bit like signing a document with a secret pen. This signature is checked against the public key, which is like a name in a secure online directory. If it matches, it confirms that the user is the authenticated and authorized one. It is extremely secure because the secret key is owned by the respective individual, making it very hard for anyone else to impersonate.

Blockchain-based authentication offers several advantages. First, it's incredibly secure because user data is stored in a tamper-proof digital ledger. This makes it nearly impossible for hackers to alter or steal information. Second, it eliminates the need for vulnerable passwords, relying instead on cryptographic keys that are much harder to crack. Third, it enhances transparency and trust because anyone can verify transactions on the blockchain, promoting accountability. Fourth, it's decentralized; this means there is no single point of failure as mentioned by Khan et al [1] in their work on smart contracts in blockchain technology.

Finally, blockchain improves privacy and provides fine-grained access control system when integrated with smart contracts. Security, privacy, and trust in the authentication process is potentially high when used with smart contract systems. For the intruder, it's a highly challenging task to view, modify, or access the data. Even if accessed, the records are assigned with traces or signature. Once accessed, the records are traceable and the root cause can be investigated. Even when an unauthorized user tampers the data, the original data is restored and will be available. In the blockchain-based authentication system, the personal information is maintained in a secured manner and remains safe. The disadvantages of PINs are eliminated when the system is implemented with blockchain-based authentication. PINs are easily compromised or recovered by using

brute force approach or cryptanalysis. Blockchain-based authentication
systems replace PINs with secret keys that are asymmetric and thus
difficult to compromise. Since the keys cannot be compromised in the
blockchain systems, the data is secured and integrity is maintained.

The rules are enforced in the form of digital agreements as the security
of the system is increased with smart contract implementation. Smart
contract agreements are executed only when the agreed conditions are
satisfied and this does not involve any human intervention or mediating
agent system. This feature reduces the risk of error or fraudulent activity.
Based on the agreed conditions, the data is revealed or shared or allowed
to be modified or no access. Security is advanced when smart contracts
and IVR systems are integrated. In the smart contract system, based on
the authentication, the agreements are self-executed by applying the
well-defined rules and conditions. When an IVR call is made or received,
both parties have to prove the identify or share the credentials, and this
information are verified before the exchange of data. The automation
of authorization using the smart contract system reduces human error
and avoids the fraudulent activities. In case of financial transactions,
negligence and lack of awareness in sharing the credential systems over
the phone or IVR system even when captured the loss in terms of money is
avoided. This is due to the fact that the configured conditions are not met
and the smart contracts act as the digital gatekeeper and are highly reliable
and secured. Based on the conditions, the resources or data is shared and
hence the unauthorized sharing of data is prevented.

# Role-Based Authentication

Role-based authentication systems enable users to access only specific
contents that are given access. For instance, a medical practitioner can
access only the patients records and not the financial/maintenance
records. In a similar manner every domain has restricted access based on
various roles. The security with IVR and a smart contract system is beyond

strong passwords, biometric systems, or physical security system in which
there is always a chance of comprising the system. The overall security
and the system integrity against intruders is significantly improved and
risks are minimized or nil when a blockchain system plus a smart contract
system is implemented. The trust, security, and sharing of information
of services are protected when the system is integrated with IVR and
blockchain-based smart contract systems. The integration makes the IVR
system highly secure, reliable, available, effective, and efficient and the
integrity of the data is maintained. It's like upgrading from a basic lock
to a state-of-the-art security system, revolutionizing how we safeguard
important information. Figure 7-1 demonstrates the working of smart
contract-based IVR application. The IVR interacts with the web-based
application and the blockchain service provider.

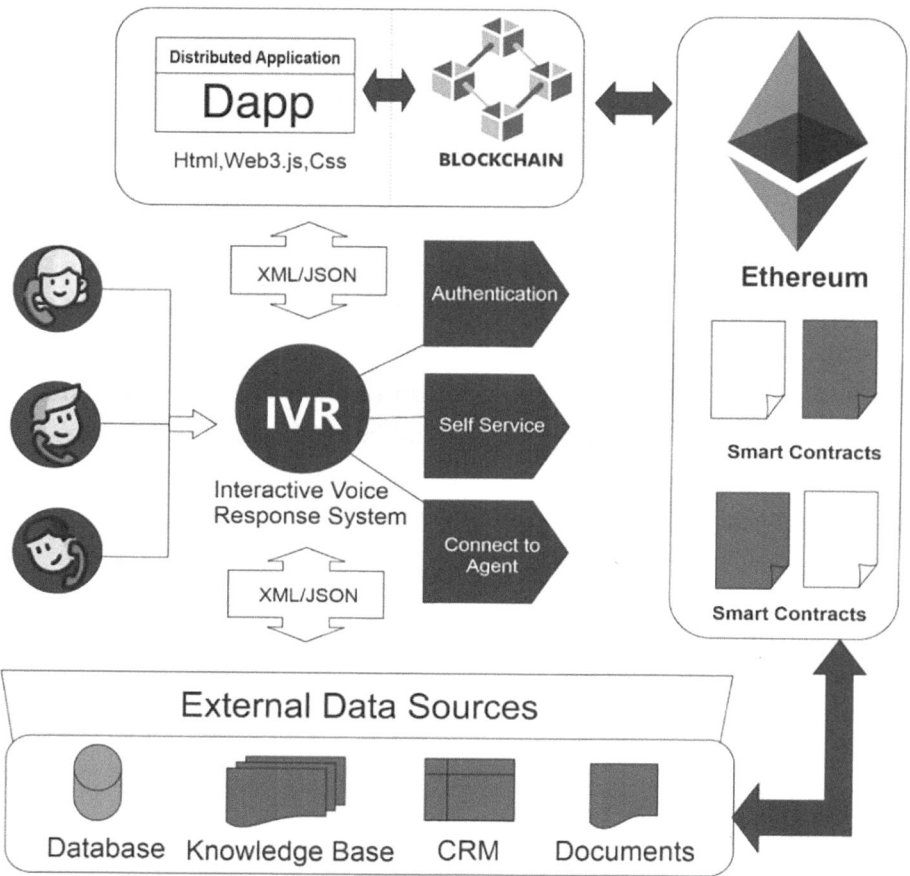

***Figure 7-1.*** *IVR and smart contract workflow*

Using the smart contract, the credentials are shared in a secured manner. Figure 7-2 shows the use case diagram on the sequence of tasks involved in the communication between the client and the blockchain system.

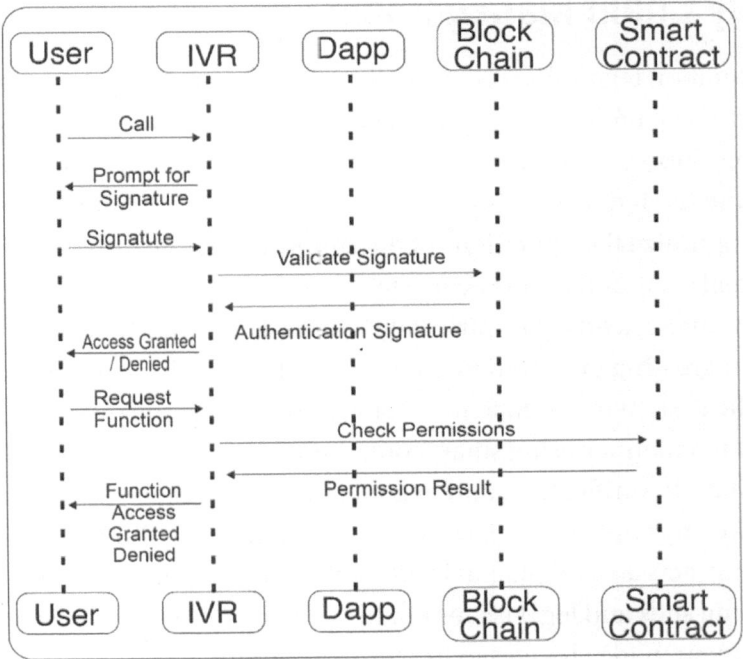

***Figure 7-2.***  *UML with user and blockchain*

The reminder of the sections discuss the literature survey, machine
learning algorithms for detection of a malicious IVR systems, smart
contract and supply chain management, observations, and the conclusion.

# Literature Survey

The significance of supply chain management, blockchain technology,
machine learning algorithms and interactive voice response systems
and the integration of these technologies is discussed in this section in a
detailed manner.

# Supply Chain Management

As information technology continually advances, machine learning and
other artificial intelligence technologies have been steadily evolving and
maturing. Supply chain management plays a pivotal role in the business
world, and its significance is evident to all. Supply chain management
aims to optimize the operations of the supply chain, ensuring it operates
at minimal costs and covers every step from procurement to meeting the
end customer's needs. It is intricately intertwined with China's economy
and is progressing in a rapid manner. Many domains have influenced
the application of blockchain technologies in sharing the digitized data
in a secured manner using smart contracts (a collection of protocols
for facilitation, verification, and negotiation of agreements between
untrustworthy applications). Despite the enhanced methodologies, the
smart contracts are still plagued with security threats and are vulnerable
to phishing sites and legal issues [1]. In 1998, the Council of Logistics
Management made changes to its logistics definition, clarifying that
logistics is just one component of supply chain management, emphasizing
that these terms are not interchangeable. With this acknowledgment by
a leading organization in the field of logistics, the next task is to figure
out how to effectively put supply chain management into practice [2].
In the contemporary and dynamic world we live in, the enterprises that
formerly revolved around inadequate data have now been replaced
with worries about an excess of data in the environment of force chain
operation. The sheer volume of data generated across all angles of
the force chain has brought about a metamorphosis in how SCM is
anatomized. As data volumes have surged, the conventional styles have
endured a decline in effectiveness and effectiveness. The constraints of
these styles in handling and decoding vast datasets have urged scholars
to concoct new approaches with a heightened capacity to dissect and
make sense of expansive data. Thus, the primary ideal of the work is to
probe the operation of machine literacy (ML) in SCM, an extensively

honored artificial intelligence fashion. Through the development of an abstract frame, the exploration work aims to delineate the benefactions of ML ways in several aspects of SCM, including the selection and categorization of suppliers, the expectation of force chain pitfalls, and the estimation of variables similar as demand and trade of products, product operation, stock and force operation, delivery and distribution of products, sustainable development (SD), and indirect frugality (CE). The article also discusses the repercussions of the study on the primary limitations, which is followed by presenting managerial insights and outlining directions for future research [3].

Supply chain management (SCM) encompasses the integration of all components and business processes and is managed by a separate supply chain based information management system. The integration of artificial intelligence algorithms into the SCM system enables the visualization process, automation controls, and intelligent action in every aspect within the supply chain. Consequently, this can significantly assist the industries by reducing the operational costs and improving response time related to market demands. This ultimately leads to overall improved performance in operation procedures. A supply chain member selection algorithm is being introduced for addressing challenges like processing large number of decision attributes and data samples. This algorithm is a dynamic one and is based on conditional generative adversarial networks (CGANs). The principle objective of this algorithms is to reduce the dimension of the data and also the complexity involved in the classification process without comprising the performance measures. Additionally, machine learning is employed to analyze and predict procurement and inventory aspects within the supply chain. For the vehicle scheduling module, an optimized path planning approach is implemented to enhance operational efficiency. The complete workflow of the SCM system is carried out by applying the Secured Socket Shell (SSH) framework [4].

# Supply Chain Management and Machine Learning

The COVID-19 pandemic presented an unprecedented challenge for global supply chains (SCs). Shipments of crucial and life-saving products, including pharmaceuticals, agricultural goods, healthcare supplies, and manufacturing materials, experienced significant disruptions and delays, rendering global SCs highly vulnerable. To alleviate this concern, a better comprehension of shipment risks is imperative. The research suggests a collection of deep learning (DL) technologies for handling the risks in the shipment process by forecasting the possibility of exporting shipments from the given location to another location, irrespective of the constraints that were laid during the pandemic in the year 2019 (COVID-19). These DL techniques consist of four main stages: data acquisition, noise reduction or preprocessing, feature extraction, and classification. The feature extraction phase relies on two primary variations of DL models. The first variant encompasses three recurrent neural networks (RNN) structures, namely long short-term memory (LSTM), bidirectional long short-term memory (BiLSTM), and gated recurrent unit (GRU). The second variant involves the temporal convolutional network (TCN). In the classification phase, six distinct classifiers are employed to assess the entire methodology, namely SoftMax, random trees (RT), random forest (RF), k-nearest neighbor (KNN), artificial neural network (ANN), and support vector machine (SVM). The performance of the proposed DL models is evaluated using an online dataset (used as a case study). Numerical results indicate that one of the proposed models, specifically TCN, achieves approximately 100% accuracy in predicting shipment risk to a specific destination under COVID-19 restrictions. Undoubtedly, the outcomes of this research will aid decision-makers in proactively predicting supply chain risks to enhance the resilience of SCs. The objective of this work is that in the recent times, there has been a growing number of practical applications of ML, particularly within the realm of SCM. This paper aims to connect the practical use of ML techniques to the SCM task model, shedding light on current SCM applications and pinpointing areas where further research is needed. To achieve this goal, a literature review was conducted between 2009 and 2019 to identify relevant papers that describe the applications of ML in SCM. Connections were established between the ML methods employed and the various components of the SCM model, creating a two-way mapping. By bridging the SCM task model with the current practical implementations of ML, SCM offers a comprehensive perspective on the role of ML within SCM. This not only assists businesses in identifying potential areas where ML can be applied but also pinpoints areas for future research in the academic realm [6].

In the intricate and ever-evolving landscape of today's business world, SCM has become increasingly pivotal for companies across all industries in this global era. The surging interest in applying DL to SCM has underscored the need for a current, systematic review of research developments in this field. The articles focuses on the comprehensive overview by evaluating 43 papers that explore the use of DL methods in SCM. It also examines the current inclination, viewpoints, and the various possible research ideas. The review employs the concept of content analysis for addressing the major research questions: What are the challenges that are address by DL for SCM applications? What are the DL algorithms that are applied in solving the identified issues? In place of DL algorithms, what are the other efficient and effective algorithms available for addressing the challenges? If alternate algorithms are outperformed by DL algorithms, what are the reasons and root cause and the considered evaluation metrics? Furthermore, the article reveals the demand in establishing a value-driven conceptual framework that presents a comprehensive landscape of how and where DL can be integrated into the SCM context. This framework not only facilitates the identification of possible applications for businesses but also highlights potential areas for future research in academia. Importantly, it could grant

businesses a competitive edge over rivals by enabling them to extract quick
and precise insights from their data, thus adding significant value [7].
The article focusses on the potency of machine learning algorithms
when compared to traditional demand forecasting models. Notably,
it underscores that neural networks are among the most frequently
utilized algorithms in the domain of demand forecasting. Ultimately,
the robust capabilities of machine learning techniques in addressing
demand forecasting challenges across various domains underscore their
significant potential for enhancing supply chain efficiency. This, in turn,
has the potential to inspire both decision-makers and stakeholders to
strategize corrective actions grounded in the applications of machine
learning within supply chain management and demand forecasting.[8]. AI
is increasingly recognized as a potential source of competitive advantage
within operations and supply chain management (OSCM). Nevertheless,
many organizations still encounter difficulties in effectively integrating
AI, and there is a scarcity of empirical studies offering clear insights in
the existing literature. The authors aimed to find how AI applications
can enhance the OSCM processes and identify the advantages and
disadvantages while implementing the system. The input data was
considered from six organizations with structured questionaries and a
total of 17 implementation cases. The research was based on the supply
chain operations reference (SCOR) model and focused on the more
specific processes in data analysis phases. The results revealed that the
ability of AI techniques in OSCM supports organizations by reducing
costs and lead times and by enhancing service levels, quality, safety,
and sustainability. However, the authors also identified the drawbacks
in the AI implementation, and this includes that the requirement for
ensuring data quality, the need for domain experts with AI knowledge,
substantial investment requirements, and uncertainty in the profit/loss
for the organization [9]. Decision-making in the realm of supply chains
faces formidable challenges due to its intricate nature and is marked by
a combination of continuous and discrete processes. The integration

and interdependence of operations are also other challenges faced by the organizations. The dynamic and adaptable characteristics of supply chain processes overcome these challenges. The enormous increase in the quantity of data and in the computing power and the emergence of sophisticated algorithms have revealed new opportunities for adaptive, data-driven decision-making [10]. Recent technological advancements, particularly in ML, have demonstrated the potential to mitigate supply chain risks by reducing the dependency in organizing and maintain the laborers (mainly humans), effective and efficient response systems, and identification and elimination of possible risks. Despite these promising developments, the existing literature lacks a comprehensive analysis of the relationship between ML and SCRM. The authors addresses this gap by conducting an extensive review of the relatively limited literature in this field by considering current research landscape, enabling researchers to identify the existing gaps in this domain [11].

The authors [12] delved into the intersection of machine learning techniques and supply chain management and then investigate the application of support vector machines and decision trees within the realm of supply chain management, highlighting various successful cases. The article concludes by outlining potential future directions for the development of machine learning technology. In the context of overseeing and controlling contemporary supply chain systems, the Internet of Things holds significant importance. To ensure the security and automation of IoT, two advanced technologies, namely blockchain and machine learning, are pivotal. The authors suggested the integration of blockchain into modern supply chains to facilitate effective cooperation among all involved parties and employed a model based on multi-head attention (MHA) combined with gated recurrent units (GRU) for predicting inbound logistics tasks. The numerical results substantiate that the proposed approach exhibits an effective model that fits with high efficiency and the level of accuracy in the prediction process is high when compared with the other alternative approaches[13]. This research paper aimed to analyze and highlight the

191

contributions of AI to the field of SCM by conducting an orderly review
of the existing literature survey. Addressing the current gap in scientific
knowledge regarding AI in SCM, this study sought to identify the current
AI techniques in use and those with potential for enhancing both the
theoretical and practical aspects of SCM. Furthermore, it identified areas
within the literature that require further research. The study specifically
delved into four aspects: the most commonly utilized AI techniques within
SCM; AI techniques with the potential for application in SCM; the subfields
of SCM that have already been improved by AI; and the subfields with high
potential for enhancement through AI [14]. Over the past two decades,
there has been a significant surge in research interest at the integration
or combination of ML and SCM, leading to a substantial volume of
publications. However, within the existing literature, there has been a lack
of a systematic exploration of the research developments in the specific
realm of ML application, particularly in the context of SCM [15] The article
initially addressed the necessity of gathering data in accordance with
the SC strategy and outlined methods for data collection. Several types
of forecasting by considering the time frame or most important supply
chain objects were also discussed. Furthermore, it recommended using SC
KPIs and error-measurement systems to enhance the performance of the
top-performing forecasting model. The article sheds light on the negative
consequences of inventory (which are unknown/unreliable) on forecasting
and how the decision processes are influenced by supply chain KPIs in
determining the behavior of the model with the help of the indicators
and thereby enhanced the management related to operations, involving
transparency and an effective planning system. The framework proposed
in this research creates a cyclical connection that involves optimizing
preprocessing based on post-process KPIs, leading to the improvement of
control processes such as managing inventory, allocation of workforces,
cost analysis, effective production environment, and planning at
various levels. This research contributed by offering a standardized

SC process framework, suggesting best practices for forecasting data analysis, highlighting the effects of forecasting on SC performance, optimizing machine learning algorithms, and providing insights for future research [16].

# Blockchain Technology

Through the utilization of smart contracts, which are essentially scripts securely embedded in decentralized blockchain or similar systems, it becomes feasible to render the execution of predefined processes transparent to external observers. Smart contracts enable the programmability of assets like money, which was not possible before, and the automation of previously manual business logic. The article addressed the gaps and challenges existing in the related literature, with a particular emphasis on its limitations [17]. Blockchain-based smart contracts are computer programs designed to encode agreements between participants who may not trust each other. These contracts are automatically executed on a blockchain when specific conditions are met, eliminating the need for a trusted third party. Blockchains and smart contracts have garnered increasing attention in recent years, particularly within academic circles. The authors conducted a systematic mapping analysis of all peer-reviewed research focused on technology-oriented aspects of smart contracts. The block chain has application in distinct areas, including security, privacy, software engineering, applications, performance, and scalability [18]. The integration of platforms that support blockchain technologies with the regular or existing programming languages for establishing smart contracts are at the peak of gaining momentum and increase in popularity. However, the development of smart contracts and blockchain applications follows non-standard software development lifecycles, which can make it challenging to update delivered applications or fix bugs through the traditional approach of releasing new software versions. The articles focused on software engineering that aims to bring attention to current issues and build potential solutions concerning the development of smart contracts and blockchain applications. Testing, code analysis, metrics evaluation, security, decentralized application (Dapp performance) of smart contract formulates the basic block application [19].

As time progresses, our lives are increasingly shaped by digitization and technology, with their diverse applications and uses. Smart cities, along with their associated technologies and services, have become an integral part of our daily existence. The concept of smart cities relies on various mechanisms to deliver dependable services. Among these, blockchain technology has emerged as a highly reliable and secure approach. The article outlined an approach in order to elucidate the implementation of smart contract by utilizing the blockchain paradigms, with the aim of enhancing reliability, data security, and various other advantageous attributes as an integral component of the numerous services offered in the smart city environment. The article also provided significant insights into blockchain technology and its role in the entire administrative process, the governing services when implemented using the smart contracts. Furthermore, the authors addressed a realistic application on how to electronically manage the real estate rental agreements to demonstrate the benefits of applying the blockchain technology. Using this case study, how blockchain technology can effectively resolve existing issues in such contracts and services was discussed [20]. Smart contract technology is revolutionizing traditional industry and business operations. These contracts, integrated into blockchains, have the ability to autonomously enforce the terms of an agreement, eliminating the need for a trusted third party to oversee the process. Consequently, smart contracts have the potential to streamline administrative tasks, reduce service costs, enhance the efficiency of business operations, and mitigate risks. While smart contracts hold promise for ushering in a new era of innovation in business processes, they also present several challenges that need to be addressed. This paper conducted a survey on smart contracts, beginning with an introduction to blockchains and smart contracts. It then delved into the challenges associated with smart contracts and highlighted recent technical advancements in this field. Additionally, the paper offered a comparison of typical smart contract platforms and provided a categorization of smart contract applications, accompanied by representative examples [21].

# Interactive Voice Response Systems

In recent times, advancements in telecommunications technology have opened up new possibilities for improving the value of healthcare services by implementing the telehealth, which involves the applications of information systems and telecommunication systems for building a good healthcare system. However, the wide array of technologies and applications associated with telehealth has led to some confusion when discussing the effectiveness of these initiatives. One such telehealth solution is the interactive voice response system (IVRS), which, despite its simplicity, proves to be an effective tool for expanding access to healthcare beyond the confines of a hospital, offering readymade software that are readily available to patients for 24x7 and 365 days. Often it is similar to a phone interlinked with a system that can speak. IVRSs allow patients to interact with the system for tasks such as gathering data or receiving well-defined/stored voice telephone messages that correspond to medication adherence or behavior alteration. IVRS systems are still not famous or unused due to lack of awareness even though there is a sufficient availability of touchtone telephone services. An IVRS offers a range of services from basic reminders to interactive data handling. The IVRS systems provide solutions without user input or new information or initiating a new process and provide reminders for routing clinical tasks. Several algorithms are being developed for combining the features of reminders about physician schedule for treatment or lab testing or collection of data and educating the system. For instance, a user might have various options for accessing supplementary data on a chosen topic

by selecting the numbers on a touchtone telephone. It functions like a
"telephone banking" system where customers can check their account
balances and make transfers. With IVRS, a patient acquires the current
or live data about their thyroid level, blood sugar level, blood cholesterol
level, blood pressure, nicotine levels, or adjusted risk scores. The users/
patients can then select information on topics like thyroid, cholesterol,
hypertension, and smoking and choose to respond to preconfigured
queries or submit a message to a real-time assistant, as all are using a
touchtone telephone. The computer programs within IVRS are guided
by preconfigured call-flow algorithms that collect the data and provide
individual responses in the form of feedback to the patients. In the
healthcare industry, there is a growing need to improve customer
service quality while managing or reducing costs. Telehealth, including
telephone-based IVRS, offers numerous opportunities in this regard. When
used effectively, IVRS technology can help healthcare providers expand
their interactions with customers, increase access to healthcare, lower
operational costs, and enhance staff efficiency. Much like live telephone
follow-up extends the care of a patient, IVRS can be seen as an extension
of live telephone follow-up, encompassing both one-to-one and real-time
communication on the phone and providing a sequential message-based
communication to support the provision of good service in the healthcare
services [22]. The article [23] focused on identifying the vulnerabilities
in the interactive voice response system. The vulnerability list includes
improper system configuration, platform dependency, loss of preexisting
functionality due to upgradation of software version/hardware equipment,
improper voice recognition engine, mismatch between voice recognition
engine and voice packs versions, generation of personal information in
log files, spyware, vendor back doors, poor disaster recovery systems, poor
password recovery systems, undetected bugs in the software, and spoofing
attacks. The eight-step generic process of a web-based IVRS system is
defined by Vrishabhsagar Ruikar [24] as follows: identify and finalize the
protocol; select IxRS service provider; validate IxRS; unit testing at the

service provider end; build the IxR system; configure the requirements
based on the initial protocol identification; validate the protocol,
requirements, call in/out flow, log the issue trackers and generate the
report; and deploy the IxR system into the production environment by the
service provider. Heart failure (HF) stands as the primary contributor to
cardiovascular health issues and medical resource utilization on a global
scale. A significant portion of the expenses related to HF treatment is
linked to hospital stays, making it crucial to focus on reducing the chance
of getting readmitted in nursing homes or specialist hospitals. In order
to track the status of the patient health condition and other diagnosis, an
IVR system is implemented, which uses the current telephone lines. This
feature provides an early intervention whenever there is a deviation in the
health condition of the patient. The data used in this research work is from
the patients of the University of Ottawa Heart Institute (UOHI) who are
enrolled in the IVR program; mainly they are heart patients. The system
analyses the data received based in patient symptoms, confirming with the
treatment and day-to-day behavior or lifestyle, and computes the chance
of getting admitted back in the hospital. The study encompassed 902 HF
patients with an average age of 70 years, of which male patients are 60%
(approximately). For a period of three months of IVR utilization, it was
observed that the patients strictly consumed the prescribed medicines, a
reduction in reoccurrence of heart failure symptoms, a maintenance of the
Body Mass Index, and low chance of getting admitted to the hospital again.
Medication adherence had the highest compliance rate, while exercise had
the lowest. In general, aged female patients who are not from urban areas
(mainly from rural hospitals) are more motivated in utilizing the IVR; they
complete the calls and they follow the medication procedure, management
of weight, and the lifestyle system. These findings indicate that the use of
IVR systems can positively impact the management of HF patients. The
increased adoption of IVR in remote patient monitoring offers a more
cost-effective and accessible approach to home-based monitoring. The

adoption of IVR systems especially during the pandemic in supporting the
health status was of great advantage as it reduced visits to the hospital and
the complications involved in providing medication [25].

The current clinical trial process often lacks the means to effectively
monitor and maintain the integrity of the collected data. We suggest
the implementation of a blockchain-based system to establish data
immutability, traceability, and potentially enhance reliability. The authors
applied the raw data collected from a completed clinical trial, replicating
the trial on a proof-of-concept web portal service, and testing its resilience
against data tampering. Also, the authors evaluated the approach and its
potential in providing a transparent and valuable audit trail for regulatory
authorities, while also offering a versatile service for all participants in the
clinical trials network [26].

To summarize the literature review, advancements in technology,
particularly in artificial intelligence and machine learning, are
transforming supply chain management. The complexity and importance
of supply chain management are evident, spanning from procurement
to customer satisfaction. China's economy heavily relies on supply
chain management and it's rapidly evolving. The distinction between
logistics and supply chain management has been clarified, highlighting
their interconnected but distinct roles. In the supply chain management
context, the surge in data volume has necessitated the use of machine
learning for analysis, impacting various aspects of SCM, from supplier
selection to demand forecasting. Blockchain technology is being explored
to secure and make clinical trial data immutable and traceable, addressing
concerns about data integrity. However, challenges like security threats
and legal issues persist. The COVID-19 pandemic has disrupted global
supply chains, emphasizing the need for predictive models to manage
shipment risks. Deep learning techniques have been proposed for this
purpose. Machine learning and data analysis play a crucial role in demand
forecasting, with neural networks being frequently used for this purpose.
The integration of AI in operations and supply chain management (OSCM)

has the potential to reduce costs, improve efficiency, and enhance various aspects of operations. The intersection of machine learning and supply chain management is explored, focusing on support vector machines and decision trees' successful applications. The combination of blockchain and machine learning in supply chain management is proposed to enhance reliability and data security. The study offers practical insights into the management of real estate rental agreements using blockchain technology. Smart contracts on blockchains automate agreements, offering potential benefits but also posing challenges. The paper surveys smart contracts, highlighting platforms and applications. Blockchain-based systems are proposed to enhance data integrity in clinical trials, providing traceability and security. These developments in technology and data analysis have the potential to revolutionize various aspects of supply chain management, healthcare, and clinical trials.

# Secured Smart Contract Architecture

The section focusses on two components. The first phase discusses the impact of machine learning algorithms in detecting malicious calls using the IVR system and the model's performance is analyses. The second phase discusses in the supply chain management system how the smart contracts using blockchains are implemented in a secured manner after identifying the genuine enquiries.

## Machine Learning Algorithm for Detection of Malicious IVR Systems

Amirah Alshammari and Abdulaziz Aldribi [27] considered the network traffic dataset. It comprises flow network traffic attributes outlined in Aldribi et al.'s work [28] and it lacks labels. This dataset has been generated from network traffic collected during various time periods and

encompasses details such as frame time, source and destination MAC
address, source and destination IP address, source and destination port,
IP length, IP header length, TCP header length, frame length, offset, TCP
segment and acknowledgment, and in- and out-frequency numbers. These
attributes serve to distinguish between normal and anomalous packets.
Equations are formulated in order to compute the in-frequency number
and, likewise, the out-frequency number. Additionally, the ISOT-
CID dataset incorporates other essential features, including APL (average
payload packet length) for a given time interval, PV (variance of payload
packet length) for a time interval, and TBP (average time between packets)
within that time interval. A new type of feature labelled as rambling is
applied in the training process while building the machine learning model,
which calculates the instance flow for the interval time t and reduces the
flow packet size difference and supports in the classification process.
Preparation of the dataset, building the model, and evaluating it are
the three phases involved in this work. The features extracted from the
network traffic includes the following: source MAC address in the data link
frame (S_MAC), destination MAC address in the data line frame (D_MAC),
source IP of the data packet (S_IP), source port of the data packet (S_PT),
destination IP of the data packet (D_IP), destination port of the data packet
(D_PT), length of the IP packet (IP_LEN), IP header length of the IP packet
(IP_HLEN), TCP header length (TCP_HLEN), packet's length including the
header data identification for the current data in a packet (FR_LEN), offset
of the IP packet (IP_OFFS), data location of the TCP segment (TCP_SEQ),
and number of data received (TCP_ACK) from the data set ISOT-CID [29].
From this dataset, it is possible to extract the following features:

- Frequency number (T_IN) represents the total number
  of incoming packets directed to the destination IP
  address within a specified observation time window.

- Frequency number (T_OUT) corresponds to the total count of outgoing packets originating from the destination IP address within a specified observation time window.

- Average payload packet length for the time interval (APL) signifies the mean length of payload in packets within a specific time interval.

- Variance of payload packet length for the time interval (PV) indicates the degree of variation or spread in payload packet lengths.

- Average time between packets in a time interval (TBP) refers to the mean duration between the arrival of packets.

- Rambling amount of payload packet length means in a time interval (RAMBLING) describes the extent of inconsistency or randomness in payload packet lengths.

The renowned algorithms include the decision tree, neural networks, K-nearest neighbor, naïve Bayes, support vector machine, and random forest are considered by the authors for developing a model whose performance measures are reliable and high.

Cross-validation is a method used for validating machine learning algorithms by dividing the dataset into multiple segments, referred to as "folds" to ensure that all types of dataset instances are used for both training and testing. The parameter K indicates the number of these divisions. For instance, when K is set to 5, the dataset is decomposed into five parts, with the first part used in the training process and the second part for testing in the first fold. In the second fold, the second part is considered for the training the model, and the third part is considered in testing the model, and so on. This process continues until all parts have been utilized for both training and testing. The overall accuracy of the model is determined by averaging the accuracies across all five folds. This technique is crucial for assessing whether there is overfitting during the training process. In machine learning, overfitting occurs when the model performs poorly on new data because it has learned to fit the training data too closely, resulting in a lack of clear separation between data instances, making attribute values closely resemble each other, and potentially causing the model to classify the same instance into multiple classes. The ANN algorithm results with an accuracy of 94% when k-fold is set to 15. The algorithms decision tree, random Forest, and KNN achieved the accuracy to 100%, SVM yielded 84% and naïve Bayes only 60%. As per the experiment, naïve Bayes is not a reliable approach in detecting the anomalies.

Figures 7-3 and 7-4 provide an insight about the performance of the algorithms for the normal and malicious traffic.

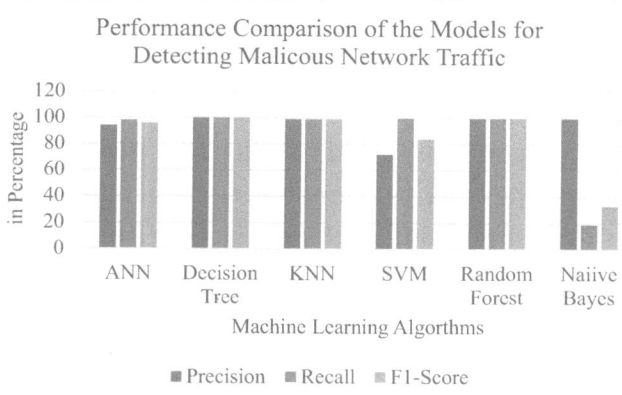

*Figure 7-3.* *Normal Traffic – Evaluation of Models [27]*

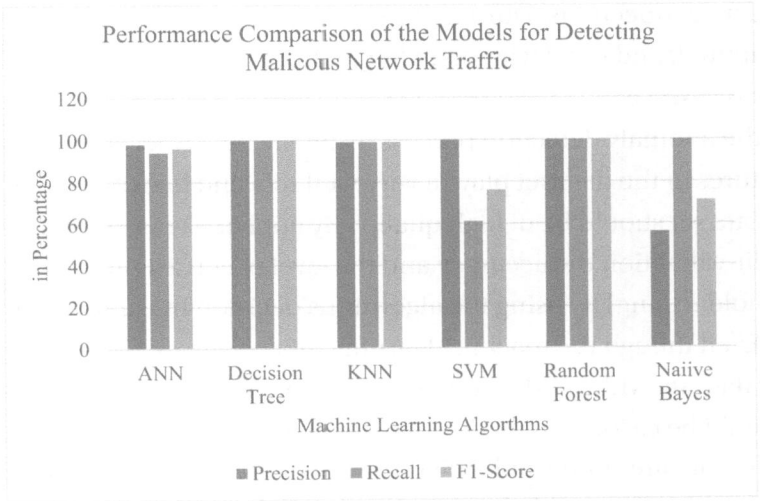

***Figure 7-4.*** *Malicious Traffic – Evaluation of Models [27]*

Network security is of major concern today in the communication
medium due telecommunication in various forms and the different
types of high speed system networks, which are cost effective, simple to
implement, and offer good availability.

As a result, the field of intrusion detection has gained significance,
with both research and corporate organizations moving their focus on
finding solutions for effective intrusion detection systems (IDSs) capable
of safeguarding critical system components against intruders. In this study,
we introduce a robust real-time model for identifying malicious data flow
traffic using supervised machine learning techniques, specifically based
on the dataset ISOT-CID, which is available with the features related
to network traffic data. The objective of this research is to identify the
anomalies in the data instances, distinguishing between malicious and
normal properties. The authors [27] introduced six additional features that
are related to the properties of network traffic in diagnosing the malicious
traffic for building the model using machine learning algorithms. One
features is termed as "rambling," which calculates the interval time of

traffic data connections. During this time, the packet payload length can
be computed, and the deviation in length from the mean of all packet
lengths is assessed.

In the anomaly detection process using the machine learning models,
the features in the data set plays a very vital role and hence the quality
of the data set should be of high quality. By applying cross-validation
and split-validation the accuracy and the level of consistency is also high
(multi-fold testing) by using the algorithms decision tree and random
forest. Even though the machine learning models are developed using high
quality data set with good feature sets, there is still a lot of improvisation
that should be carried out in detecting the anomalies. The computer
networks that are supported with intrusion detection system have to
operate at a higher speed in the real-time environment and the extraction
of information about the network traffic and responding to the collected
attributes needs to be carried out in an effective manner. The developed
machine learning model uses a large volume of data and this leads to the
degradation in the systems performance if the deployed environment does
not meet the minimum hardware requirements. If these requirements
are compromised, then the implemented model does not produce the
expected results.

With the increasing emphasis on individual privacy and encrypted
data, the use of secured or encoded information traffic has become
commonplace in the digital realm. However, this secured data transfer
also serves to protect mischievous and illicit traffic generated by
adversaries from being easily detected. This issue has become particularly
pronounced in the post-COVID-19 environment, where the prevalence
of malicious traffic encryption is increased in a higher note. Traditional
security solutions that rely on analyzing the content of plain payloads,
such as inspection of data packets, are no longer effective in this context.
Consequently, machine learning-based approaches have emerged as a
crucial avenue for detecting malicious encrypted traffic. Wang et al. [30]
presented a comprehensive framework for machine learning-based

techniques in the detection of encrypted and illicit traffic and offer an
orderly review of the field. Moreover, current research in this area often
employs different datasets for training their models, primarily due to the
absence of well-established datasets and feature sets. Consequently, it
becomes challenging to reliably compare and analyze the performance of
these models. The authors addressed this issue by analyzing, processing,
and amalgamating datasets from five distinct sources to create a
comprehensive and equitable dataset that can aid future research in
this domain. Building on this foundation, the authors implemented and
compared ten different algorithms for detecting encrypted malicious
traffic.

Liu et al. (2021) [31] proposed a concurrent neural network-based
approach for detecting illicit traffic structure. The data flow segment is
derived through data preprocessing, leading to the proposal of a novel
structure for detecting malicious traffic using a combined deep neural
network with a hierarchical attention mechanism. This innovative model,
grounded in the effective and reliable deep recurrent neural network,
demonstrates superior accuracy detection rate, reduced negative response
rate, and offered commendable live data performance compared to
traditional methods. The hierarchical attention model for detection of
illicit traffic detection is composed of five components: the input layer,
feature conversion part, bidirectional gated memory unit part, hierarchy
part, and multi-layer perceptron output part. The term "hierarchy" in
this work refers to performing additional operations on the hidden state
of the bidirectional gated recurrent neural network. Based on the data
flow segment obtained from preprocessing, three distinct operations are
applied to the hidden state information: attention mechanism hierarchy,
maximum pooling hierarchy, and average pooling hierarchy. The attention
mechanism hierarchy, containing a single layer, focuses on recognizing
malicious flow in the data flow segment using a soft attention mechanism
with a singular attention weight. The outcomes of these operations are
stacked to generate more comprehensive traffic features, facilitating

the model's identification of malicious traffic. The attention hierarchy
primarily concentrates on recognizing malicious flow within the data
flow segment. The soft attention mechanism at this level employs a single
attention weight, emphasizing the importance of the data flow level in
the data flow segment. The introduction of abstract expressions in the
maximum pooling hierarchy alleviates overfitting during model training,
while the average pooling level reduces variance and enhances the model's
generalization ability. Both maximum pooling and average pooling
hierarchies contribute to a reduction in model learning parameters,
thereby lowering the cost of model inference.

The GRU network, derived from the LSTM network variant, exhibits a
distinct characteristic in that it lacks a gate, resulting in fewer parameters
compared to LSTM. The traffic detection model prioritizes two key
features: (1) the capacity to minimize parameters, and (2) the ability to
handle time-series data. The GRU model is primarily characterized by
the update gate and the reset gate. In contrast to the LSTM model, GRU
features one less gating signal, leading to a reduction in the number of
parameters. The update gate regulates the extent to which previous state
information influences the current state, with a higher value allowing
more input from the previous moment. Meanwhile, the reset gate controls
the information from the previous state written to the current candidate
set, where a smaller reset gate implies less information from the previous
state is incorporated. In the network unit, the input is multiplied by its
weight, and similarly, the hidden state contains information from the
preceding units and is multiplied by its weight. The results are combined,
and a Sigmoid activation function is applied to constrain the outcome
between 0 and 1. This involves multiplying input gate with weight and
reset gate with weight, followed by calculating the Hadamard product
between the reset gate and update gates previous term. The final memory
at the current time step involves two steps: Step 1 includes element-wise
multiplication of reset gate and previous hidden gate, and Step 2 involves
element-wise multiplication of reset gate and hidden state, followed by

summing the results from both steps. The proposed GRU is bidirectional
and is time sequential with two sequences for the feature extraction of
the traffic segments which are from front to back and from back to front
and finally merged into the first hidden state. Within the neural network
framework, the activation function plays a crucial role in executing a
nonlinear transformation on the numerical values of neural network
units. Its primary function is to enhance the nonlinearity within the
neural network model, thereby improving the expressive capabilities of
the model. Additionally, the activation function finds utility in attentional
mechanisms. ReLU (Rectified Linear Unit) is the activation function
applied in the proposed model.

The hierarchical attention mechanism for detecting the malicious
network in this work is applied using maximum pooling (applied on the
hidden later) and average pooling (similar to max pooling which calculates
the value of the hidden state and results in a single dimensional vector).
The multi-class classification is achieved by applying soft max function.
The proposed approach is compared with XGBoost, light gradient
boosting (Swift Intrusion Detection System), deep packet (CNN and SAE),
multi-CNN and multi-LSTM. The performance measures considered are
detection rate (DR), false positive rate (FPR) and F1 score on the datasets
NSL-KDD, CES-CIC-IDS2017 and CES-CIC-IDS2018. The attacks in the
data set are Benign, DDoSattacskLOICHTTP, Bot, DDoSattack-
HOIC, DoSAttack-Hulk, FTP-BruteForce, SSH-BruteForce, Infilteration,
DoSAttackslowHTTPtest, DoSAttacks-GoldenEye, DoSAttacks-SlowLoris,
DDoSAttack-LOICUDP, Web-Attack, Macro. Figures 7-5 through 7-7 give
the performance measure of various models in the data set NSL-KDD,
CIC-IDS2017, and CIC-IDS2017, respectively. In this study, the DR and
F-score of the proposed HAGRU model surpass those of the compared
models. Notably, the HAGRU model demonstrates superiority over the
compared models in the U2R category, contributing to an overall sample
evaluation index with a DR of 94.12% and an F-score of 95.61%. Despite
challenges posed by unbalanced data samples in the NSL-KDD dataset,

particularly in categories like Normal, DoS, Probe, and R2L, the HAGRU model excels in performance compared to the other models, especially in addressing unbalanced datasets.

In a separate experiment involving the reclassification and sampling of the CIC-IDS2017 dataset, the HAGRU model continues to outperform compared models in terms of total samples, achieving a DR of 96.32% and an F-score of 96.71%. However, it's essential to acknowledge that not every evaluation indicator excels in all categories. The unbalanced categories are effectively handled by the HAGRU model, since the F-Score is 98.52% for the web attack category which is better than the other models. The model also exhibits low false alarm rate (FPR), however this doesn't guarantee the models performance is good, since the SAE based deep packet model developed for the Bot classification performance is poor even though the FPR is good.

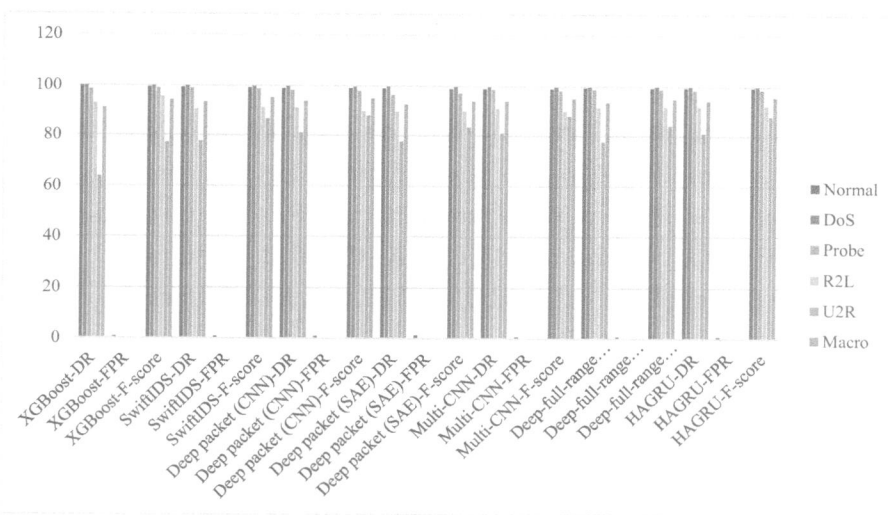

***Figure 7-5.***  *NSL-KDD – performance measure of machine learning models [31]*

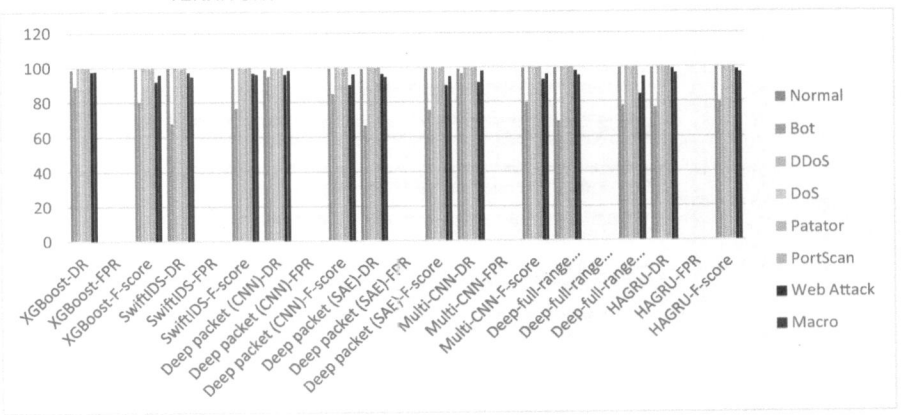

**Figure 7-6.** *CIC-IDS2017 – performance measure of machine learning models [31]*

The HAGRU model when implemented for the data set CSE-CIC-IDS2018 yields good performance for detecting the malicious traffic attacks. The imbalances in the data set, label definition, recognition of various types of attacks are successfully computed by the model. The DR and F-Score the HAGRU model is 93.06% and 93.95% respectively. The FPR is ZERO for the attacks DDoS attack-HOIC, SSH-Brute Force, DoS Attacks-SlowLoris, DDoSAttack-LOIC-UDP and the F-Score is almost close to 100%.

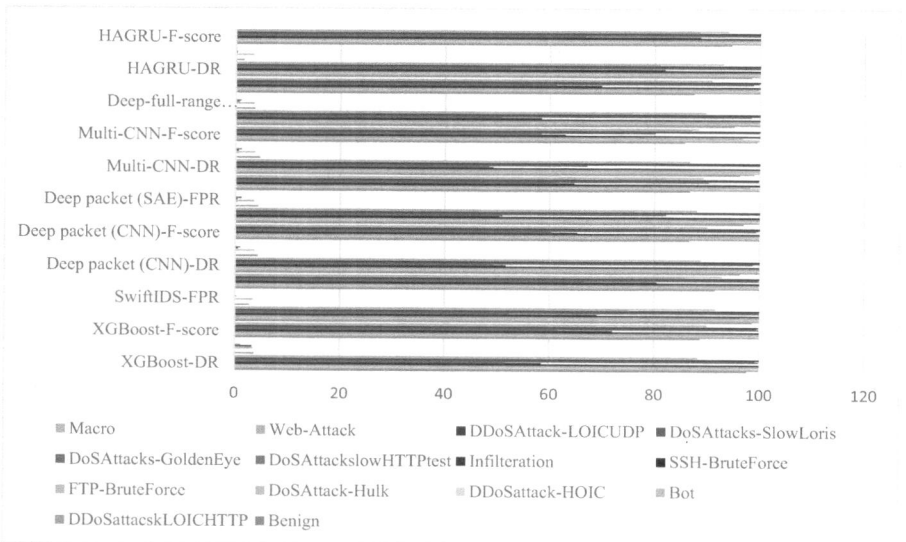

***Figure 7-7.*** *CIC-IDS2018 – performance measure of machine
learning models [31]*

From the comparative experimental analysis, the performance of
the HAGRU model results in an exceptional performance for classifying
the type of attacks in the network. However, the performance of the
algorithm purely depends on the size of the data set for multiple categories
(i.e., when the data set is of large volume is directly proportional to the
performance of the algorithm). Also, if a single category to be detected,
then it is evident from the results that with small volume of data the
performance of the model is good when compared with the traditional
algorithms. By incorporating attentional mechanism and hierarchy
features, the algorithm is capable of detecting the network traffic
anomalies even with smaller size data set.

The authors have introduced the real-time supervised machine
learning model (mainly decision tree and random forest) for detecting
the malicious data flow traffic using the ISOT-CID dataset, which consists
of high quality features plus the feature called "rambling." The rambling

feature supports the model in diagnosing the traffic with anomalies.
However, the model relies on a large dataset, considered as big data, and
may compromise speed when deployed in real networks. The HAGRU
model showcases exceptional performance in classifying overall samples,
particularly as data set size and the number of data categories increase.
The model's advantages become more evident with larger and more
diverse datasets. It excels in identifying categories with limited data,
surpassing traditional models due to its attentional mechanisms and
hierarchies. The HAGRU model's ability to extract rich information even
from small data samples enables robust traffic identification, especially in
scenarios characterized by data imbalance.

## Smart Contracts and SCM

Dobrovnik and Herneth (2021) [32] state that the advancements in
technology, efficient business processes, and collaboration among the
various stakeholders in the supply chain process are essential for fostering
the growth of a sustainable and socially inclusive society. Both the
enterprise (non-government organizations) and the governmental entities,
along with academia, have to enhance the digital capabilities and gain a
comprehensive understanding of the challenges and opportunities posed
by technology, as well as its impact on society, to actively contribute to
societal goals. Currently, literature on smart contracts, blockchain, and
sustainability pursues divergent activities.

**Technology**: The emergence of technological innovation facilitates
novel methods for generating value through the restructuring of business
models and processes. The blending of industry boundaries and the
simultaneous application of diverse technologies results in what is
known as technology convergence. The readiness of technology and
decreasing costs contribute to its widespread use throughout the supply
chain, facilitating the smooth combination of information technology
and operational technologies. When viewed through a sustainability

lens, it becomes crucial to acknowledge and weigh the trade-offs
between diminished consumption of resources resulting from enhanced
operational efficiency and the resource consumption associated with the
convergence in the technology innovation.

**Business process**: Supply chains are designed to meet customer
requirements through collaborative value creation involving various legal
entities. The complexity of a supply chain is determined by the interface
count and the coordination of these activities. Key factors influencing this
complexity include the characteristics of the underlying goods or services,
the number of involved actors, and their geographical distribution. In highly
fragmented environments, a significant challenge arises from the lack of
synchronization among individual business processes. The integration of AI-
driven automated collaboration and decentralized decision-making enhances
alignment across supply chain processes, paving the way for the exploration
of digitized "situational awareness" in research. From a sustainability
standpoint, it becomes imperative to carefully weigh the trade-offs between
process performance and the social impact on environmental issues.

**Sustainability**: For emerging technologies to gain widespread
acceptance and be widely adopted across various sectors, they must
showcase economic advantages. The primary emphasis in developing
hardware and algorithms lies in achieving economic progress in terms
of speed, capacity, and costs. However, real sustainability challenges
arise from energy-intensive consensus algorithms, e-wastage, and the
environmental factors that are associated with cloud hosting nodes/
locations/centers.

To bridge the research gap on block chain and supply chain management,
the authors [32] put forth research propositions that encompass technology,
business process and supply chain management, and sustainability. These
propositions are organized in a chronological sequence, spanning short-to
long-term perspectives. These proposition aims to elucidate the primary
trade-offs that should be taken into account, providing guidance for future
research endeavors. The propositions [32] are listed in Table 7-1.

***Table 7-1.*** *Smart Contracts and SCM Research Propositions*

| | | |
|---|---|---|
| 1. | Technology | The convergence cf innovation in key technologies, such as 5G, blockchain, IoT, and AI, facilitates the integration and widespread use of smart contracts in supply chains to meet business requirements. |
| 2. | | Achieving Society 5.0 involves establishing socially inclusive Industry and Logistics 4.0 with highly parallelized operations. Progress in technology and the maturation of smart contracts contribute to reduce the costs involved during the transaction and improving the visibility and security in the supply chain. |
| 3. | | Commercial, proprietary and other open source solutions (or) alternatives will compete to become accepted as prevailing standards or dominant designs in markets and global supply chains. |
| 4. | | The emergence of elegant designs will simplify the dissemination of smart contracts in supply chains by lowering the risk of technological obsolescence (or) malfunctioning and gaining the importance in the business needs. |
| 5. | Business Process | The significant fragmentation within certain supply chains and the ensuing coordination necessity by creating a substantial opportunity for adopting the smart contract standards using the standard information technology infrastructure and bridging the integration of supply chain within the organization. |
| 6. | | The incorporation of smart contracts into supply chain management will occur gradually, starting from individual business processes and eventually evolving into comprehensive, industry-specific frameworks. |
| 7. | | Smart contracts are formulated with reference to the industry and are evolving into industry-agnostic blueprints, enabling decentralized formation and autonomous business networks. |

*(continued)*

213

*Table 7-1.* (*continued*)

| | | |
|---|---|---|
| 8. | Sustainability | The initial short and mid-term adoption due to disproportionate resource consumption of smart contracts may result in rebound of effects. |
| 9. | | Over the long term, eco-efficient smart contracts will progressively replace existing proof-of-work-based solutions. |
| 10. | | Environmental challenges associated with smart contracts will provided with solutions by considering various societal factors. |
| 11. | | The widespread incorporation of smart contracts into the existing manual supply chains and the subsequent development of autonomous self-organizing systems may have negative impact in the employment levels at various levels of organization functionalities, which may lead to social repercussions. |
| 12. | | With the integration of AI and the incorporation of autonomy into smart contracts, ethical considerations in computing, governance, and societal values will become increasingly significant. |
| 13. | | The deployment of smart contracts throughout the supply chain presents a novel framework for corporate and governmental sustainability strategies aligned with societal development objectives. |

The introduced technology [32] provides novel solution in the production environment by reducing the cost and values are also generated. The cost involved in the individual contract for concluding and enforcing the contract (for example, labor costs) is reduced. But the implementation of smart contract in the production environment leads to incurring additional expenses through tool deployment, operations cost, and the activity ownership. Sustainability considerations encompass the management of environmental impacts across the entire supply chain of smart contracts. There are also possible changes in the various levels of the employment, which is more provident in the administrative routines such as legal departments, the procurement region, and logistics management. Smart contracts are still in primitive or the early development process when implemented by using cutting-edge technologies. However, several smart contract supporting technologies/platforms are available in order to establish an effective business solution with more accurate algorithms and good design of functionality. When smart contracts are implemented with good design functionality, they are energy efficient, they reduce the investment risk, and the concerns related to the socio-economic impact of major vendors in the market are also included. Relatively advanced business models with enhanced technology and algorithms are always introduced for facing various security challenges in the business process and or requirements. Vision, strategy, speculation, and proper mapping are required for implementing the digital end-to-end supply chain systems. Value-added networks with similar objectives and values are the need of the hour in the adaptive and automatized supply chain management system. The efficiency in process, environment-specific goas, societal relationships, and various other approaches are some of the trade-offs between the consumer and the producer; this is a challenging task in the current digital platforms or the ecosystem. The implementation of AI systems in various domains leads to an "open living system" in which one has to focus on understanding the vital dimensions of a human being and the introduction of cybernetic, creation of values in the developed or developing process. Economic objectives may be short or medium and this is also to be addressed while implementing the smart contract as it may have effects in the societal environment and the organization. Another consideration is the environmental aspect of the technology. The environmental context can be applied by developing green smarter contracts, which is highly competitive and thereby the reducing the risk. When creating the new business opportunities, various supporting strategies may change the customer preference towards achieving sustainable service and increase in the discovery rate in the supply chain model.

Terzi et al. [33] developed algorithms designed for smart contracts in scenarios related to a) supply chain, specifically focusing on logging raw materials and products and b) agile manufacturing, addressing aspects such as platform logging and registration processes. The smart contract for raw material logging takes the input as the raw material data (name of the raw material, quantity (preferable integer), meta data (string)), assigns a unique material identifier (UID) by checking the signers permission (block chain process for smart contract, returns the Boolean value based on the signers permission), and appends that includes any supplementary metadata provided. Similarly, the process of product logging involves the following inputs: Product name (string), Material ID (integer), and Material quantity (integer). During the blockchain contract phase, the transaction is signed. If the signing process is successful, a unique identifier and the retrieved materials metadata are generated. The blockchain record is then created with the following fields: Product name, Unique identifier, Material ID, Material quantity, and Material metadata. In the registration process of the agile manufacturing phase, the input data collected is username (in string), firstname/last name (in string), email id (string), password (string), and the consent (as Boolean). The transaction is signed only if the consent is set to 'True" and the smart contract record is signed by considering the input. The blockchain record is created with username, firstname, lastname, email id, password, consent, and the generated key pair. Finally, the platform logging consent takes the username (in string), platform name (in string), and the consent (Boolean) as the input. In the blockchain process, the signer permission is and the consent is verified and should be 'True" for generating the following items: a) public key (generated using username), b) platform id (using platform name), and the c) user signature (generated using username, platform id

216

and the consent). The signed record is returned. These smart contracts can
be applied as a template for functional implementation of blockchain in
supply chain management.

# Prototype for Secured IVRS and Supply Chain Management

The proposed secured interactive voice response system by integrating the
machine learning approach and the block chain technology in shown in
Figure 7-8.

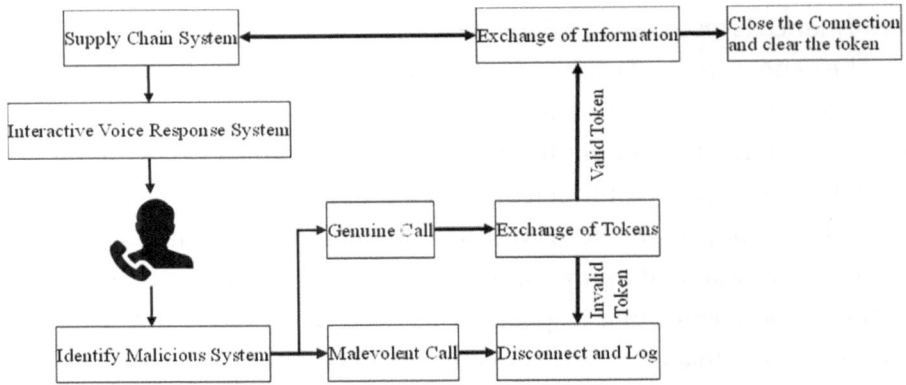

***Figure 7-8.*** *Secured IVR in SCM system using a machine learning*
*algorithm*

The sequence of steps in the secured interaction between the supply
chain management system and the consumer is as follows: the supply
chain system initiates a call to the consumer; the call tracking module is
executed for identifying whether the call is genuine or malevolent call;
if the call is malevolent, then it is disconnected and the log information
about the call is stored. If the call is genuine, tokens are generated by
applying the block chain contracts between the consumer and the IVRS
system. If the tokens are valid, then the exchange of information between

the SCM and the consumer commences and the call continues. If the
token is invalid, then the information about the issues in exchanging
the tokens is logged. On successful completion of the communication,
the system disconnects the call and the generated tokens are marked as
expired.

The major part in this proposed process is the detection of malicious
calls from the IVRS. In order to detect this, several machine learning
algorithms were implemented and tested as per the available literature.
From the review, it is evident that the random forest, XGBoost, and
decision trees algorithms were successful in detecting the malicious
network traffic. Hence these algorithms were implemented and their
performance is also compared in this work.

The generation and exchange of token using the blockchain smart
contract system is the next challenging task. In the blockchain smart
contract system, the user has to submit (or) deposit the token with the
blockchain. If required or based on the contract, commercials may
be involved. They notify the SCM system to update the token/ledger
details in the system. Both the consumer and the SCM have to exchange
the transaction using their respective digital signatures. On successful
transaction, the tokens are exchanged between the consumer and the SCM
system. The sequence of steps is shown in Figure 7-9.

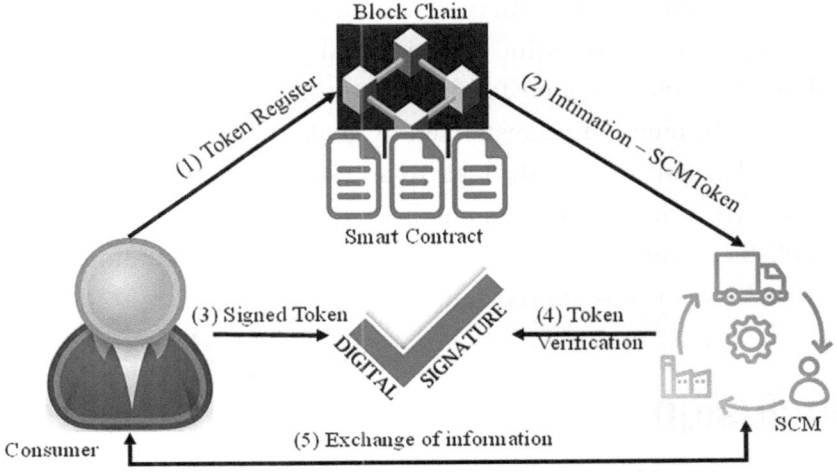

***Figure 7-9.*** *Smart contract – consumer and SCM*

Ethereum [34] for the blockchain smart contract and digital encryption standard is applied in the process. Solidity [35] is one of the most power languages in building the smart contract on Ethereum blockchain. It involves commercials by paying the computing cost, which are referred to as "gas fees."

# Results and Discussion

The growing AI capabilities and the convergence of operational and information systems leading to autonomous, self-learning systems. Ethical, social, and legal discussions are crucial for introducing new governance paradigms in a digitally transforming world. Smart contracts present a significant opportunity for corporate sustainability management and SSCM. Aligning sustainability goals with supply chain partners in global supply chains is challenging due to network complexity and partner anonymity. Smart contracts offer a means to operationalize sustainability goals as coded elements, necessitating research on assessing supply chain sustainability and trusted data sources, especially in raw material extraction, processing, logistics, and product end-of-life phases. Developing societal concepts forms the foundation for future human coexistence. Implementing sustainability goals in governmental and corporate decision-making through smart contracts requires collaboration between civil society, governmental institutions, academia, and industry to establish common societal goals, norms, and implementation-related rules to achieve overarching societal objectives.

# Conclusion

The significance of blockchain and smart contract authentication by collaborating with IVR systems plays a vital role in many industries. The combination of these technologies yields solution for securing the entire system and not only the individual APIs or modules. This results in enhancing the security, privacy, and efficiency, making digital interactions in any kind of online transaction. The complete SCM system will be of highly secure and trustworthy application by integrating blockchain and smart contracts in the business process. The technology can safeguard the IVR systems that are implemented in healthcare, finance, and more, revolutionizing how to protect and manage sensitive data. In future, deep learning techniques using cloud computing can be explored to leverage the dataset, in conjunction with the various calculated features for detecting malicious networks in the supply chain management system.

# CHAPTER 8

# Blockchain and IoT Integration-Based Transparency of Supply Chain Social Sustainability

*S. Porkodi, Research Scholar, Department of Computer Science and Engineering, Dr. Sivanthi Aditanar College of Engineering, Tiruchendur, Tamilnadu, India.* ishwaryaporkodi6296@gmail.com.

*Dr. D. Kesavaraja, Associate Professor, Department of Computer Science and Engineering, Dr. Sivanthi Aditanar College of Engineering, Tiruchendur, Tamilnadu, India.* dkesavaraja@gmail.com.

In the era of digitalization and automation, the integration blockchain and the Internet of Things has emerged as a powerful solution for addressing supply chain challenges such as enhancing transparency and social sustainability. The integration ensures maintaining immutable records at every step in the supply chain from raw material acquisition until it reaches the consumer end, providing much-needed product authenticity.

© The Editor(s) (if applicable) and The Author(s),
under exclusive license to APress Media, LLC, part of Springer Nature 2024
Dr. V. Grover et al. (eds.), *Blockchain, IoT, and AI Technologies for Supply Chain Management*,
https://doi.org/10.1007/979-8-8688-0315-4_8

This transparency enables product traceability and accountability besides mitigating issues like counterfeit products, fraud, illegal hoarding of products, and unethical labor practices. Moreover, trust is stimulated among stakeholders unknown to each other by providing both real-time access and tamper-proof data regarding the product to be purchased. It enhances the business reputation of the stakeholder and simultaneously contributes to the overall betterment of the society by enhancing fair labor practices and reducing the environmental footprint of the supply chain. In this chapter, the critical role of blockchain in securing the digital world is highlighted with the integration of IoT in the supply chain. The challenges of integrating blockchain and IoT are also discussed.

# IoT in the Digital Revolution

IoT devices around the world are utilized to collect humongous data for performing data analysis. The information extracted from the obtained data is utilized to recognize patterns, identify risks, and provide quick and efficient recommendations. As the world progresses with the digital revolution, the number of IoT devices and sensors increases day by day. According to Statista [1], there were approximately 15.14 billion IoT devices connected to the Internet in 2023 and this is projected to double in the year 2030. The evolution of technologies in numerous fields such as healthcare, farming, finance, manufacturing, energy, transportation, education, fashion, and various smart city projects will rapidly raise the IoT device count. The efficient and right usage of IoT has a huge capability to improve the human lifestyle with personalized solutions, automation, wellness, environmental sustainability, safety and security [2]. Yet there are major vulnerabilities including data management and data security when using IoT devices.

# Blockchain to Secure the Digital World

Blockchain was initially developed as a backbone to support a
cryptocurrency application called Bitcoin, which was launched by
Nakamoto [3] in 2008. Blockchain records all the transactions and data
with a time stamp in a chronological order. Once a transaction (Tnx) is
made, it is distributed to all the nodes in the network in peer to peer (P2P)
fashion and, after being verified by the miners, the records are stored
immutably in the ledger. All the records are cryptographically encrypted
where the hash value of the previous block n- 1 is chained to the current
block n, as shown in Figure 8-1, so that the blocks are chained to each
other. This makes any modification or alteration of data within the
blockchain almost impossible. Even a small change in a user's block
would result in changing all the hash values of the subsequential blocks.
The change is easily notable as the original copy of the digital ledger is
distributed across the network and the change is seen only with a single
user's data. If such scenario occurs, then the strained copy of the user is
considered an orphan and is replaced by the original copy of the ledger,
eliminating the chance of deleting or altering records. This also improves
the data security. A block consists of header, nonce, timestamp, Merkle
root, and hash value of the previous block. All the transactional data are
stored in a Merkle tree structure for easy search of data at the time of
need [4, 5].

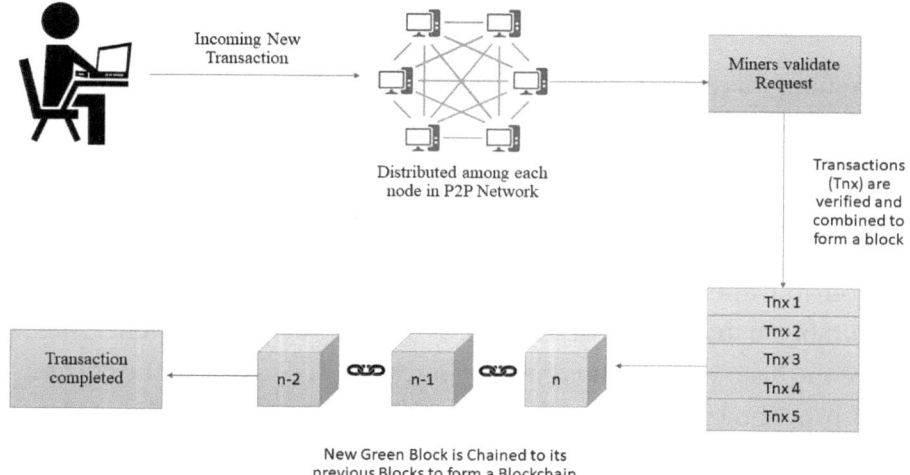

***Figure 8-1.*** *Working of the blockchain mechanism*

The introduction of Ethereum [6] created an impactful revolution in utilizing the blockchain ecosystem along with the introduction of smart contracts, which is basically a digital agreement between two parties such as seller and a buyer [7]. This concept eradicates all third parties or agents in real-world systems and promotes a direct, trusted way for two unknown nodes to interact. The discussed predefined conditions are set in the smart contract and deployed; the digital contract executes automatically whenever the conditions are satisfied, resulting with the outcome initially set. For example, if the buyer transfers money to the seller's wallet via a smart contract to buy a house, then the smart contract automatically checks for the correctness of the transaction and transfers the ownership rights to the buyer. All these records can be viewed by any nodes in the network, improving transparency. The smart contract plays a vital role in supply chain applications, due to its ability to avoid manual errors, and every record gets stored immutably in the blockchain. Furthermore, usage of smart contract speeds ups the entire process, also saving money [8].

# What Is Social Sustainability in a Supply Chain?

Identifying the positive and negative impacts of the business to understand
the need of the people involved in the system for promoting wellbeing and
a positive environment is termed as "social sustainability," which is crucial
for a company or an organization in its long run. With the rising global
demands from the side of the stakeholders such as consumers, investors,
or governments, providers of businesses hold a tremendous opportunity
to deliver services and products at a large scale and provide a trustable
service. However, it is also paramount to protect the dignity and rights
of the workers throughout the supply chain. Blockchain is preferred [10]
along with the integration of IoT to raise the standard of businesses with
decent labor work, proper human rights, fair trade, social equality, more
security, better delivery, enhanced product accessibility, and improved
data management. This enriches the lives of everyone involved in the
network.

# Related Research Works

In the recent years, a huge number of decentralized applications (DApps)
have been created based on blockchain mainly to solve data management
issues and security issues in various fields. After the COVID-19 pandemic,
the focus shifted to making the blockchain environment sustainable
and green [9, 11]. Various researches have focused on green supply
chains for environment sustainability, economic sustainability, and
social sustainability [13]. In 2020, Köhler, S., & Pizzol [10] performed
a case study on six food supply chains looking for environmental and
social sustainability. The proposed work gave insights on the benefits of
the sustainability. In 2021, Mangla et al. [14] assessed blockchain on its
social impact in the milk supply chain. The social impacts of blockchain
identified in the proposed work were listed as transparency, rural

development, food security, food quality, reduction of food fraud, and
better animal health and welfare. Lotfi et al. [17] in 2022 suggested an
optimized and sustainable blockchain to manage medical inventory in the
health care supply chain in which only energy consumption was discussed
for sustainability. Even in 2023, IoT and a blockchain-based supply chain
was developed by Nygaard et al. [12] for tracking hazardous material end
to end. But the proposed work focused only on the green sustainability
and not on social sustainability even when hazardous substances such
as radioactive materials were involved. In the same year, Wang et al. [15]
adapted blockchain for developing sustainable supply chain for industrial
purposes where businesses value, consumer value, and social reputation
were discussed as social barriers and other social aspects were not
explored. The shift towards sustainability is at its early phase contributing
towards various fields [16, 18] but the papers still lack exploring social
sustainability in the supply chain.

# IoT and Blockchain Integrated Supply Chain Architecture and Applications

The supply chain consists of five layers: data acquisition, communication,
stakeholders, blockchain, and application. In the data acquisition layer,
wearables and biometric authentication can be given to all employees to
detect their age, working time, temperature, heartbeat, movement, and
more. The data from the wearables and biometric authentication can be
used to eradicate child labor, direct people with bad health for a checkup,
maintain fair labor work, and continuously provide proper human rights
and social equality. The GPS attached to the smart containers consisting
of products can help in tracking the goods between the travel among
stakeholders and actively alert the stakeholder when the path of the
vehicle deviates drastically, indicating a possible vehicle hijack. The
pressure sensor can alert when the smart container is opened between the

deliveries or when the products are stored in the warehouse. All the other
sensors, cameras, and RFIDs can be used to collect data about materials
and environmental conditions and assist in decision-making.

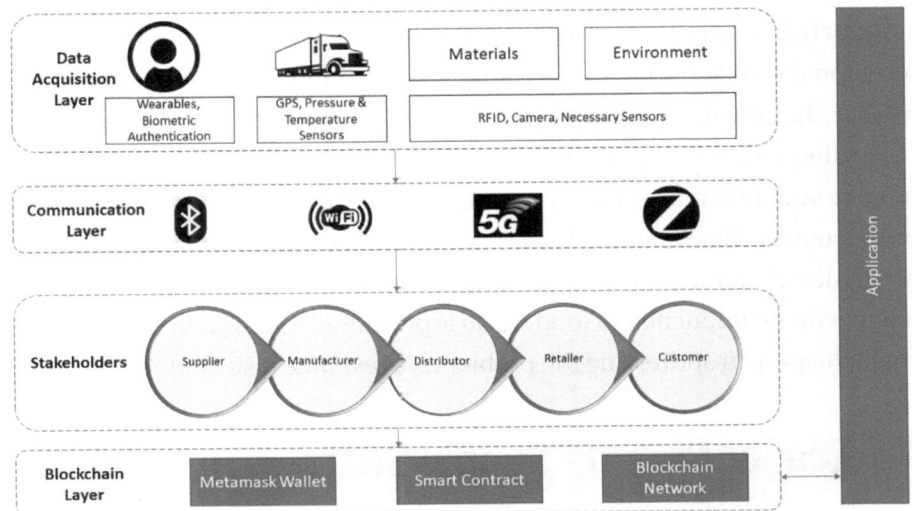

***Figure 8-2.*** *Supply chain architecture*

The communication layer consists of Bluetooth, Wi-Fi, ZigBee, or 5G
networks for transmitting the diverse data collected from the acquisition
layer. The data are cleaned and processed in the stakeholder's side, after
which the data are stored in the blockchain network via smart contracts.
The stakeholders initially are registered to the blockchain using their
metamask wallet accounts and are also granted access to the network
according to the role assigned. All the information and transactions are
stored as blocks, enabling better data management and providing security
to the data with an immutability feature; also, the data can be viewed
by the stakeholders at any time, ensuring transparency. The application
layer is built on the top to manage the supply chain, human resources,
traceability of the products, health, and a safe work environment, as shown
in Figure 8-2.

# Food Supply Chain

One of the important and basic needs of humans is a food supply chain where social and ethical responsibility are followed. In any food or agricultural supply chain from a rice chain [19] to frozen foods [20], the products can be monitored with IoT sensors and transferred from food production until it reaches the consumer. As the farmers are listed as stakeholders in supply chain, they can be recognized as essential contributors to the production process and this enables the farmers to receive a fair price for their agricultural production via blockchain, which is not only an ethical practice but also a fundamental element of fair trade and socially responsible supply chain management. Reduction of food waste is promoted throughout the supply chain, helping in addressing the problems of resource distribution and hunger.

# Medical or Pharma Supply Chain

The need for doctors and drugs is paramount for a healthy lifestyle, and during pandemic situations the demands for supplies are huge. Blockchain-based medical or pharma supply chains [21, 22] will ensure people obtain the necessary medical supply such as drugs, vaccines, and protective equipment regardless of preference to their economic or social status. As all the users are registered with their wallet address, their real identity regarding the economic or social status will not be know; if a user tries to buy too many products at a time of high demand, it will be considered hoarding. Health and safety standards can be followed by the workers in medicine manufacturing facilities, preventing accidental illness. The usage of IoT can prevent any stakeholder from hoarding the necessary medical supplies at the times of need. There are more and more counterfeiting drugs circulating even in developed countries, which can be completely eradicated with the use of blockchain because every authentic product can be found in the record of the digital ledger. Thus, unnecessary health issues caused by counterfeits can be avoided.

# Industrial Supply Chain

According to UNICEF [23, 24], 78 countries still have child labors, so it is
mandatory to check the age of the workers in the supply chain. Biometric
sensors can be used to verify their identity in the industrial supply chain
[25]. Blockchain and IoT device data can be utilized to provide fair wages
to the workers, to maintain safe working conditions, and to explore
fundamental labor rights including addressing issues like child labor,
forced labor, and worker exploitation.

# Radioactive Supply Chain

Social sustainability is way too crucial in the radioactive supply chain
[26, 27] considering the wellness and equitable treatment of the people
involved in the handling, transporting, and disposal of radioactive
materials. As the radioactive substance or products consist of potential
hazards, it is essential to implement responsible practices using IoT
sensors for protecting all the workers, communities, and environments.
IoT wearables can continuously monitor the health of the workers, and
people should be given the right equipment and guidelines to handle
such radioactive materials. A robust emergency response system can be
developed along with blockchain so that in case of accidents, immediate
aid can be given to the people affected. Since the IoT devices are
connected to the blockchain, any emergency alert from the IoT devices
will automatically trigger the smart contract in two ways. Alerts can be
sent to other stakeholders such as healthcare providers and emergency
responders with information such as severity and location. Evacuation
plans and emergency contact details can be sent to the affected people as
the emergency response.

# Why Social Sustainable Supply Chains Need IoT and Blockchain

The integration of blockchain and IoT enables different aspects of maintaining social sustainability in the supply chain as listed in Figure 8-3.

**Traceability:** The immutable digital ledger of the blockchain tracks the voyage of a product starting from the origin until it reaches the final destination. Traceability is vital to verify the authenticity of products and to ensure that the social ethical responsibilities are followed.

**Transparency:** The real-time information from the IoT sensors is used to track the location and its condition along the entire supply chain path. Each collected information point is recorded in the blockchain, promoting transparency and thus enabling fair trade, ethical sourcing, and social stability.

**Fair labor:** The working conditions and health of every employee is recorded with wearable devices and stored transparently in the blockchain. The salaries of the employees are also recorded in the blockchain as the amount is deposited in the employee wallet, thus ensuring ethical treatment and maintaining a fair labor system.

**Accountability:** Since the blockchain has the immutable feature, unethical activities such as human rights violations and fraud can be reduced, also making the stakeholders responsible for their actions. The IoT devices continuously monitor the health conditions of the laborers and the details are stored as transactions in the blockchain and can never be erased. So, if the laborers are exposed to hazardous materials or hazardous waste disposal and an unusual change in their health is observed, the industry could be held accountable for their actions with the real-time data collected by IoT devices and stored in the blockchain network. Likewise, IoT-enabled surveillance can be used to identify forced labor. Also, any counterfeit products can also be identified because the counterfeited product won't be registered on the blockchain.

**Why Social Sustainable Supply
Chain Needs IoT and Blockchain**

☑ Traceability

☑ Transparency

☑ *Fair Labor Practices*

☑ *Accountability*

☑ *Waste Reduction*

☑ *Fair Product Pricing*

☑ *Safety and Health Management*

☑ *Ethical Sourcing*

☑ *Security*

***Figure 8-3.***  *Why social sustainable supply chains need IoT and
blockchain*

**Waste reduction:** Parameters like temperature, pressure, humidity,
and expiring conditions are observed continuously with IoT devices and
all the information is immediately stored on blockchain. Waste reduction
can be made possible; this also improves inventory management. By
collecting real-time parameters, IoT devices can provide insight on
conditions that degrade the quality of the product and the life span
of the product, and this information is stored continuously. So, the
product condition can be audited via blockchain. When the humidity
or temperature value exceeds the safe threshold during the storage in

warehouse or transportation, immediate alerts can be sent to assigned stakeholders and this prevent spoilage. Expiry dates of the product help the sellers to not overstock products, leading the efficient resource usage.

**Fair pricing of products:** Since product prices are recorded in the blockchain, a customer can check the rate even before buying the product. So cases of unfair pricing can be identified easily, thus ensuring a fair pricing system.

**Safety and health management:** Employee health conditions are recorded using healthcare wearables like smart watches or smart bands and monitored continuously. The data is maintained in the blockchain, helping the organization follow all safety and health standards.

**Ethical sourcing:** The details regarding the origin of the data can be identified since the data is collected using IoT devices and is recorded in the blockchain. The acquired information can be useful when handling raw data like hazardous or radioactive materials and during the process of ethical sourcing verification that includes abolishing child labor completely from the supply chain system.

**Security:** Two essential features, integrity and authenticity of the product, must be maintained throughout the supply chain system to avoid any risks and fraud, further enhancing the security of the overall system. With the help of blockchain-integrated IoT systems, better solutions can be found focusing on the social sustainability by reducing the interference of the counterfeit market and by promoting fair trade. For example, a counterfeit medicine in the medicine supply chain can be found by checking the credibility of the product, which can be easily verified with the help of a unique ID. If the entered ID is not found on the system, then the medicine can be considered counterfeit. Here, the IoT devices help in maintaining all the details about the medicine along the supply chain. Also, if a thief tries to break open a contain filled with supply chain products, the pressure sensor in the smart container will send an alert along with the location details. The theft could be immediately reported

and actions can be taken by the police and authorities. Hence, the
proposed system improves risk management and minimizes company-
community conflicts.

# Barriers in Integrating Blockchain and IoT Technologies

Even as the world adapts to the various new technologies, there are still
many barriers, as shown in Figure 8-4.

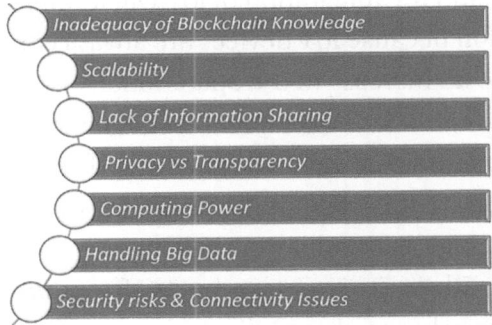

*Figure 8-4.* *Barriers in integrating blockchain and IoT technologies*

**Inadequacy of blockchain knowledge:** Organizations and people
does not possess the necessary understanding or expertise to deal with
blockchain. This hinders the utilization of blockchain solutions and also
impacts the integration of blockchain and IoT technologies.

**Scalability:** Networks of IoT devices are increasing tremendously and
will expand further in the future when more organizations delve into them,
making every basic thing smart. Blockchain is preferred by IoT experts for
its capacity in providing security. IoT systems involving micro payments
tremendously hike the volume of blockchain transactions, resulting in
scalability challenges.

**Lack of information sharing:** Accurate and effective decision-making requires a lot of information gathered from the users and the environment. But information sharing is restricted due the fear of misusing the information and various confidential policies of the organizations.

**Privacy vs. transparency:** Blockchain furnishes transparency and security in recording and transferring data in some applications. Yet certain user data from eHealth applications must maintain both privacy and transparency for which either encryption or access control policies via smart contracts are necessary.

**Computing power:** Blockchain requires high computational power to run algorithms, and the integration of IoT will immensely increase the energy consumption because IoT devices are always connected to the Internet, leading to an increase in the operational cost.

**Handling big data:** IoT devices generate huge amounts of real-time data. Blockchain maintains a digital ledger comprising all the transactions where the same copy of the ledger is distributed to every node in the network. Handling big data could be a challenge.

**Security risks:** Ethereum smart contracts offer automation in various DApps; however, they have vulnerability issues such as loopholes and backdoors if not written carefully, leading to hack where a hacker can drain out all the ether in the wallet. The user can not even stop the hacker because the smart contracts cannot be deleted or updated as they are stored immutably in the blockchain network. Cybercriminals continuously try to exploit vulnerabilities in smart contracts so blockchain experts are expected to develop tools to identify such vulnerabilities.

**Connectivity issues:** Instant processing and real-time decision-making require IoT devices and sensors to be connected to the Internet and blockchain all time. But various developing and even developed countries faces internet connectivity issues. 5G is expected to be adopted, providing more connectivity to all the IoT devices.

# Conclusion

After the pandemic era, the research focus has shifted to sustainability of businesses. Social sustainability is one of the main keys to be considered in improving the wellness of all the users in the network. This chapter details the role of blockchain in securing the digital world. You explored the architecture of the integration of blockchain and IoT in the supply chain system. You also looked at the ways advanced technologies can improve social sustainability in the supply chain and the challenges of doing so. The purpose of the chapter was to focus on contributing to the efficient utilization of blockchain and IoT for attaining advancement towards socially sustainable supply chain systems.

# CHAPTER 9

# Integrating Blockchain, IoT, and AI in Supply Chain Management

*Dr. Kumar Aditya, Assistant Professor in Commerce, GGV, Bilaspur, India.*

*Dr. Subhadeep Chakraborty, Assistant Professor in Commerce, Digboi College, Assam, India.*

*Akash Dahire, Research Scholar, Department of Commerce, GGV, Bilaspur, India.*

*Anmol Kumari, Research Scholar, Department of Commerce, GGV, Bilaspur, India.*

*Dr. Mariofanna (Fanny) Milanova, IEEE Senior Member, NVIDIA Deep Learning Instructor, Fulbright Scholar and Professor, Computer Science Department, University of Arkansas, Little Rock, AR 72204, USA.*

This chapter compares how blockchain, the Internet of Things (IoT), and artificial intelligence (AI) technologies are used in supply chain to promote sustainability. The chapter starts with explaining the concept of supply chains and its increasing importance in today's business world.

Dr. V. Grover et al. (eds.), *Blockchain, IoT, and AI Technologies for Supply Chain Management*,
https://doi.org/10.1007/979-8-8688-0315-4_9

237

It explores the challenges and objectives involved in managing supply chains, which sets the foundation for examining how blockchain, IoT and AI contribute to this transformative approach. The study extensively analyses how blockchain advances the sustainability of supply chains. It provides insights into real-world implementations and evaluates their social impacts. Additionally, it explores applications of IoT that utilize sensor technology for monitoring conditions, tracking assets, and reducing waste within supply chains. The study also investigates how AI contributes to sustainability through activities like demand forecasting, optimization, resource management, predictive maintenance, and energy conservation. This research highlights the potential of blockchain, IoT, and AI in advancing supply chain management. It offers a nuanced understanding of these technologies' strengths and weaknesses plus their cost effectiveness and adaptability in supply chain. It draws on real life examples from organizations that have successfully utilized these technologies to improve integration opportunities and overcome challenges. This research contributes to the understanding of the critical role played by blockchain, IoT, and AI technologies for the achievement of sustainability goals within supply chains. It offers practical recommendations for researchers, policymakers, and supply chain practitioners, enabling them to optimize the use of technologies in achieving sustainable supply chains. In conclusion, this study predicts the trends in integration of technology for supply chain sustainability.

# Sustainable Supply Chains

In today's rapidly evolving global business landscape, the concept of sustainable supply chains has emerged as a critical imperative for organizations across industries. (Martins and Pato, 2019) The traditional view of supply chains primarily focused on cost efficiency and timely delivery. However, the ethical, social, and environmental dimensions of supply chain management have gained unprecedented prominence, making sustainability a cornerstone of modern business practices.

# Significance in Today's Business Environment

Sustainable supply chain management represents a strategic shift in the way companies conduct their operations and interact with the world. It encompasses a holistic approach that aims to minimize adverse impacts on the environment, promote fair labor practices, and foster responsible sourcing of materials. This paradigm shift is propelled by several interrelated factors:

- **Environmental concerns**: Escalating environmental issues such as climate change, resource depletion, and pollution have raised alarms globally. Organizations are increasingly accountable for their ecological footprint, necessitating a re-evaluation of supply chain practices.

- **Consumer expectations**: Modern consumers are nowadays conscious of the ethical and environmental implications of their purchasing choices. They demand transparency, ethical sourcing, and sustainability in products, compelling companies to adopt sustainable supply chain strategies to remain competitive.

- **Regulatory compliance**: Governments and regulatory bodies worldwide have introduced stringent laws and regulations pertaining to environmental protection, labor rights, and responsible sourcing. Compliance with these regulations is not just a legal obligation but also a moral imperative.

- **Resource scarcity and cost efficiency**: With finite resources becoming scarcer and more expensive, sustainable supply chains emphasize responsible resource utilization. This approach leads to cost savings through reduced resource consumption, efficient processes, and waste reduction.

- **Innovation and efficiency**: Sustainability drives innovation in supply chain processes and technologies. Businesses that embrace sustainability tend to find more efficient ways of doing business, reducing costs, and enhancing overall productivity.

- **Ethical considerations**: Ethical supply chain practices, such as fair labor conditions and responsible sourcing, resonate with stakeholders. Businesses that prioritize these values align with broader ethical considerations and support social justice causes.

- **Global supply chain visibility**: In an interconnected world, understanding every aspect of a product's journey from source to consumer is vital. Sustainable supply chains offer improved visibility, enabling companies to make informed decisions and address potential issues proactively.

- **Brand image and reputation**: Companies with strong commitments to sustainability are often viewed more favorably by the public and investors. A positive brand image translates into increased brand loyalty, higher market valuation, and access to a broader investor base.

- **Competitive advantage**: Businesses that implement sustainable supply chains can gain a competitive edge. They are better positioned to adapt to market shifts, attract top talent, and meet the changing expectations of customers and investors.

In conclusion, sustainable supply chains are not only an ethical choice but also a strategic one. They align with evolving consumer preferences, regulatory requirements, and global challenges, and they offer cost savings and brand advantages. As sustainability continues to shape the business environment, sustainable supply chains have become essential for businesses to thrive, adapt, and demonstrate their commitment to a better future.

# Key Challenges of Sustainable Supply Chain Management

While the benefits of sustainable supply chain management are evident, it is not without its challenges. (Madhogarhia, 2022) Some of the primary challenges include the following:

- **Complexity**: Supply chains are intricate networks involving multiple stakeholders, making it challenging to trace and mitigate environmental and social impacts throughout the entire chain.

- **Data and technology**: Effectively monitoring and managing sustainability metrics require advanced data collection, analysis, and reporting capabilities. Emerging technologies like IoT and AI play a pivotal role in addressing this challenge.

- **Supply chain visibility**: Achieving sustainability objectives necessitates end-to-end visibility into the supply chain, from raw material extraction to the end consumer. This visibility is often lacking in traditional supply chains.

- **Cost considerations**: Sustainable practices may entail higher initial costs, making it imperative for organizations to balance sustainability with economic viability.

In essence, sustainable supply chain management is a multifaceted approach aimed at aligning social, economic, and environmental considerations to create a more responsible and resilient global supply network. It is a journey that requires continuous commitment, collaboration, and innovation to navigate the evolving landscape of today's business environment. In the subsequent sections, we will explore how emerging technologies such as IoT, AI, and blockchain are being leveraged to advance sustainability within supply chains.

# Research Design

This research is both descriptive and empirical in nature. The paper starts with explaining the concept of supply chains and their increasing significance, in contemporary business environments. It highlights the challenges inherent in sustainable supply chain forming the basis for an investigation into how blockchain, IoT, and AI contribute to this paradigm shift. The analysis goes in depth into the blockchain's role in improving supply chain sustainability, offering insight into real-world implementations and examining the environmental and social impacts. Furthermore, it explores the various IoT applications, demonstrating how sensor technology is used to monitor environmental conditions, track assets, and reduce waste in supply chains. The study also discusses AI's contribution to sustainability through demand forecasting, optimization, and resource management, as well as its role in energy conservation and predictive maintenance. The research focuses on a comparative assessment of these technologies, evaluating their strengths, weaknesses, cost-effectiveness, and scalability in various supply chain contexts. The research aims at integration challenges and opportunities, as well as best practices from organizations that have successfully combined blockchain, IoT, and AI for long-term supply chain management. The paper concludes by forecasting future trends in technology integration for supply chain sustainability and providing practical recommendations for supply chain practitioners, policymakers, and researchers.

# Blockchain For Supply Chain Sustainability

Blockchain technology, originally devised to underpin cryptocurrencies like Bitcoin, has emerged as a transformative force in supply chain management, offering promising solutions to enhance sustainability. (Nair and Praveena T., 2021) (Ante, 2020) This section delves into how blockchain can be harnessed to enhance sustainability in supply chains, drawing insights from real-world examples, evaluating its environmental and social impact and also discussing the associated challenges and limitations.

# Improving Sustainability Through Blockchain

Blockchain's distributed ledger technology provides an immutable, transparent, and tamper-proof record of transactions and events (Sharifpour et al., 2022). This inherent feature can significantly bolster sustainability efforts in supply chains in the following ways:

- **Traceability**: Blockchain enables end-to-end traceability of products and materials, allowing consumers and stakeholders to trace the origin, journey, and lifecycle of a product. This traceability is instrumental in verifying claims related to sustainability, such as organic or fair-trade certifications (Centobelli et al., 2022).

- **Transparency:** The transparent nature of blockchain means that supply chain participants can access a shared ledger containing all relevant data. This fosters accountability and trust because it becomes more challenging for unethical practices, such as child labor or illegal logging, to remain hidden.

- **Authentication**: Through the use of cryptographic signatures, blockchain ensures the authenticity of products and documents. Counterfeiting and fraudulent practices are deterred, thus promoting the use of genuine sustainable materials.

- **Smart contracts**: Smart contracts, which are self-executing agreements with predefined rules, automate processes in the supply chain (Tyagi et al., 2023; Singh and Dadhich, 2023). These contracts can enforce sustainability criteria, such as fair trade or responsible sourcing, ensuring compliance without the need for intermediaries.

# Real-World Examples and Case Studies

Several pioneering companies have successfully harnessed blockchain technology to advance supply chain sustainability (S. P. Yadav et al., 2022). **Walmart**, in collaboration with IBM, has implemented a blockchain-based system to trace the origins of food products (S. Yadav et al., 2021). This innovative initiative not only enhances food safety but also minimizes waste through precise recalls, providing consumers with valuable insights into the sources of their groceries (S. K. Sharma and Singh Vinay, 2022). **IBM Food Trust,** another notable player, has seen adoption across various food producers and retailers. By utilizing IBM's blockchain platform, these entities enable consumers to access detailed product information, fostering transparency and sustainability throughout the supply chain. **De Beers**, a prominent diamond company, employs blockchain technology to meticulously track the provenance of diamonds, guaranteeing that they are conflict-free and ethically sourced. This application aligns perfectly with social and ethical sustainability objectives (S. P. Yadav et al., 2022). **Nestlé,** a global food and beverage conglomerate, utilizes blockchain technology to enhance supply chain visibility. This technology offers transparency from "source" (raw materials such as coffee or cocoa) across every stage to "shelf" (finished products) in the supply chain, reinforcing responsible supply chain management. It ensures ethical sourcing practices and adherence to sustainability goals. Furthermore, **Unilever** has embraced blockchain within its palm oil supply chain, with a focus on tracing palm oil production and ensuring adherence to sustainable practices, including the prevention of deforestation and human rights violations (M. Sharma and Kumar, 2021). These real-world examples exemplify how blockchain is actively contributing to sustainable supply chain management across various industries.

# Environmental and Social Impact

Blockchain-based supply chain solutions have the potential to exert both positive and negative impacts on the environment and society. On the positive side, blockchain can significantly reduce waste, combat fraud, and promote responsible sourcing. These attributes contribute to a reduction in environmental degradation and improvements in labor conditions throughout supply chains. However, it is essential to acknowledge the potential negative environmental consequences. (Sasikumar et al., 2022; Wang et al., 2020) The energy-intensive nature of blockchain networks, especially those reliant on proof-of-work consensus mechanisms, has raised concerns about their carbon footprint. Striking a delicate balance between blockchain's computational demands and environmental sustainability remains a notable challenge in the adoption of this technology.

# Challenges and Limitations

Blockchain technology holds immense potential to enhance supply chain sustainability by improving traceability, transparency, and accountability. Real-world examples demonstrate its effectiveness, but challenges related to scalability, integration, data accuracy, energy consumption, and cost must be carefully addressed to fully realize its potential in sustainable supply chain management.

- **Scalability**: Current blockchain networks may not handle the vast volume of transactions in complex supply chains efficiently.

- **Integration**: Integrating existing supply chain systems with blockchain can be complex and costly.

- **Data accuracy**: Blockchain relies on accurate data input; if incorrect data is entered, it will be stored perpetually.

- **Energy consumption**: Energy-intensive consensus mechanisms can contradict sustainability objectives.

# IoT Applications For Sustainability

The IoT has revolutionized supply chain by providing real-time data and insights that enable organizations to monitor environmental conditions, track assets, reduce waste, and enhance sustainability (Menon and Shah, 2019). This section explores the diverse applications of IoT sensors and devices in promoting sustainability in supply chains, offering real-world examples, analyzing the impact of real-time data, and addressing security and privacy considerations.

# Examples of IoT-Enabled Sustainable Supply Chain

The IoT has emerged as a transformative force in enhancing sustainability within supply chain management (Houshang Tajfar and Gheysari, 2016). Here, we explore real-world instances where IoT technology is deployed to promote sustainability:

The agricultural machinery giant **John Deere** employs IoT sensors to optimize farming practices (Bhat et al., 2022). These sensors collect data on soil conditions, weather, and crop health, enabling precise irrigation, reduced pesticide usage, and enhanced resource efficiency. **Coca-Cola** employs IoT technology to monitor and optimize the energy usage of its cooling equipment. By remotely monitoring cooler temperatures and adjusting settings as needed, the company reduces energy consumption and carbon emissions. **FedEx** uses IoT sensors and telematics to monitor its fleet of delivery vehicles. These sensors track vehicle performance, fuel consumption, and driver behavior (Gromovs and Lammi, 2018). The data collected aids in route optimization, reduces fuel consumption, and lowers carbon emissions. **Pfizer** utilizes IoT sensors to monitor temperature-sensitive pharmaceuticals during transport (Kumar and Pundir, 2020). If temperature deviations are detected, the system triggers alerts, ensuring the integrity of vaccines and medicines. This technology is instrumental in maintaining product quality and reducing waste. **Waste Management Inc.** deploys IoT sensors in waste bins to optimize collection schedules (Hrouga et al., 2022). The sensors alert waste collection teams when bins are nearing full capacity, reducing unnecessary pickups and minimizing fuel consumption. Fast- fashion retailer **Zara** employs RFID technology, a subset of the IoT, to enhance inventory management. RFID tags on clothing items enable real-time tracking, reducing excess stock and minimizing waste through more efficient inventory control. The **Ocean Cleanup** initiative utilizes IoT sensors to monitor and collect data on ocean plastic waste. These sensors are integrated into floating cleanup systems and buoys, providing valuable insights into the location and density of plastic debris. This data informs cleanup efforts and aids in the development of more effective waste reduction strategies. **Pharma Secure**, a pharmaceutical technology company, uses IoT to ensure the authenticity of medicines in supply chains. Patients can verify the legitimacy of a medication by sending an SMS with a unique code found on the packaging. This technology safeguards against counterfeit drugs and promotes safe and ethical pharmaceutical supply chains. **Levi's**, a renowned denim manufacturer, incorporates IoT sensors in its production processes. These sensors help in optimizing water usage during the denim finishing process, reducing water waste by up to 96%, thus promoting more sustainable manufacturing.

# Monitoring Environmental Conditions and Asset Tracking

IoT sensors plays an important role in monitoring environmental conditions, and tracking assets in supply chains:

- **Temperature and humidity sensors**: These sensors help maintain the quality and safety of perishable goods during transportation and storage, reducing spoilage and waste (Khan et al., 2022).

- **GPS and RFID tags**: IoT-enabled asset tracking devices provide real- time location data, improving inventory management, and reducing the risk of theft or loss (Reyes et al., 2020).

- **Air quality sensors**: Monitoring air quality within supply chain facilities can contribute to healthier working environments and reduced emissions (M. Bublitz et al., 2019).

# Real-Time Data and Supply Chain Efficiency

The real-time data generated by IoT devices is invaluable for supply chain sustainability and efficiency (Atlam et al., 2020):

1. **Proactive decision-making**: Access to real-time data allows for proactive decision-making. For example, adjusting transportation routes based on traffic conditions can reduce emissions and delivery times (Rejeb et al, 2019).

2. **Predictive maintenance**: IoT sensors can predict equipment failures, enabling timely maintenance and reducing downtime, waste, and costs.

3. **Inventory optimization**: Real-time inventory data helps prevent overstocking or stockouts, minimizing waste and improving supply chain efficiency (Soori et al., 2023).

# Security and Privacy Considerations

While IoT enhances sustainability, it also introduces security and privacy concerns:

- **Data security**: IoT devices can be vulnerable to cyberattacks. Ensuring robust cybersecurity measures is essential to protect sensitive supply chain data.

- **Data privacy**: Collecting and sharing data from IoT devices may raise privacy concerns, especially when personal or confidential information is involved. Compliance with data protection regulations is crucial.

- **Interoperability**: Ensuring IoT devices from different manufacturers can securely communicate and integrate within the supply chain ecosystem is vital for security.

In summary, IoT sensors and devices have revolutionized supply chains by providing real-time data that contributes to sustainability and efficiency. Through monitoring environmental conditions, asset tracking, and proactive decision-making, IoT empowers organizations to reduce waste, save resources, and minimize their environmental footprint. However, it is essential to address security and privacy considerations to harness the full potential of IoT in supply chain sustainability.

# AI's Contribution To Sustainability

AI is revolutionizing supply chains by offering advanced capabilities for demand forecasting, optimization, resource management, and sustainability improvements (Min H., 2010). This section explores how AI and machine learning algorithms are applied in supply chains to achieve sustainability objectives, including energy efficiency, emissions reduction, waste reduction, and predictive maintenance. It also addresses the ethical implications associated with AI in supply chain sustainability.

# Real-World Examples and Case Studies

Here, we delve into instances where AI has been leveraged to drive sustainability in supply chain management.

E-commerce giant **Amazon** has harnessed AI's predictive capabilities to refine demand forecasting. By analyzing vast datasets and customer behavior, AI assists in inventory management (Ahmad Tass, 2023). This not only reduces overstock and understock situations but also curtails waste and contributes to efficient resource utilization. The maritime industry leader **Maersk** deploys AI for route optimization in its shipping operations (Shaw et al., 2021). AI algorithms analyze real-time data, weather conditions, and traffic patterns to identify the most fuel-efficient routes. This leads to substantial reductions in fuel consumption and, consequently, lower carbon emissions in the logistics sector. In the automotive sector, **Ford** employs AI-driven analytics to optimize manufacturing processes. AI models analyze every aspect of the production line, identifying opportunities for energy savings and resource conservation. This contributes to both cost reduction and a more sustainable production footprint. These real-world examples vividly demonstrate the transformative potential of AI in enhancing sustainability within supply chains. Whether through demand forecasting, route optimization, supply chain visibility, or manufacturing efficiency, AI offers versatile tools to achieve sustainability goals.

# Demand Forecasting, Optimization, and Resource Management

AI plays a pivotal role in enhancing supply chain sustainability:

- **Demand forecasting**: AI leverages historical data, market trends, and external factors to provide accurate demand forecasts. This reduces overproduction, minimizes waste, and ensures optimal resource allocation.

- **Optimization**: Machine learning algorithms optimize various supply chain processes, such as transportation routing, inventory management, and production scheduling, leading to reduced resource consumption and increased efficiency.

- **Resource management**: AI helps manage resources like water, energy, and raw materials efficiently by analyzing data from IoT sensors and making real-time adjustments based on demand and availability.

# AI and Sustainability Goals

AI plays a significant role in contributing to sustainability goals, particularly in the areas of energy efficiency, emissions reduction, and waste minimization.

- **Energy consumption reduction**: AI-driven algorithms analyze energy consumption patterns in supply chain operations. By identifying inefficiencies and recommending energy-saving measures, AI reduces energy consumption and associated costs.

- **Emissions control**: AI can optimize transportation and logistics operations to reduce carbon emissions by choosing more fuel-efficient routes, load optimization, and managing vehicle fleets for lower environmental impact.

- **Waste reduction**: AI analytics identify waste generation points in the supply chain, facilitating waste reduction initiatives, and promoting recycling and reuse.

# Predictive Maintenance for Sustainability

Predictive maintenance powered by AI minimizes disruptions and contributes to sustainability by the following:

- **Reducing downtime**: AI-powered predictive maintenance uses sensor data and machine learning to anticipate equipment failures. This proactive approach minimizes disruptions, reducing downtime and the environmental impact of emergency repairs.

- **Prolonging asset life**: Predictive maintenance ensures that assets are maintained optimally, extending their lifespan and reducing the need for replacements.

- **Resource efficiency**: By preventing over-maintenance and resource overuse, predictive maintenance enhances resource efficiency and minimizes environmental impact.

# Ethical Implications of AI in Supply Chain Sustainability

The ethical use of AI in supply chains is crucial. Consider the following:

- **Algorithm bias**: AI algorithms may inherit biases present in training data, potentially leading to unfair decisions in areas like hiring, sourcing, or pricing. Careful algorithm design and data bias mitigation techniques are essential.

- **Transparency and accountability**: Ensuring that AI decision-making processes are transparent and accountable is vital for maintaining ethical supply chain operations.

- **Data privacy**: AI relies on extensive datasets for training, which can lead to unauthorized usage of copyrighted content. This infringes on copyright law and raises concern about data privacy when the output includes personal data. Supply chains must navigate privacy regulations while collecting and using data for sustainability.

- **Fairness and transparency**: AI must be programmed to ensure fairness in various aspects of supply chain management, including supplier relations and employee treatment. Ethical AI practices involve regularly auditing models for bias, ensuring diverse data sources, and transparently disclosing decision-making criteria.

In conclusion, AI's contributions to supply chain sustainability are substantial, encompassing demand forecasting, optimization, energy reduction, emissions reduction, waste reduction, and predictive maintenance. However, it is crucial to address the ethical implications associated with AI in supply chains, such as bias and fairness, as organizations harness the power of AI to drive sustainability improvements.

# Comparative Analysis

The convergence of blockchain, IoT, and AI technologies in supply chain management offers a multifaceted approach to achieving sustainability goals. In this comparative analysis, we assess the strengths and weaknesses of each technology, evaluate their cost-effectiveness and scalability, discuss integration challenges and opportunities, and identify best practices from successful implementations.

## Strengths and Weaknesses of Blockchain, IoT, and AI in the Supply Chain

Let's explore the strengths and weaknesses of blockchain, IoT, and AI in supply chain management. See Table 9-1.

*Table 9-1.* *Strengths and Weaknesses*

| Strengths | Weaknesses |
|---|---|
| **Blockchain** | |
| Immutability, transparency, and traceability enable accountability and ethical sourcing. Smart contracts automate sustainability criteria enforcement. | Scalability issues, energy-intensive, consensus mechanisms, and data privacy concerns can hinder widespread adoption. |
| **IoT** | |
| Real-time data collection and monitoring enhance resource efficiency, reduce waste, and enable precise decision-making. | Security vulnerabilities, data privacy risks, and the potential for data overload pose challenges. |
| **AI** | |
| Predictive analytics, machine learning, and optimization algorithms improve resource allocation, demand forecasting, and sustainability strategy development. | AI implementation requires substantial computational resources and skilled personnel. Ethical considerations, such as algorithm bias, need attention. |

In summary, these technologies offer various strengths, they also come with challenges and limitations. Successful implementation requires addressing these weaknesses while leveraging the technologies' unique strengths to create sustainable and efficient supply chains.

# Cost-Effectiveness and Scalability of Blockchain, IoT, and AI in the Supply Chain

The cost-effectiveness and scalability of blockchain, IoT, and AI technologies in supply chains can vary depending on factors like the specific use case, implementation, and industry. Table 9-2 provides an overview of their cost-effectiveness and scalability.

*Table 9-2.* *Cost-Effectiveness and Scalability*

| Blockchain | IoT | AI |
| --- | --- | --- |
| The initial setup cost can be high, making it less accessible for smaller businesses. Scalability issues may limit its effectiveness in large supply chains. | IoT solutions vary in cost but can offer a rapid return on investment through waste reduction and efficiency gains. Scalability depends on the availability of infrastructure and cost considerations. | AI adoption can be costly due to the need for specialized talent and computational resources. The scalability of AI applications depends on the complexity of algorithms and data availability. |

Organizations should carefully assess their specific requirements and consider both the initial costs and long-term benefits when implementing these technologies in supply chain operations.

# Integration Opportunities and Challenges

The integration of blockchain, IoT, and AI technologies in supply chains offers numerous opportunities and challenges (Zhao et al., 2016). See Table 9-3.

*Table 9-3.* *Integration Opportunities and Challenges*

| Opportunities | Challenges |
| --- | --- |
| **Data synergy**: Combined data from blockchain, IoT, and AI offers a comprehensive view of the supply chain, enhancing insights and decision-making. | **Data interoperability**: Integrating data from various IoT devices can be challenging due to differing protocols and formats. |
| **Traceability and transparency**: Blockchain complements IoT's data gathering by providing a secure and transparent record of product movements, fostering trust and accountability (Centobelli et al., 2022; Tsang et al., 2021). | **Scalability**: Scalability issues in blockchain networks can arise, especially in public networks, when integrating numerous IoT devices and AI processing. |
| **Smart contracts**: Blockchain's smart contracts automate actions based on IoT data, optimizing processes like inventory management and payments (Wamba and Queiroz, 2020). | **Data consistency**: Ensuring consistent data across blockchain, IoT, and AI platforms is essential to prevent errors in insights and decisions. |
| **Real-time decision-making**: AI processes IoT data in real-time, enabling quick, data-driven decisions for predictive maintenance, demand forecasting, and routing. | **Complexity**: Integration can be complex, requiring expertise in multiple domains, posing challenges in finding skilled personnel. |
| **Enhanced security**: Blockchain's security features protect IoT data and AI models from tampering, ensuring data integrity and confidentiality. | **Security concerns**: In the IoT, the expanded attack surface due to increased connectivity raises cybersecurity concerns, necessitating robust security measures (Furneaux, 2018). |

Integrating blockchain, IoT, and AI can create synergies. (Parker and Bach, 2020) IoT data can feed into AI models for predictive analytics, while blockchain ensures data integrity. However, integration of these technologies can be complex due to differing protocols technical requirements and data formats. Achieving interoperability and ensuring data consistency across systems is a challenge.

In conclusion, blockchain, IoT, and AI technologies offer unique strengths and weaknesses in achieving sustainability goals in supply chain management. The cost-effectiveness and scalability of each depend on various factors. While integration presents challenges, successful organizations demonstrate that combining these technologies can lead to enhanced transparency, efficiency, and sustainability, setting a precedent for future supply chain practices.

# Future Trends and Recommendations

The convergence of blockchain, IoT, and AI in supply chain management is poised for significant advancements. Here are some future trends and recommendations for stakeholders.

## Emerging Trends and Developments

- **Convergence of technologies**: The future will likely see the development of interoperable ecosystems where blockchain, IoT, and AI seamlessly integrate, allowing for more streamlined data flow and collaboration across supply chains.

- **AI-driven decision-making**: AI will increasingly drive real-time decision-making, not just in optimization but also in sustainability. AI models will provide insights for reducing environmental impact, optimizing resources, and ensuring ethical practices.

- **Edge computing for IoT**: Edge computing will gain prominence in IoT deployments, allowing data processing closer to the data source. This will enhance real-time analytics and reduce latency, which is crucial for sustainability applications.

- **Edge computing and data privacy**: Through the ability to process data locally, edge computing improves privacy. It reduces data exposure during transmission by handling tasks closer to the source. Also, edge nodes allow for more private interactions because data stays in the local network instead of being transferred to remote cloud services.

- **Hybrid blockchain solutions**: Organizations may adopt hybrid blockchain solutions, combining the transparency of public blockchains with the control and scalability of private or consortium blockchains (Miraz and Ali, 2018).

# For Supply Chain Practitioners

- **Collaborate**: Engage in collaborative efforts with supply chain partners to share the benefits and costs of implementing these technologies (Chauhan et al, 2023). Cross- industry collaborations can foster innovation.

- **Data governance:** Develop robust data governance policies to ensure data quality, security, and compliance. This is critical for maintaining trust in sustainability initiatives.

- **Continuous learning:** Invest in training and development for employees to ensure they have the skills to manage and utilize these technologies effectively.

# For Policymakers

- **Standardization:** Promote the development of industry-wide standards for data formats, security, and interoperability to facilitate technology adoption and ensure compliance with sustainability regulations.

- **Incentives:** Consider providing incentives or tax benefits to encourage businesses to adopt sustainable supply chain technologies.

- **Regulatory frameworks:** Develop and update regulatory frameworks that address data privacy, cybersecurity, and ethical considerations associated with these technologies.

# For Researchers

- **Multi-disciplinary research:** Encourage multi-disciplinary research that combines expertise in technology, sustainability, and supply chain management to address complex challenges.

- **Longitudinal studies**: Conduct longitudinal studies to track the long-term impact of these technologies on sustainability outcomes, both positive and negative.

- **Emerging technologies**: Explore emerging technologies, such as quantum computing and advanced sensors, and their potential integration into sustainable supply chains.

# Conclusion

The convergence of blockchain, IoT, and AI holds tremendous promise for transforming supply chains into more sustainable and efficient systems. The comparative analysis highlighted their strengths, weaknesses, and the potential for synergy when integrated effectively. As we look to the future, it is imperative for stakeholders to collaborate, adopt best practices, and remain adaptable to emerging trends. A holistic approach to sustainability through the integration of these technologies will not only drive competitive advantage but also contribute to a more responsible and resilient global supply chain ecosystem.

The following are some additional key takeaways:

- The traditional supply chain primarily focuses on cost efficiency and timely delivery. On the other hand, the modern supply chain also focuses on the environmental, social, and ethical dimension of the supply chain.

- Sustainability is a strategic choice in the supply chain to align with evolving customers, regulatory requirements, environment concerns, and global challenges to thrive, adapt, and demonstrate commitment to a better future.

- Blockchain technology has immense potential to enhance supply chain sustainability with its inherent characteristic like traceability, transparency, and accountability. Real-world examples (Walmart, De Beers, IBM Food Trust, and Unilever) demonstrate its effectiveness, but challenges related to scalability, integration, data accuracy, energy consumption, and cost must be carefully addressed.

- IoT sensors and devices have revolutionized supply chains by offering real-time data to improve sustainability and efficiency through environmental monitoring, asset tracking and data driven decisions. However, the security and privacy concern must be considered to harness the full potential of IoT in supply chain sustainability.

- AI encompasses demand forecasting, optimization, energy reduction, emissions reduction, waste reduction, and predictive maintenance and has made significant contributions to sustainable supply chains. However, it is crucial to address the ethical implication of AI in supply chain, such as biasness and transparency.

- On comparing blockchain, IoT, and AI we found that blockchain's inherent features of transparency, traceability, and immutability enable accountability in the supply chain. In IoT, real-time data collection and monitoring enhance efficiency and reduce waste. AI's machine learning, predictive analytics and optimization algorithms improve demand forecasting, resource allocation, and sustainable strategy development.

- However, all these technologies have data privacy, scalability, cost-effectiveness, complexity, and interoperability issues. Convergence of these technologies is still in its early stage and the practical potential has not been realized yet. There are great opportunities in the future.

# CHAPTER 10

# Challenges of Supply Chain Management Post COVID-19

*Lipsa Das, Amity University, Greater Noida, UP, India.*
`lipsaentc9@gmail.com.`

*Veena Grover, NIET, Greater Noida, India.* `veena.grovere@gmail.com.`

*Rishit Jain, Amity University, Greater Noida, UP, India.*
`rishitjain4874@gmail.com.`

*Aryan Gulati, Amity University, Greater Noida, UP, India.*
`aryann2708@gmail.com.`

This chapter's goal is to present a thorough examination of the difficulties supply chains encountered following the COVID-19 epidemic, as well as a thorough analysis of the mitigating measures that businesses put in place. This chapter intends to aid practitioners, researchers, and decision-makers in establishing strong strategies for a more resilient and adaptive supply chain by exploring the practical lessons acquired from these experiences. It also hopes to bring important insights to the area of supply chain management as outlined here:

- **Contextualizing post-COVID-19 supply chain dynamics**: Examining the unique challenges and disruptions posed by the COVID-19 pandemic to supply chains globally and highlighting the evolving nature of supply chain dynamics in the post-pandemic era and the need for adaptive strategies.

- **Setting the stage for mitigation strategies**: Establishing a foundation for understanding the critical role of supply chain management in responding to and recovering from unprecedented disruptions and emphasizing the interconnected nature of mitigation strategies in addressing various facets of supply chain challenges like supply chain disruption, inventory management, demand forecasting, logistic and transport management.

- **Analyzing the practical implications of mitigation strategies**: Providing a detailed analysis of specific mitigation strategies employed by organizations in response to post-COVID-19 challenges. Also assessing the effectiveness and adaptability of these strategies across different industries and supply chain models.

- **Extracting lessons for future supply chain resilience**: Drawing practical lessons from real-world experiences, successes, and failures in supply chain management post-COVID-19 and offering actionable insights for organizations to enhance their resilience and responsiveness in the face of future uncertainties.

- **Contributions to academic and practical knowledge**: Contributing to the academic discourse on supply chain management by synthesizing current research, industry practices, and post-pandemic experiences with providing practical recommendations and guidelines to aid professionals in optimizing their supply chain strategies.

# Defining Supply Chain Management

The comprehensive planning, execution, and oversight of the complete process of locating, producing, distributing, and returning goods or services is known as supply chain management (SCM). For goods or services to move smoothly from the place of origin to the final client, a number of parties must cooperate and coordinate, including suppliers, manufacturers, distributors, retailers, and customers (J. T. Mentzer et al., 2001).

SCM, to put it simply, is the strategic and operational management of the interdependent web of activities that go into the development and provision of a good or service. Purchasing raw materials, manufacturing procedures, inventory control, logistics of transportation, and information system integration are all included in this to enable effective communication and decision-making along the supply chain.

Enhancing overall efficiency, cutting costs, cutting lead times, optimizing inventory levels, and quickly adapting to shifts in demand or market conditions are the main objectives of efficient supply chain management. Over time, SCM has changed as a discipline, adjusting to globalization, technology breakthroughs, and shifting market conditions.

Following the COVID-19 pandemic, supply chain management has become even more important as businesses struggle with hitherto unseen obstacles. This has led to a critical reassessment of established procedures and the investigation of novel approaches to guarantee flexibility and resilience in the face of setbacks.

# Importance of Effective Supply Chain Management

In today's dynamic and linked global economy, supply chain management is essential to a company's success and sustainability. The importance of SCM will be discussed in detail in this section with a focus on how it helps firms achieve their strategic goals (Wisner et al., 2021)

## Enhancing Operational Efficiency

- **Streamlining processes**: SCM involves optimizing and integrating various operational processes from procurement to distribution to eliminate bottlenecks and enhance overall efficiency.

- **Cost reduction**: Well-managed supply chains help in minimizing operational costs through effective resource utilization, inventory management, and process optimization.

## Customer Satisfaction and Service Levels

- **Timely delivery**: SCM ensures that products or services reach customers in a timely manner, meeting or exceeding their expectations regarding delivery speed and reliability (Dong Won et al., 2012).

- **Quality assurance**: Through effective supply chain practices, organizations can maintain consistent product quality, enhancing customer satisfaction and loyalty.

# Strategic Decision-Making

- **Data-driven insights**: SCM involves the collection and analysis of data throughout the supply chain, providing organizations with valuable insights for informed decision-making (Cabral et al., 2012).

- **Agility and adaptability**: A well-designed supply chain allows organizations to adapt quickly to market changes, emerging trends, and unexpected disruptions.

# Globalization and Market Expansion

- **Access to global markets**: SCM facilitates the expansion of businesses into new markets by managing the complexities of international trade, compliance, and diverse cultural considerations (Mangan et al., 2026).

- **Supply chain network optimization**: Global supply chains require strategic network design to balance cost-effectiveness and responsiveness.

# Risk Mitigation

- **Identifying and managing risks**: SCM involves proactively identifying potential risks followed by risk assessment and prioritizing the risk based on the likelihood of occurrence and severity. By developing and implementing the required mitigation strategies throughout the supply chain, it can contribute to enhance organizational resilience (Gurtu at al., 2021).

- **Contingency planning**: Effective supply chain management includes the development of contingency plans to address disruptions and uncertainties.

# Impact of COVID-19 on Global Supply Chains

The COVID-19 pandemic of 2019 exposed vulnerabilities and upended long-standing standards with significant and far-reaching effects on global supply networks. This section will look at the particular difficulties and interruptions that supply chains faced after the pandemic (Laoucine Kerbache et al., 2020).

# Disruptions in the Global Supply Chain

- **Overview of pandemic-induced disruptions**: Analyzing the immediate and long-term disruptions caused by the pandemic across industries and geographical regions (Magableh et al., 2021).

- **Supply chain fragility**: Understanding how the pandemic highlighted the fragility of global supply chains and the interconnectedness of various components (Ozdemir et al., 2022).

# Demand Fluctuations and Uncertainties

- **Shifting consumer behavior:** Exploring changes in consumer preferences and behavior during the pandemic and their impact on demand forecasting and fulfillment (Sarkis et al., 2020).

- **Unpredictable market dynamics:** Assessing the challenges posed by sudden shifts in market dynamics, including demand spikes, supply shortages, and changes in product priorities (Ivanov et al., 2020).

# Transportation and Logistics Issues

- **Border closures and trade restrictions:** Examining how border closures and trade restrictions affected the movement of goods, leading to delays and increased costs (Adel Elomri et al., 2020).

- **Disruptions in freight and transportation networks:** Analyzing challenges faced by transportation and logistics providers, including disruptions to air, sea, and land freight (Christopher et al., 2022; Adel Elomri et al., 2020).

# Inventory Management Challenges

- **Stockouts and shortages:** Investigating instances of stockouts and shortages due to production halts, distribution challenges, and increased demand for essential goods (Luis Miguel et al., 2020).

- **Excess inventory and overstocking issues**: Discussing the consequences of overestimating demand and the accumulation of excess inventory during periods of uncertainty (Samir K. Srivastava et al., 2022).

# Challenges Faced by Supply Chains Post COVID-19

All sectors had global supply chain (GSC) interruptions. Items can often be divided into two categories: inventive items and utilitarian products. In normal times, there is a stable supply and demand for functional products. But because of the erratic nature of supply and demand, some products—like masks—have evolved from useful items to creative works of art. During the epidemic, GSCs' high earnings and ability to respond quickly to clients become critical characteristics. Addressing the COVID-19-related disruptions in the GSCs of all product groups is imperative, on the one hand (Fonseca et al., 2020). Figure 10-1 shows the features of the damage of the COVID-19 pandemic on GSCs.

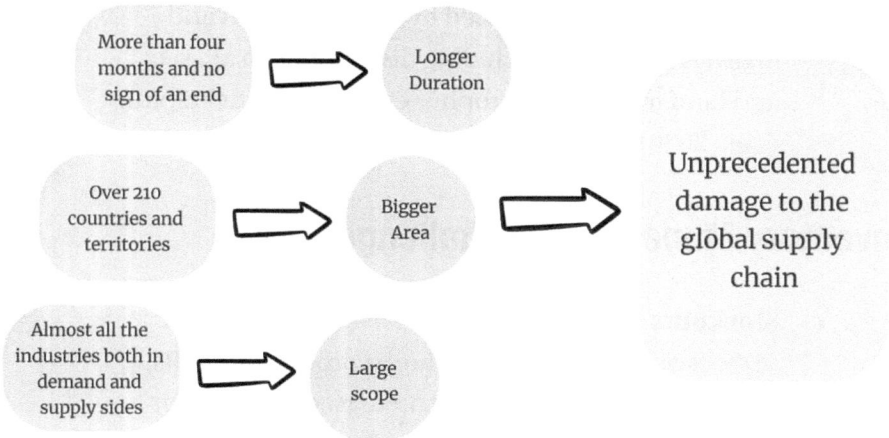

***Figure 10-1.*** *Features of the damage of the COVID-19 pandemic on GSCs*

Almost all industries experienced shutdowns or suspensions of operations due to limited availability of raw materials, consumables, and human resources as a result of the lockdown in numerous cities. On the other hand, client requests pertaining to COVID-19 prevention increased. While demand for electronics declined, there was a great demand for things such as masks. Large-scale travel restrictions and border closures caused delays, postponements, cancellations, and blockages in international logistics for sea, aviation, and terrestrial routes (Atif Saleem et al., 2021).

# Disrupted Commodities and Supply Chain High-Tech Products

The shortage of various components wreaked havoc on the supply chains within the high-tech industry, impacting the production of essential devices such as virtual reality headsets, cellphones, and other technological accessories. Notably, the temporary closure of Foxconn factories in China had a cascading effect, leading to Apple's postponement of product releases. This disruption extended to major players like Samsung and LG, with production halts reported in their facilities in South Korea and India. The reverberations of the supply chain disruptions reached even prominent electric vehicle manufacturer Tesla Motors, which had to cease operations in locations like Shanghai, California, and New York. The aviation sector faced similar challenges, witnessing production halts in facilities belonging to major players like Airbus, Boeing, and Lockheed in the United States and Europe, as documented by Saleheen et al. (2022). This multifaceted crisis underscores the interconnectedness of global supply chains and the vulnerability of industries to disruptions, revealing the critical need for robust contingency planning and risk management strategies.

# Automotive Parts

Production stoppages occurred at several of the major automakers' facilities in China and other nations. A 13% decline in global automotive sector output was anticipated. Volkswagen closed its car factories in China because of travel restrictions and parts shortages. For essentially the same reasons, General Motors reactivated its operations in China, albeit at a very modest output pace. Hyundai closed its assembly facilities in South Korea, primarily as a result of Chinese component shortages. Production was suspended at Nissan facilities in the Middle East, Asia, and Africa (Ishida et al., 2020).

# Medicines and Medical Devices

Approximately 40% of the global supply of active pharmaceutical ingredients (API) is believed to originate from Chinese producers. India, the third-largest exporter of pharmaceuticals globally, plays a crucial role in providing essential COVID-19 drugs. However, the heavy reliance of Indian pharmaceutical companies on Chinese suppliers, responsible for over 70% of India's bulk medication production, resulted in acute material shortages due to halted output from these suppliers. This interdependence underscores the vulnerability of the pharmaceutical supply chain, emphasizing the need for diversified sourcing strategies and increased resilience measures to mitigate disruptions in the future.

Beyond pharmaceuticals, there was a significant shortage of personal protective equipment (PPE), impacting the global efforts to contain the virus. This scarcity encompassed medical masks, respirators, protective clothing, footwear, gowns, and goggles, all of which were vital for safeguarding frontline healthcare workers. The shortage was exacerbated by the unfortunate loss of numerous medical and paramedical personnel in countries like Spain, Italy, and the United States. Factors such as panic buying, misinformation, and stockpiling further contribute to the surge in global demand for PPE. Chinese suppliers, being key players with almost exclusive dominance in PPE production, prioritized meeting local demand. In response, various governments and organizations urged manufacturers to fill the current PPE shortages. Notable companies, including Tesla Motors and Peugeot, stepped up by modifying their production processes to contribute to the production of ventilators and other essential goods, collaborating with PPE providers in a collective effort to address the ongoing shortages (Miller et al., 2020; Liza et al., 2023). This adaptive response highlights the importance of global collaboration and innovative solutions to overcome critical supply chain challenges during a crisis.

## Food Supply Chain

Global food supply chains (GSCs) grapple with profound challenges primarily rooted in cultivation and transportation, impacting a spectrum of food items encompassing seeds, staples like rice and wheat, as well as perishables such as meat, vegetables, and fruits. The intricacies of food production, spanning from seeding through picking to delivery, intensified amid the disruptions caused by the ongoing pandemic (Alabi et al., 2023). Notably, India, the world's foremost rice exporter, curtailed exports due to a confluence of labor shortages and logistical complications, while Vietnam, ranking third globally, contemplated a 40% reduction in quotas from the preceding year. Critical disruptions in fresh food distribution further compounded the challenges, marked by shortages of truck drivers, flight cancellations, protracted inspections, and quarantine measures within customs departments.

The implications were grave, raising the specter of a worldwide famine if swift resolutions remained elusive. The ramifications of COVID-19-induced interruptions to food supplies were projected to double the prevalence of chronic hunger globally. According to the Global Report on Food Crises, 135 million people grappled with food insecurity in 2019, a figure poised to triple to 265 million by 2020 (Hobbs et al., 2020). Urgent and concerted efforts are imperative to address these complexities, ensuring the stability of global food supply chains and avert a precipitous escalation of global hunger. The interconnected nature of the global food system underscores the need for collaborative strategies at local, regional, and international levels to mitigate the far-reaching impact of any pandemic on global food security.

# Disrupted International Logistics

The COVID-19 pandemic exacerbated disruptions in international logistics, hindering the global flow of products. Various facts that contributed for the same are discussed below.

## Shortages in the Labor Force

The logistics industry faced a profound labor shortage throughout the supply chain due to quarantine restrictions and infections, affecting both white- and blue-collar workers. The impact of COVID-19 on critical roles within the supply chain was exacerbated by quarantine measures, travel restrictions, and temporary plant shutdowns. Notably, Chinese specialists and technicians encountered difficulties reaching a camera manufacturing facility in India, disrupting operations. Similarly, South Korean technicians were denied access to the Samsung facility in Vietnam, further underscoring the challenges posed by the pandemic on global supply chain operations (Zhitao et al., 2020). The widespread disruptions to labor availability and logistical constraints emphasize the need for adaptive strategies and resilience in supply chain management to navigate uncertainties during such global crises.

# Shutdown of Commercial Aviation

The suspension of commercial flights during the pandemic had a profound impact on global logistics, significantly reducing the availability of air cargo and posing challenges in transporting essential supplies, particularly medical equipment, worldwide. Air cargo, constituting over 35% of the value of global trade, plays a crucial role, with an estimated annual delivery value of $6.25 trillion. However, the suspension of passenger flights, which typically carry 50 to 60 percent of all flying freight in their cargo holds, led to a drastic reduction in available air cargo capacity. The US Department of Transportation Security Administration reported a staggering 95% decrease in passenger flights compared to the previous year (Belhadi et al., 2021; Sudan et al., 2021). This disruption underscores the vulnerability of global supply chains to external shocks and emphasizes the need for innovative solutions and contingency plans to ensure the efficient transportation of essential goods, particularly during times of crisis.

# Sealed Borders and Trade Restrictions

Global logistics grapples with formidable challenges arising from border closures and stringent export-import regulations, significantly disrupting international trade (Curran et al., 2021). The intricacies of logistics are further compounded by delays in transactions and, in certain instances, the outright prohibition of products leaving one country or entering another due to imposed export restrictions. Nations including the US, France, Germany, India, and others imposed such restrictions on specific medications and medical equipment. Maritime freight, representing 90% of global commerce volume, faced delays due to a shortage of available truck drivers for container pickup and the imposition of rigorous customs inspections and quarantine procedures. The diminishing demand for container transportation services, attributed to the overall decline in global container trade, was exacerbated by blank sailings, removing more than

30% of the market's container capacity, with a staggering 45% rate of blank sailings announced for transpacific trade. These multifaceted disruptions underscore the critical need for agile and adaptable logistics strategies, emphasizing the importance of international collaboration to navigate the complexities of the current global trade landscape effectively.

## Distorted Demand in Pharmaceuticals and Medicines

- The COVID-19 pandemic caused substantial disruptions to the pharmaceutical and medical industries, especially as a result of skewed demand patterns.

- Fears of shortages and panic buying increased demand for drugs like chloroquine and hydroxychloroquine, which are frequently used to treat COVID-19.

- In order to meet the higher-than-normal demand, governments limited the amount of drugs they bought, which upset the system that supplies medications (Tavakol et al., 2023).

## Increased Demand for Personal Protective Equipment (PPE) and Ventilators

- There were serious shortages of PPE, including masks, gloves, and coveralls, worldwide as a result of the COVID-19 epidemic (Finkenstadt et al., 2021).

- Medical masks, gloves, and goggles were estimated to be significantly needed each month by the World Health Organization (WHO).

- There were reports of 4- to 6-month production backlogs for PPE orders, and demand for ventilators increased from 77,000 in 2019 to a projected 250,000 in 2020.

## Airline Industry Challenges

- Travel restrictions and border closures enforced by the government seriously affected demand for air travel (Raj et al., 2022).

- In 2020, the International Civil Aviation Organization projected a significant decline in the number of available airline seats, ranging from 57% to 64%.

- Global airlines, such as US carriers and Qatar Airways, experienced financial difficulties, requested government assistance and reduced their international travel schedules (Hasaney et al., 2023).

## Impact on the Textile and Apparel Industries

- The labor-intensive and globally integrated textile and garment sector struggled as a result of store closures, quarantine restrictions, and declining consumer spending (Paul et al., 2021).

- Forecasts suggested that the textile and apparel industry in the European Union might experience a 50% decline in sales by 2020 (Anner et al., 2022).

- 2020 was predicted to see a 27%–30% decline in revenues for the clothing and footwear industries, with many manufacturers not reaching their full potential.

## Retailing Activities and Consumer Behavior

- During the early phases of the COVID-19 outbreak in the US, panic buying—especially for non-perishables and toilet paper—caused a 53% spike in sales.

- Nonetheless, drops in consumer confidence led to lower sales of products including electronics, furniture, clothing, and home goods in China and the US (Sarkis et al., 2020).

## Analysis of Industry Disruptions and Mitigation Plans:

- Disruptions to the GSC caused by unseen lower-tier suppliers were common; Wuhan-based vendors were one example of this.

- Under time restrictions, mitigation plans were crucial, highlighting the significance of alertness and responsiveness to COVID-19 benchmarks on a global and local scale.

- With examples from Wuhan, the US, and Germany, the response time and relative response time were critical indicators for organizations to plan and minimize risks (Zhitao et al., 2020).

# Mitigation Strategies for Supply Chain Challenges

Understanding that preventative steps are necessary, this section carefully describes mitigation techniques intended to increase supply chain resilience. Every tactic, from embracing technology integration and digitalization to redefining supplier relationships and encouraging openness, is a cornerstone in the development of a strong, flexible supply chain.

# Digital Transformation and Technology Integration

It is obvious that supply networks must go beyond conventional paradigms at a time of unparalleled upheavals. The key cornerstone in the variety of mitigation techniques is the continual pursuit of digital transformation and the seamless integration of state-of-the-art technology (Attaran et al., 2020). As supply chain experts struggle to navigate the complexities of a post-COVID-19 world, utilizing technology turns becomes a vital survival skill as well as a competitive advantage.

- **The digital imperative**: More than just implementing new tools and systems, the digitalization of supply chain operations is a fundamental shift (Javaid et al., 2020). It represents a thorough change in the way businesses plan, carry out, and maximize their supply chain activities. Unmatched visibility, efficiency, and flexibility are possible with digital technologies—factors that are vital for strengthening supply networks against unanticipated interruptions.

- **Technology integration:** Moving beyond platforms and tools to establish a responsive and intelligent supply chain ecosystem involves more than just implementing stand-alone technical solutions. It also entails establishing a seamless integration of interconnected tools, platforms, and systems. From blockchains boosting transparency to the Internet of Things providing real-time tracking, each integration constitutes a key layer in establishing a robust supply chain architecture (Attaran et al., 2020).

- **Handling the data flood:** The clever use of data is the fundamental element of this revolution. Organizations are able to get meaningful insights from the massive amounts of data created across the supply chain thanks to the use of big data analytics and machine learning algorithms. In addition to increasing forecasting accuracy, data-driven decision-making allows for flexible reactions to changing circumstances (Ali et al., 2023).

- **Redefining supply chain dynamics:** Digital transformation goes beyond simple process improvement to radically alter the supply chain's basic dynamics. Businesses may move away from reactive models and toward proactive ones by using technology to plan ahead, maximize inventories, and improve overall agility.

# Adoption of Advanced Analytics and AI: Enhancing Predictive Capabilities

To improve the predictive capabilities and transform various sectors, the use of AI and advanced analytics has proven to be a great help. By harnessing vast amounts of data and leveraging these cutting-edge technologies, organizations can unlock insights, streamline and optimize the operations, and make more informed decisions, driving innovation, anticipate future trends and competitive advantage.

- **The rise of predictive analytics**: The application of AI and advanced analytics is a game-changer in the dynamic field of supply chain management, transforming traditional operational approaches. At its core, this is about using predictive analytics, whereby companies make use of complex algorithms and machine learning models to foresee future disruptions, variations in demand, and logistical challenges (Zamani et al., 2023).

- **Quick decision-making**: Using AI helps with real-time decision-making, which is important when dealing with changing market situations. Supply chain workers may make timely and well-informed choices with the help of these technologies, which offer insights derived from the study of historical data, current trends, and external variables. This helps to improve operational efficiency by reducing the effect of disruptions and allowing for proactive changes (Shah et al., 2023).

- **Demand forecasting precision**: AI's capacity to improve demand forecasting accuracy is a significant benefit for supply chain management. Especially in uncertain markets, traditional methodologies frequently fail to capture the nuances of customer behavior. AI-powered advanced analytics is excellent at spotting trends and abnormalities, which leads to more accurate demand forecasts. In turn, this helps businesses minimize the risk of stockouts, optimize inventory levels, and cut down on excess stock (Awan et al., 2021).

- **Adaptive routing and inventory management**: The optimization of logistics and inventory management is greatly aided by AI-driven solutions. Through real-time analysis of variables such as supplier performance, traffic patterns, and weather, these systems suggest the best routes for transportation and modify inventory levels. This flexibility guarantees a streamlined supply chain that can quickly address unanticipated obstacles (Modgil et al., 2022; Jibrin et al., 2022).

## Illustrative Example: Transformation in the Retail Industry

Inventory management in the retail industry has changed as a result of the use of AI-driven analytics. In order to predict demand, retailers may now examine consumer buying habits, seasonality, and outside variables like social media trends. This degree of information enables prompt inventory adjustments, lowering the possibility of overstocking or understocking and eventually raising profitability and customer satisfaction (Preindl et al., 2020).

## Future Prospects and Challenges

While adopting AI and advanced analytics has enormous potential, there are drawbacks as well, such as worries about data security, moral dilemmas, and the need for a trained labor force. In order to fully utilize AI in supply chain management, companies must overcome these obstacles as they proceed through this revolutionary path.

# IoT and Blockchain in Supply Chain Management: Revolutionizing Transparency and Traceability

Transparency and traceability in supply chain management are being revolutionized by the combination of blockchain and IoT technologies. These developments are changing the way companies track and verify the movement of goods across international supply chains by fusing secure decentralized ledgers with real-time data tracking.

- **The intersection of IoT and blockchain**: The convergence of blockchain and IoT technologies is a game-changer in the quest for a transparent and robust supply chain. The IoT offers real-time information on the flow, state, and status of items across the supply chain through its network of linked sensors and devices. In the meanwhile, recorded data is guaranteed to be transparent, unchangeable, and trustworthy thanks to blockchain, a decentralized and secure ledger. When combined, they bring forth a synergistic revolution that tackles enduring issues in supply chain management (Latif et al., 2021).

- **Unprecedented real-time visibility and condition monitoring**: IoT sensors integrated into goods, containers, and cars produce a constant data stream. This visibility goes beyond traditional checkpoints, allowing supply chain participants to follow the path of commodities across the network. The IoT improves entire supply chain visibility with anything from temperature and humidity sensors that guarantee the integrity of perishable items to GPS trackers that give exact position information (Chatterjee et al., 2021).

- **Automated procedures and smart contracts**: Smart contracts are self-executing contracts with predetermined rules that are made possible by blockchain technology (Grida et al., 2023). Smart contracts are used in supply chain management to automate procedures like compliance checks, quality assurance, and payment verification. Because of this automation, there is less need for middlemen and a lower chance of fraud and mistakes. For example, a smart contract may be set up to pay automatically when IoT sensors verify that the products have been delivered successfully.

- **Supply chain integrity**: One of blockchain's most important contributions to supply chain management is its ability to guarantee the chain's integrity. Every transaction is captured on an immutable blockchain, from the creation of the product to its ultimate delivery. The supply chain's integrity is less likely to be compromised by unauthorized changes, fake goods, or other fraudulent actions thanks to this tamper-proof record, which also increases stakeholder trust.

# Illustrative Example: Pharmaceutical Industry Evolution

IoT and blockchain together have transformed supply chain integrity in the pharmaceutical sector, where product authenticity is critical. Medication that is sensitive to temperature is tracked by IoT sensors while it is in transit, and the data is stored on a blockchain (Chen et al., 2023). As a result, medications are guaranteed to remain in the necessary conditions along the supply chain, giving all parties involved the unquestionable ability to track a drug's full path from manufacturing to distribution.

## Future Implications and Challenges

IoT and blockchain integration has potential, but there are drawbacks as well, such as interoperability problems, scalability issues, and the requirement for industry-wide standards. Reaching the full potential of these technologies in improving supply chain resilience and transparency requires overcoming these obstacles.

# Introduction to Supplier Diversification and Sourcing Strategies

Building robust and flexible systems within the intricate web of international supply chains requires a key strategy of supplier diversification and sourcing technique optimization (Argiyantari et al., 2020). Diversification becomes a proactive undertaking, purposefully dispersing risks and fortifying supply networks against unforeseen obstacles, going beyond just responding to disturbances. This section examines the critical roles that diversity and strong sourcing strategies play, examining how these actions provide the groundwork for a supply chain that can both weather shocks and position itself for long-term success in a changing business environment.

# Reducing Dependency on Single Suppliers

- **Breaking the cycle of dependency**: Diversification reduces reliance on a single supplier, which helps to mitigate the risks that come with concentrated sourcing. Businesses that rely solely on one supplier run the risk of being vulnerable to events such as interruptions in the supply chain, changes in geopolitics, and unanticipated changes in the market (Haishang et al., 2022). Organizations may spread risk by purposefully diversifying their supplier base, which helps to prevent the entire supply chain from being crippled by the collapse or interruption of a single supplier.

- **Increasing resilience with source redundancy**: Creating a supply chain with redundancy is necessary to lessen reliance on a single source. An example of this redundancy is different vendors for essential parts or supplies. Having several sources for critical inputs acts as a safety net against disruptions, allowing businesses to quickly adjust and continue operations (Tucker et al., 2022). Supplier redundancy not only guards against unanticipated events but also encourages healthy competition among suppliers, driving higher performance and reliability.

# Regionalization and Nearshoring

- **Taking a regional approach and moving past globalization**: In addition to economic benefits, the current trend of globalization has increased supply chain risks because of long delivery times, tense geopolitical situations, and challenging logistics (Clinton et al., 2021). Organizations are using nearshoring and regionalization as a reaction, reevaluating their sourcing methods. Regionalization is the process of obtaining supplies and components from vendors that are located closer together, which allows for faster response times and less vulnerability to interruptions caused by great distances.

- **The return of nearshoring**: Nearshoring is the practice of moving production or sourcing operations to nations that are geographically adjacent to one another, expanding on the idea of regionalization. This method lessens lead times, shipping expenses, and the difficulties involved in overseeing suppliers across great distances. In addition, nearshoring responds to the increasing focus on sustainability as businesses work to reduce the environmental effects of long-distance transportation.

# Robust Risk Management Frameworks: Safeguarding the Supply Chain Resilience

A company's ability to precisely and resiliently manage risks becomes critical to its success in the intricate dance of global supply chains, where opportunities and uncertainties coexist. Building and implementing strong risk management systems is more than just a reaction to events; it is a strategic requirement (El Baz et al., 2021). This section explores the critical role that comprehensive risk management plays in strengthening the supply chain's resilience and offers an organized method for identifying, evaluating, and mitigating risks in a constantly changing business environment.

## Identifying and Assessing Supply Chain Risks

- **Identifying hazards in the environment**: The systematic identification of possible hazards affecting the supply chain is the cornerstone of a robust risk management system (Emrouznejad et al., 2023). This calls for a careful analysis of a wide range of elements, such as market pressures, geopolitical dynamics, internal processes, and external impacts. In order to encourage stakeholders at all levels to actively participate in the identification process, organizations must foster a culture of alertness. This might entail doing regular risk assessments, creating scenarios, and using data analytics to find any weak points.

- **Thorough risk assessment**: After hazards are identified, evaluating their possible effect and probability is an essential next step. Every risk that has been discovered is taken into account in both quantitative and qualitative ways in a thorough risk assessment. Prioritizing risks according to their possible impact allows businesses to assign severity and likelihood metrics. Supply chain experts may plan for lower severity risks by creating backup plans and allocating resources to reduce high-impact, high-probability threats through this methodical examination.

- **Continuous observation and adjustment**: Supply chain hazards are dynamic, quickly changing in reaction to outside events. A strong foundation for risk management requires ongoing supply chain environment monitoring. Organizations may remain proactive against new threats by adjusting their risk mitigation methods in real-time thanks to this monitoring (Bechtsis et al., 2022). Utilizing technology, data analytics, and collaborative intelligence ensures that risk identification and assessment stay nimble, enabling rapid reactions to altering conditions.

## Implementing Resilience Strategies

- The process of moving from identification to action involves a shift from identifying and analyzing risks to actually executing real resilience solutions (Ahmed et al., 2021). This is when a robust risk management framework truly shines. Resilience methods are preemptive actions meant to lessen the effects of hazards that have been recognized and guarantee that the supply chain will continue to run. These tactics can include the design of redundant logistical channels, the development of alternate sourcing techniques, and the construction of adaptable manufacturing schedules.

- **Cooperation and supplier resilience**: The supply chain ecosystem as a whole benefits from resilience, which is not limited to internal initiatives. In order to increase group resilience, organizations and suppliers need to work closely together. This entails exchanging risk data, working together to create backup plans, and promoting a supportive community. Supply chain resilience as a whole depends critically on supplier resilience as any link in the network can be disrupted and have far-reaching consequences.

- **Technology integration for increased resilience**: Using technology effectively is essential for putting resilience methods into practice (Patel et al., 2023). The incorporation of cutting-edge technology, such blockchain, IoT, and artificial intelligence, improves responsiveness, visibility, and traceability. Automation expedites procedures and shortens the time needed to initiate backup plans, while real-time data analytics enable businesses to take well-informed choices quickly. The supply chain becomes a dynamic and flexible network when technology and resilience methods operate together.

# Agile and Flexible Supply Chain Structures: Navigating Dynamic Business Realities

The traditional supply chain model is changing as a result of rapid changes, unpredictability, and increased consumer demands in the corporate world (Enrique et al., 2022). Organizations hoping to thrive in unpredictable and dynamic environments must strategically need supply chain systems to be agile and flexible. This section explores the critical role that flexible and agile supply chain systems play, where resilience in the face of changing business realities is based on responsiveness and adaptation.

# Responsive Manufacturing and Distribution Processes

- **Dynamic production systems**: Agile supply chain architectures require a shift away from rigid manufacturing procedures and toward flexible, adaptable production systems. The capacity to quickly modify assembly line configurations, scale production quantities, and modify production schedules in response to real-time demand signals is known as responsive manufacturing. In order to foresee changes in the market and modify manufacturing procedures accordingly, this calls for the integration of cutting-edge technology like machine learning and predictive analytics.

- **Lean inventory management**: Being responsive in an agile supply chain requires effective lean inventory management (Patil et al., 2023). Companies strive to keep their inventory levels at ideal levels, eliminating surplus stock while guaranteeing that necessary items are always accessible. Demand-driven replenishment, just-in-time implementation, and real-time monitoring are all components of lean inventory procedures. Reducing carrying costs, improving cash flow, and strengthening the supply chain's flexibility to adapt to shifting consumer needs are the objectives.

# Flexibility in Supply Chain Networks

- **Multi-tiered supplier relationships:** Building multi-tiered supplier relationships that go beyond transactional exchanges is a key component of supply chain networks' flexibility. Agile supply chains place a high value on cooperation, openness, and communication with different levels of providers. This strategy makes it easier to share information, make decisions together, and respond swiftly to supply chain interruptions or changes in the market.

- **Modular and scalable network architecture:** Supply chain network architecture is a key factor in attaining flexibility. Scalable and adaptable network architectures that provide effortless growth or reduction in response to market fluctuations are embraced by agile structures. To maximize responsiveness and save lead times, this entails the strategic location of suppliers, production sites, and distribution centers. Organizations can easily adjust to changes in the business environment or in demand because to the network's flexibility.

- **Demand-driven procurement:** Demand-driven procurement techniques help supply chain networks become even more flexible. Organizations use real-time data to modify orders and inventory levels, closely coordinating their procurement procedures with actual demand. By reducing the possibility of overstocking or stockouts, this demand-driven strategy makes sure that the supply chain can adapt to changes in consumer demand.

# Practical Lessons Learned from the COVID-19 Experience: Navigating Disruptions and Building Resilience

The COVID-19 pandemic's worldwide disruption served as a testing ground for supply chain management techniques employed in a variety of businesses (Asha et al., 2023). This crisis crucible produced useful insights that go beyond the short-term problems and offer guidance for building resilient supply networks in the face of unpredictability. This part tells a story of flexibility, creativity, and foresight by examining the priceless lessons learned from the COVID-19 experience. These useful insights work as markers, steering businesses toward approaches that strengthen supply chains against future uncertainty while simultaneously navigating the current storms (Bryce et al., 2022).

## Case Studies and Real-World Examples: Extracting Wisdom from Experience

Understanding the intricacies of supply chain management involves more than just theoretical frameworks; it also requires insights derived from struggles and victories in the real world. We examine case studies and real-world examples taken from the COVID-19 pandemic's crucible in this section (Benis et al., 2021). These stories provide concrete insights by highlighting the achievements of businesses that are skilled at overcoming obstacles as well as the priceless lessons that can be learned from errors and setbacks.

### Companies Successfully Adapting to Challenges

Amidst the pandemic's disruptions, a few businesses stood out as examples of resilience. Case studies shed light on the tactics these companies use to quickly adjust to shifting conditions. These success stories, which range from inventive supply chain networks to flexible manufacturing methods, offer practical insights into the ideas and procedures that support robust supply chains. Organizations may extract the core of successful strategies that withstood extraordinary obstacles by scrutinizing these case studies.

Case studies explore the tactics used by businesses that were able to withstand the storm. These examples, which included changing production lines to accommodate new demand patterns, implementing cutting-edge technologies for improved visibility, and forming strategic alliances to strengthen supply chain resilience, provide a useful manual for businesses looking to protect their supply chains from unforeseen shocks (Fedushko et al., 2022).

# Mistakes and Failures As Learning Opportunities

Mistakes and failures leave behind priceless learning chances. The significance of accepting failure as a driving force for progress is shown by case studies that look at errors and shortcomings made throughout the epidemic (Eriksson et al., 2022). These instances highlight potential hazards to avoid, such as poor risk mitigation strategies, a dependence on a single source provider too much, or communication breakdowns. Organizations may become more resilient by learning from the mistakes of others by drawing valuable lessons from their failures.

Supply chain management is an iterative process, as demonstrated by real-world instances of errors and failures. One of the characteristics of resilient businesses is their capacity to quickly alter direction in the event of a setback. This category's case studies provide insight into how businesses adjusted their tactics, improved workflows, and put remedial measures in place. Organizations may cultivate a culture of perpetual learning and adaptability by seeing setbacks as essential to the process of progress.

The main objective is to extract knowledge that can influence future resilience as we examine case studies and real-world situations (Sakurai et al., 2020). These useful lessons, whether gained from mistakes or from success stories, serve as the cornerstone upon which businesses may construct flexible, robust, and agile supply chain systems. In the next chapters, we dissect the accounts of businesses that successfully traversed the pandemic terrain, distilling the guiding principles that might steer the path toward supply chain resilience in an uncertain commercial milieu.

# Importance of Collaboration and Communication: Foundation for Resilient Supply Chains

In the complex web of international supply chains, cooperation and communication show up as essential components for flexibility and resilience. The changing character of contemporary corporate environments is shown by the COVID-19 pandemic's difficulties, which highlight the critical importance that effective cooperation and communication play (Frederico et al., 2021). The importance of developing solid alliances, open lines of communication, and cooperative ecosystems within the supply chain is explored in this section. We investigate how these components serve as the cornerstone for robust supply chains that are prepared for the future by looking at actual cases and taking lessons from past experiences.

## Strengthening Collaboration Across the Supply Chain

- **Strategic alliances as activators:** Successful cooperation goes beyond transactional connections to form strategic alliances that strengthen resilience. This subpoint looks at how businesses may build alliances with distributors, manufacturers, and suppliers to build a highly integrated supply chain network. Collaborative activities, via the development of a common vision, goal alignment, and resource pooling, become an effective means of managing disruptions, sharing risks, and leveraging group strengths.

- **Planning and decision-making together**: Enhancing cooperation calls for integrated planning and decision-making procedures in addition to high-level interactions. This subpoint looks at how businesses should coordinate planning efforts across the supply chain to make sure all parties involved are on the same page about the overall goals. The supply chain's agility is increased through integrated decision-making, which is made possible by shared data and real-time insights. This allows for quick adjustments in reaction to changing conditions.

- **Cross-functional cooperation**: Cross-functional cooperation occurs within an organization in addition to external relationships. This entails dismantling organizational silos and encouraging collaboration and communication across several divisions, including manufacturing, logistics, and procurement. When internal teams collaborate well to achieve shared objectives, the supply chain as a whole responds to obstacles and becomes more flexible.

# Transparent Communication with Stakeholders

- **Developing transparency**: In the supply chain ecosystem, open and honest communication is the cornerstone of trust. This subpoint highlights the significance of freely exchanging information with all relevant parties, such as internal teams, suppliers, and customers. Organizations may build trust, lessen uncertainty, and create a more conducive atmosphere for efficient collaboration amongst all stakeholders during regular business operations and unexpected disruptions by fostering openness.

- **Real-time information sharing**: Transparent communication is important in the context of resilient supply chains, and this includes real-time information sharing. This subpoint examines the ways in which businesses might use digital platforms and technology to promote smooth information flow. Real-time data sharing improves the supply chain's overall responsiveness and flexibility by empowering stakeholders to take well-informed decisions quickly.

- **Crisis communication techniques**: In times of crisis, open communication is especially important. This subpoint explores crisis communication tactics and highlights the significance of timely, clear, and consistent message. During interruptions, good communication reduces uncertainty, builds trust, and enables stakeholders to work together to quickly and effectively address unanticipated issues.

# Building Adaptive and Resilient Supply Chains: A Strategic Imperative

In the fast-paced world of global business, the ability to withstand uncertainties, disruptions, and shifting client expectations is not only a wish but also a strategic necessity (Moktadir et al., 2023). This section goes into detail on the basic concepts and techniques for building robust, adaptable supply chains. Drawing on insights from the COVID-19 pandemic and beyond, we explore how companies might transform their supply chains into flexible, dynamic ecosystems that can withstand the constantly shifting dynamics of the modern business landscape. The creation of supply networks that can actively adapt to shifting conditions and thrive even in the face of disruptions is the aim of this research work.

## Developing a Culture of Continuous Improvement

- **Cultivating a proactive mindset**: Creating a culture of continuous improvement is the first step in building resilient and flexible supply chains. This subpoint emphasizes how important it is to establish a proactive mindset inside the organization. It means promoting a common commitment to continuously assess, enhance, and develop strategies, tools, and procedures. A culture of continuous improvement ensures that the supply chain is adaptable, always altering to meet new demands and take advantage of changing market conditions.

- **Agile process optimization**: Optimal processes are an example of ongoing development and enhancement. Organizations must adopt strategies that allow for quick iterations and adjustments in response to input received in real time and changing circumstances. This subpoint looks at how companies can reduce inefficiencies, streamline procedures, and proactively address potential disruptions before they worsen by implementing agile methodologies like Six Sigma or lean.

- **Innovation as a driver**: In the quest for continuous improvement, innovation plays a significant role. This subpoint highlights the ways in which innovation fosters adaptability and resilience. Organizations should embrace a culture that values and encourages innovation. Whether through technological advancements, inventive business plans, or imaginative problem-solving, innovation becomes a catalyst for staying ahead of the curve and successfully responding to shifting market conditions.

# Learning from Adversity for Future Preparedness

- **Post-crisis reflection and analysis**: Resilience is more than just getting over losses; it also includes learning from hardship to improve future preparation. This subpoint highlights the importance of doing post-crisis reflection and analysis. Companies need to assess how successfully their responses to disruptions worked, identify any weak points, and assess the effects of the disruptions. By drawing lessons from the past, organizations can gather useful insights to strengthen their supply networks against similar challenges in the future.

- **Risk reduction**: To learn from adversity, risk reduction and scenario planning are crucial. The key is prevention. This subpoint examines how companies can analyze different scenarios, foresee potential disruptions in advance, and develop risk-reduction strategies. By predicting, preparing for, and overcoming future unpredictability, organizations can enhance their supply chains by using the lessons learnt from previous setbacks..

- **Adaptive capacity building**: Learning from adversity is a necessary step in developing adaptive capacity. It is recommended that businesses invest in gaining the competencies, know-how, and skills necessary to respond swiftly to changing circumstances. This could mean offering cross-training to employees, promoting a flexible work schedule, and leveraging technology to increase flexibility. With adaptive capacity, the supply chain is ensured to be resilient in the face of unforeseen challenges.

# Conclusion

Since the COVID-19 pandemic, the global supply chain landscape has changed significantly, bringing with it previously unheard-of challenges that have tested the adaptability and resilience of businesses. To effectively overcome these challenges, organizations need to create workable mitigation plans and learn from their mistakes. The rising volatility of the global supply chain is one of the primary challenges, calling for a reevaluation of traditional models with an emphasis on better risk management strategies. Demand fluctuations are a result of quick changes in customer behavior, which highlights the necessity for businesses to use artificial intelligence and data analytics to manage their supply chains nimbly and adaptably.

The utilization of technologies such as blockchain and the Internet of Things, together with digitization, has become increasingly significant in enhancing communication and visibility across the supply chain. Mitigation strategies address geopolitical concerns and go beyond the present problems, emphasizing the value of diversifying suppliers and manufacturing locations. Cooperation is essential since alliances encourage resource sharing and support from one another in case of disruptions. Practical lessons emphasize the need for robust scenario planning and contingency planning, transparency enabled by real-time information, and agility and adaptation in supply chain systems. In summary, a comprehensive mitigation approach that integrates advanced technologies, diverse sourcing, and collaborative projects can enhance the resilience of the supply chain. The practical experience acquired provides the foundation for creating adaptable, transparent, and durable supply chain solutions—all of which are necessary for handling unforeseen obstacles in the evolving post-COVID-19 landscape.

# CHAPTER 11

# Autonomous Vehicles and Delivery Robots in SCM

*D. Preethi, Associate Professor, Vel Tech Rangarajan Dr. Sagunthala R&D Institute of Science and Technology, Chennai, India.*

*R. S. Valarmathi, Dean SoEC, Vel Tech Rangarajan Dr. Sagunthala R&D Institute of Science and Technology, Chennai, India.*

*G. Sasikala, Professor, Department of ECE, Vel Tech Rangarajan Dr. Sagunthala R&D Institute of Science and Technology, Chennai, India.*

This chapter revolves around the changes or transformations happening in SCM over the past few years. In the 1990s and early stages of the 2000s, supply chains and logistical operations underwent significant and quick changes. The goods-shipping business faced serious hurdles as a result of these changes. Two major issues faced by the sector were just-in-time processes and the need for client responsiveness. This fast trend of economies and markets becoming more globalized has an impact on the distribution and purchase of commodities. New information technologies, such as decision support systems (DSS), electronic data interchange (EDI) and the Internet, and GPS via satellites, arose in response to these difficulties facing the logistics sector. Freight forwarders responsiveness capacity and their ability to make decisions in real time significantly grew as they implemented this fresh technology. SCM can be performed manually or in an automated manner, and the choice between the two depends on various factors, including the size of the operation, the complexity of the supply chain, cost considerations, and the specific goals of the business.

# Inbound and Outbound Logistics in SCM

The movement of raw materials from suppliers to producers is referred to as inbound logistics. Receiving, storing, and distributing goods that are entering a business from within illustrates inbound logistics activities. Freight management, materials handling, warehouse consolidation, and backhaul management are among the decisions made in inbound logistics management. The physical distribution of completed items, including the gathering, storing, and delivery of goods from producers to consumers, is covered by outbound logistics. Outbound logistics tasks include order processing, scheduling and routing of vehicles, materials handling, network planning and administration, and finished goods warehousing [1]. Product attributes are the primary distinction between inbound and outbound logistics. Outbound logistics handles resources that are finished goods, whereas incoming logistics handles raw materials or incomplete things.

Due to rigorous client expectations including on-time delivery and greater production values than incoming logistics, outbound logistics involves more complex operations. The branch of company management known as "physical distribution" is in charge of creating movement systems and moving completed goods and raw materials. "Physical distribution" is a more comprehensive term that encompasses both incoming and outbound movements, even though it is typically connected to outgoing product movements from a company. The logistics activities that are inbound and outgoing are displayed in Figure 11-1.

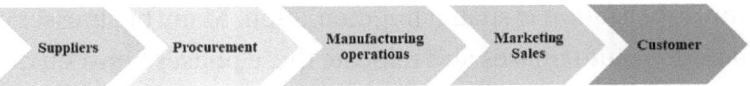

*Figure 11-1.* *Process depicting inbound and outbound logistics activities in SCM*

The convergence of technologies such as machine learning, deep learning, and robotics is required at each and every instance of inbound as well as outbound activities with data integrity and security of prime importance.

# Trade Services and Their Impact on Supply Chains

Supply chains nowadays span international borders, making supply chain management an international phenomenon rather than a domestic one. Businesses that benefit from globally dispersed supply chains for their new or existing product lines face additional hurdles as a result of the expansion of supply chains. In the process of developing supply chains, globalization presents both tremendous potential and high hazards. Some supply chains benefit from these opportunities, but others suffer harm from the hazards brought about by globalization. Accordingly, while creating a global supply chain network, opportunities and risks should both be considered. In addition to providing businesses with the chance to promote in new areas and attract potential clients, globalization allows them to expand their operations to less expensive nations, which can result in significant cost savings [2].

These chances, meanwhile, are typically accompanied by possible hazards that could sabotage a supply chain's flow. Natural disasters, a lack of trained personnel, unpredictability in geopolitics, terrorists infiltrating cargo, fluctuations in fuel prices, and fluctuations in currency values are a few of these risk factors. It is believed that one of the primary drivers of globalization is spatial fragmentation. Many businesses divide their operations into phases and relocate these phases between different areas. A company's supply chain is made up of a number of commercial operations that are coordinated and carried out in various states or nations. Businesses use the spatial fragmentation as one of the primary drivers of economic globalization in order to capitalize on variations in technology, wages, and other costs. A comparison of manual vs. automated SCM is shown in Table 11-1 to analyze the merits of automation in logistics and services in SCM.

***Table 11-1.*** *Comparison of Manual vs. Automated Supply Chain Management*

| Features | Manual SCM | Automated SCM |
| --- | --- | --- |
| ***Decision making*** | It relies on human intervention for decision-making, planning, and execution of tasks. | Automation enables real-time decision-making based on data analytics and algorithms. |
| ***Labor intensive*** | It needs a significant amount of human labor, including data entry, communication, processing of order, and physical handling of goods. | It can lead to cost savings by optimizing resource utilization and minimizing inventory-holding costs. |
| ***Scalability*** | As the supply chain grows, expanding operations may necessitate additional labor and resources. | Additional workloads can be managed without a direct linear increase in labor. |

*(continued)*

***Table 11-1.*** (*continued*)

| Features | Manual SCM | Automated SCM |
|---|---|---|
| *Risk of errors* | It's prone to errors, such as data entry, miscommunication, and inaccuracies in inventory management. | It uses automated data entry, integration with sensors, and real-time tracking to improve data accuracy. |
| *Efficiency* | It leads to higher operational costs and potentially slower delivery times. | It utilizes software and technology, leading to greater efficiency. |
| *Response time* | Quick response to real-time changes in the supply chain can be challenging with manual processes. | Automation provides better visibility into the entire supply chain, from procurement to delivery, allowing for better planning and optimization. |
| *Integration* | The entire process including document maintenance is manual and does not have a standard ERP. | It integrates with ERP software to provide a cohesive view of business operations. |

It's important to note that many organizations today employ a combination of manual and automated supply chain management (Table 11-2). For instance, they may use automation for routine, repetitive tasks while relying on human expertise for complex decision-making. The choice between manual and automated supply chain management should be based on the specific needs and goals of the organization, balancing the advantages of automation with the costs and investments required.

A 2020 global assessment by McKinsey & Co. of corporate executives across multiple industries found that 66% were investigating solutions to automate at least one business function; this is an increase from 57% two years earlier, as Table 11-2 illustrates. It is worth noting that the percentage of organizations that have completely automated one or more functions has grown more slowly, from 21% in 2018 to 31% in 2020 [3]. Employers who have successfully finished BPA initiatives, according to McKinsey, tend to overcommunicate and involve their staff in training automated systems: "When implementing automation efforts, respondents from companies that have had success are seven times more likely than others to say they formally involve the communications function, and they are more than twice as likely to say the HR function is involved."

***Table 11-2.*** *Statistics Depicting the Adaption of Business Units Undergoing Transformation from Manual to Automated Supply Chain Management over the Years*

| Response of business units to new technology | 2018 | | 2020 | |
|---|---|---|---|---|
| Have established an automation program and are expanding automation technology throughout many company divisions | 16 | **57** | 15 | **66** |
| Have at least one business unit's process completely automated but haven't expanded automation technologies to other business units | 13 | | 16 | |
| Laying out a plan for automating business procedures in at least one business division | 28 | | 35 | |
| Are still in the planning stages and have not started automating company processes | 18 | **38** | 14 | **30** |
| Have no plans to automate company processes and haven't started yet | 20 | | 16 | |

The shift from manual to automated supply chain management can be attributed to the significant obstacles encountered during the pandemic, when transportation of products was a laborious task. Due to the rising demand for contactless delivery services, the COVID-19 pandemic hastened the deployment of autonomous delivery robots. Many businesses and organizations began using these robots to maintain social distancing, though these experiments and prototypes had begun to emerge in the early 2000s. These early robots were often large and not very practical for real-world use but laid the groundwork for future developments. In the mid-2000s, smaller, more practical ground-based delivery robots began to appear with basic sensors and cameras to navigate and avoid obstacles, and they were tested on university campuses and in controlled environments.

Continuous advancements in AI, machine learning, and computer vision have enabled delivery robots to navigate complex urban environments with more precision. Improved obstacle avoidance, human interaction capabilities, and real-time decision-making became key features. Beyond retail and food delivery, autonomous robots have found applications in healthcare, logistics, and more. These robots have been used for medication delivery in hospitals, parcel delivery in warehouses, and more. As environmental concerns became more prominent, autonomous delivery robot manufacturers focused on creating eco-friendly designs and efficient delivery routes.

# Adopting SCM in Product Delivery

The issue of effective product delivery to the customer is brought up by the e-commerce market's continued growth in volume. Three parties are involved in the last-mile delivery: the client, the intermediary, and the supplier. The persistence in tackling the last-mile issue in traditional B2C and e-commerce settings were addressed, stating that unattended product receipt may lead to a 60% cost savings for home delivery [4]. The unattended delivery approach is based on the concepts of the delivery box and the reception box. The receiving box is located in the customer's garage or garden, whereas the delivery box is a shielded, insulated box with a docking mechanism.

Following the initial excitement surrounding drone deliveries, land-based delivery robots have become the main emphasis for last-mile delivery in recent times. The underlying business strategy emphasizes the last-mile delivery's cost advantage, which is projected to be less than 1€ per unit/delivery and can be up to 15 times less expensive than existing expenses depending on the location's salary level. Autonomous delivery robots are more competitive than traditional delivery methods in certain regions.

The major players in last-mile delivery today include both well-known delivery firms such as DHL and UPS as well as a number of recent startups that are concentrating on the global development of delivery robots. Right now, perishable items like food and flowers are the most significant markets for delivery robots; however, automated warehouses may also find use in the retail and warehousing industries. Upon detailed examination of the primary startup funding landscape, it can be observed that around 50% of total investment amounts are allocated towards enterprise robots [5].

Articles about Industry 4.0 are related to online connected machine-to-machine communication and interaction, as well as the ability to work in a networked production and logistics environment and integrate into intercompany processes. According to research, machine-to-machine (M2M) technologies are currently only partially implemented. Consider the RoboVan system, in which the delivery robots function as feeders and the van acts as a center for communication. On the other hand, an M2M delivery robot that can navigate on its own and connect with the entire supply chain might accomplish the final mile of delivery on its own without requiring human labor. This type of system is modelled after the experimental project AMATRAK at ISL Bremen. It established a self-directed system for container relocation, enabling users to choose and reserve the best means of transportation in accordance with their own requirements. Autonomous delivery robots offer a competitive advantage over other delivery modalities since they can be up to 15 times less expensive than traditional delivery services [6]. Less than 1€ is spent on delivery expenses of each unit. Due to their small delivery radius and need to share the pavement with other vehicles and pedestrians, land-based delivery robots prefer to operate in suburban regions and low-density traffic locations. As such, they are primarily used as a supplement to existing delivery services.

The extent to which society would actually be willing to allow an overuse of delivery robots is another significant issue that has not received much attention in robot-friendly groups. In many locations, the coexistence of delivery robots and walkers on sidewalks has already resulted in significant acceptability issues. These issues are reflected in varying legal framework conditions, contingent upon the area. Some of them have the potential to gravely jeopardize the delivery robots' economic model. While some countries are still hesitant, Estonia, for instance, has already changed its traffic laws to permit people and robots to share space (see the June 14, 2017 reform act on the Estonian traffic legislation, which modifies Section 2 of the same act).

In certain cities where there is a greater "population" of delivery robots, public attitude is beginning to change. For example, in early December 2017, the municipal government in San Francisco approved severe restrictions limiting authorization to "three per company, and nine total at any given time for the entire city" [7]. The few examples that are still free roaming some towns' sidewalks are revered and eagerly observed in these locales. The robots require constant human supervision and will only be permitted to operate on six-foot-wide pavements in specific industrial zones.

The manufacturing and industrial sectors will remain the biggest users of robots and associated services, according to a study by International Data Corporation. Global robotics spending, which hit $100 billion in 2017 and is expected to more than double until 2021, is also anticipated. However, the robot industry has now realized that, with a compound annual growth rate of almost 60%, deliveries to the consumer sector are expected to constitute the fourth highest increase until 2021. A closer look at the land-based delivery robot market reveals that startups like Marble, Tele retail, Dispatch, or Starship Technologies were successful in securing finance in the region of several million Euros [8].

The debate over the legal framework governing delivery robots is still ongoing. While there are opportunities to advance the development of a legislative framework for Industry 4.0, there are also opportunities to keep up with the conversations around autonomous mobility. When creating a framework for laws governing autonomous driving, Scheurs and Stewer looked at the social, legal, political, and sustainable facets of mobility. Their investigations placed a strong emphasis on innovation, safety, harmonization, coordination, and competitiveness. Their research is based on empirical data from development projects in several countries as well as the United Nations convention on road traffic.

Delivery robots, which are a part of last-mile business-to-consumer distribution, are currently receiving a lot of attention and are a developing industry that is being driven by both established logistics service providers and several international start-ups. The gadgets currently in use are still in the testing stage [9], and the cases studied indicate that the food, flower, and grocery industries are the primary areas of operation, with people handling the charging and unloading of the robots. Given that they are internet-connected, self-organizing, and 90% autonomous, the delivery robots in the Starship Technologies example can be classified as cyber-physical systems (CPS). However, complete self-organization is still a work in progress.

The challenges in logistics, which can vary depending on the industry, region, and specific circumstances and also pertaining to the delivery of services and security are demand variability, inventory management, transportation costs and efficiency, technology adoption, and, most importantly, data security. To overcome these challenges, organizations need to be agile, adaptable, and willing to invest in technology and talent. They should also focus on risk mitigation, sustainable practices, and constantly improving their supply chain processes. Hence the industries are transforming to adapt new technologies [10]. Through the description of growing automation and intelligent machinery/factories, the Industry 4.0 revolution is also supporting business units. Productivity is increased throughout the value chain and commodities are produced more effectively thanks to the informed data.

The adoption of autonomous robots and delivery vehicles is a key enabler of Industry 4.0, offering the potential to create more efficient, flexible, and responsive manufacturing and supply chain processes.

# Industry 4.0 and Its Impact on SCM

The concept of Industry 4.0 represents the fourth industrial revolution, following the previous three industrial revolutions, each marked by significant advancements in technology, manufacturing, and industry. The stage-by-stage development of industry from 1.0 to 4.0 is shown in Figure 11-2.

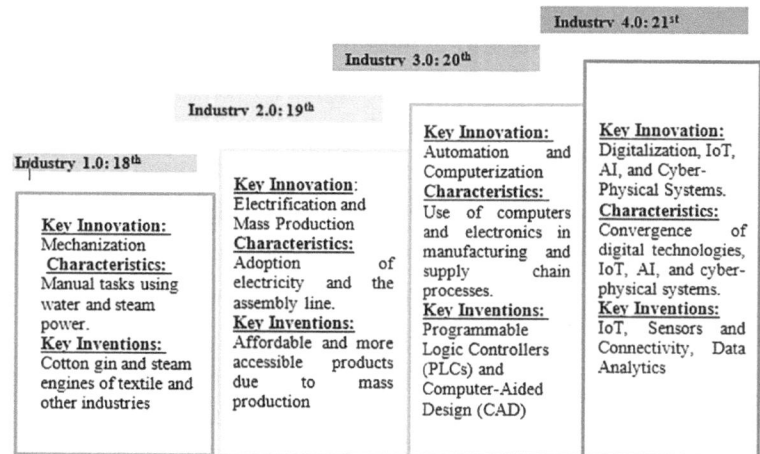

**Figure 11-2.** *Step-by-step evolution from Industry 1.0 to Industry 4.0*

# Investigations on System Integration

Autonomous systems such as vehicles and delivery robots fall under the category of system integration. Autonomous vehicles and delivery robots are playing increasingly important role as one of the pillars in supply chain management. They offer several benefits, including efficiency improvements, cost savings, and enhanced safety. Autonomous vehicles and delivery robots are impacting supply chain management for last-mile delivery. They can navigate through crowded urban environments and deliver packages to customers' doorsteps. This reduces delivery times and costs, making it more efficient for businesses. They can operate without human drivers or delivery personnel, reducing labor costs associated with transportation and logistics. They are destined to operate around the clock, improving supply chain efficiency and meeting consumer demands for faster delivery times, especially in e-commerce [12].

AI algorithms and real-time data analysis allow autonomous vehicles and robots to optimize their routes, taking into account traffic, weather, and road conditions. This minimizes delays and ensures timely deliveries, thereby ensuring optimization. These bots can be used within warehouses and fulfilment centers to manage inventory. They can pick and transport items, improving order accuracy and speed. The integration of advanced sensors in AI systems enhances the safety during transportation by reducing the risk of accidents caused due to human error. Autonomous electric vehicles can be more environmentally friendly than traditional delivery trucks with internal combustion engines, contributing to sustainability efforts in supply chain management.

# Autonomous Delivery Vehicles and Robots: A Paradigm Rise

The use of automated systems and robots in manufacturing and warehousing can improve efficiency and reduce the risk of human error. Automated guided vehicles (AGVs), robotic process automation (RPA), and autonomous drones are examples of technologies used to streamline SCM. Autonomous robots and delivery vehicles are integral components of Industry 4.0, playing a significant role in transforming various aspects of manufacturing and supply chain operations.

## Autonomous Delivery Vehicles

DHL has been investing in electric delivery vehicles that are suitable for autonomous operations. These electric vehicles are designed to be more environmentally friendly and can be adapted for autonomous technologies. They have tested and deployed autonomous last-mile delivery robots in select locations. These robots are designed to navigate urban environments and deliver parcels to customers' doorsteps. They are equipped with sensors and cameras for safe and efficient navigation.

DHL has explored the use of drones for autonomous delivery of small packages and medical supplies to remote or hard-to-reach areas. These drones have the potential to significantly improve delivery speed and accessibility.

317

A robotics business called Starship Technologies specializes in creating autonomous delivery robots for local and last-mile delivery of products and packages. These robots are made to deliver goods to customers by navigating neighborhood streets and sidewalks. The Starship Robot is an autonomous delivery robot that can navigate streets and pavements. Starship Technologies created it with the intention of delivering shipments and food to both businesses and customers. In 2015, it made its American premiere. Items up to four miles (6 km) in radius can be carried by the Starship Robot [13]. The recipient must use their smartphone to unlock the cargo bay while it is being delivered. Starship Robots are equipped with a range of sensors, cameras, and other technology that enables them to autonomously navigate urban environments. They can travel at a pedestrian pace and are designed to operate on sidewalks and local roads [4]. The comparison of various autonomous delivery vehicles is listed in Table 11-3.

***Table 11-3.*** *Comparison of Autonomous Delivery Vehicles*

| Feature | Autonomous Delivery Vehicles | | | | |
|---|---|---|---|---|---|
| | Amazon Scout | KiwiBot | Starship Robot | FedEx Roxo | Nuro R2 |
| *Height* | 29" \| 73.7 cm | 22" \| 55.9 cm | 21.8" \| 55.4 cm | 58" \| 147.3 cm | 73" \| 186 cm |
| *Width* | 24" \| 61 cm | 17" \| 43.2 cm | 22.4" \| 56.9 cm | 28" \| 71.1 cm | 43" \| 110 cm |
| *Length* | 30" \| 76.2 cm | 22" \| 55.9 cm | 26.7" \| 67.8 cm | 36" \| 91.4 cm | 108" \| 274 cm |
| *Weight* | 100 lb \| 45 kg | 40lb\| 14 kg | 50 lb \| 23 kg | 200 lb \| 91 kg | 2535 lb \| 1150 kg |

(*continued*)

***Table 11-3.*** (*continued*)

| Feature | Autonomous Delivery Vehicles | | | | |
|---|---|---|---|---|---|
| | Amazon Scout | KiwiBot | Starship Robot | FedEx Roxo | Nuro R2 |
| *Max. Payload* | 50 lb \| 23 kg | 15 lb \| 7 kg | 22 lb \| 10 kg | 100 lb \| 45 kg | 419 lb \| 190 kg |
| *Max. Speed* | 15 mph \| 24 km/h | 1.5 mph \| 2.4 km/h | 3.7 mph \| 6 km/h | 10 mph \| 16 km/h | 25 mph \| 40 km/h |
| *Designer* | Amazon | KiwiBot | Starship Technologies | FedEx | Nuro |
| *Use* | Last-mile package delivery | Food and small-item delivery | Delivery of grocery and packages | Local and same-day deliveries | Local and last-mile deliveries |
| *Layout* | | | | | |

The flowchart in Figure 11-3 shows that the robot's program begins with the Bluetooth module, GPS, and compass sensors initialized. This sensor initialization serves to adjust the speed at which data is transmitted to the Arduino microcontroller. The robot operates on the following stages [14]:

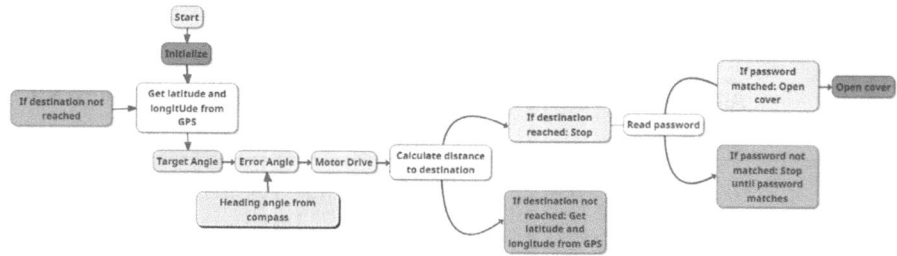

***Figure 11-3.*** *Flowchart of working mechanism in autonomous delivery vehicles*

**Step 1:** The GPS module measures latitude and longitude in addition to looking for satellites. The GPS module must lock onto at least four satellites in order to calculate the latitude and longitude with any degree of accuracy.

**Step 2:** Next, using the latitude and longitude information, the robot determines the goal angle. Radians are the unit of measurement for angles.

The algorithm to find the target angle is

```
Comparison of location_longitude = radians(destination
                           location - source location);
Location_latitudeA = radians(source latitude);
Location_latitudeB = radians(destination latitude);
x = sin(Comparison of location_longitude) ×
                           cos(Location_latitudeB);
y = cos(Location_latitudeA) × sin(Location_latitudeB) -

sin(Location_latitudeA) × cos(Location_latitudeB) ×
           cos(Comparison of location_longitude);

destination_angle = atan2(x, y) × (180/3.14159);
if (destination_angle < 0) target angle += 360;
```

*Step 3:* The compass module determines the angular difference between the goal and the current heading and then generates an error angle.

*Step 4:* The error angle helps us in deciding whether the robot has to turn left or right. The robot's motors are aligned with the desired angle through L298N motor driver.

*Step 5:* The latitudes of the current location and the intended destination are used to determine the distance to the target.

*Step 6:* The robot calculates if it has travelled the required distance to arrive at its destination. If it doesn't, the robot keeps calculating the target angle, current heading angle, and destination distance until it gets there.

*Step 7:* An authenticated password has to be entered when the robot reaches its destination. Until then the recipient cannot take the delivered goods.

*Step 8:* To start or restart the input password, press the "*" key. Enter # to end the password entry. The key is added to the password string that the customer enters if neither of these two keys is typed.

*Step 9:* When the # key is pressed, the comparison between the recipient input password string with the input password is verified to conclude whether the entered password is correct or incorrect. Once the decision is taken, then the recipient password will be cleared for privacy and security reasons. To alert that the entered password of the recipient is incorrect, the buzzer beeps three times.

*Step 10:* The container lid opens and the servo motor receives a pulse width modulated signal if the password matches.

*Step 11:* The robot goes back to its starting point and the container lid closes after a ten-second pause.

Autonomous delivery vehicles have the potential to transform the logistics and transportation industry by making deliveries more efficient, reducing the need for human drivers, and potentially improving environmental sustainability through more efficient route planning and energy use. However, the widespread adoption of these technologies may still be several years away, as they face technical and regulatory challenges that need to be overcome.

## Autonomous Robots in Industry Applications

Autonomous robots in industrial applications are becoming increasingly common and play a significant role in various industries, including manufacturing, logistics, and agriculture. These robots are designed to operate without human intervention, performing tasks that range from material handling to quality control. They are frequently used in manufacturing environments to perform tasks like assembly, welding, painting, and quality control. These robots are equipped with sensors, vision systems, and precision control mechanisms to ensure they can carry out tasks with high accuracy and consistency. In warehouses and distribution centers, autonomous robots are used for material handling, such as moving goods, picking and packing, and transporting items to and from storage locations. These robots can optimize storage space, reduce manual labor, and improve the efficiency of order fulfillment.

Autonomous robots equipped with vision systems and sensors are employed to inspect and assess the quality of products in real time. They can identify defects, measure dimensions, and ensure products meet the required quality standards. In the agricultural sector, autonomous robots are used for tasks like planting, harvesting, and monitoring crops. Agricultural robots can enhance productivity, reduce labor costs, and help optimize resource usage [15].

In mining operations, they are used to perform tasks such as excavation, drilling, and ore transportation. They can operate in challenging and hazardous environments, improving safety and productivity. In addition to material handling, autonomous robots are used for sorting and transporting items within logistics and warehousing facilities. They are essential in e-commerce fulfillment centers for efficiently processing and shipping customer orders. They are used for tasks such as inspecting pipelines, monitoring equipment, and performing maintenance in remote or hazardous locations. Equipped with cameras and sensors, they are used for patrolling and monitoring large areas such as industrial facilities and outdoor spaces.

In Figure 11-4, the direction and azimuth angles are used to compute the angle difference in the autonomous navigation method.

***Figure 11-4.*** *Flowchart of working mechanisms in autonomous robots in industries*

The robot can be guided in the desired direction in this fashion. The distance between the target site and the robot location is then computed. The robot reaches its destination when the heading angle equals the azimuth angle and the distance equals zero. The quadrant in which the current point was found is identified in quadrant control using the compass dial. The target point's quadrant might be identified with the aid of the computed azimuth angle.

Amazon has been a pioneer in using autonomous robots for supply chain management in its warehouses and fulfillment centers. These robots play a crucial role in optimizing operations, reducing costs, and increasing efficiency in the e-commerce giant's vast logistics network. Amazon acquired Kiva Systems in 2012 and rebranded it as Amazon Robotics. These robots are used extensively in Amazon's warehouses for various tasks such as picking, packing, and sorting. They autonomously move shelves of products to human workers, eliminating the need for workers to navigate through the warehouse to find items. This significantly accelerates the order fulfillment process.

Amazon's newer generation of autonomous robots, known as Pegasus and Xanthus, have been developed to further enhance its operations. These robots are designed to work together to transport large and heavy inventory items in a coordinated manner, improving efficiency in sorting and inventory management.

Amazon uses a variety of autonomous mobile robots for tasks like inventory replenishment and material transport within its facilities. These robots can navigate through complex and dynamic warehouse environments while avoiding obstacles and other robots. These robots can unload trucks, sort products, and deliver them to the appropriate storage locations.

They are used for managing and organizing inventory within Amazon's vast fulfillment centers. They can efficiently locate, retrieve, and restock products as needed. Automated sorting systems, combined with autonomous robots, are used to quickly sort packages and route them to the appropriate delivery stations. Robotic workstations that assist human workers with tasks like packaging and labeling increase the efficiency of order processing. They improve order fulfillment, reduce labor costs, minimize errors, and handle a large volume of orders efficiently, especially during peak shopping seasons. The company continues to invest in research and development to further advance and expand its use of robotics in supply chain management, allowing for faster and more reliable delivery of products to its customers.

The adoption of autonomous robots in industrial applications is driven by the desire to improve efficiency, reduce operational costs, enhance safety, and maintain consistent quality. These robots are often connected to the Industrial Internet of Things (IIoT) and can be managed and monitored remotely. However, their implementation may require substantial upfront investment and integration with existing systems, and they also need to comply with safety regulations and standards specific to their industry.

# Case Study: Autonomous Delivery Bots using AI Technology

For a mobile robot, the solution to finding an optimal path between the source and the destination is difficult to figure out since it wanders freely by picking the quickest and safest paths. Hence in this work, the focus was to use optimization algorithms such as ant colony optimization (ACO) to train the mobile robots to choose a wise path and plan a route so that the robot can operate in both static and dynamic situations. The mimic of the route planning done by ants through the secretion of pheromones was adopted for optimization. Also, the age of the ant inhibited the intelligence and training. The results were validated using MATLAB simulations and their performance are monitored. To guide the movement of robot, two navigation methods were utilized such as reactive and map-based. Initially when the mobile robot started navigation, it didn't understand the current location and further footsteps to take for moving forward in navigation. Hence, the robot made use of the installed sensors to realize and sense the environment. Later, the random locomotion started with the help of touch sensors, hence the name reactive navigation. The path creation was crucial in terms of choosing shortest distance or a path that utilizes least resources, called map-based navigation. Therefore, for better path planning, the machine had to sense, plan and act accordingly.

The A* algorithm generated a grid map and an improved visible graph, helps to aid in global path. For an indoor setting, Reference [3] used the modified A* algorithm for autonomous robot navigation along shortest path by taking parent node influence on the A* algorithm's heuristic function. Reference [4] illustrated the selection of shortest path in less time and memory using memory-efficient A* (MEA*) algorithm for the grid applications. The environment was constructed with nodes and edges in grids of rows and columns along with high resistance obstacles. To find the optimal path, the least resistive path between the source and target sites was determined. By utilizing the crossover function and special selection, the genetic algorithm (GA) was improved and its computing time was reduced. In addition to the identification of the shortest and smoothest safest path in a static and dynamic environment, the Hybrid PSO-MFB algorithm and a local search were employed. Furthermore, for obstacle detection and avoidance (ODA), the shortest global path in the hexagonal grid was constructed. For an explosion-proof robot (EPR), the likelihood of choosing the best path was increased to generate target attraction using a ACO path planner and other optimization algorithms via pheromone updating. The Flower Pollination Algorithm (FPA) was used to identify and solve low convergence problem for the purpose of directed path learning.

A 5kg mobile robot of wheel radius 0.015m with distances apart of 0.1m between wheels having torque of 1000N. m was considered for simulation of static and dynamic environments. Assume that in order to meet specific performance requirements, the mobile robot (MR) traveled from the start position (SP) to the goal position (GP) across an environment filled with both static and dynamic impediments, as shown in Figure 11-5a. Finding the best or nearly best route for the mobile robot while avoiding collisions with surrounding obstacles was the goal of a path planner.

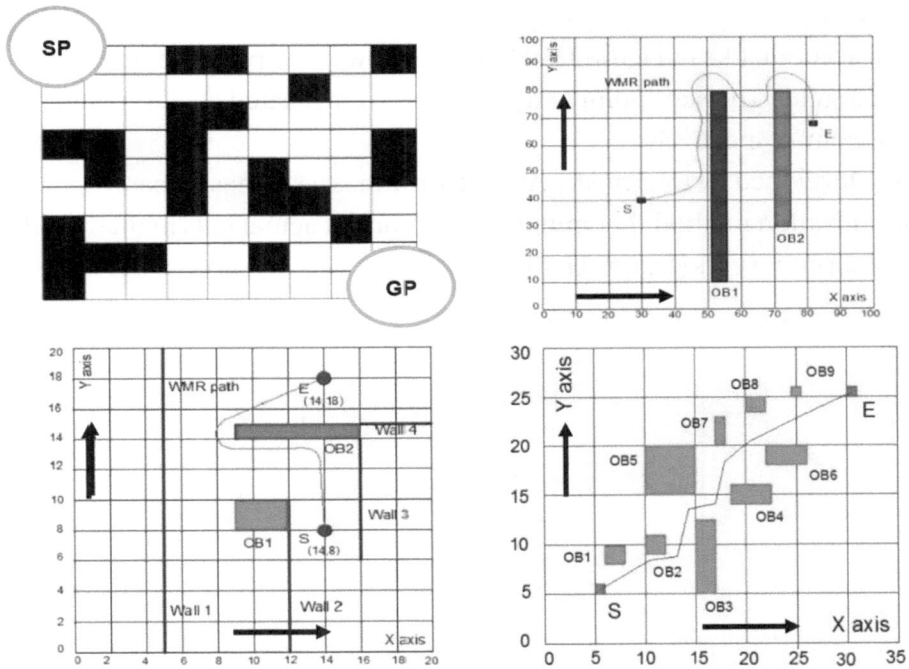

***Figure 11-5a.*** *2D grid map with source and destination points; 11-5b. Case 1: Two obstacles; Figure 11-5c. Case 2: Four walls and two obstacles; 11-5d. Case 3: Nine obstacles*

***Case 1:*** Two vertical stationary impediments were taken into consideration, as in Figure 11-5b, which shows two boxes. They are seen as two prisms that are rectangular. The start point and target point were located at (30,40) cm and (83,67) cm, respectively. The first obstacle measures 5 cm x 70 cm. The second obstacle is 5 cm x 50 cm.

***Case 2:*** Four permanent walls and two stationary barriers (two boxes) were taken into consideration, like in Figure 11-5c., which shows six prisms that are rectangular. The start point and goal point were located at (14.8)m and (14.18)m, respectively. Within a room, the robot was in motion.

***Case 3:*** Nine stationary impediments (two boxes) were taken into account, like in Figure 11-5d, which shows nine prisms that are rectangular. The start point and goal point were located at (5,5)m and (30,25)m, respectively.

Developed by Dorico, the ACO algorithm is a stochastic-based optimization method that mimics the actions of actual ants in their food-finding endeavors (Figure 11-6).

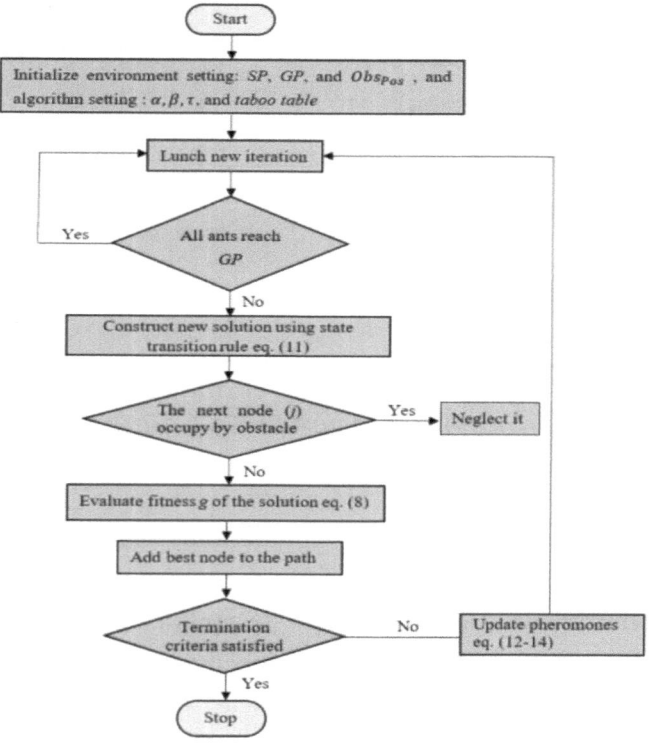

***Figure 11-6.*** *Determining the shortest and best path using the ACO algorithm*

Through cooperative information sharing, it determines the quickest path from an ant colony to food sources. The ants follow each other, travelling in unison along the same path. This is due to the fact that, as they go down the trail, all ants leave behind a chemical known as pheromone. The other ants follow the path with a higher concentration of pheromone after sensing the intensity of the pheromone. This is how they try to figure out the best route. The ants initially travel aimlessly in an attempt to reach their target. The ants detect the strength of the pheromone while on their back tour and select the path with the highest pheromone concentration. Since pheromone evaporates over time, the concentration of pheromone is higher along the shortest path since it takes less time to travel there than it does to follow other routes. As a result, practically all ants would choose the optimal path because they are drawn to the pheromone that is stronger along the shortest path. The flowchart in Figure 11-6 depicts the ACO-based shortest and best path finder for mobile robots in industries.

In this case study, an ACO path planner based on grid-based modelling was suggested to determine the mobile robot's best or nearly optimal path in both static and dynamic situations. The design of mobile robot path planning made use of a novel form of ACO optimization that was created by accounting for the ant's age. Grid-based modelling has been demonstrated to be less flexible in dynamic conditions when compared to free-space-based modelling. Still, it did a good job of simulating the moving robot and the obstacles in the two-dimensional scene.

# Legal Challenges

Autonomous delivery vehicles and robots must comply with a complex web of existing regulations, which were often developed before the technology existed. Ensuring compliance with local, state, and federal regulations related to road safety, vehicle classification, and operation is a significant challenge. Determining liability in the event of an accident or damage caused by an autonomous delivery vehicle or robot can be complex. Traditional insurance models may need to be adapted to account for autonomous technology, and questions about who is responsible (the manufacturer, operator, owner, or software developer) can arise. Autonomous vehicles and robots can collect a vast amount of data, both about their surroundings and the people they interact with. Privacy concerns related to data collection, storage, and usage need to be addressed. There may be a need for clear policies regarding data handling and user consent.

Issues related to intellectual property can arise, especially in cases where autonomous technology relies on patented algorithms, sensors, or hardware. Companies must navigate licensing agreements and potential disputes. Autonomous systems can be vulnerable to hacking and cyberattacks, which can result in safety risks and data breaches. Establishing robust cybersecurity measures is crucial. Autonomous vehicles may need to make ethical decisions in emergency situations. Determining how these decisions are made and who is responsible for programming them is a challenge.

To address these challenges, governments, companies, and legal experts are working together to develop new laws, regulations, and standards specific to autonomous vehicles and robots. Legal frameworks will continue to evolve as the technology becomes more widespread and integrated into daily life.

# Conclusion

Autonomous delivery vehicles represent a transformative technological advancement with the potential to revolutionize the way goods are transported and delivered. However, their widespread deployment is not without its challenges and considerations. Autonomous delivery vehicles have the potential to enhance delivery efficiency and convenience.

They can operate around the clock, reduce delivery times, and optimize routes, leading to cost savings and improved customer experiences. Autonomous delivery vehicles have the potential to revolutionize the delivery industry, offering improved efficiency, convenience, and potentially positive environmental impacts. However, their deployment and acceptance are accompanied by various challenges and considerations that must be addressed through collaboration between governments, businesses, and the public. It is estimated that around 9.6% growth has been recoded between 2020 to the previous year owing to adoption of autonomous bots. Overall, the integration of autonomous vehicles and delivery robots into supply chain management can result in streamlined operations, reduced costs, and improved customer satisfaction. However, successful implementation requires careful planning, investment, and consideration of regulatory and safety concerns. The successful integration of autonomous delivery vehicles into our transportation systems will depend on how well these challenges are navigated and how the technology is adapted to meet the needs and expectations of society.

# CHAPTER 12

# Using Blockchain for Sustainable Supply Chain Management in Industry 4.0

*Akshay Bhuvaneswari Ramakrishnan, School of Computing, SASTRA Deemed University, Thanjavur, Tamil Nadu, India.* akshayramakrishnan.sas@gmail.com.

*Mukunth Madavan, School of Computing, SASTRA Deemed University, Thanjavur, Tamil Nadu, India.* mm.2612@outlook.com.

*R. Manikandan, School of Computing, SASTRA Deemed University, Thanjavur, Tamil Nadu, India.* srmanimt75@gmail.com.

*Subrato Bharati, Institute of Information and Communication Technology, Bangladesh University of Engineering and Technology, Dhaka 1205, Bangladesh.* subratobharati1@gmail.com.

This chapter examines how blockchain technology might be used to reinvent sustainable supply chain management within the context of Industry 4.0 while also critically addressing the numerous security concerns that are currently existing. It achieves this by exploring

the intricate connection between blockchain technology and long-
term viability, emphasizing the profound impact that blockchain
technology has on confidence, tracking, and openness across intricate
global supply networks. The problems and potential, with the goal of
addressing concerns regarding security, are addressed. It envisions a
future in which blockchain technology, when reinforced by solid security
measures, strengthens supply chains that are resilient, transparent, and
environmentally responsible. It paves the way for a broad discussion
on how to maximize the promise of blockchain technology while also
minimizing the hazards associated with Industry 4.0.

# The Shifting Paradigm

Businesses are going through a paradigm shift, as a result of Industry 4.0,
which is to leverage emerging technology in order to drive efficiency and
innovation. In this era, we are witnessing the convergence of artificial
intelligence, the Internet of Things, and automation, which is radically
transforming the landscapes of operating environments [1]. Technology
has been a big contributor to the fundamental alteration of both the
economic world and mainstream culture, according to scholars who are
in agreement with this statement. Nevertheless, the way in which these
developing technologies tackle challenges relating to ecology and security
has gained a limited bit of press recently [2]. Technology has been a big
contributor to the fundamental alteration of both the economic world
and mainstream culture, according to scholars who are in agreement
with this statement. A revolutionary component that stands out within
the framework of this revolution is the implementation of blockchain
technology into the management of supply chains [3]. In order to
revolutionize the conventional methods of supply chain management,
blockchain technology, which is a decentralized ledger system, offers
unparalleled levels of accountability, reliability, and security [4].

In addition to providing a rigorous system for authenticating transactions and tracing items throughout complex supply networks, its immutable nature guarantees that records cannot be altered because they cannot be altered. But the question that needs to be answered is whether or not supply chains actually need to embrace concepts like blockchain. Having a firm grip on the answer to this sort of inquiry is absolutely necessary. It may be expensive to adopt and apply a new technical concept in order to replace an existing practice when dealing with supply networks, particularly ones that are on a smaller or medium scale. This is especially true when working with supply chains [5]. The influence that global supply chains have on both the environment and ethics is becoming an increasingly important concern in the context of the pursuit of operational excellence. Through the guarantee of ethical sourcing, the reduction of environmental footprints, and the enhancement of responsibility across the production cycles, the synergy among blockchain technology and environmentally friendly supply chain management is an absolute necessity. However, despite the potential that blockchain technology holds, security continues to be a significant obstacle. Even if it is durable, the decentralized architecture is not immune to attacks using flaws. Within supply chains that are built on blockchain technology, there are significant dangers that include defects in smart contracts, threats to data privacy, and consensus procedures. The purpose of this chapter is to go on a detailed examination with the intention of addressing these difficulties by presenting effective security mechanisms. Through the dissection of security concerns, the examination of technological solutions, and the analysis of successful case studies, this chapter sheds light on a road that can lead to the secure integration of blockchain technology inside supply chains that are environmentally responsible. The following sections will guide you through a technical understanding of security challenges, proposed strategies, and real-world implementations.

# Literature Review

Many academic publications highlight the significant capacity of
blockchain technology to bring about profound changes in supply
chain management. The authors in [6] specifically examine the process
of choosing suppliers that are sustainable, taking into account the
implementation of circular economy practices and Industry 4.0 projects. In
order to evaluate and select sustainable suppliers, this decision framework
incorporates the principles of both the fourth industrial revolution and
the circular economy. The study utilizes a mixed-method approach,
which includes reviewing literature and gathering insights from experts.
The study used the best-worst method (BWM) and VIKOR approach to
determine criterion weights and rank suppliers. The findings highlight
the importance of technology infrastructure, favorable organizational
culture, and supportive government regulations in the process of selecting
sustainable suppliers. The framework presents an innovative strategy that
combines circular economy with Industry 4.0 activities. It contributes
to the advancement of theoretical understanding and provides practical
instructions for managers. This comprehensive framework fills the gaps
in existing literature regarding the circular economy, Industry 4.0, and
sustainability. It improves both the theoretical understanding and practical
implementation of supply chain operations. The study [7] examines the
management of the Halal supply chain, with a focus on its significance in
maintaining the integrity of Halal products throughout the entire process
from production to consumption. This text examines the incorporation
of supply chain management with the fourth industrial revolution and
emphasizes the significance of SCM for enterprises. The study highlights
the shortcomings in the existing literature concerning supply chain
management methods in small and medium-sized enterprises (SMEs) and
agroindustry SMEs. The text outlines the primary operations and elements
of the Halal SCM, encompassing warehousing, sourcing, managing
transportation of halal items, inventory management, lean management,

and value-based management. The text discusses the concepts of halal logistics, the elements of a unified halal supply chain system, and the influence of supply chain management methods on competitive advantage and organizational performance. The empirical study validates the correlation between supply chain management methods, competitive advantage, and organizational success. This text offers an understanding of the evolution of halal supply chains and highlights the advantages of adopting supply chain management, such as decreased expenses and enhanced customer contentment. The study advocates for additional research that takes into account wider industry viewpoints and proposes the possibility of applying effective supply chain management to provide lasting advantages. The resource-based viewpoint theory is the foundation for the model that is presented by the authors in [8]. Within the context of green supply chain management, the model explores the relationships between supply chain relationship, supply chain information exchange, commitment from management, and acceptance of green logistics and procurement initiatives. The research substantiates the clear relationships between supply chain connections and information exchange within supply chains, as well as the commitment of top management and the acceptability of environmentally responsible procurement and logistical measures. Additionally, the study substantiates the positive connections that exist between the dedication of top management and the acceptance of environmentally responsible procurement and logistics, in addition to green supply chain administration principles. In this work, real-world insights and theoretical advancements are presented, including a novel and cutting-edge scale for the management of environmentally friendly supply chains. It is a type of resource-based thinking that serves as the basis for the framework that has been suggested in the research [9]. The findings of the study provide more evidence that there is a favorable correlation between supply chain connection and the sharing of information about supply chain operations, as well as top management commitment, green procurement, and logistical acceptance. In addition,

337

the study provides evidence that top management commitment is
positively associated with green procurement and logistics adoption
as well as green supply chain management. The research provides
both theoretical and practical advances, including a novel scale for the
management of green supply chains. Authors in [10] make reference to the
benefits associated with the use of blockchain technology in non-
financial industries and supply networks. Increased productivity in supply
chains can be achieved through the use of smart contracts and distributed
decision-making procedures. The state that is decentralized demonstrates
a huge improvement in comparison to the one that is centralized. The
proposed model decreases the amount of time and money spent on
solving problems, hence improving both economic and environmental
sustainability.

# Overview of Sustainable Supply Chain Management

The term "sustainable supply chain management" (SSCM) refers to a
strategic strategy that incorporates activities that are both ecologically
and socially responsible [11] throughout the entirety of the supply chain
lifecycle. Figure 12-1 depicts the supply chain life cycle illustrating the end-
to-end processes. Throughout the production and distribution processes,
the primary goals of SSCM are to maximize efficiency, minimize negative
effects on the environment, and encourage ethical business practices.

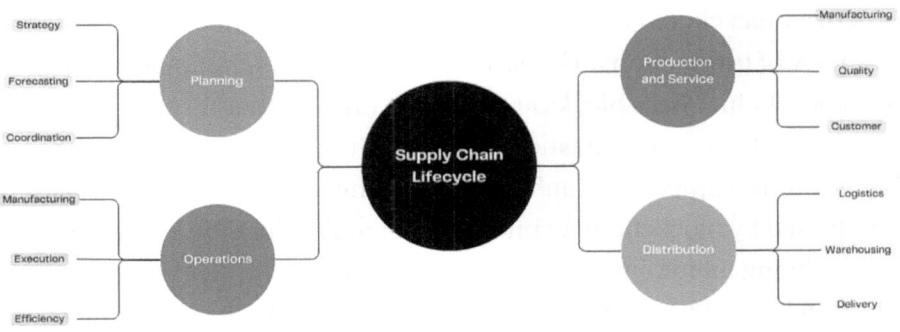

***Figure 12-1.*** *Supply chain lifecycle*

Growing environmental concerns like the effects of global warming and societal problems such as equality and safety have driven numerous companies to go beyond strictly economic-related goals and incorporate a broader range of objectives into their logistics decisions. Among the most important aspects are the responsible procurement of raw materials, the reduction of waste, the optimization of energy efficiency, and the guarantee of fair labor standards. The goal of SSCM is to provide long-term benefit for enterprises, society, and the environment [12]. This goes beyond simply complying with rules. In order to promote transparency, traceability, and accountability, it requires collaboration with various stakeholders, including customers, suppliers, and other interested parties. Through the adoption of a comprehensive viewpoint, SSCM links economic success with social responsibility and environmental stewardship. As a result, it is a crucial strategy in the aim of providing global supply networks that are both resilient and sustainable.

# Understanding Blockchain Technology

The blockchain technology is a distributed and decentralized ledger system that enables record-keeping [13] that is safe, transparent, and immune to tampering represented in Figure 12-2. The most fundamental form of a blockchain is a series of blocks, each of which includes an inventory of transactions. This structure is the most fundamental form of a blockchain. These blocks are linked to one another through the utilization of encryption hashes, which result in the formation of a link that is uninterrupted and can't be altered. The distributed ledger that is maintained by blockchain technology isn't maintained by a single entity instead being maintained by a collection of nodes [14]. This decentralized aspect of blockchain technology is one of its defining characteristics. This approach guarantees transparency and reduces the likelihood of fraudulent activity. As a result of the fact that every participant in the blockchain network owns a copy of the whole ledger, the blockchain is robust against hacking and manipulation.

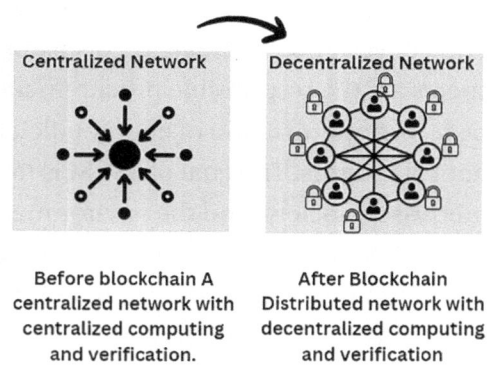

Centralized Network          Decentralized Network

Before blockchain A          After Blockchain
centralized network with     Distributed network with
centralized computing        decentralized computing
and verification.            and verification

***Figure 12-2.*** *Evolution from centralized to decentralized blockchain architecture*

Transaction verification is carried out by consensus processes, which are often carried out on public blockchains through a process known as mining. Due to the fact that it is incredibly impossible to change prior blocks after a block has been added to the chain, the level of security that is provided is quite strong. Beyond the realm of cryptocurrencies, blockchain technology [15] has a wide range of applications, including supply chain management, healthcare, and banking. Another essential characteristic is the existence of smart contracts, which are contracts that automatically carry out their terms and are coded. These contracts automate and guarantee the execution of predetermined conditions in a trustworthy and safe manner. In general, blockchain technology has the potential to revolutionize a variety of different industries by improving the safety, transparency, and efficiency of data storage and transactions.

# Need for Sustainability and Security in Industry 4.0

It is essential to place a strong emphasis on the convergence of sustainability and security in this era of Industry 4.0 [16]. In the context of Industry 4.0, sustainability refers to the optimization of processes with the goals of minimizing negative effects on the environment, increasing resource efficiency, and maintaining ethical standards. At the same time, the intricate integration of networked technologies that is characteristic of Industry 4.0 (as in Figure 12-3) necessitates the implementation of stringent security measures in order to protect against cyber threats and guarantee the integrity of data.

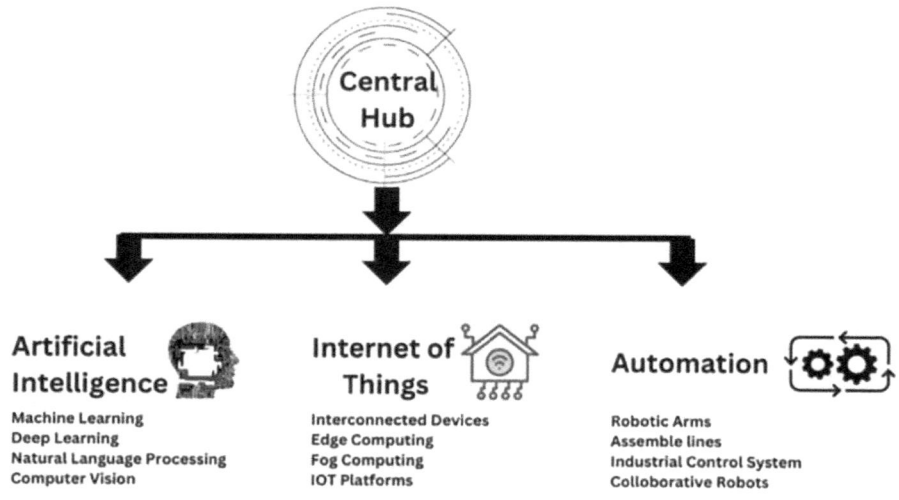

***Figure 12-3.*** *Environment of Industry 4.0*

As a result of the fact that secure practices defend sustainable efforts
and sustainable technology assists in decreasing environmental effects,
which in turn indirectly enhances security, the interplay between
sustainability and security is readily apparent. One of the most important
things that needs to be done in order to support responsible technological
growth, ensure the long-term viability of operations, and fulfil the ethical
standards of a globally cognizant marketplace is to achieve a harmonious
balance between sustainability and security in Industry 4.0 [17].

# Integrating Blockchain with Sustainable Supply Chains

It is absolutely necessary to take a systematic approach in order to
successfully navigate the issues of security inside the sustainable supply
chains of Industry 4.0. [18] The foundation of increased security is the
implementation of a blockchain architecture that is decentralized and is

strengthened by consensus methods. Not only does this structure protect against unauthorized changes, but it also helps to build confidence by dispersing control throughout the network of the supply chain (represented in Figure 12-4). In addition, the implementation of smart contracts within the framework of blockchain technology allows for the automation and protection of essential supply chain transactions [19], thereby guaranteeing transparency and conformity to predetermined specifications. The integration of these technical solutions results in an integrated approach that not only reduces the potential for security breaches but also facilitates the smooth integration of blockchain technology into environmentally responsible supply chains, thereby ushering in a paradigm shift towards Industry 4.0 that is both robust and transparent.

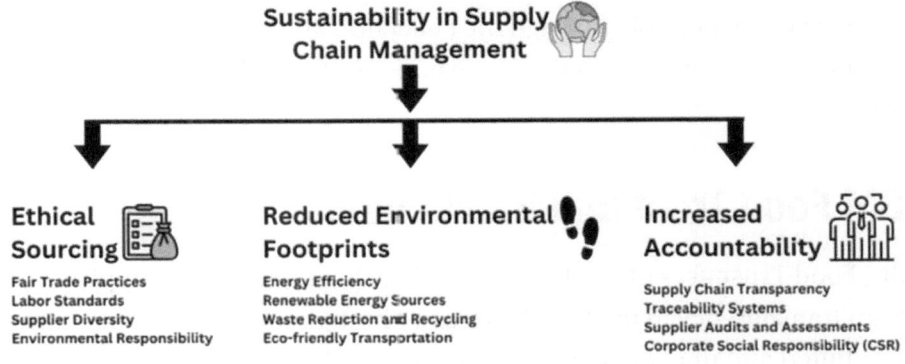

*Figure 12-4.* *Network representing the outcomes of sustainable supply chain management*

# Innovative Applications and Case Studies

The world of creative applications and case studies offers a dynamic insight into the practical manifestations of cutting-edge technologies, and it is possible to gain this understanding by exploring the domain. Examples from the real world that demonstrate the transformative power of innovation are discussed in this section. These examples range from the use of artificial intelligence to revolutionize healthcare diagnoses to the use of blockchain technology to revolutionize financial transactions.

# The Autopilot Technology of Tesla

The Autopilot system that Tesla has developed is a prime example of groundbreaking innovation in the automobile sector [20]. The capabilities of semi-autonomous driving are made possible by Autopilot, which makes use of sophisticated sensors, cameras, and artificial intelligence components. Over-the-air updates are used to continuously improve the system, which also includes the addition of new functionality and enhancements to existing safety features. Continuous learning of the system is made possible through the collection and analysis of data in real time, which results in a driving experience that is both dynamic and inventive.

# IBM Food Trust and Blockchain

IBM Food Trust uses blockchain technology to revolutionize supply chain transparency in the food business. Through the establishment of a distributed and unchangeable ledger, it is possible to achieve complete visibility throughout the whole food supply chain [21]. Food waste may be reduced, quality control can be maintained, and consumer trust can be increased through the use of real-time tracking of items from the farm to consumption. This unique technology has been accepted by major retailers and food producers such as Walmart and Nestlé in order to establish a food supply chain that is more transparent and traceable.

## Zoom Video Communications During the COVID-19 Pandemic

Zoom's stratospheric rise during the COVID-19 pandemic is a prime
example of the transformative influence of video conferencing technology.
Zoom had growth that was unparalleled as the benefits of remote work and
virtual communication became increasingly important [22]. Because of its
cutting-edge capabilities, user-friendliness, and scalability, the platform
was able to successfully meet the ever-increasing demand for online
education, social gatherings, and participation in virtual meetings. This
particular case study demonstrates how technology can fast adapt to the
requirements of society, thereby promoting global connectedness even in
the face of difficult circumstances.

# Conclusion

According to the findings of the investigation into the role that blockchain
will play in determining the future of environmentally responsible
supply chain management within the framework of Industry 4.0,
its transformative potential has been revealed. Not only does the
implementation of blockchain technology improve transparency,
traceability, and efficiency, but it also addresses critically important pillars
of sustainability. Blockchain technology helps to contribute to ethical
sourcing, lower environmental footprints, and more accountability. This
is accomplished through the use of decentralized ledgers and smart
contracts respectively. But security risks continue to exist, just like they
do with every disruptive technology, which is why it is necessary to make
a deliberate effort to install effective measures. Looking ahead, the future
of blockchain in sustainable supply chain management shows promise,
particularly with continued developments in consensus methods,

interoperability, and scalability. This is especially true when considering
the future of cryptography. A dynamic landscape for innovation
and collaboration is presented by the convergence of blockchain,
sustainability, and Industry 4.0. This landscape offers a pathway towards
supply chain ecosystems that are more resilient, transparent, and
ecologically responsible.

# CHAPTER 13

# Managing the Dynamics of New Technologies in the Global Supply Chain

*K. Santhi, School of Computer Science Engineering and Information Systems, Vellore Institute of Technology, Vellore, India.*

*Saurya Raj Pandey, School of Computer Science Engineering and Information Systems, Vellore Institute of Technology, Vellore, India.*

*M. Lawanyashri, corresponding author, School of Computer Science Engineering and Information Systems, Vellore Institute of Technology,* `lawanyaraj@gmail.com`.

*Balamurugan Balusamy, Shiv Nadar University Noida, Uttar Pradesh, India.*

*Dr. Veena Grover, Noida Institute of Engineering & Technology, Greater Noida, Uttar Pradesh, India.*

Global supply chains are becoming increasingly intricate, constantly evolving, and spanning across borders. This dynamic nature is beneficial for companies worldwide, facilitating their production and expansion. As someone who is deeply involved in the advancement of supply chain management, I'm excited to witness the transformative impact of emerging technologies such as cloud computing and blockchain on this critical aspect of business.

This chapter will begin by providing an overview of the key characteristics and challenges facing modern global supply chains. It's important to understand the intricate web of interconnected processes and the myriad of obstacles that supply chain professionals must navigate on a daily basis.

Next, we will delve into the rise of cloud computing and examine how it has impacted software development and data management in supply chain contexts. While cloud-based solutions have brought many benefits, such as improved efficiency and reduced costs, the chapter will also discuss some of the security and transparency limitations that have been observed.

The main focus of this chapter, however, will be an in-depth analysis of blockchain technology and its potential to address these issues as a "Cloud 2.0" solution for global supply chains. We will explore the core attributes of blockchain, such as its distributed ledger and decentralized architecture, and unpack the various blockchain-enabled services and applications that can be leveraged to enhance supply chain management. Finally, we will conclude by considering the broader implications of these new technological paradigms for the future of global supply chain operations, management, and optimization. By the end of this chapter, you will have a comprehensive understanding of how the convergence of cloud computing, blockchain, and global supply chain dynamics is shaping the future of this critical business domain.

# Supply Chain Overview

The main objective of blockchain s concerning however it is employed
within the net service. Web service area unit created, printed and
accessed by net mistreatment normal net protocols, net assistance plays a
significant part within Service Oriented Architecture (SOA) by facilitating
the composition of diverse composing varied work net assistance proceeds
along that performed work because every actuation after service-oriented
computing (SOC). The goal of net assistance coordination is to integrate
various diverse trade forms to meet client demands that cannot be satisfied
by a single network service. Examples for complicated net assistance
applications are online travelling memos, websites for buying books, and a
protection handling framework. To attain the same user necessities, many
net assistance area units organized ideally to attain a client objective. net
service composition method (WSC) net service composition is that the
mechanism for combining and reusing existing net assistance to make new
net assistance.

## Service Discovery

Service discovery, which is shown Figure 13-1, is the method of
mechanical detection devices and assistance on a network. The assistance
discovery protocol (SDP) may be a networking normal that accomplishes
detection of networks by distinguishing resources. Historically, service
discovery helps scale back configuration efforts by users World Health
Organization area unit conferred with compatible resources, like a
Bluetooth-enabled printer or server.

349

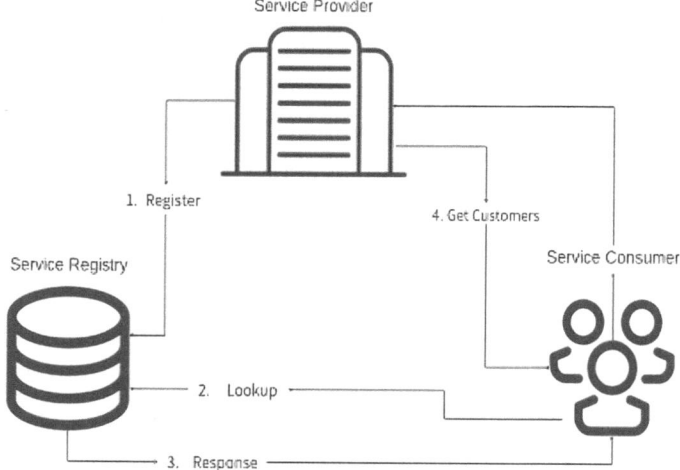

***Figure 13-1.*** *Service discovery*

The regions consist of two benefit disclosures, which are server-side
and client-side. Server-side benefit licenses buyers applications help to
look for out help through a switch or a stack balancer. Client-side benefit
revelation licenses buyers' applications to look for out help by looking
through or questioning a benefit composed record, amid which benefit
occurrences and endpoints square measure all at interims the benefit
composed record.

# Service Selection

Enterprises heavily trust progressive info technologies, user behaviors,
and social structure to sustain business aggressiveness. SoA and the
cloud enable enterprises to utilize dynamic distributed assistance
across enterprise boundaries and even people. Supported the wants of
society, enterprise will turn out a virtual enterprise for brand spanking
new businesses wherever the commanded producing resources area
unit obtained through service choice and advancement composition

over the net. Associate in Nursing increasing range of web of Things
(IoT) assistance create enterprises facing the challenge to pick preferred
assistance for his or her business workflows. we tend to improve
advancement compositions ways at three major aspects:

- We tend to gift Associate in Nursing integrated
  approach for service choice and composition to satisfy
  the wants of users and social structure.

- We tend to extend Service Work flow Specification
  (SWSpec) as a proper command specification to work
  out a style house of assistance.

- We tend to introduce the Fuzzy Analytic Hierarchy
  method (F-AHP) to judge nonfunctional specifications
  quantitatively with less uncertainty. applicable
  rankings may be appointed to on the market assistance
  supported non-functional necessities to work out the
  best-suited assistance with less uncertainty which is
  shown in Figure 13-2.

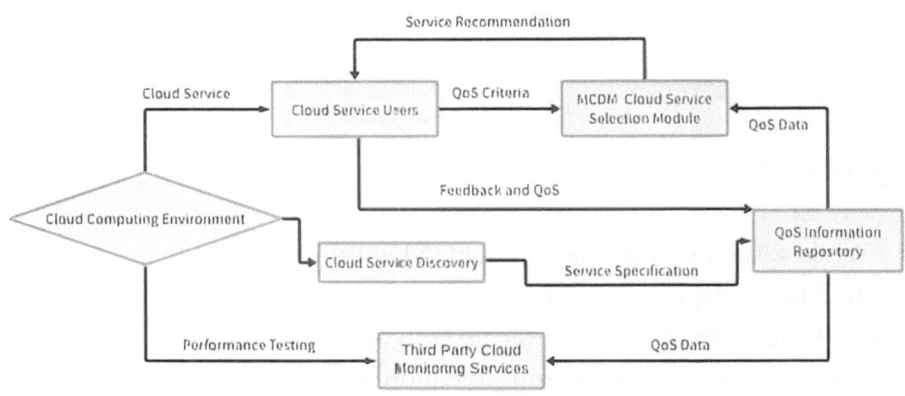

***Figure 13-2.*** *Service selection*

# Service Composition

Benefit composition, Relate in Nursing rising subject in net help, talks around the adaptability to blend net help into a commerce strategy. this will be furthermore talked as benefit coordination or benefit course of action. Benefit composition is that the capcom ability to arrange and control talk between net help into a greater bunch activity. for occasion, a gather activity that includes a client to a checking account benefit may also deliver numerous accounts in conjunction with including the client data to the client service. All of those demands unit of measurement control inside the setting of a greater commerce strategy stream that either succeeds or falls flat as a full.

Service composition means composing a greater benefit by combining a few littler helps. This could be an identical rule utilized once composing a greater computer program bundle portion from a few littler components. Figure 13-2 shows a graph outlining benefit composition.

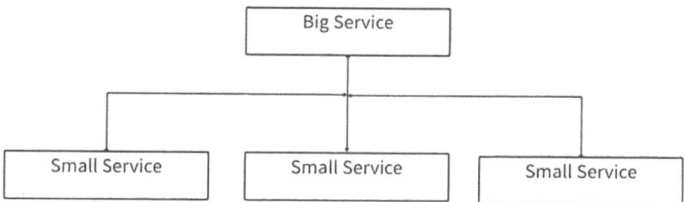

**Figure 13-3.**  *Service composition*

While service composition shown in Figure 13-3 might look compelling on paper, similar to part composition would, confine mind that assistance usually communicate with one another via the network. meaning that inter-service communication is far slower than typical inter-component communication, which usually takes place within an equivalent address house (application/process). moldering your larger

assistance into too several smaller assistances might hurt performance.
particularly if the assistance communicates internally via associate in
nursing enterprise service bus (ESB).

## Service Execution

Online social media assistance, like Facebook and Twitter, have set new
standards on how individuals communicate with one another online
and share their everyday activities. Whereas current mobile assistance
supporting social interaction area unit usually primarily for inaccessible
communication, comparable help may be presented to co-located social
intuitive. In such a setting, people and proactive, setting detecting versatile
gadgets sort current very a socio-digital framework wherever the portable
gadgets unit dynamic members and might start interaction among the
gadgets and other individuals. Physical nearness of the gadgets gets to be a
key enabler to advance users' interaction with one another conjointly the
supporting portable help. amid this paper, we tend to present the thought
of Social Gadgets and its execution. The Social Gadgets Stage encourages
independently made agreeable help in co-located gadgets wherever the
customer half is simple and essentially deployable to completely diverse
styles of gadgets which is shown in Figure 13-4.

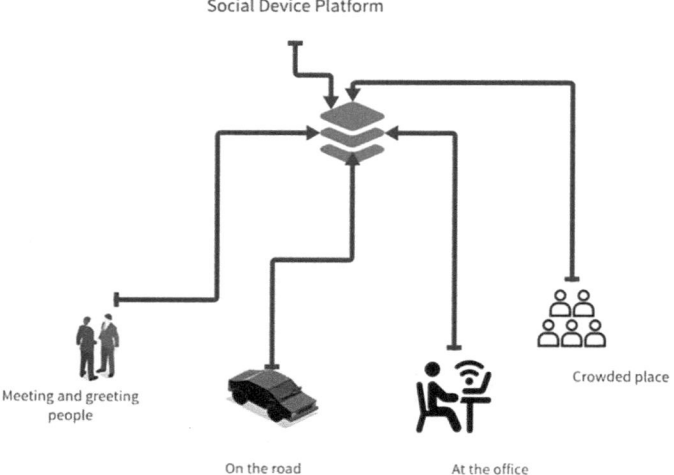

***Figure 13-4.*** *Service execution*

The blockchain technology is revolutionizing how assets are
exchanged and web services are organized. A smart contract-enabled
blockchain creates a self-executing community that ensures secure
access to web services through public-key cryptography. Drawn from
the remarkable achievement by integration containing smart contracts
powered by blockchain technology, which finds utilities across a range of
application, the overall aim of this paper is to integrate intelligent solutions
contracts into Quality of Service (QoS)-aware historical web service
composition processes. Service-level agreement (SLA) assertions lack
the authority to manage the establishment and initiation of web services,
leaving room for potential data breaches. Initially, a new trustworthy SLA
based on first-party assertions is introduced which is then reserved in the
decentralized alternative, which is blockchain, instead of a traditional
consolidated network. Table 13-1 provides information about user
information and service provider information stored on the blockchain.
The economic logic of web services cannot be altered, so service providers
tend to represent higher QoS, assigning significance towards enhancing

the services within the range of choices on the list. To prevent the range of choices of undesirable services, a smart contract is utilized to establish successful conditions for the QoS-aware online service architecture procedures, ensuring a reliable, effective, and secure online solution. We conduct empirical tests using OWLS-TC datasets using the Truffle Ethereum framework to evaluate the effectiveness of our approach, which focuses on contracts provided by an intelligent algorithm of QoS alert composition.

***Table 13-1.*** *SLA agreement*

| User Information in Blockchain | Service Provider Information in Blockchian | | |
|---|---|---|---|
| User Registration | Service Profile OWL-S | Serice Model OWL-S | Serice Model OWL-S |
| username user ID publick key ethereum address timestamp email address | Provider providerID ethereum address service category IOPE functional catergories non-functional Values | Access points WS business category control flow Logical flow A hash value of a supplementary class | Access points WS business category control flow Logical flow A hash value of a supplementary class |

# Ethereum Blockchain-Based Design for Semantic Web

The advantage supplier makes a SLA assertion near to an advantage event record (OWL-S record) and hold on it in Ethereum Blockchain. At that point, the made extraordinary contract mechanically dead by the diggers interior the Ethereum blockchain organize victimization Affirmation of Stake (VAoS) assertion instrument to favor the advantage over the data

provided is validated and affirms the authenticity shown in Figure 13-5.
The assertion of advantages is securely recorded and transmitted through
Blockchain, acting as a transaction endorsed by the supplier of the
advantages. Following this, the resulting SLA declaration is retrieved from
the Blockchain. Subsequently, the SLA, derived from OWL-S records
stored within the Blockchain, is made available in the UDDI registry to
facilitate business interactions with clients. Notably, as all disseminated
Blockchain data remains immutable, this implies that they are not much
acknowledged to change the online advantage events data. Hence, an
advantage supplier has not much acknowledged to deny the permitted
net advantage deliberateness, non-functional data enables a fair sensible
agreement is established.

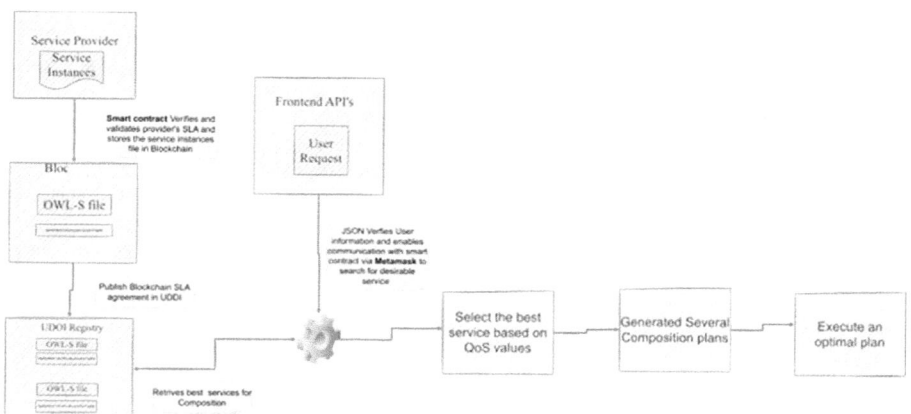

**Figure 13-5.**  *ETHEREUM blockchain for a web service*

# The Drawbacks of Traditional Semantic Web Service Composition Handling

The constancy of services the benefit supplier might alter the SLA useful and values that are not tied to functionality by means of integrated hub director Whenever client filling a complaint regarding advertised obnoxious benefit.

- Copied information

- Introducing a middleman to facilitate the selection of advantages through coercion

- Trustless stage for benefit execution

- Cost-fraudulent

The traditional way of doing things has some problems, so people are looking into other options. One idea is to use cloud computing and blockchain technology for web services. In the next part, we'll talk about how combining cloud computing with blockchain can help fix some of the problems with traditional web service setup.

# Cloud Computing Can Be Used in the Blockchain as a Webservice

Cloud technology has become a favored option for both individuals and businesses, presenting a myriad of advantages including cost-effectiveness, heightened productivity, accelerated operations, enhanced efficiency, superior performance, and fortified security. The concept revolves around shifting computing functions and data storage from local clients to remote data centers managed by expert teams. Blockchain technology serves as the intermediary for service composition and transaction recording within the cloud infrastructure. Additionally, a QoS-aware model for service

357

composition is proposed within the blockchain-based cloud architecture. A particle swarm optimization (PSO) algorithm is introduced to address this model effectively. Furthermore, simulations have been conducted to demonstrate the application of service composition in blockchain-based cloud computing. Web assistance comprises self-contained, modular, and distributed applications with dynamic features. These applications can be described, shared, found, or accessed through networks to enhance products, processes, and supply chains. They can take the form of native, distributed, or web-based applications. Furthermore, web assistance is built upon foundational open standards including TCP/IP, HTTP, Java, HTML, and XML. The online service will be applied in blockchain as can, that has created numerous topic which may be employed in numerous fields that's being developed. the online service is

(i)   Code as a service

(ii)  Platform as a service

(iii) Infrastructure as a service

(iv)  Blockchain as a service

# Blockchain As a Service (BaaS)

Blockchain as a service (BaaS) reflects as a third-party creation and control of cloud-based networks for firms within the business of building blockchain applications. These third-party services represent a recent advancement in the expanding realm of blockchain technology, addressing the need for hosting support. Essentially, BaaS provides third-party cloud infrastructure and management for companies engaged in developing and operating blockchain applications. It operates akin to a web host, facilitating the setup and maintenance of blockchain networks. BaaS serves as a catalyst driving the widespread adoption of blockchain technology, as shown in Figure 13-6.

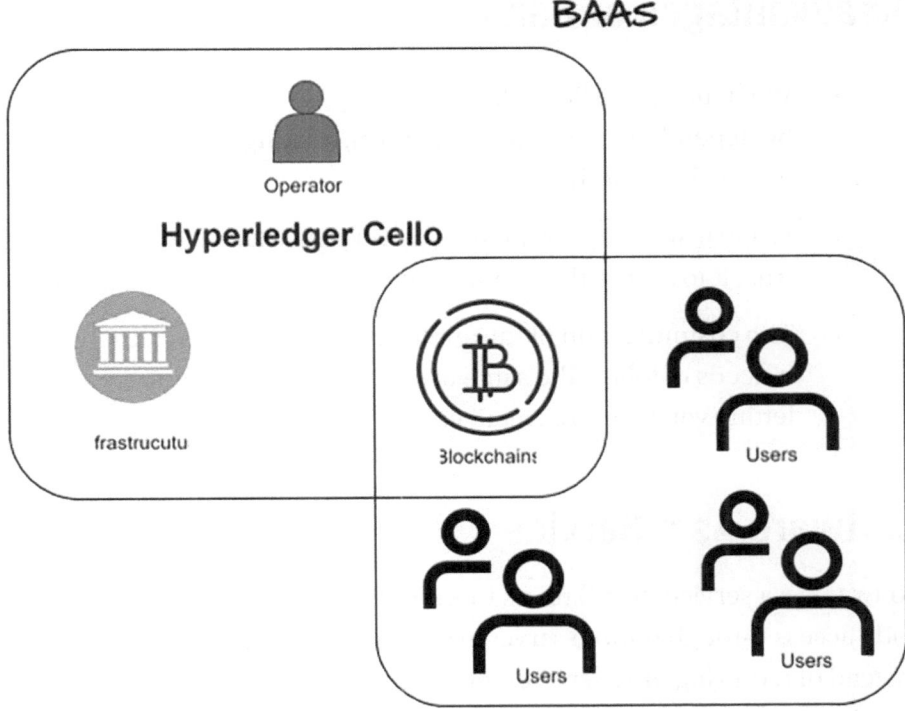

*Figure 13-6.* *Blockchain as a service*

## Advantages of BaaS

- It eliminates the maintenance costs for businesses to
  set up and maintain their own infrastructure, which
  reduces the initial and continuing costs related to
  building and maintaining a proper blockchain network.

- It has a faster deployment as it offers a prebuilt
  blockchain solution.

- It meets the growing demands of businesses because it
  helps them scale.

# Disadvantages of BaaS

- When using the Baas platform, many businesses may be dependent on a certain platform, making it difficult to switch to another platform.

- While using the Baas platform, every business needs to trust it to secure the application.

- The customization of the application is limited because it needs to follow the same use cases every time, not letting you be more creative.

# Software As a Service

Software as a service (SaaS) refers to a model of code licensing that allows code access through remote server exploitation on a subscription basis. Instead of requiring the user to enter the code on their computer, SaaS enables users to access programs through the Internet. In addition to file sharing, email, schedules, client retention control, and human resources, SaaS offers a number of commercial applications.

The rise of cloud-based computing and SaaS, as depicted in Figure 13-7, are related. Cloud computing is a net-based innovation support technique that often involves servers, networking, and data storage. Businesses wishing to update code on their computers had to purchase CDs, carrying the changes and transferring them into their systems prior to SaaS being available on the market. Changing code was a time-consuming process for large companies. With time, code updates were made available for download via the Internet, and businesses began to receive additional licenses rather than additional disks. All devices that needed access to that, though, still needed to have a duplicate of the code entered. Users are not forced to install or update any code when using SaaS. To use the actual service, they instead check in via the Internet or application software and connect to the service provider's network.

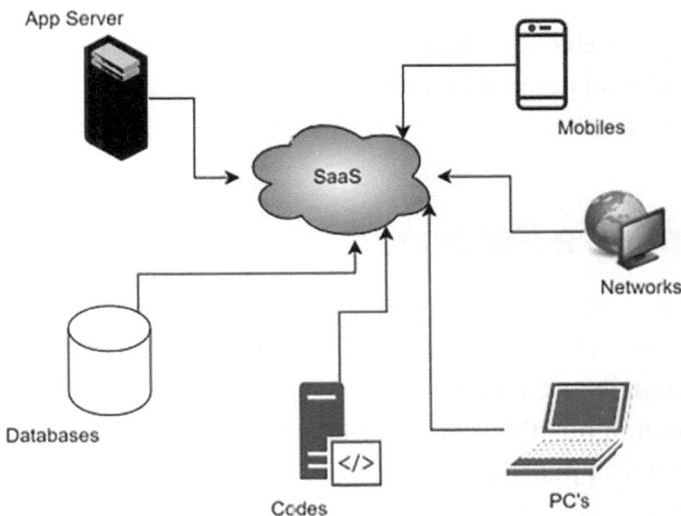

***Figure 13-7.***  *Software as a service*

# Advantages of SaaS

SaaS offers a range of benefits over the ancient code authority models. as a result of the code doesn't continue to exist the Authority of the company's servers, there is less command for the corporate to speculates the device. It's simple to implement, simple to update and rectify, and may be more cost-effective since users get it as they're working rather than getting multiple code licenses for multiple computers. Applications used by SaaS are

- Email

- Auditing

- Auto sign-in

- Managing documents

## Disadvantages of SaaS

- Businesses should guarantee that it is secure and inaccessible to unauthorized individuals.

- Poor web connections will reduce functionality. Internal networks tend to be quicker than web connections.

# Platform As a Service

One of the benefits of PaaS is its adaptability and quantify combability. Designers will construct apps exploitation their determination of manufactured dialect or system. They will be run any frame of app on a PaaS, whether or not it's a web or portable app, web of Things (IoT) app, or relate degree application programming interface (API) that interfaces apps and frameworks. PaaS help area unit planned to essentially measure; apps will start out small and consistently extent to handle enterprise-level command. relate degree app on a PaaS might too be a back-end benefit that gives a particular operate, like to validate clients or thrust notices. A few organizations these days unit of measurement taking a micro assistance method to their application engineering; they're building applications that unit of measurement made of a group of stars of person back-end and front-end help. PaaS types it less demanding to rapidly send and control person micro assistance, especially on the off chance that they're designed exploitation numerous totally diverse dialects and system shown in Figure 13-8.

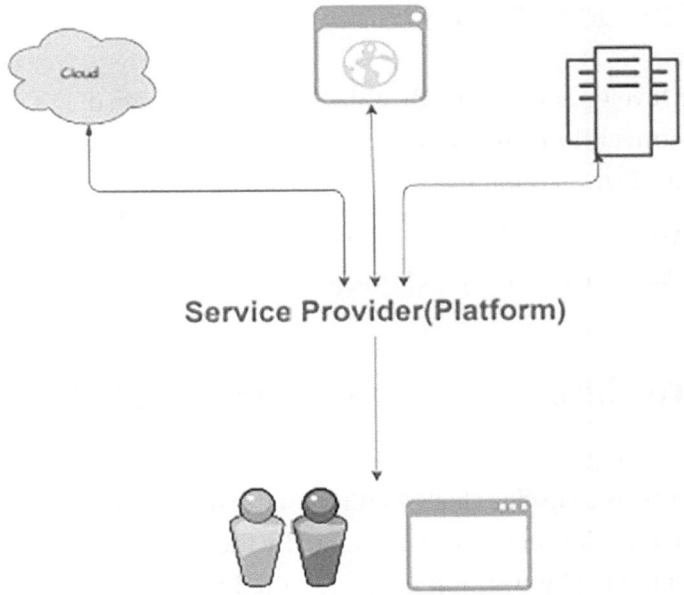

Service Provider(Platform)

Application Clients(End Users)& Applications

*Figure 13-8.*  *Platform as a service*

## Advantages of PaaS

- Less coding time

- Add improvements without involving staff

- Handel it topographically disseminated
  advancement groups

- Productively control the application lifecycle

- Use sophisticated tools affordably

## Disadvantages of PaaS

- Developers may not be able to use a full range of
  conventional tools, such as a relational database with
  unrestricted joins.

- You are locked into a certain platform. However, most
  PaaS are relatively lock-in-free.

# Infrastructure as a Service in Blockchain

Rather than being based in a traditional on-premises data center,
Infrastructure as a service (IaaS) is built on the open and private
clouds. The foundation is fully controlled by the service provider but is
communicated to clients upon request. It might be a cloud computing
service where businesses rent or lease servers to use for processing power
and capacity. Clients are able to use a variety of operating systems and
apps on the servers they rent without any limitations, performing tasks and
actively contributing to server costs. Giving customers access to servers
located in close proximity to their final clients is a benefit. As a result,
IaaS offers assured service-level understanding in terms of uptime and
execution, and it scales both up and down in response to commands. It
eliminates the need to physically set up and manage the physical servers in
the information centers, as depicted in Figure 13-9.

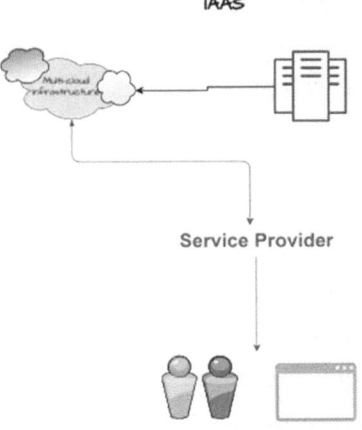

*Figure 13-9.* *Infrastructure as a service*

## Advantages of IaaS

For a small business, IaaS could be more cost-effective than purchasing
and maintaining its own infrastructure. It's possible that new applications
are using an associate degree IaaS supplier instead of testing the
infrastructure.

- Quick recovery from disasters and continuity
- Quicker scaling

# Conclusion

Blockchain is very popular among people because it's decentralized
and lets us trade directly with each other. But most people only think of
Bitcoin when they hear about blockchain. Blockchain can be used in lots
of different ways, not just for Bitcoin. It's good at changing how things work

in regular businesses because it's decentralized, it keeps things going even if some parts fail, it keeps things private, and it's easy to check everything that's happened. In this research paper, the research we have done is about blockchain and web assistance and how blockchain in connected to the web service and how important it is in our daily use of applications. As blockchain is a grad it platform where everything can be protected and is will be very hard for hackers to go through the system as if any changes is done every member in that block needs to grant the permission of the changed done. Although, there might be numerous escapes and restricts in shrewd agreement dialects, numerous inventive programs might be a little tough to execute right now but its growth is so much and being used everywhere, people are not caring about the limitation cause mostly it consist of benefits.

# CHAPTER 14

# Future Trends and Challenges in Supply Chain Technology

*Dr. Imran Ali, Assistant Professor, Noida Institute of Engineering and Technology, Greater Noida, India.*

*Dr. Mohammad Naushad, Associate Professor, College of Business Administration, Prince Sattam Bin Abdulaziz University, Al-Kharj, Saudi Arabia.*

New digital technologies are highly accepted and adopted by both manufacturing and service organizations. Intensity of competition is increasing day by day due to the urge for high profit, more market share, and market leadership. The supply chain is one of the important dimensions to focus upon to make an organization competitive and responsive. New digital technologies improve the supply chain efficiency and make the organization more resilient. The enabling technologies of the supply chain such as blockchain and IoT will make the supply chain more efficient. This chapter intends to distinguish between traditional and modern supply chains and examine the role of new digital technologies to make the supply chain more efficient.

# Role of the Digital Supply Chain

The digital supply chain (DSC) is a customer-focused platform that gathers and makes the most of real-time data coming from a range of sources. In order to have optimal performance and reduced risk, the digital supply chain enables demand stimulation, sensing, matching, and management. The foundation of the DSC is web-enabled capabilities. A lot of supply chains combine IT-enabled and paper-based procedures. In order to fully utilize connectivity, system integration, and the information-producing capabilities of "smart" components, a true DSC goes far beyond this hybrid model.

Worldwide, supply chains are involved in everything from the procurement of raw materials to the direct distribution of goods to consumers. However, because of their intricate structure, every link in the supply chain needs to work correctly for shipments to arrive by the deadline. Digital supply chains can help with this. Digital supply chains make use of digital technologies to collect large amounts of data generated at every stage of the process. Data analytics is then used to make sure logistics experts have the knowledge and tools necessary to efficiently plan, manage, and strategize supply chains. A digital supply chain is one that uses data analytics and digital technologies to inform decisions, maximize efficiency, and react rapidly to conditions that change. Fundamentally, data generated by current supply networks, which are kept in data warehouses and examined to provide useful insights, powers digital supply chains. In the upcoming years, there is anticipated growth in digital supply chains. For example, the value of the worldwide digital supply chain market is expected to expand by more than three times to $13.7 billion by 2030 from the current 2020 estimation of $3.9 billion.

Conventional supply chains depend on products and services moving in a straight line from the point of material sourcing through manufacturing, distribution, and finally point of sale. Regrettably, because every stage in the supply chain depends on the one before it, delays in one can lead to expensive delays in other steps. Each step essentially entails a planning and assessment process that is easily disrupted. Traditional supply chains are frequently hindered by an insufficient amount of actionable information, whereas digital supply chains are strengthened by a constant flow of big data in real time that permits more effectively managed logistics and transportation. Businesses that are dedicated to supply chain execution excellence should already be implementing a digital strategy. This includes optimizing all available supply chain assets, controlling costs at every stage, and delivering goods to customers on schedule and in accordance with specifications. One noteworthy finding from McKinsey's report is that there isn't yet a "Toyota way" for the digital supply chain that other companies can use as a model. Businesses might be prone to becoming mired in a single process or metric. Alternatively, the project might become overly dependent on IT, fail to find a strong business partner, and never progress past the pilot stage. Others have trouble getting money and hiring the right people to lead the digitization process.

The two primary enablers required for the conversion to a digital supply chain are the environment and capabilities. The company needs to strengthen its digitization capabilities (refer to the chapter on capability building), which typically necessitates the selective hiring of individuals with specialized skills. The second crucial prerequisite is the creation of a two-speed architecture or organization. This suggests that while the organization and IT landscape are being established, an innovation environment with a start-up mentality needs to be established. This "incubator" must provide state-of-the-art IT systems (a two-speed architecture independent of current legacy systems) along with a high degree of organizational freedom and flexibility to enable rapid cycles of solution development, testing, and deployment. Implementing a pilot program quickly is essential to get business input on suitability and impact. See Figure 14-1.

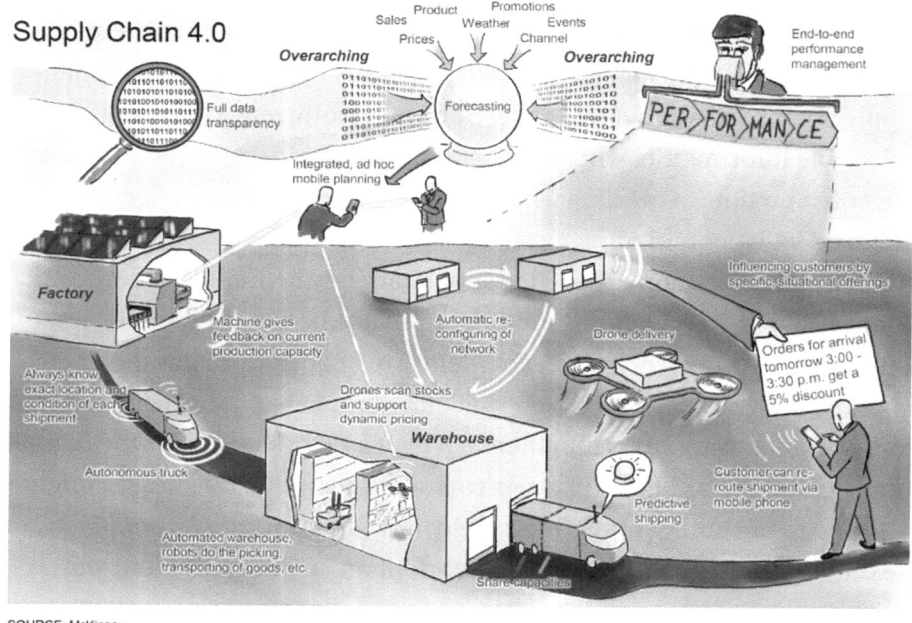

SOURCE: McKinsey

***Figure 14-1.*** *Supply chain 4.0*

A supply chain is the system that businesses and their suppliers use to produce and distribute a particular good. It stands for the actions required to provide or offering a good or service to clients. The supply chain operations reference (SCOR) model optimizes the supply chain decisions. The Supply Chain Council claims that the SCOR model can be used to help manage different phases of supply chain management. Plan, source, make, deliver, and return are the different phases of digital supply chain. Supply chain management is an important procedure since Enhanced supply chains will result in reduced expenses and quicker cycles of production. But the conventional supply chain lacks certain qualities that are necessary in the worlds of today's and tomorrow's business prerequisites. The conventional supply chain is made up of a sequence of mainly isolated, identifiable steps. As more and more businesses understand the impact of digitization on their corporate performance and, consequently, their competitiveness, they should support and participate in these initiatives. This circumstance reduces the possibilities for responding by undermining the ability of diverse supply chain operations to collaborate effectively and efficiently and by raising the likelihood of problems developing later on. A wide range of businesses from various industries are making significant investments in digitalizing their supply chains and business processes. Consider significant logistics service providers like DHL, which track and report on developments that may affect the logistics sector going forward. Gati Limited, Mahindra Logistics, and Delhivery are augmenting their supply chain capabilities. Their logistics service provider making an investment in a digital mobility. Strong cargo-operating airlines like Emirates, Lufthansa, and Turkish Airline are growing their paperless e-freight services with data cleansing for clients.

The conventional supply chain depends on a combination of paper-based and electronic processes records and paperwork. Organizational silos that are resistant to change are frequently used to illustrate organizational structures. Open communication of information can result in less-than-ideal performance. Conversely, the digital supply chain has the potential to make widespread information accessibility, excellent teamwork, and communication across digital platforms, leading to improved dependability and flexibility and efficiency.

Digital supply chains are made up of the systems (hardware, software, and communication networks) that facilitate communication between geographically dispersed businesses and coordinate the actions of supply chain partners. These tasks involve purchasing, producing, transporting, storing, and selling goods. Digitalization has the power to change supply chains by increasing the value, accessibility, and affordability of services.

Therefore, in order for digital technologies to open up new supply chain opportunities, a different viewpoint is required. Businesses should rethink their supply chains as a digital supply network that connects talent, information, and financial flows in addition to the actual flows of goods and services. In a broad sense, all resources—including people, data, and supplies, materials, and products—must be transported throughout the extended enterprise.

# Characteristics of Digital Supply Chain

The majority of globally prosperous enterprises possess exceptional supply chains, and some even contend that the rivalry between organizations stems from the competition between their supply chains. For example, Woodworths and Coles, Australia's two biggest supermarket chains, are in direct competition with their international chains when it comes to high agility, better service, and cost productivity. An additional illustration of this can be found in the supply chain for the iPad, where the device's semiconductors are produced in three different nations, assembly is carried out in a different nation, monitors are imported from a different group of nations, and design and branding are completed in the United States, home of Apple Inc. Supply chains are changing and becoming more innovative.

The speed of delivery of goods is essential for suppliers as well as digital supply chain participants. Organizations want the stock delivered as soon as possible, but those employees at digital supply chains desire to be able to move more quickly. One of a DSC's most crucial pillars will be its capacity to respond swiftly to demand, as businesses search for innovative techniques for speedy product delivery. As an example, Amazon (Prime Air) and Google (Project Wing) have both conducted delivery drone tests of systems to deliver parcels to clients in 30 minutes or less in order to break the mysterious delivery obstacle.

Supply chain digitalization suggests the requirement for operational flexibility and ease of adaptation to shifting conditions. This outlines how to respond to issues in supply chains rather than how goods are delivered. For instance, the political unrest in Syria, natural catastrophes like earthquakes, or the Ebola outbreak can be terrible. However, anticipating such occurrences or taking appropriate action and responding quickly and effectively can be managed seamlessly through digital supply chain.

The world has become smaller as a result of the Internet. Businesses must swiftly deliver goods and services to every corner of the globe. This means that in order for organizations to ensure a local response in addition to delivery, they must have a truly global supply chain. It will be inefficient to have a product shipped all the way from Europe to the United States at the precise moment it is needed if that product is made in Europe and is in demand in the United States. It would need a significant amount of time and possible financial loss. Consequently, DSC provides a means of creating efficient global hubs to supply goods and services locally rather than transporting them across the globe for a single order.

Technological enablers of the new generation offer intelligent products with sufficient processing power to allow for autonomous decision-making and self-learning using predefined algorithms. This feature, which enables better decision making, automated execution, and supports operational innovations, is included in DSC.

A DSC offers the tools to guarantee that the inventory on hand is enough—not too much—to satisfy demand. With the aid of numerous sensors and other cutting-edge technologies, DSC improves warehouse management efficiency and continuously tracks stock levels. Even though consumer behavior is changing quickly, supply and demand must always be met. Orders can be placed by customers at any time and from any location, so inventory control should be done in real time. It is not necessary to maintain the same level of inventory at each distribution center. To make well-informed decisions, it actually means anticipating future demand for goods and services as well as purchasing trends. These resources are made available by DSC for advanced analytics.

Supply chains can be scaled up or down based on the required conditions that frequently cause organizations to struggle greatly. When traditional supply networks are combined with digitization, scalability is less of a concern. This makes process duplication and optimization easier; and the detection of mistakes and anomalies easier too.

A crucial component of DSCs is excellence, which keeps DSCs open to improvement. It seems like new technologies are entering the world quicker than ever before. To maintain its competitiveness and guarantee supply chain excellence, a DSC should constantly be searching for fresh approaches to integrate these innovations into operations. The innovations of today will eventually become the idle, dead technologies of tomorrow. Examples include the transition from black and white to smart TVs in television technology or the use of smart glasses in warehouse management instead of paper and pen for efficient picking. Innovation is the driving force behind the inevitable change of technologies. A commercial enterprise that hasn't changed in thousands of years is built on information. DSC enforces preventative measures in order to avert possible disruptions. This can be achieved not only by troubleshooting but also by conducting research to find latent issues beforehand. To coordinate these issues, a significant amount of knowledge and preparation are required. A DSC provides operational intelligence, an efficient analytics framework, and proactive solutions to anticipate problems before they arise in order to satisfy digitally savvy customers.

The environment is somewhat impacted by supply chains. Inadequate attention to the environment by a DSC could cause business disruption for a variety of reasons, including bad press, environmental regulations, and public awareness. It is a difficult task to find a traditional supply chain that incorporates eco-friendly practices at every level. The capabilities of environmentally friendly processes can be expanded by next-generation DSCs.

# New Digital Technology in Supply Chain

Digital supply chains have been created and are continuing to grow as a result of the quick development of IT technologies. You can customize a good or service with the aid of digital supply chains. Additionally, it enables adaptation to customer needs and the reduction of price of transporting goods through a logistics chain. Managers require access to real-time supply chain data in order to make informed decisions. Businesses will be able to gather, examine, compile, and decipher current, high-quality data with the aid of digital technologies. Robotics, automation, and forecasting—all innovations that will supersede conventional supply chain management—will be built using this data. Therefore, some of the popular new digital technologies in supply chain are discussed in detail.

## Drone Technology

Ever pondered how your internet orders arrive so quickly? Drones—well, soon-to-be drones—may be the solution! The logistics and supply chain sectors are undergoing a revolution thanks to those tiny unmanned aerial vehicles. Drones have revolutionized the industry and are transforming the way we conduct business, from carrying goods to giving real-time inventory information. But there are still some obstacles to be solved, especially with regard to last-mile deliveries and FAA regulations. To fully utilize drones for timely and effective mile deliveries, these adjustments are required.

In response to worries about security and safety in air traffic systems, the Federal Aviation Administration (FAA) has put restrictions on the use of drones into effect. Drones, however, can increase productivity on the production line by giving real-time information on inventory, raw materials, and completed goods, according to research. This may result in lower costs, modified production procedures, and new shipping routes.

Customers are happier and orders are more accurate for businesses that use unmanned aerial systems (UAS) in their supply chain operations. More precisely and quickly than before, they can now deliver goods, particularly in the final mile. It is important to note, though, that UAS must abide by FAA regulations and should not be used on factory floors.

Precise margins, careful handling, and total transparency are necessary in the complex and vital pharmaceutical supply chain. Pharmaceutical companies may suffer significant financial losses if these priorities are not met. To reduce these risks and improve supply chain performance, executives should give infrastructure and technology investments top priority. Sensitive cargo transportation necessitates a highly customized logistics system that can satisfy strict specifications, offer total visibility, and adhere to strict regulations. Businesses all across the world are utilizing the cutting-edge technology of drone logistics to make sure these demands are met. The pharmaceutical supply chain is undergoing a rapid transformation due to this emerging field, resulting in a delivery system that is more efficient, dependable, and timely. Businesses can increase supply chain visibility, expedite operations, and shorten delivery times by utilizing drone technology.

The timely delivery of pharmaceuticals while adhering to stringent transportation regulations presents special challenges for the pharmaceutical industry. Pharmaceutical deliveries, in contrast to other packages, necessitate precise scheduling and careful planning, which makes it challenging for conventional logistics systems to handle. Drone delivery services give businesses a dependable and effective system by removing many of the obstacles associated with pharmaceutical delivery. Imagine a world in which unmanned aerial systems deliver your online orders to your doorstep in a matter of hours rather than days. Drone technology is making this a reality rather than just a dream. Furthermore, you can be certain that your packages will arrive safely and without misplaced items because of FAA regulations.

# Warehouse Robotics

Usually, warehouse robots are used for a single task, like automatically selecting items from shelves. These were strict tasks in the past, with little opportunity for customization. Artificial intelligence, computer vision, and machine learning have made warehouse robotics capable of dynamic task performance and environment adaptation. Automation of every warehouse task is still a long way off with robotic technology. When humans and robots collaborate, businesses can still experience significant cost savings and performance gains. Modern warehouses are being forced to seriously consider using robotics due to technological advancements and an increasingly competitive business landscape. Warehouse robots are now essential to smooth warehouse operations due to their increased productivity, accuracy, and operational efficiency. They are no longer just nice-to-have accessories. All warehouse automations enhance the value of warehousing operations by automating the completion of tedious, repetitive tasks, freeing up human workers to concentrate on more difficult jobs.

# Machine Learning

Traditionally, business intelligence has focused on generating insights from historical data, such as sales from the previous week, overtime from the previous month, and trends from the previous quarter. While those realizations remain valuable, they are insufficient today. In many sectors today, a level of business agility that would have made headlines 20 years ago is the bare minimum required to survive.

Contrarily, supply chain management that makes use of machine learning's predictive powers assists buyers and suppliers in anticipating changes and remaining resilient in the face of significant disruptions. Demand, delivery, customer behavior, and forward and reverse supply flow can all be forecasted at a high level and at a granular level using machine learning technology, which can process and analyze data from every layer of an enterprise. The fundamental ideas of machine learning are well suited to offer previously unavailable insights into enhancing supply chain management performance. Machine learning, which combines the best aspects of supervised, unsupervised, and reinforcement learning, is showing itself to be a very useful technology that is constantly looking for the critical elements that have the biggest impact on supply chain performance. Since all of the endpoints listed in the taxonomy below are solely derivable from algorithmic reasoning, algorithms are guaranteed to scale across an international organization.

# Internet of Things

Imagine an e-commerce company's warehouse that manages several thousand products. The warehouse uses information from its Internet of Things (IoT) devices to track the quantity of each product automatically. When the stock drops below a predetermined level, the devices automatically raise an alert or place an order to replenish the stock. That is only one of the numerous changes that IoT can bring about in logistics and supply chain management. A few businesses that have effectively utilized the IoT include Amazon, Volvo, and Nissan Motor Company. Volvo tracks the components of its cars from multiple nations and the delivery of those vehicles to its customers around the world using an IoT supply chain. Nissan connects its various industrial facilities via an IoT supply chain. By scanning the QR code on packages, Amazon's fleet of IoT-enabled robots has been managing warehouse operations. For a business to expand, supply chain management must leverage the Internet of Things. Supply chains are not as robust as one might have thought, as the COVID-19 pandemic and the subsequent global geopolitical events have shown. There is a greater chance of disruptions when goods move farther and touch more people. IoT can assist businesses in handling such extraordinary circumstances in such a case.

# AR and VR Technology in Supply Chain

The success of any organization depends heavily on supply chain management in the quickly changing business environment of today. Sustaining competitiveness and satisfying customer demands require the supply chain's flow of information and goods to be effectively managed and optimized. With the development of technology, augmented reality (AR) and virtual reality (VR) have become potent instruments that can completely change the way this industry conducts training and visualization. Supply chain visualization is the process of representing intricate logistical operations—such as inventory management, transportation, and warehousing—in a clear, understandable way. Historically, 2D computer-aided design models or static diagrams have been used for this. These approaches can give a basic understanding of the supply chain, but they frequently fall short of capturing the system's dynamic nature and practical complexity. Here's where AR and VR become useful. While VR creates a fully immersive virtual environment, AR overlays virtual elements onto real-world objects to integrate digital information into the real-world environment. These technologies present special chances to improve training and supply chain visualization. Supply chain experts can visualize and engage with the supply chain in real-time with AR, giving them a comprehensive understanding of the whole process.

# Challenges in Managing Digital Supply Chain

It is the goal of every manager and business owner to think that staff members are enthusiastic about changes. Regretfully, things aren't always like this. Any link in the supply chain may be the source of resistance to change. This increases the difficulty of the system's implementation process. Early on, you might discover that major obstacles to a successful implementation are institutional knowledge gaps and resistance to using the new system effectively and giving up control. Integrating current systems into a single, global system is one of the primary implementation challenges of supply chain digitization. A multitude of planning, production, and data management applications comprise many traditional supply chain systems. Put differently, there's no global software catalog that unites these disparate systems under a single roof. As a result, digitization becomes challenging because it must interact with multiple systems. As a result, it splits up into fragments instead of being a cohesive system. Ineffective integration causes a number of issues, such as poor user experience and ineffective company coordination. For supply chain digitization to be successful, real-time data sharing, collaboration, and communication at every level of the chain are required. Data can be accessed at various points in the digital supply chain. It also makes it easier and faster to upload and share that data. By doing this, the lengthy wait times associated with traditional supply chains are eliminated for data review and system-wide communication. But without appropriate planning, preparation, and intervention, effective communication, coordination, and good visibility are not things that will just happen in the organization. If this isn't done, there may be breakdowns, bottlenecks, and supply chain disruptions.

# Conclusion

The digitization of the supply chain is a quickly expanding trend that has the power to completely change how businesses run. A digital supply chain has many advantages, including enhanced sustainability, better decision-making, and increased efficiency. But businesses also need to be cognizant of the difficulties that come with it, like integration, data security, integration costs, and resistance to change. Through careful consideration of these obstacles and collaboration with knowledgeable partners, businesses can effectively adopt a digital supply chain and enjoy enhanced productivity, heightened competitiveness, and an improved future. Businesses that adopt this trend will be well-positioned to meet the challenges of a market that is changing quickly and propel success in the years to come.

The academic and professional community of logistics and supply chain management considers the digitalization of the supply chain to be a strategically important topic. There are still a number of organizational, technological, and strategic obstacles that must be addressed to ensure the DSC's successful implementation. The development of emergent research on technology adoption and its effects on the supply chain is imperative. Additionally, it is critical to investigate new DSC directions, DSC configurations, the role of customer-supplier integration, the contribution of fresh project management techniques and skills, and the development of an integrated DSC performance measurement tool. In order to furnish a thorough comprehension of the concerns associated with DSC, forthcoming studies ought to incorporate diverse theoretical frameworks, such as technology acceptance models.

# CHAPTER 15

# Real-World Applications of Generative AI For Data Augmentation

*Dr. Veena Grover, Professor, Noida Institute of Engineering and Technology, Greater Noida, India.*

*Naved Ahmad, Assistant Professor, Dr. Akhilesh Das Gupta Institute of Technology and Management, New Delhi, India.*

*Ms. Iram Fatima, Assistant Professor, Dr. Akhilesh Das Gupta Institute of Technology and Management, New Delhi, India.*

*Mehtab Alam, Scholar, Jamia Hamdard, New Delhi, India.*

*Dr. Ihtiram Raza Khan, Professor, Jamia Hamdard University, New Delhi, India.*

Generative artificial intelligence (generative AI) is a paradigm within the 'field of artificial intelligence that focuses on creating models and algorithms capable of generating new, 'often realistic, data instances. Generative AI marks a significant advancement in machine learning, going beyond the usual limits. It enables machines not only to learn from existing data but also to create entirely new and realistic data instances. One of the most promising applications of generative AI is data augmentation. This aspect is crucial, effectively generating extra synthetic data to enhance the variety and size of training datasets for machine learning models.

Generating additional data instances through the application of diverse transformations to existing data characterizes data augmentation. This approach proves particularly advantageous in scenarios with limited or imbalanced datasets. In classification tasks, data is often categorized into different groups. However, in imbalanced datasets, one group (the majority class) dominates the data, while another group (the minority class) is significantly underrepresented. Models trained on imbalanced data tend to prioritize accuracy by favoring predictions of the majority class, potentially overlooking the importance of recognizing the minority class, which could be crucial in real-world applications. Nevertheless, conventional data augmentation techniques may require manual intervention and may not consistently yield realistic outcomes. The integration of generative AI addresses these challenges.

# Fundamentals of 'Data Augmentation'

Data augmentation is a technique of artificially increasing the training set by creating modified copies of a dataset using existing data. It includes making minor changes to the dataset or using deep learning to generate new data points" The key principles of data augmentation include:

- **Diversity**: Data augmentation is a technique employed to enhance the variety of the training dataset by generating extra synthetic data instances. The goal is to enable models to build more versatile representations, enhancing their capacity to adapt to variations in real-world data by generating diverse samples through transformations.

- **Robustness:** The objective of data augmentation is to enhance the performance and resilience of a model by expanding the training dataset. This process assists models in forming more generalized representations and boosts their capability to handle variations in real-world data through the generation of diverse samples via transformations.

- **Efficiency**: Utilizing data augmentation can decrease the need for extensive collection and preparation of training data, leading to the quicker development of more precise machine learning models.

- **Cost-effectiveness**: The implementation of data augmentation can lower the operational expenses associated with the collection and labelling of data, a process that can be both laborious and expensive.

- **Data quality**: By mitigating overfitting and enhancing the model's generalization, data augmentation contributes to elevating the quality of the training dataset.

# Generative AI for Data Augmentation

Generative AI is a powerful tool that can generate additional synthetic data to enhance the diversity and size of training datasets for machine learning models [1]. Generative AI has found its stride in various applications, unleashing its creative potential across different domains. In the realm of text generation, AI researchers have begun training generative adversarial networks (GANs) to produce text that resembles human speech. Notable examples, like ChatGPT [3] showcase the remarkable feats of generative AI in generating natural language text. The allure of generative AI is equally evident in image generation, where AI models can create novel images based on natural language prompts. Text-to-image generation protocols, as demonstrated by DALL-E 2 [4], are becoming increasingly sophisticated and hold immense promise for creative industries. Video generation has also found its stride with generative AI, as exemplified by tools like Stable Diffusion. These tools can breathe life into existing videos, seamlessly creating music videos and generating transitions between text prompts.

Generative AI has emerged as a powerful force for transforming multiple industries, and its potential to tackle existing challenges is undeniable. For instance, it holds promise in generating rich academic content, making education more accessible and engaging [2]. On the flip side, the rise of generative AI in creating synthetic data raises ethical concerns related to cybersecurity and data privacy [5]. However, with the advent of transformers and large language models, generative AI is marching forward, enabling more accurate and sophisticated operations [6].

# Understanding Generative AI: Unravelling GANs and VAEs

Generative adversarial networks (GANs) are a class of machine learning frameworks designed by Ian Goodfellow and his colleagues in 2014' [7]. Variational autoencoders (VAEs) are a type of generative model that has gained popularity due to their ability to learn complex data distributions and generate new data samples (Figure 15-1). What sets VAEs apart from GANs is their approach to generating new data [1]. While GANs use an adversarial process with two competing networks, VAEs use a probabilistic framework that models the underlying data distribution. This allows VAEs to generate new data by sampling from the learned distribution, which can be more mathematically rigorous and easier to interpret than the adversarial process used by GANs.

There are scenarios where VAEs can outperform or complement GANs in data augmentation tasks. For instance, VAEs tend to perform better than GANs when the goal is to model the entire data distribution, as VAEs explicitly model this distribution [1]. Moreover, VAEs can complement GANs in tasks where both variability and realism are important. For example, in image data augmentation, a VAE could be used to generate variations of an image and then a GAN could be used to refine these images to make them more realistic.

VAEs offer a powerful and flexible approach to data augmentation. By modelling the underlying data distribution and generating samples with inherent variability, VAEs can enhance the diversity and richness of datasets for machine learning tasks.

The following sections take a closer look at both models.

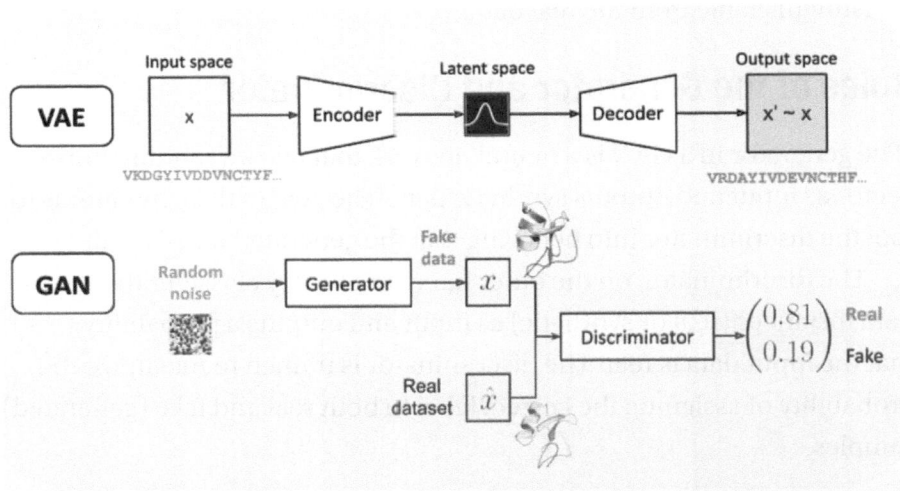

***Figure 15-1.***  *VAE and GAN*

# Generative Adversarial Networks

The foundational principle of GANs lies in its unique adversarial training mechanism, which pits two neural networks against each other in a zero-sum game framework.

The adversarial training mechanism is a novel approach to training generative models. It involves models: a generative model (the generator) and a discriminative model (the discriminator) [7]. The generator's goal is to produce data that the discriminator cannot distinguish from real data, while the discriminator's goal is to accurately classify data as real or fake'.

The generator and discriminator are trained simultaneously. The generator learns to produce more realistic data, while the discriminator becomes better at distinguishing fake data. This creates a dynamic equilibrium, where the generator eventually learns to generate data that is indistinguishable from the real data'.

## Roles of the Generator and Discriminator

'The generator in a GAN is a neural network that takes a random noise vector as input and outputs synthetic data. The goal of the generator is to fool the discriminator into believing that the generated data is real'.

The discriminator, on the other hand, is a binary classifier that takes data instances (real or synthetic) as input and outputs a probability that the input data is real. The discriminator is trained to maximize the probability of assigning the correct label to both real and fake (generated) samples.

## Applications in Data Augmentation

GANs have found significant applications in the field of data augmentation, where they are used to generate synthetic data that can augment existing datasets.

'Data augmentation is a strategy used to increase' the diversity and amount of training data. Traditional data augmentation techniques include transformations like rotation, scaling, and flipping for image data, or synonym replacement for text data. GANs provide a sophisticated approach to data augmentation. They can generate realistic synthetic data that maintains the same underlying distribution as the original data [6]. This makes GANs particularly useful for augmenting datasets in domains where data is scarce or imbalanced.

## Examples of GAN-Generated Data

GANs have been used to generate a wide variety of data for augmentation purposes. In the field of computer vision, GANs have been used to generate synthetic images for tasks like object recognition. 'For instance, a GAN can be trained on a dataset of car images and then used to generate new images of cars in various colors, from different angles, and in different lighting conditions.

In natural language processing, GANs have been used to generate synthetic text data. This can help in augmenting datasets for tasks like sentiment analysis or machine translation.

In healthcare, GANs have been used to generate synthetic medical imaging data, which can help improve the performance of diagnostic algorithms [6].

# Variational Autoencoders

VAEs are based on the principles of probabilistic modelling and the encoding-decoding mechanism. They are a type of autoencoder, a 'neural network used for data compression and' noise reduction. However, unlike traditional autoencoders, VAEs are designed to model the underlying probability distribution of the input data [1].

# Probabilistic Modeling and the Encoding-Decoding Mechanism

'The architecture of a VAE consists of two main parts: an encoder and a decoder. The encoder takes the input data and encodes it into a lower-dimensional latent space. This latent space is modelled as a Gaussian distribution, with the encoder outputting the mean and variance parameters of this distribution' [1].

'The decoder then takes a sample from the latent space and decodes it back into the original data space. The goal of the VAE is to optimize the parameters of the encoder and decoder such that the reconstructed data is as close as possible to the original data, while also ensuring that the latent space has good properties (i.e., follows a Gaussian distribution).'

# Role in Data Augmentation

VAEs have a significant role in data augmentation due to their ability to generate new data samples that inherently contain variability.

In data augmentation, VAEs 'can generate new samples by sampling from the latent space' [1]. Because the latent space is a continuous distribution, small changes in the latent variables can result in realistic variations in the generated samples [1]. This makes VAEs particularly useful for tasks where variability in the data is important.

For example, in image data augmentation, a VAE can generate new images that contain variations in lighting, pose, or color. In text data augmentation, a VAE can generate new sentences that maintain the same semantic meaning but have different syntactic structures.

# Image Data Augmentation

Generative AI has revolutionized the field of image data augmentation, providing innovative techniques to enhance and diversify image datasets (Figure 15-2). It has emerged as a powerful tool in image augmentation, including the generation of new training samples from the available data to increase the performance and robustness of the models. It includes a number of techniques. We discuss style transfer, super-resolution and conditional GANs in the subsections below.

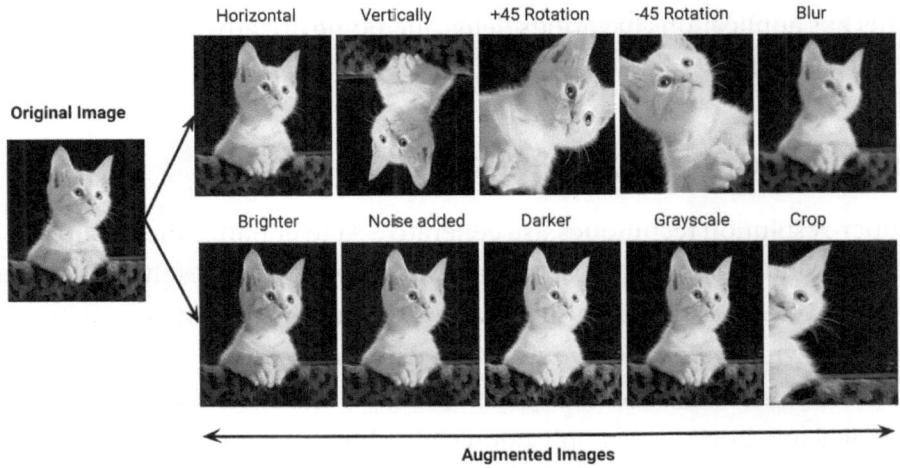

*Figure 15-2.*  *Original vs augmented images*

# Style Transfer

Style transfer is a technique that leverages generative AI to modify the style of an image while preserving its content [6]. This is achieved by separating the style and content features in an image using a pretrained convolutional neural network. 'The style of one image is then applied to the content of another, resulting in a new image that combines the content of the original image with the style of the second.

Style transfer has been used to augment image data by imparting diverse artistic styles, thereby increasing the diversity of the dataset. This has applications in various fields, including art, advertising, and entertainment.

# Super-Resolution Techniques

Super-resolution techniques use generative AI to enhance the quality of low-resolution images. These techniques generate high-resolution images from low-resolution inputs, improving the image quality and detail [6].

Super-resolution techniques have significant relevance in real-world applications. For instance, they can be used to enhance satellite imagery, medical imaging, or any application where high-quality images are required but only low-resolution images are available.

# Conditional GANs for Image Synthesis

Conditional 'generative adversarial networks' (cGANs) are a variant of GANs that can generate images based on specific criteria. Unlike traditional GANs, which generate data from random noise, cGANs take additional input from a label or condition [6].

cGANs have been employed in various industries to generate images that meet specific requirements. For example, in the fashion industry, cGANs can be used to generate images of clothing items in different colors or styles. In the automotive industry, cGANs can generate images of cars in different colors, from different angles, or under different lighting conditions.

# Top Three Data Augmentation Libraries in Python for Images

Several Python libraries provide augmentation functionality for machine learning tasks. Here are some of the most popular ones for image processing: Keras, albumentations, and imgaug.

## Keras ImageDataGenerator

This library provides an easy-to-use interface for image augmentation in Keras, a popular deep-learning framework. It supports a variety of augmentation techniques such as rotation, shearing, zooming, and flipping.

```
from keras.preprocessing.image import ImageDataGenerator

datagen = ImageDataGenerator(
    rotation_range=20,
    width_shift_range=0.1,
    height_shift_range=0.1,
    shear_range=0.2,
    zoom_range=0.2,
    horizontal_flip=True,
    fill_mode='nearest'
)
```

# Albumentations

This powerful and flexible library for image augmentation supports a wide range of transformations. It can be used with various deep learning frameworks and supports both CPU and GPU acceleration.

```
import albumentations as A

transform = A.Compose([
    A.Rotate(limit=20),
    A.RandomCrop(width=256, height=256),
    A.HorizontalFlip(),
    A.RandomBrightnessContrast(),
    A.Normalize()
])
```

# Imgaug

This library provides a flexible and extensible platform for image augmentation with support for various transformations. It also supports batching and multiprocessing for the efficient processing of large datasets.

```
import imgaug.augmenters as iaa

seq = iaa.Sequential([
    iaa.Rotate((0, 45)),
    iaa.Flipud(),
    iaa.GaussianBlur(sigma=(0, 3.0)),
    iaa.AdditiveGaussianNoise(scale=(0, 0.1*255)),
    iaa.Crop(px=(0, 16))
])
```

These libraries provide a variety of augmentation techniques that can be combined and customized to suit the specific needs of your machine-learning task.

# Benefits and Outcomes

The use of generative AI for image data augmentation offers numerous benefits. By generating synthetic images, generative AI can increase the size and diversity of image datasets, which can improve the performance and robustness of machine learning models.

Moreover, generative AI can generate images that are difficult or expensive to collect in the real world, such as rare animal species for wildlife image classification, or specific weather conditions for autonomous driving systems.

# Text Data Augmentation

Generative AI has brought about a paradigm shift in the field of text data augmentation, providing innovative techniques to enhance and diversify text datasets.

## Language Modeling'

Language modeling is a fundamental task in natural language processing (NLP) that involves predicting the next word in a sentence (Figure 15-3)'. Generative AI, particularly deep learning models like Transformers, has significantly improved the performance of language models [5]. These models can generate diverse and coherent text, which can be used to augment text datasets.

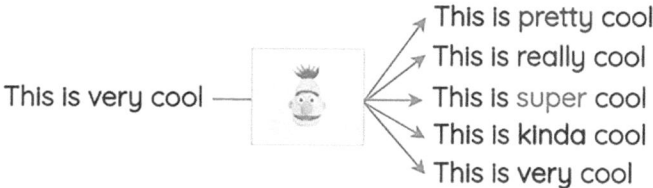

**Figure 15-3.** *Language modeling*

# Paraphrasing

Paraphrasing is another technique where generative AI has made a substantial impact [2]. It involves generating a sentence that conveys the same meaning as the original sentence but with different wording. Paraphrasing can increase the diversity of text datasets, thereby improving the robustness of NLP models.

These techniques contribute significantly to natural language understanding (NLU), a branch of NLP that focuses on machine understanding and generation of human languages. By generating diverse linguistic constructs, generative AI helps in creating more comprehensive and robust NLU models.

# Text-to-Image Synthesis

Generative AI has also made strides in bridging the gap between textual and visual domains through text-to-image synthesis. This involves generating an image from a textual description, which is a complex task requiring an understanding of both language and visual elements [5].

Text-to-image synthesis has valuable applications in various fields. For instance, in e-commerce, it can be used to generate images of products based on textual descriptions. In the entertainment industry, it can be used to create visual scenes based on script descriptions.

# Top Three Data Augmentation Libraries in Python for Text

Data augmentation for text can help improve the performance of NLP models by increasing the diversity and quantity of training data. The following are some popular Python libraries for text augmentation:

- NLpaug

- TextBlob

- AugLy

## NLPaug

This library provides various text augmentation techniques, including word embeddings, back translation, and contextual word embeddings. It supports various NLP tasks such as text classification, sentiment analysis, and machine translation.

```python
import nlpaug.augmenter.word as naw

aug = naw.ContextualWordEmbsAug(
    model_path='bert-base-uncased',
    action="substitute"
)
augmented_text = aug.augment("This is a sentence.")
```

## TextBlob

This library provides simple and easy-to-use methods for text augmentation, including synonym replacement and random word insertion.

```python
from textblob import Word

word = Word("happy")
augmented_word = word.synsets[0].lemma_names()[0]
```

## AugLy

This library provides a range of augmentation techniques for various data types, including text. It supports spelling correction, keyboard noise, and random word deletion techniques.

```
from augly.text.augmenters import (
    apply_levenshtein_distance,
    apply_typo,
    insert_punctuation_chars,
)

augmented_text = apply_levenshtein_distance("This is a
sentence.")
```

These libraries provide a variety of text augmentation techniques that can be used to generate additional training data for NLP tasks, improving the model's ability to generalize and perform well on unseen data. It is important to note that text augmentation can sometimes lead to semantically incorrect or nonsensical text, so it is important to carefully evaluate the generated data before using it for training.

# Benefits and Outcomes

The use of generative AI in text data augmentation offers numerous benefits. It can generate diverse and novel text, helping to overcome the limitations of manual data collection and annotation. This can lead to improved performance of NLP tasks like sentiment analysis, text classification, and summarization [5][2]. Moreover, generative AI can generate text data that is difficult or expensive to collect in the real world, such as multilingual text or text with specific stylistic properties.

# Audio Data Augmentation

Generative AI has brought about a paradigm shift in the field of audio data augmentation, providing innovative techniques to enhance and diversify audio datasets.

## Pitch Modulation

Pitch modulation is a technique that leverages generative AI to modify the pitch of an audio signal without affecting its temporal structure. This is achieved by transforming the frequency components of the signal. Pitch modulation can increase the diversity of audio datasets, thereby improving the robustness of audio processing models.

## Genre Transformation

Genre transformation involves changing the genre of a music piece using generative AI. This is a complex task that requires an understanding of both the musical structure and the characteristics of different genres. Genre transformation can be used to augment music datasets by generating diverse versions of the same music piece.

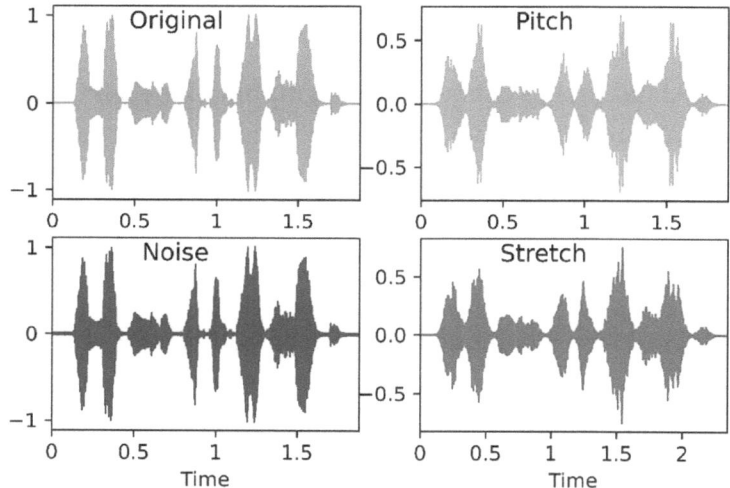

***Figure 15-4.*** *Pitch modulation*

# Speech Synthesis

Speech synthesis, or text-to-speech, is a task that involves generating human-like speech from text. Generative AI, particularly deep learning models, have significantly improved the performance of speech synthesis systems, enabling them to generate speech that is almost indistinguishable from human speech.

# Speech Recognition

Speech recognition involves transcribing spoken language into written text. Generative AI can contribute to speech recognition by generating diverse linguistic constructs, which can be used to train more robust speech recognition models [4].

Generative AI has been employed in various industries for speech synthesis and recognition tasks. For example, in the telecommunication industry, it can be used for voice assistants and automated customer service. In the healthcare industry, it can be used for transcribing medical dictations.

# Benefits and Outcomes

The use of generative AI in audio data augmentation offers numerous benefits. It can generate diverse and novel audio data, helping to overcome the limitations of manual data collection and annotation. This can lead to improved performance of audio processing tasks like speech recognition and audio classification [4].

# Challenges and Ethical Considerations: Navigating the Generative Landscape

As we navigate the generative landscape, it's crucial to address the challenges and ethical considerations associated with generative AI.

## Bias, Fairness, and Transparency
### Bias in Generative AI-Generated Data

Generative AI models learn from the data they are trained on. If the data contains biases, the models can inadvertently learn and perpetuate these biases [4]. For instance, a language model trained on biased text data might generate text that reflects these biases. Similarly, an image generation model might produce images that favor certain demographics over others if the training data is skewed in that direction.

Bias in AI-generated data can have serious implications, leading to unfair outcomes and perpetuating existing inequalities. It's therefore crucial to examine and address bias in AI-generated data (Figure 15-5).

# Enhancing Fairness and Transparency

Strategies to enhance fairness and transparency in data augmentation processes include:

- **Diverse and representative training data:** Ensuring that the training data is diverse and representative can help reduce bias. This includes considering various demographics and scenarios in the data [7].

- **Bias mitigation techniques:** Techniques such as reweighting the training data, modifying the learning algorithm, or post-processing the model's predictions can help mitigate bias [4].

- **Transparency in AI systems:** Making AI systems transparent can help users understand how the AI makes decisions [4]. This includes explaining the AI's workings in understandable terms and disclosing the nature and source of the training data.

***Figure 15-5.*** *Enhancing fairness and transparency*

# Responsible Development and Deployment

## Ethical Considerations

Deploying generative AI in real-world applications comes with several ethical considerations. These include privacy concerns (as AI models can generate realistic personal data), the potential for misuse (such as generating deep fakes or disinformation), and the impact on jobs and society [4][7].

## Responsible Development and Deployment

Frameworks for responsible development and deployment of generative AI should consider the following:

- **Privacy-preserving techniques:** Techniques such as differential privacy can help protect an individual's data during the AI training process.

- **Robustness and security measures:** Implementing measures to ensure the robustness and security of AI systems can help prevent misuse.

- **Regulations and guidelines:** Adhering to regulations and guidelines can help ensure the ethical use of AI. This includes respecting data protection laws and following ethical AI guidelines set by reputable organizations.

- **Stakeholder involvement:** Involving stakeholders, including the public, in AI development and deployment decisions can help consider societal impact and ensure the technology is used responsibly [3][7].

In conclusion, navigating the generative landscape requires addressing these challenges and ethical considerations. By doing so, we can harness the power of generative AI in a way that is fair, transparent, and beneficial for all.

# Future Directions and Emerging Trends
## Advancements in Generative Models

Generative AI has been a transformative force in the realm of artificial intelligence, with models like GANs and VAEs leading the charge. However, the field is continually evolving, with ongoing research and advancements pushing the boundaries of what's possible with generative AI [7].

## Ongoing Research and Advancements

Beyond GANs and VAEs, several other generative models are gaining traction in the AI community. One such model is the **transformer-based generative model**. Originally designed for natural language processing tasks, transformer models have shown remarkable results in generative tasks due to their ability to model long-range dependencies in data. Models like GPT-3 and BERT are prime examples of transformer-based generative models that have achieved state-of-the-art results in text generation and understanding.

Another promising area of research is **self-supervised learning**, where models learn to generate data by predicting parts of the input data from other parts. This approach has been successful in various domains, including computer vision and natural language processing, and is seen as a step towards more general and flexible AI systems [4].

## Novel Architectures and Techniques on the Horizon

Looking ahead, we can expect to see more novel architectures and techniques that enhance the capabilities of generative AI. For instance, **neuro-symbolic generative models** are an emerging area of research that combines neural networks with symbolic reasoning to generate data. This approach holds promise for tasks that require both high-level reasoning and low-level perception.

Another exciting development is the advent of **generative models for graph data**. Graphs are a common data structure in many domains, including social networks, biological networks, and the World Wide Web. Generative models for graph data can help in understanding the structure of these networks and predicting future interactions [4].

The field of generative AI is ripe with opportunities for innovation and advancement. As we continue to explore and refine these technologies, we can look forward to a future where AI not only learns from data but also creates it.

# Future Directions and Emerging Trends in Interdisciplinary Applications of Generative AI

In the ever-evolving landscape of artificial intelligence, generative AI stands at the forefront, captivating researchers, practitioners, and industries alike. As we explore the future directions and emerging trends in the interdisciplinary applications of generative AI, a profound shift becomes apparent, one that transcends traditional boundaries and fosters unprecedented collaboration between disparate domains.

The amalgamation of generative AI with diverse disciplines heralds a new era of innovation and problem-solving. In this section, we delve into the burgeoning trends that signify the transformative potential of generative AI in bridging gaps between traditionally siloed fields (Figure 15-6).

# Bridging Divides: Generative AI in Interdisciplinary Applications

## Healthcare and Biotechnology Integration

The intersection of generative AI with healthcare and biotechnology holds immense promise. Advanced generative models are now being utilized to unravel the complexities of genomic data, facilitating the identification of potential biomarkers and accelerating drug discovery processes. The ability of generative AI to simulate molecular structures opens doors to novel drug design, ushering in a paradigm shift in personalized medicine [3]

Moreover, generative AI finds application in medical imaging, where it aids in generating high-resolution images, contributing to more accurate diagnostics. The fusion of medical expertise and generative AI prowess is poised to redefine healthcare practices, offering tailored solutions for individual patient needs.

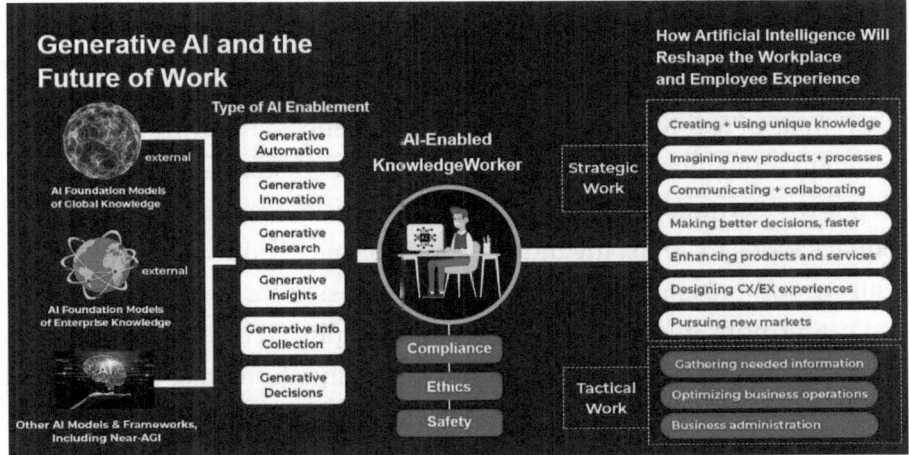

*Figure 15-6.*  *Generative AI*

## Urban Planning and Smart Cities

The advent of smart cities necessitates a holistic approach to urban planning, and generative AI emerges as a key facilitator in this realm. By analyzing vast datasets encompassing urban infrastructure, traffic patterns, and environmental variables, generative AI models can generate predictive simulations for city planners. This interdisciplinary synergy enhances the efficiency of urban systems, optimizing resource allocation and mitigating potential challenges.

Generative AI, coupled with geographic information systems (GIS), enables the creation of dynamic models that respond to changing urban dynamics. This collaborative approach not only fosters sustainable urban development but also addresses the intricate challenges posed by the growing urbanization trend.

## Education and Cognitive Science

The marriage of generative AI with education and cognitive science holds the promise of revolutionizing learning experiences. Tailoring educational content to individual learning styles, generative AI facilitates the creation of adaptive learning platforms. These platforms leverage real-time feedback loops to adjust the difficulty and format of educational materials, ensuring optimal engagement and comprehension for each student.

Furthermore, generative AI models are employed in simulating cognitive processes, offering valuable insights into human cognition. This interdisciplinary synergy paves the way for a deeper understanding of learning mechanisms, influencing the design of more effective educational interventions and cognitive therapies.

# Navigating the Horizon: Emerging Trends in Generative AI Applications

- **Explainable generative models:** As generative AI permeates various domains, the demand for transparency and interpretability becomes paramount. The evolution of explainable generative models represents a pivotal trend, addressing concerns related to the "black-box" nature of complex AI systems. Researchers are actively developing models that not only generate high-quality outputs but also provide insights into the underlying decision-making processes, fostering trust and accountability.

- **Human-AI collaboration:** The synergy between human intelligence and generative AI capabilities is emerging as a cornerstone in interdisciplinary applications [3]. Rather than replacing human expertise, generative AI is increasingly seen as a collaborative tool augmenting human creativity and problem-solving skills. This trend is particularly evident in creative industries, where generative AI collaborates with artists, writers, and designers to push the boundaries of creative expression.

- **Ethical AI integration:** In the pursuit of interdisciplinary applications, the ethical implications of generative AI cannot be overlooked. An emerging trend involves the integration of ethical considerations into the development and deployment of generative AI models. Initiatives are underway to ensure fairness, accountability, and transparency, preventing inadvertent biases and ethical dilemmas in diverse applications, from healthcare to urban planning.

# The Road Ahead: Nurturing Collaborative Innovation

Generative AI's foray into interdisciplinary applications marks a paradigmatic shift from isolated endeavors to collaborative innovation. The synthesis of expertise from traditionally distinct domains not only accelerates progress but also introduces novel perspectives and approaches to problem-solving.

As we navigate the future directions of generative AI in interdisciplinary applications, fostering a collaborative ecosystem becomes imperative. Interdisciplinary research centers and collaborative initiatives must be nurtured, providing a fertile ground for the convergence of diverse talents. The synergy between computer scientists, domain experts, and ethicists is the crucible in which the future of generative AI applications will be forged.

The intersection of generative AI with diverse fields is not merely a convergence of technologies; it is a fusion of ideas, perspectives, and possibilities. The journey into interdisciplinary applications is an exciting expedition, unveiling new horizons and redefining the boundaries of what generative AI can achieve [3][4].

# Call to Action

As we conclude this exploration into the transformative realms of generative AI for data augmentation, the journey forward beckons researchers, developers, and practitioners to embark on a sustained exploration of its potential. A proactive stance in research, development, and responsible implementation is not merely encouraged but essential for unlocking the full promise of generative AI.

This call to action is a collective plea to the scientific community, industry stakeholders, and policymakers to actively engage in shaping the trajectory of generative AI. The potential is immense, and with responsible research, development, and implementation, generative AI can not only redefine the landscape of machine learning but also contribute positively to societal progress. As the torch passes to those ready to explore the next frontiers, the transformative power of generative AI for data augmentation becomes a beacon guiding the way to a future where innovation, ethical considerations, and the following responsible practices coalesce to shape a new era in artificial intelligence:

- **Innovative architectures and techniques**: Encourage researchers to delve into innovative architectures and techniques that push the boundaries of generative AI beyond existing models. Novel approaches could uncover new avenues for enhancing the generative capabilities of models.

- **Interdisciplinary collaboration**: Recognize the interdisciplinary nature of generative AI's impact and encourage collaborative efforts across domains. Interactions with experts from diverse fields may reveal novel applications and innovative solutions.

- **Ethical considerations**: Emphasize the integration of ethical considerations into the fabric of generative AI research and development. Responsible AI practices, transparency, and bias mitigation strategies should be integral components of the research agenda.

- **Mitigate bias and fairness**: Highlight the importance of addressing biases in generative AI-generated data. Researchers should actively work on developing strategies to mitigate biases and ensure fairness in data augmentation processes.

- **Transparent deployment**: Advocate for transparent deployment practices. As generative AI models find their way into real-world applications, transparency in deployment is crucial for building trust and ensuring responsible use.

- **Continuous monitoring and improvement**: The importance of continuous monitoring and improvement in generative AI models. Given the evolving nature of the field, it is essential to establish frameworks for ongoing evaluation, addressing challenges, and incorporating advancements.

# Conclusion

In navigating the expansive realms of generative artificial intelligence and its application in data augmentation, a tapestry of innovation and transformative potential unfolds. As we reflect on the key findings, it is evident that generative AI stands at the nexus of reshaping the landscape of machine learning, particularly in the augmentation of datasets across image, text, and audio domains.

**CHAPTER 16**

# Revolutionizing Supply Chain Dynamics: A Comprehensive Case Analysis of Synergies in Blockchain, IoT, and AI Integration

*Sonal Trivedi, VIT Business School, VIT Bhopal University, Bhopal-Indore Highway, Kothrikalan, Sehore Madhya Pradesh, India.*

*Balamurugan Balusamy, Associate Dean - Student Engagement, Shiv Nadar Institute of Eminence, Delhi-NCR, India.*

*Veena Grover, School of Management, Noida Institute of Engineering and Technology, Greater Nodia, India.*

© The Editor(s) (if applicable) and The Author(s),
under exclusive license to APress Media, LLC, part of Springer Nature 2024
Dr. V. Grover et al. (eds.), *Blockchain, IoT, and AI Technologies for Supply Chain Management*,
https://doi.org/10.1007/979-8-8688-0315-4_16

This chapter embraces an inclusive case study analysis of synergistic assimilation of AI, IoT, and blockchain technologies in the context of supply chain management. The convergence of these cutting-edge technologies has the prospective to revolutionize traditional process of supply chain, enhancing transparency, traceability, and overall efficiency.

The case study focuses on a real-world implementation within a global supply chain network, where IoT devices are strategically deployed to collect real-time data on inventory levels, transportation conditions, and product status. AI algorithms are used to process and analyze the collected data, enabling predictive analytics for demand forecasting, inventory optimization, and route optimization. Simultaneously, blockchain technology is employed to establish an immutable and transparent ledger, ensuring data integrity and traceability throughout the supply chain.

The findings highlight the tangible benefits of this integrated approach, including reduced operational costs, minimized errors, and enhanced responsiveness to dynamic market demands. The study also explores the challenges encountered during the implementation phase, such as interoperability issues and data privacy concerns, and proposes strategies to address these challenges.

This research contributes to the existing body of knowledge by offering practical insights into the successful integration of IoT, AI, and blockchain in supply chain management. It serves as a valuable reference for industry practitioners, policymakers, and researchers seeking to harness the full potential of emerging technologies for optimizing supply chain processes in an increasingly complex and interconnected global marketplace.

# Introduction

The modern global economy is characterized by its intricate web of interconnected supply chains, where the efficient movement of goods and information is paramount for success (Sandybayev and Bvepfepfe,

2022). Traditional supply chain management faces challenges such as opacity, inefficiency, and the inability to adapt rapidly to dynamic market conditions. To address these issues, organizations are increasingly turning to emerging technologies, including the IoT, AI, and blockchain, as catalysts for transformative change (Sodhi et al., 2022). This research paper delves into a compelling case study that examines the convergence of these technologies in a real-world supply chain context, exploring their collective impact on transparency, traceability, and overall operational efficiency.

The assimilation of IoT, AI, and blockchain represents a paradigm shift in how supply chains are managed and optimized. The Internet of Things facilitates the seamless connection of physical devices, enabling real-time data collection and communication across the supply chain (Gohil and Thakker, 2021). Artificial intelligence, with its advanced analytics capabilities, processes this influx of data to derive actionable insights, from demand forecasting to route optimization. Concurrently, blockchain technology offers a decentralized and secure ledger, ensuring the immutability and transparency of transactional data (Wamba and Queiroz, 2020). This research focuses on unraveling the intricacies of this integrated approach, offering a deep understanding of its implications for supply chain dynamics.

The case study chosen for analysis is set within a global supply chain network, offering a practical examination of the implementation and impact of IoT, AI, and blockchain integration. By leveraging real-time data, predictive analytics, and an immutable ledger, this integrated system aims to enhance supply chain visibility, reduce operational costs, and improve overall responsiveness to market fluctuations. The study not only highlights the potential benefits but also addresses the challenges encountered during the implementation phase, providing valuable insights for organizations looking to navigate the complex landscape of integrating these transformative technologies into their supply chain strategies.

# Purpose Behind the Research

This research was designed to address the overarching question, how does the integrated application of AI, IoT, and blockchain technologies in a global supply chain milieu contribute to enhanced transparency, traceability, and overall operational efficiency? By focusing on a case study, the research aims to investigate synergistic effects of these technologies on supply chain processes, shedding insight on the practical implications, problems found during execution, and the resultant improvements in areas such as demand forecasting, inventory management, and response to market dynamics. The research question delves into the multifaceted impact of this convergence, providing a comprehensive understanding of its transformative potential and guiding organizations in their pursuit of optimized and resilient SCM strategies in the digital era.

The research methodology employed for the study on the integrated usage of IoT, AI, and blockchain in SCM involves a mixed-methods approach, using quantitative and qualitative research techniques to provide a comprehensive perceptive of the complex interactions and outcomes.

Firstly, a detailed literature review is carried out to set up the theoretical groundwork and discover key concepts, challenges, and best practices related to IoT, AI, and blockchain in SCM. This phase lays the groundwork for the subsequent empirical investigation.

The primary research data is gathered through a case study analysis of a real-world implementation of the integrated technology solution within a global supply chain network. Qualitative data collection methods include in-depth interviews with key stakeholders involved in the implementation, such as supply chain managers, IT specialists, and decision-makers. These interviews aim to capture insights into the decision-making processes, challenges faced, and perceived impacts on operational efficiency and transparency.

# Literature Review

The literature review on the integrated application of IoT, AI, and blockchain in supply chain management reveals a landscape characterized by theoretical enthusiasm and practical challenges. While existing research highlights the potential benefits of enhanced visibility, transparency, and efficiency, a critical analysis points to a gap between theoretical frameworks and activities which are useful for people in real world. Concerns over privacy and data security, particularly in the context of blockchain, persist, necessitating a careful balance between technological advancements and regulatory compliance (Min, Zacharia, and Smith, 2019). Furthermore, the absence of standardized evaluation frameworks impedes the comparability of findings across studies, calling for a more systematic approach to assessing the impact of these technologies on supply chain performance. Addressing these gaps is crucial for advancing research and facilitating the effective implementation of integrated solutions, emphasizing the need for a more holistic and practical understanding of the implications of IoT, AI, and blockchain in modern supply chain management.

# Theoretical Framework

The integration of AI, IoT, and blockchain technologies in supply chain management has emerged as a transformative paradigm, promising unprecedented levels of efficiency, transparency, and security. AI, with its advanced analytics and machine learning capabilities, plays a pivotal role in optimizing supply chain processes by analyzing vast amounts of data to predict demand, optimize inventory levels, and enhance decision-making. By leveraging AI algorithms, supply chain managers can gain valuable insights, enabling them to make informed and proactive decisions to streamline operations and reduce costs (Arunmozhi et al., 2022).

In conjunction with AI, the IoT introduces a new dimension to SCM by facilitating immediate monitoring and tracking of physical assets. IoT devices, such as sensors and RFID tags, provide a continuous stream of data throughout the supply chain, offering visibility into the movement and condition of goods. This real-time data allows for better tracking of shipments, identification of potential bottlenecks, and swift responses to unforeseen events. The seamless connectivity facilitated by IoT enhances the overall agility of the supply chain, enabling businesses to respond dynamically to changing market conditions and customer demands (Bhargava et al., 2022).

Blockchain technology serves as a foundational pillar in securing and validating transactions within the supply chain. Its decentralized and immutable nature ensures transparency, traceability, and trust among participants in the supply chain ecosystem. By implementing blockchain, supply chain stakeholders can establish a single, shared ledger which records every movement and transaction. This not only reduces the risk of fraud and errors but also enhances the authenticity of product information. The combination of AI for data analytics, IoT for real-time tracking, and blockchain for secure transactions establishes a robust theoretical framework for revolutionizing supply chain management, fostering efficiency, and instilling a new level of confidence in the global supply chain network (Xu et al., 2021).

# Key Concepts

The IoT is a major concept in supply chain management, representing the interrelated arrangement of physical devices entrenched with software, sensors, and other technologies. These devices, ranging from RFID tags to heat sensors, facilitate immediate data capture and communication all over the complete supply chain. By seamlessly integrating IoT devices, supply chain stakeholders gain unprecedented visibility into the movement, condition, and status of goods, allowing for efficient monitoring and optimization of logistics processes. This enhanced connectivity facilitates proactive decision-making, reducing lead times, minimizing disruptions, and ultimately optimizing the overall supply chain performance (Reyes, Visich, and Jaska, 2020).

AI is another crucial concept reshaping supply chain dynamics. AI encompasses advanced data analytics, machine learning, and predictive modeling capabilities that empower supply chain managers to make informed decisions. Through the analysis of massive datasets, AI algorithms can forecast patterns of demand, optimize stock levels, and enhance forecasting accuracy. AI-driven systems also facilitate dynamic routing and scheduling, adapting to changing conditions and improving the efficiency of transportation and logistics operations. By harnessing the power of AI, supply chain management becomes more adaptive, responsive, and capable of addressing the complexities inherent in modern global supply networks (Rodriguez-Espindola et al., 2020).

Blockchain technology introduces a foundational shift in the way transactions and information are managed within the supply chain. The concept of a decentralized and distributed ledger ensures transparency, traceability, and security in supply chain processes. Each transaction, from the production of goods to their delivery, is recorded in a tamper-resistant and immutable blockchain. In addition to reducing fraud risk, this also increases the level of trust between supply chain actors. Blockchain's smart contract functionality further automates and enforces predefined agreements, streamlining processes such as payments, contract fulfillment, and compliance. Together, these key concepts of IoT, AI, and blockchain form an integrated framework that revolutionizes supply chain management, fostering agility, transparency, and resilience in an increasingly complex global marketplace (Girija et al., 2023).

# Challenges with IoT, AI, and Blockchain in SCM

The adoption IoT technologies in SCM introduces several challenges that organizations must navigate. One significant hurdle is the sheer amount of data generated by IoT devices. Managing and analyzing the massive influx of immediate facts from sensors and devices throughout the supply chain can overwhelm traditional IT infrastructure. This challenge extends to issues of data quality, security, and privacy. Ensuring the veracity and privacy of IoT-generated facts is crucial to avert unauthorized access or exploitation, particularly as the interconnected nature of IoT devices increases the attack surface for potential cybersecurity threats (Javaid et al., 2021).

AI implementation in SCM faces challenges related to data quality and availability. AI algorithms heavily depend on accurate and diverse datasets for training and decision-making. Inconsistent or biased data can lead to flawed predictions and suboptimal decision outcomes. Additionally, the scarcity of skilled AI talent within organizations poses a challenge. Developing, deploying, and maintaining AI systems requires expertise that is often in high demand. Organizations must invest in training or hiring skilled professionals to successfully leverage AI in their supply chain processes (Wamba and Queiroz, 2020).

The execution of blockchain in SCM presents challenges related to scalability, interoperability, and regulatory frameworks. Blockchain networks can face scalability issues when handling a large number of transactions, impacting the speed and efficiency of the supply chain. Ensuring interoperability between different blockchain platforms and legacy systems is also a concern, as supply chain ecosystems involve numerous stakeholders using diverse technologies. Moreover, the lack of standardized regulatory frameworks poses challenges in terms of legal acceptance and compliance. Harmonizing regulations across borders and industries is essential to realizing the full prospective of blockchain in increasing precision and trust in the supply chain. Addressing these challenges requires a collaborative effort among industry stakeholders, technology providers, and policymakers.

# Best practices for IoT, AI, and Blockchain in SCM

Implementing best practices in the integration of IoT in SCM involves a strategic approach to data management and security. Organizations should prioritize defining clear objectives for their IoT implementation, ensuring that the deployment aligns with specific business goals. Leveraging IoT data for actionable insights requires robust data governance practices, including data quality assurance, standardized formats, and protocols for secure data sharing. Additionally, organizations should invest in cybersecurity measures to shield the veracity and discretion of IoT-generated data, implementing encryption, secure access controls, and continuous monitoring to mitigate potential threats (Min, Zacharia, and Smith, 2019).

In the realm of AI in supply chain management, best practices revolve around developing a well-defined strategy for AI adoption. It's important for organizations to assess their current data infrastructure and make sure it's capable of supporting AI applications. Investing in data quality and establishing a data governance framework are critical steps to ensure that AI algorithms receive accurate and unbiased data for training and decision-making. Furthermore, organizations should prioritize employee training and change management initiatives to cultivate a workforce that can effectively collaborate with AI systems, fostering a culture that embraces innovation and continuous improvement (Sandybayev and Bvepfepfe, 2022).

When implementing blockchain in supply chain management, best practices involve collaboration and standardization. Organizations should work collaboratively with supply chain partners to define common standards and protocols for data exchange and smart contracts.

This collaborative approach helps in creating a unified and interoperable blockchain network across the supply chain ecosystem. Transparency is a key principle in blockchain, and organizations should design their blockchain networks with considerations for data visibility and accessibility while ensuring that sensitive information is appropriately protected through cryptographic techniques. Finally, staying informed about evolving regulatory frameworks and compliance requirements is crucial to ensure that blockchain implementations adhere to legal standards and foster trust among all contributors in the supply chain (Xu et al., 2021).

From the above discussion, it can be said that the best practices outlined for the assimilation of IoT, AI, and blockchain in SCM reflect a comprehensive approach to addressing the complexities inherent in modern supply chain ecosystems. The emphasis on strategic alignment with business objectives, robust data governance, and cybersecurity measures in IoT implementation underscores the importance of a well-defined and secure data infrastructure. Similarly, the focus on AI strategy, including data quality assurance and employee training, acknowledges the need for a holistic approach that considers both technological and organizational aspects. The best practices for blockchain highlight the significance of collaboration, standardization, and regulatory awareness, emphasizing the importance of transparency and data protection. However, it is crucial to recognize that the successful implementation of these technologies requires not only technical proficiency but also a commitment to ongoing adaptation and collaboration within a rapidly evolving landscape. Continuous monitoring of emerging challenges and advancements will be essential to ensuring the long-term effectiveness of these best practices in enhancing supply chain efficiency and resilience.

# Case Study: Synergistic Assimilation of AI, IoT, and Blockchain Technologies in SCM

Walmart has been at the vanguard of adopting innovative technologies to enhance its supply chain processes (Zawish et al., 2022). The company deployed IoT devices, such as RFID tags, on its products to track inventory in real time. These devices generate a continuous stream of data, providing insights into product movement, shelf availability, and customer preferences (Mehta et al., 2021). AI algorithms process this vast amount of data to optimize inventory levels, improve demand forecasting, and streamline logistics.

In addition to IoT and AI, Walmart also employed blockchain technology to augment the lucidity and traceability of its supply chain (Charles, Emrouznejad, and Gherman, 2023). The decentralized and tamper-resistant character of blockchain ensures the integrity of transactions and product information throughout the supply chain. This lucidity is crucial in addressing issues like food safety as it allows for rapid traceability in the event of product recalls.

Moreover, Walmart has recently submitted a patent application for a shopping cart equipped with a biometric handle. This innovative feature aims to monitor customers' stress levels, pulse rate, and temperature. Furthermore, the carts are designed to alert store associates when assistance may be required by the customers.

By integrating IoT, AI, and blockchain, Walmart has achieved significant improvements in operational efficiency, reduced stockouts, and enhanced customer satisfaction (Tan et al., 2018). This real-life example serves as a rich case study for examining the holistic impact of these technologies on a global scale, offering practical insights and lessons for other organizations seeking to leverage similar technological integrations in their supply chain management strategies.

# Description

Walmart's execution of IoT, AI, and blockchain technologies in its SCM exemplifies a comprehensive and successful assimilation of cutting-edge solutions to enhance operational efficiency and transparency (Gohil and Thakker, 2021). In the sphere of the Internet of Things, Walmart employed RFID tags on its products, enabling the real-time tracking of inventory and facilitating data-driven decision-making. These IoT devices continually generate data streams, providing invaluable insights into product movement, stock levels, and consumer preferences (Kshetri, 2018). AI algorithms analyze this wealth of data, offering the ability to optimize inventory management, refine demand forecasting, and streamline logistics operations (Alalwi et al., 2021). Walmart's use of AI in conjunction with IoT showcases the transformative potential of data-driven decision-making in a large-scale retail supply chain.

In parallel, Walmart employed blockchain technology to fortify the lucidity and traceability of its supply chain (Bhandari, 2018) By utilizing a tamper-resistant and decentralized ledger, blockchain makes certain the veracity of transactional data and product information at every stage of the supply chain (Hassija et al., 2020). This transparency is particularly vital in addressing food safety concerns because it allows for rapid and precise traceability of products in the event of recalls. The integration of blockchain technology inserts an additional layer of security and faith, demonstrating the applicability of distributed ledger technology in enhancing supply chain visibility and reliability ( Xu et al., 2021).

Walmart's success in harmonizing IoT, AI, and blockchain technologies underscores the transformative impact of an integrated approach (Subramanian et al., 2020). The implementation has led to tangible improvements in operational efficiency, reducing stockouts and enhancing overall customer satisfaction (Vishwakarma and Singh, 2022). This real-life example stands as a robust case study, offering valuable insights for organizations seeking to navigate the complexities of integrating these technologies into their supply chain management strategies. The Walmart case demonstrates the practical benefits and challenges associated with such technological convergence on a global scale.

# Analysis

While Walmart's execution of IoT, AI, and blockchain technologies in its SCM is widely lauded for its success, a critical analysis reveals several nuanced aspects. One notable aspect is the significant upfront investment required for such an integration. While the benefits of enhanced efficiency and transparency are evident, not all organizations may have the financial resources or infrastructure to undertake a similar technological transformation. This raises questions about the scalability and accessibility of these advanced technologies for businesses of varying sizes.

Additionally, the case of Walmart highlights the critical role of data governance and privacy in IoT and AI applications. The huge volume of data produced by IoT devices must be managed and secured appropriately to mitigate privacy risks. The use of AI algorithms also raises questions about the potential biases in decision-making processes and the need for ethical considerations in deploying these technologies. A critical analysis should delve into how Walmart addresses these issues and the broader ethical implications linked with the use of AI in SCM.

Moreover, the success of Walmart's integration may be influenced by its market dominance and centralized control over its supply chain. Small and medium-sized enterprises (SMEs) may encounter more significant challenges in implementing similar solutions due to resource constraints such as lacking infrastructure, less investment in R & D, less availability of information, and complex supply chain ecosystems. This raises questions about the generalizability of the findings and the adaptability of the integrated approach to diverse organizational contexts.

Despite these considerations, Walmart's case remains a valuable example of how the strategic assimilation of IoT, AI, and blockchain can yield substantial benefits. The critical analysis serves as a reminder for organizations to carefully evaluate their specific contexts, address ethical considerations, and weigh the costs and benefits when considering a similar technological integration in their supply chain management strategies.

# Implication of Study

The study on the integrated usage of IoT, AI, and blockchain in SCM, exemplified by Walmart's case, carries several implications for both academia and industry. Firstly, from an academic perspective, the study underscores the need for more research that bridges the gap between theoretical frameworks and real-world implementations. While theoretical foundations are crucial, a deeper understanding of the practical challenges, contextual nuances, and actual outcomes of integrating these technologies is necessary to notify future studies and contribute to the evolving field of SCM.

In the realm of industry, the study provides actionable insights for organizations considering or undergoing digital transformations in their supply chain processes. The consequences highlight the need for a strategic and multi-faceted approach to tech integration. Businesses need to assess their individual requirements, evaluate the scale and scalability of integrations, and consider the ethical implications of data management and AI decisions. The study also highlights the significance of regulatory compliance, as seen in the case of blockchain, and the need for a well-defined framework that ensures alignment with existing legal standards.

Furthermore, the study's implications extend to technology vendors and solution providers, emphasizing the importance of developing interoperable and scalable technologies. As organizations look to implement integrated solutions similar to Walmart's, technology providers should consider offering flexible and customizable solutions that can adapt to diverse supply chain environments.

Overall, the implications of this study encourage a nuanced and informed approach to the acceptance of IoT, AI, and blockchain in SCM. Organizations and researchers alike can benefit from understanding the complexities, challenges, and potential benefits of such integrations, fostering a more robust and practical foundation for the ongoing evolution of supply chain technologies.

# Future Research Direction

This study suggests several promising directions for future research:

- **Interdisciplinary studies**: Future research should embrace interdisciplinary approaches, bringing together insights from fields such as information technology, operations management, ethics, and legal studies. This would enable a more comprehensive understanding of the multifaceted implications of integrating IoT, AI, and blockchain in supply chains.

- **Socio-economic impacts**: Explore the broader socio-economic impact of these integrated technologies. Investigate how the widespread adoption of these technologies influences employment dynamics, economic structures, and societal well-being. Understanding the social implications is crucial for responsible and sustainable technological advancements in supply chain management.

- **Standardization and framework development**:
  Address the existing gap in standardized frameworks
  for evaluating the performance and impact of
  integrated solutions. Future research should focus
  on developing standardized metrics and evaluation
  criteria, facilitating cross-study comparisons and
  providing a foundation for best practices in the
  integration of IoT, AI, and blockchain technologies.

- **Ethical considerations**: Delve deeper into the ethical
  considerations associated with the use of AI in decision-
  making processes within supply chains. Explore ways
  to mitigate biases, ensure fairness, and establish
  ethical guidelines for the responsible execution of AI
  technologies in diverse supply chain contexts.

- **Small and medium-sized enterprises (SMEs)**:
  Investigate the challenges and opportunities faced
  by small and medium-sized enterprises in adopting
  integrated IoT, AI, and blockchain solutions. Given
  that SMEs may encounter resource constraints,
  understanding how these technologies can be adapted
  and scaled down to suit their operational contexts is
  crucial for inclusive technological advancements in
  supply chain management.

- **Long-term sustainability**: Assess the long-term
  sustainability of integrated solutions. Investigate how
  these technologies evolve over time, considering
  factors such as technological obsolescence,
  maintenance costs, and environmental impacts. This
  long-term perspective is essential for organizations
  making substantial investments in technology
  integration.

- **Global supply chain resilience**: Explore the role of
  integrated technologies in enhancing global supply
  chain resilience, especially in the face of unforeseen
  disruptions such as pandemics, geopolitical events, and
  natural disasters. Investigate how these technologies
  contribute to adaptability and agility in supply chain
  responses to ensure continuity in operations.

By focusing on these future research directions, scholars and
practitioners can contribute to a more nuanced understanding of the
implications and potential advancements associated with the assimilation
of IoT, AI, and blockchain in SCM. This knowledge will be invaluable in
guiding organizations towards effective and responsible implementation
strategies in an ever-evolving technological landscape.

# Conclusion

The case study in this chapter underscores the transformative potential
of technology convergence in enhancing transparency, efficiency, and
responsiveness within global supply chains. While the case highlights
notable successes, a critical analysis reveals challenges related to
scalability, data governance, and ethical considerations. The implications
of the study suggest a need for interdisciplinary research, standardized
evaluation frameworks, and a deeper exploration of the socio-economic
impacts of these technologies. As organizations embark on digital
transformations, lessons from this study emphasize the importance of
strategic planning, ethical awareness, and a holistic understanding of the
complexities involved in integrating IoT, AI, and blockchain technologies
into contemporary supply chain practices. The following are key
takeaways:

- AI optimizes supply chain processes through data analysis, demand prediction, and decision-making. AI best practices include a well-defined strategy, data quality assurance, and employee training.

- IoT enables real-time tracking, monitoring, and improved agility in responding to market changes. IoT best practices involve clear objectives, robust data governance, and cybersecurity measures.

- Blockchain ensures transparency, traceability, and trust in supply chain transactions. Blockchain best practices emphasize collaboration, standardization, and regulatory awareness.

# Correction to: AI-Enabled Supply Chain Planning and Execution: A Pathway to Sustainability

## Correction to:

**Chapter 5 in: Grover, D. V., Balusamy, D. B. B., Milanova, D. M., Felix, D.A.Y. (eds) Blockchain, IoT, and AI Technologies for Supply Chain Management**
**https://doi.org/10.1007/979-8-8688-0315-4_5**

This chapter was inadvertently published with affiliations and names clubbed for Vaishnavi Gadi, Pathik Govani. It is now corrected to reflect individual affiliations.

---

The updated version of this chapter can be found at
https://doi.org/10.1007/979-8-8688-0315-4_5

# References

## Chapter 1

- Kozlenkova, Irina et al. "The Role of Marketing Channels in Supply Chain Management," *Journal of Retailing*. 91 (4): 586–609. doi:10.1016/j. jretai.2015.03.003. 2015.

- Ghiani, G., Laporte, G., and Musmanno, R. "Introduction to Logistics Systems Planning and Control" [PDF]. doi:10.1002/0470014040. 2003.

- Handfield, R. B. and Nichols, E. L. *Introduction to Supply Chain Management*. Retrieved from www.worldcat.org/title/301072523. 1998.

- Mentzer, J. T., DeWitt, W., Keebler, J. S., Min, S., Nix, N. W., Smith, C. D., and Zacharia, Z. G. "Defining supply chain management," *Journal of Business Logistics*, 22(2), 1–25. 2001. doi:10.1002/j.2158-1592.2001.tb00001.x

- La Londe, B. J. and Masters, J. M. "Emerging logistics strategies," *International Journal of Physical Distribution & Logistics Management*, 24(7), 35–47. doi:10.1108/09600039410070975. 1994.

- Enver Yücesan, *Competitive Supply Chains a Value-Based Management Perspective*, PALGRAVE MACMILLAN, ISBN 9780230515673. 2007.

- Blanchard, D. *Supply Chain Management Best Practices* (2nd ed.; D. Blanchard, Ed.) [PDF]. doi:10.1002/9781119202912. 2010.

# Chapter 2

[1] Wisner, J. D., Tan, K. C., and Leong, K. *Principles of Supply Chain Management: A Balanced Approach.* South-Western, Cengage Learning. 2021.

[2] Charles, V., Emrouznejad, A., and Gherman, T. "A Critical Analysis of the Integration of Blockchain and artificial Intelligence for Supply Chain," *Annals of Operations Research*, 1-41. 2023.

[3] Fernando, J., James, M., and Kvilhaug, S. Supply Chain Management (SCM) [Online]. *Investopedia.* www.investopedia.com/terms/s/scm.asp [Accessed September 25, 2023]. 2022.

[4] Mridul Bhardwaj "What Are the Five Basic Components of a Supply Chain Management System?" [Online]. *IIM Udaipur Chronicles.* www.iimu.ac.in/blog/what-are-the-five-basic-components-of-a-supply-chain-management-system/ [Accessed September 25, 2023]. 2020.

[5]   Habib, G., Sharma, S., Ibrahim, S., Ahmad, I.,
      Qureshi, S., and Ishfaq, M. "Blockchain Technology:
      Benefits, Challenges, Applications, and Integration
      of Blockchain Technology with Cloud Computing,"
      *Future Internet, 14*(11), 341. 2022.

[6]   Dutta, P., Choi, T. M., Somani, S., and Butala,
      R. "Blockchain Technology in Supply Chain
      Operations: Applications, Challenges, and
      Research Opportunities," *Transportation Research
      Part E: Logistics and Transportation Review, 142,*
      102067. 2020.

[7]   Khanfar, A. A., Iranmanesh, M., Ghobakhloo,
      M., Senali, M. G., and Fathi, M. "Applications
      of Blockchain Technology in Sustainable
      Manufacturing and Supply Chain Management:
      A Systematic Review," *Sustainability, 13*(14),
      7870. 2021.

[8]   Goyat, R., Kumar, G., Rai, M. K., and Saha,
      R. "Implications of Blockchain Technology in
      Supply Chain Management," *Journal of System and
      Management Sciences, 9*(3), 92-103. 2019.

[9]   Blossey, G., Eisenhardt, J., and Hahn, G. "Blockchain
      Technology in Supply Chain Management: An
      Application Perspective." 2019.

[10]  Park, A. and Li, H. "The Effect of Blockchain
      Technology on Supply Chain Sustainability
      Performances." *Sustainability, 13*(4), 1726. 2021.

REFERENCES

[11]   Bhaveshkumar N. Pasi, Subhash K. Mahajan, and Santosh B. Rane. "Smart Supply Chain Management: A Perspective of Industry 4.0," *International Journal of Advanced Science and Technology*, Vol. 29, No. 5, 3016 – 3030. 2020.

[12]   Y.P. Tsang, T. Yang, Z.S. Chen, C.H. Wu, and K.H. Tan. "How Is Extended Reality Bridging Human and Cyber-Physical Systems in the IoT-Empowered Logistics and Supply Chain Management?", *Internet of Things* [Accessed September 27, 2022].

[13]   Ozden Ozkanlısoy and E. Akkartal. "Digital Transformation in Supply Chains: Current Applications, Contributions and Challenges," *Business and Management Studies: An International Journal*, vol. 9, no. 1, Mar. 2021, 32-55.

[14]   T. E. Evtodieva, D. V. Chernova, N. V. Ivanova, and J. Wirth. "The Internet of Things: Possibilities of Application in Intelligent Supply Chain Management", *Digital Transformation of the Economy: Challenges, Trends and New Opportunities*, 395–403. 2019.

[15]   Avani Phase and Nalini Mhetre. "Using IoT in Supply Chain Management," *International Journal of Engineering and Techniques* - Volume 4 Issue 2, Mar-Apr 2018.

[16]   Mohamed Abdel-Basset, Gunasekaran Manogaran, and Mai Mohamed. "Internet of Things (IoT) and Its Impact on Supply Chain: A Framework for Building Smart, Secure, and Efficient Systems," *Future Generation Computer System*, Volume 86, 614-628. 2018.

[17]  Serge Legchekov. "IoT for Smarter Supply Chain
      Management and Logistics." www.scnsoft.com/
      blog/iot-scm-and-logistics (accessed Aug
      1, 2022).

[18]  "IoT in Supply Chain and Logistics: Role, Benefits
      and Use Cases," www.rishabhsoft.com/blog/iot-
      in-scm-and-logistics (accessed January 5, 2023)

[19]  Mediavilla, Mario Angos, Fabian Dietrich, and
      Daniel Palm. "Review and Analysis of Artificial
      Intelligence Methods for Demand Forecasting in
      Supply Chain Management," *Procedia CIRP* 107.
      1126-1131. 2022.

[20]  Dash, Rupa, Mark McMurtrey, Carl Rebman,
      and Upendra K. Kar. "Application of Artificial
      Intelligence in Automation of Supply Chain
      Management," *Journal of Strategic Innovation and
      Sustainability* 14, no. 3. 43-53. 2019.

[21]  Rob Neibauer, "AI in Inventory Management:
      Putting AI to Work to Optimize Your Inventory,"
      https://hypersonix.ai/blog/ai-in-inventory-
      management/, April 24, 2023.

[22]  Milan Panchmatia, "Enhancing Supplier
      Relationship Management with an AI Co-Pilot",
      https://comprara.com.au/enhancing-supplier-
      relationship-management-with-an-ai-co-pilot/,
      September 18, 2023.

[23]  Oh, Am-Suk. "Development of a Smart Supply-Chain Management Solution Based on Logistics Standards Utilizing Artificial Intelligence and the Internet of Things," *Journal of Information and Communication Convergence Engineering* 17, no. 3. 2019.

[24]  Soltani, Zhandark Khalife. "The Applications of Artificial Intelligence in Logistics and Supply Chain," *Turkish Journal of Computer and Mathematics Education* (TURCOMAT) 12, no. 13. 4488-4499. 2021.

[25]  Pandian, Dr A. Pasumpon. "Artificial Intelligence Application in Smart Warehousing Environment for Automated Logistics," *Journal of Artificial Intelligence and Capsule Networks* 1, no. 2. 63-72. 2019.

[26]  Abdul-Rahman, Ahmed I., and Corey A. Graves. "Internet of Things Application Using Tethered msp430 to Thingspeak Cloud," In *2016 IEEE Symposium on Service-Oriented System Engineering* (SOSE), 352-357. 2016.

[27]  Wang, M., Wu, Y., Chen, B., and Evans, M. "Blockchain and Supply Chain Management: A New Paradigm for Supply Chain Integration and Collaboration," *Operations and Supply Chain Management: An International Journal, 14*(1), 111-122. 2020.

[28]  Chawla, P., Kumar, A., Nayyar, A., and Naved, M. (Eds.). *Blockchain, IoT, and AI Technologies for Supply Chain Management.* CRC Press. 2023.

[29] Indrakumari, R., Kumar, R. L., Balusamy, B., and Asirvadam, V. S. (Eds.). *Convergence of Blockchain, AI, and IoT: Concepts and Challenges*. CRC Press. 2021.

[30] Balamurugan, B., Poongodi, T., Manu, M. R., Karthikeyan, S., and Sharma, Y. *Convergence of Blockchain, AI and IoT: A Digital Platform*. CRC Press. 2023.

[31] Kaur, A., Singh, G., Kukreja, V., Sharma, S., Singh, S., and Yoon, B. "Adaptation of IoT with Blockchain in Food Supply Chain Management: An Analysis-Based Review in Development, Benefits, and Potential Applications," *Sensors*, *22*(21), 8174. 2022.

[32] Bhat, M. S. and Dubey, S. "An Overview of The Effects of Blockchain Technology in Food Chain Supply: A Case Study on Walmart," *The Online Journal of Distance Education and e-Learning*, *11*(2). 2023.

[33] Jain, K. "Aerospace and Defence the Financial Impact of Covid-19 on the Rolls-Royce Supply Chain," *The Journal of Purdue Undergraduate Research*, *12*(1), 32. 2022.

[34] Clohessy, T. and Clohessy, S. "What's In the Box? Combating Counterfeit Medications in Pharmaceutical Supply Chains with Blockchain Vigilant Information Systems," *Blockchain and Distributed Ledger Technology Use Cases: Applications and Lessons Learned*, 51-68. 2020.

REFERENCES

[35]   Nasrat, L., Zedan, M., Ali, A. A., and Shabib,
       G. "Review on Energy Trading of Community-
       Based Projects Around the World," in *2022 23rd
       International Middle East Power Systems Conference
       (MEPCON)* (pp. 1-8). IEEE. 2022.

[36]   Milkau, U. "International Payments: Current
       Alternatives and Their Drivers." *Journal of Payments
       Strategy & Systems, 13*(3), 201-216. 2019.

[37]   Shahbaz Khan, Abid Haleem, Zafar Husain, Daniel
       Samson, and R. D. Pathak, "Barriers to Blockchain
       Technology Adoption in Supply Chains: The
       Case of India," *Operations Management Research,*
       6:668–683. 2023.

[38]   Pishdar, Mahsa, Ghasemzadeh, Fatemeh,
       Antucheviciene, Jurgita and Saparauskas, Jonas.
       "Internet of Things and Its Challenges in Supply
       Chain Management: A Rough Strength-Relation
       Analysis Method," *E+M Ekonomie a Management.*
       21. 208-222. 10.15240/tul/001/2018-2-014. 2018.

[39]   Feng Zhang, Hao Wang, Lu Zhou, Dequan Xu,
       and Liang Liu, "A Blockchain-Based Security and
       Trust Mechanism for AI-Enabled IIoT Systems,"
       *Future Generation Computer Systems*, volume 146,
       78-85. 2023.

[40]   Sylvia Marak, "Supply Chain Trends for 2023 and
       Beyond." https://www.selecthub.com/supply-
       chain-management/supply-chain-management-
       future-trends/ (Accessed October 6, 2023)

# Chapter 3

- Shri, M.L., Gangadevi, E., Santhi, K., and Chowdhary, C.L. *Hybridization of Blockchain and Cloud Computing: Overcoming Security Issues in IoT*, 1–263. 2023.

- Gupta Paluri, C., and Santhi, K., "Consensus Mechanism of Blockchain for Industrial Internet of Things (IIoT)," *Hybridization of Blockchain and Cloud Computing: Overcoming Security Issues in IoT.* 203–214. 2003.

- Lohia, G. and Santhi, K. "Blockchain-Based Distributed Transactions for Industrial Applications," *Hybridization of Blockchain and Cloud Computing: Overcoming Security Issues in IoT*, 187–202. 2003.

- Santhi, K. and Lawanyashri M. "Performance Evaluation of Transactions in Blockchain Based on Workload Using Queueing Model," *Journal of Green Engineering* Vol 10, Issue 5, 2446-2457. 2020.

- Santhi, K. and Saravanan, R. "Performance Analysis of Cloud Computing Using Series of Queues with Erlang Service," *International Journal Internet Technology and Secured Transactions* 9(1/2), 147-162. 2019.

- Santhi, K. and Saravanan, R. "Performance Analysis of Cloud Computing in Healthcare System Using Tandem Queues," *International Journal of Intelligent Engineering and Systems* 10(4), 256-264. 2017.

- Santhi, K. and Saravanan, R. "Performance Analysis of Cloud Computing Using Batch Queueing Models in Healthcare Systems," *Research Journal of Pharmacy and Technology* 10(10), 3331-3336. 2017.

- Santhi, K. and Saravanan, R. "Performance Analysis of Cloud Computing Bulk Service Using Queueing Models," *International Journal of Applied Engineering Research* 12(7), 6487-6492. 2017.

- Santhi, K. and Saravanan, R. "A Survey on Queueing Models for Cloud Computing," *International Journal of Pharmacy and Technology* 8(2), 3964- 3977. 2016.

- Santhi K. and Patel R. "Sheds: A Simple and Secure Cost Efficient Data Storage in Heterogeneous Multiple Cloud," *International Journal of Pharmacy and Technology,* Vol 8, Issue 4, 26058-26065.

- Santhi K. and Priyadarshini C., "Efficiently Allocating the Virtual Machines in Cloud Environment," *International Journal of Applied Engineering Research,* Vol 9, Issue 3, 887-392.

- Antidham, T. and Aung, Y. N. "Emergency Service for Smart Home System Using Ethereum Blockchain: System and Architecture," In 2019 IEEE International Conference on Pervasive Computing and Communications Workshops (PerCom Workshops). 888-893. March 2019.

- Li, X., Zheng, Z. and Dai, H. N. "When Assistance Computing Meets Blockchain: Challenges and Opportunities," *Journal of Parallel and Distributed Computing,* 150, 1-14. 2021.

- Mohammadzadeh, N., Nogoorani, S. D., and Muñoz-Tapia, J. L. "Invoice Factoring Registration Based on a Public Blockchain," *IEEE Access,* 9, 2422124233. 2021.

- Dai, H. N., Zheng, Z., and Zhang, Y. "Blockchain for Internet of Things: A survey," *IEEE Internet of Things Journal*, 6(5), 8076-8094. 2019.

- Yu, C., Zhang, L., Zhao, W., and Zhang, S. "A Blockchain-Based Service Composition Architecture in Cloud Manufacturing," *International Journal of Computer Integrated Manufacturing*, 33(7), 701-715. 2020.

- Park, J. H., and Park, J. H. "Blockchain Security in Cloud Computing: Use Cases, Challenges, and Solutions," *Symmetry*, 9(8), 164. 2017.

- Lawanyashri, M., Balusamy, B., and Subha, S. "Energy-Aware Hybrid Fruitfly Optimization for Load Balancing in Cloud Environments for EHR Applications," *Informatics in Medicine Unlocked*, 8, 42-50. 2017.

- Lawanya Shri, M., Ganga Devi, E., Balusamy, B., Kadry, S., Misra, S., and Odusami, M. "A Fuzzy Based Hybrid Firefly Optimization Technique for Load Balancing in Cloud Datacenters," In *Innovations in Bio-Inspired Computing and Applications: Proceedings of the 9th International Conference on Innovations in Bio-Inspired Computing and Applications* (IBICA 2018) held in Kochi, India during December 17-19, 2018. 463-473. Springer International Publishing. 2019.

- Shri, M. L., and Gangadevi, E. *Blockchain Technology-Based Industrial Internet of Things: Research Challenges. Hybridization of Blockchain and Cloud Computing*, 61-74. 2023.

- Sujigarasharma, K., Shri, M. L., Gangadevi, E., Dhanaraj, R. K., Narmatha, C., and Balusamy, B. "Detection and Classification of Speech Disorder using FOA-SCNet," In *2023 3rd International Conference on Computing and Information Technology (ICCIT)* (pp. 391-395). IEEE. September 2023.

- Hemalatha, T., Bhuvaneswari, A., Poornima, N., Shubha, B., Santhi, K., Lawanyashri, M., and Mara, G. C. "Secure And Private Data Sharing in CPS E-Health Systems Based on CB-SMO Techniques," *Measurement: Sensors*, *27*, 100787. 2023.

- Hemalatha, T., Sangeetha, K., Rani, K. S. K., Kanimozhi, K. V., Lawanyashri, M., Santhi, K., and Deepalakshmi, R. "CPS in block Chain Smart City Application Based on Distributed Ledger Based Decentralized Technique," *Measurement: Sensors*, *30*, 100906. 2023.

# Chapter 4

[1] A. H. M. Van Waes, "Platform Innovation in Urban Mobility Transitions: The Case of Dockless Bike Sharing," Utrecht University. doi: 10.33540/515. 2021.

[2] V. Albuquerque, M. Sales Dias, and F. Bacao, "Machine Learning Approaches to Bike-Sharing Systems: A Systematic Literature Review," *ISPRS Int. J. Geo-Inf.*, vol. 10, no. 2, 62, doi: 10.3390/ijgi10020062. February 2021.

[3]   Y. Chen, K. He, M. Deveci, and D. Coffman, "Health impacts of bike sharing system – A case study of Shanghai," *J. Transp. Health*, vol. 30, 101611, doi: 10.1016/j.jth.2023.101611. May 2023.

[4]   J. Park, Y. Honda, S. Fujii, and S. E. Kim, "Air Pollution and Public Bike-Sharing System Ridership in the Context of Sustainable Development Goals," *Sustainability*, vol. 14, no. 7, 3861, doi: 10.3390/su14073861. Mar. 2022.

[5]   I. Otero, M. J. Nieuwenhuijsen, and D. Rojas-Rueda, "Health Impacts of Bike Sharing Systems in Europe," *Environ. Int.*, vol. 115, 387–394, doi: 10.1016/j.envint.2018.04.014. June 2018.

[6]   W. Jiang, "Bike Sharing Usage Prediction with Deep Learning: A Survey," *Neural Comput. Appl.*, vol. 34, no. 18, pp. 15369–15385, doi: 10.1007/s00521-022-07380-5. September 2022.

[7]   A. Krishna, A. V, A. Aich, and C. Hegde, "Sales Forecasting of Retail Stores Using Machine Learning Techniques," in *2018 3rd International Conference on Computational Systems and Information Technology for Sustainable Solutions (CSITSS)*, Bengaluru, India: IEEE, 160–166. doi: 10.1109/CSITSS.2018.8768765. December 2018.

[8]   S. V. E, J. Park, and Y. Cho, "Using Data Mining Techniques for Bike Sharing Demand Prediction in Metropolitan City," *Comput. Commun.*, vol. 153, 353–366, doi: 10.1016/j.comcom.2020.02.007. March 2020.

[9]   R. Nair and E. Miller-Hooks, "Equilibrium Network
      Design of Shared-Vehicle Systems," *Eur. J. Oper. Res.*,
      vol. 235, no. 1, 47–61, doi: 10.1016/j.ejor.2013.09.019.
      May 2014.

[10]  K. Kim, "Investigation on the Effects of Weather
      and Calendar Events on Bike-Sharing According
      to the Trip Patterns of Bike Rentals of Stations,"
      *J. Transp. Geogr.*, vol. 66, 309–320, doi: 10.1016/j.
      jtrangeo.2018.01.001. Jan. 2018.

[11]  C. Feng, J. Hillston, and D. Reijsbergen, "Moment-
      Based Availability Prediction for Bike-Sharing
      Systems," *Perform. Eval.*, vol. 117, 58–74, doi:
      10.1016/j.peva.2017.09.004. Dec. 2017.

[12]  S.-H. Lee and H.-C. Ku, "A Dual Attention-Based
      Recurrent Neural Network for Short-Term Bike
      Sharing Usage Demand Prediction," *IEEE Trans.
      Intell. Transp. Syst.*, vol. 24, no. 4, 4621–4630, doi:
      10.1109/TITS.2022.3208087. April 2023.

[13]  N. Gast, G. Massonnet, D. Reijsbergen, and
      M. Tribastone, "Probabilistic Forecasts of
      Bike-Sharing Systems for Journey Planning,"
      in *Proceedings of the 24th ACM International
      on Conference on Information and Knowledge
      Management*, Melbourne Australia: ACM, 703–712.
      doi: 10.1145/2806416.2806569. October 2015.

[14]  J. Corcoran, T. Li, D. Rohde, E. Charles-Edwards,
      and D. Mateo-Babiano, "Spatio-Temporal Patterns
      of a Public Bicycle Sharing Program: The Effect of
      Weather and Calendar Events," *J. Transp. Geogr.*,
      vol. 41, 292–305, doi: 10.1016/j.jtrangeo.2014.09.003.
      December 2014.

[15]  F. Lin, J. Jiang, J. Fan, and S. Wang, "A Stacking Model
      for Variation Prediction of Public Bicycle Traffic
      Flow," *Intell. Data Anal.*, vol. 22, no. 4, 911–933, doi:
      10.3233/IDA-173443. June 2018.

[16]  J. Schuijbroek, R. C. Hampshire, and W.-J. Van
      Hoeve, "Inventory Rebalancing and Vehicle Routing
      in Bike Sharing Systems," *Eur. J. Oper. Res.*, vol. 257,
      no. 3, 992–1004, doi: 10.1016/j.ejor.2016.08.029.
      March 2017.

[17]  Z. Ergül Aydın, B. İçmen Erdem, and Z. İ. Erzurum
      Çiçek, "Prediction Bike-Sharing Demand with
      Gradient Boosting Methods," *Pamukkale Univ.
      J. Eng. Sci.*, vol. 29, no. 8, 824–832, doi: 10.5505/
      pajes.2023.39959. 2023.

[18]  P. Chen, H. Hsieh, K. Su, X. K. Sigalingging, Y. Chen,
      and J. Leu, "Predicting Station Level Demand in
      a Bike-Sharing System Using Recurrent Neural
      Networks," *IET Intell. Transp. Syst.*, vol. 14, no. 6,
      554–561, doi: 10.1049/iet-its.2019.0007. June 2020.

[19]  R. A. Acheampong, "Towards Sustainable Urban
      Transportation in Ghana: Exploring Adults'
      Intention to Adopt Cycling to Work Using Theory
      of Planned Behaviour and Structural Equation
      Modelling," *Transp. Dev. Econ.*, vol. 3, no. 2, p. 18,
      doi: 10.1007/s40890-017-0047-8. October 2017.

[20]  A. A. Kadri, I. Kacem, and K. Labadi, "A Branch-and-
      Bound Algorithm for Solving the Static Rebalancing
      Problem in Bicycle-Sharing Systems," *Comput. Ind.
      Eng.*, vol. 95, 41–52, doi: 10.1016/j.cie.2016.02.002.
      May 2016.

[21]  S. Kaplan, F. Manca, T. A. S. Nielsen, and C. G. Prato, "Intentions to Use Bike-Sharing for Holiday Cycling: An Application of the Theory of Planned Behavior," *Tour. Manag.*, vol. 47, 34–46, doi: 10.1016/j.tourman.2014.08.017. April 2015.

[22]  H. Fanaee-T and J. Gama, "Event Labeling Combining Ensemble Detectors and Background Knowledge," *Prog. Artif. Intell.*, vol. 2, no. 2–3, 113–127, doi: 10.1007/s13748-013-0040-3. June 2014.

[23]  V. Grover, M. Nandal, B. Balusamy, D. Sahu, and M. Dogra, "Proposed Hybrid Model in Online Education," *EAI Endorsed Trans. Internet Things*, vol. 10, doi: 10.4108/eetiot.4770. January 2024.

[24]  P. Pal, M. Nandal, S. Dikshit, A. Thusu, and H. Vikram Singh, "Harnessing the Power of Ensemble Machine Learning for the Heart Stroke Classification," *EAI Endorsed Trans. Pervasive Health Technol.*, vol. 9, doi: 10.4108/eetpht.9.4617. December 2023.

# Chapter 5

- *8 Ways Artificial Intelligence Can Drive Decarbonization.* (n.d.).

- *Advancing Progress Toward 2050 Net Zero Emissions Goal _ Mondelēz International, Inc.* (n.d.).

- Ahmed, M., Zheng, Y., Amine, A., Fathiannasab, H., and Chen, Z. "The Role of Artificial Intelligence in the Mass Adoption of Electric Vehicles," *Joule*, 5(9), 2296–2322. https://doi.org/https://doi.org/10.1016/j.joule.2021.07.012. 2021.

- Ali, A. *"Supplier Collaboration for Sustainability: A Study of UK Food Supply Chains."* http://uobrep.openrepository.com/uobrep/handle/10547/623363. 2018.

- Ayan, B., Güner, E., and Son-Turan, S. "Blockchain Technology and Sustainability in Supply Chains and a Closer Look at Different Industries: A Mixed Method Approach," *Logistics*, 6(4). https://doi.org/10.3390/logistics6040085. 2022.

- Casandra Okogwu, Mercy Odochi Agho, Mojisola Abimbola Adeyinka, Bukola A. Odulaja, Nsisong Louis Eyo-Udo, Chibuike Daraojimba, and Adeyinka Alex Banso. "Exploring the Integration of Sustainable Materials in Supply Chain Management for Environmental Impact," *Engineering Science & Technology Journal*, 4(3), 49–65. https://doi.org/10.51594/estj.v4i3.546. 2023.

- Chen, L., Chen, Z., Zhang, Y., Liu, Y., Osman, A. I., Farghali, M., Hua, J., Al-Fatesh, A., Ihara, I., Rooney, D. W., and Yap, P.-S. "Artificial Intelligence-Based Solutions for Climate Change: A Review," *Environmental Chemistry Letters*, 21(5), 2525–2557. https://doi.org/10.1007/s10311-023-01617-y. 2023.

- *Country Delight Sucess Story: The Story of Country Delight's Farm-to-Table Delivery Model.* (n.d.).

- Date, R., & Search, Q. No 主観的健康感を中心とした在宅高齢者における 健康関連指標に関する共分散構造分析Title. 1–154. 2019.

- Elkington, J. "Partnerships from Cannibals with Forks: The Triple Bottom Line of 21st-Century Business," *Environmental Quality Management, 8*(1), 37–51. https://doi.org/10.1002/tqem.3310080106. 1998.

- *Generative AI in Supply Chain | IBM.* (n.d.). www.ibm.com/thought-leadership/institute-business-value/en-us/report/Generative-AI-supplychain.

- Govindan, K., Mina, H., and Alavi, B. "A Decision Support System for Demand Management in Healthcare Supply Chains Considering the Epidemic Outbreaks: A Case Study of Coronavirus Disease 2019 (COVID-19)," *Transportation Research Part E: Logistics and Transportation Review, 138*, 101967. https://doi.org/https://doi.org/10.1016/j.tre.2020.101967. 2020.

- Hervani, A. A., Helms, M. M., and Sarkis, J. "Performance Measurement for Green Supply Chain Management," *Benchmarking: An International Journal, 12*(4), 330–353. https://doi.org/10.1108/14635770510609015. 2005.

- Ivanova, K. "A Review of Deep Learning Applications in Energy-Efficient Transportation Systems," *International Journal of Intelligent Automation and Computing, 5*(2), 15–28. https://research.tensorgate.org/index.php/IJIAC/article/view/36. 2022.

- Kaplan, R. S. and Norton, D. P. The Balanced Scorecard: Measures that Drive Performance," *Harvard Business Review, 83* (7–8). 2005.

- Kshetri, N. "Blockchain's Roles in Meeting Key Supply Chain Management Objectives," *International Journal of Information Management, 39*, 80–89. https://doi.org/https://doi.org/10.1016/j.ijinfomgt.2017.12.005. 2018.

- Min, H. "Artificial Intelligence in Supply Chain Management: Theory and Applications," *International Journal of Logistics Research and Applications, 13*, 13–39. https://api.semanticscholar.org/CorpusID:168157593. 2010.

- *"Mondelez Net Zero 2050: The Role of Sustainable Sourcing," Procurement Magazine.* (n.d.).

- Naz, F., Agrawal, R., Kumar, A., Gunasekaran, A., Majumdar, A., and Luthra, S. "Reviewing the Applications of Artificial Intelligence in Sustainable Supply Chains: Exploring Research Propositions for Future Directions," *Business Strategy and the Environment, 31*(5), 2400–2423. https://doi.org/10.1002/bse.3034. 2022.

- Perifanis, N.-A. and Kitsios, F. "Investigating the Influence of Artificial Intelligence on Business Value in the Digital Era of Strategy: A Literature Review," *Information, 14*(2). https://doi.org/10.3390/info14020085. 2023.

- Rae, A. A. "How Sustainable Supply Chains Are Driving Business Transformation | EY – Global," In *Ernst & Young.* www.ey.com/en_gl/supply-chain/supply-chain-sustainability-2022. 2022.

- Rajeev, A., Pati, R. K., Padhi, S. S., and Govindan, K. "Evolution of Sustainability in Supply Chain Management: A Literature Review," *Journal of Cleaner Production, 162,* 299–314. https://doi.org/https://doi.org/10.1016/j.jclepro.2017.05.026. 2017.

- Ramos, M. *What is supply chain sustainability?, IBM Blog.* 2022.

- *Regenerative Sustainable Agriculture: Mondelēz International, Inc.* (n.d.).

- Rodriguez Pepe, Gstettner Stefan, and Pathak Ashish. *"Benefits of AI Driven Supply Chain."* www.bcg.com/publications/2022/benefits-of-ai-driven-supply-chain. 2022.

- *Role of Artificial Intelligence in Supply Chain Analytics, Marketing Analytics Companies, Digital Analytics.* (n.d.).

- Sanders, N., Boone, T., Ganeshan, R., and Wood, J. "Sustainable Supply Chains in the Age of AI and Digitization: Research Challenges and Opportunities," *Journal of Business Logistics, 40.* https://doi.org/10.1111/jbl.12224. 2019.

- *Supply Chain Sustainability: Importance, Roles, and Best Practices | GEP.* (n.d.). www.gep.com/supply-chain-sustainability.

- Toorajipour, R., Sohrabpour, V., Nazarpour, A., Oghazi, P., and Fischl, M. "Artificial Intelligence in Supply Chain Management: A Systematic Literature Review," *Journal of Business Research, 122*, 502–517. https://doi.org/https://doi.org/10.1016/j.jbusres.2020.09.009. 2021.

- Transmetrics. *Logistics Demand Forecasting: The Benefits of AI & How to Implement It.* www.transmetrics.ai/blog/logistics-demand-forecasting/. 2023.

- Tukker, A., Cohen, M. J., Hubacek, K., and Mont, O. "Sustainable Consumption and Production," In *Journal of Industrial Ecology* (Vol. 14, Issue 1, 1–3). https://doi.org/10.1111/j.1530-9290.2009.00214.x. 2010.

- US EPA, & OAR. *Sources of Greenhouse Gas Emissions | US EPA.* www.epa.gov/ghgemissions/sources-greenhouse-gas-emissions. 2022.

- Villena, V. H. and Gioia, D. "A More Sustainable Supply Chain," In *Harvard Bus. Rev* pp. 84–94. https://hbr.org/2020/03/a-more-sustainable-supply-chain. 2020.

- Waters, D. *Inventory Control And Management, 2Nd Ed.* Wiley India Pvt. Limited. https://books.google.co.in/books?id=sBZgyHpcQbcC. 2008.

- *What is the Role of Chatbots in Digitizing the Supply Chain?* (n.d.).

# Chapter 6

- S.P. Afsharian, A. Alizadeh, and M. Chehrehpak. "Effects of Applying Radio Frequency Identification in Supply Chain Management: An Empirical Study of Manufacturing Enterprises," *Int. J. Bus. Inf. Syst.*, 23 (1) 97-115. 2016.

- C.C. Aggarwal, N. Ashish, and A. Sheth. "The IoT: A Survey from the Data-Centric Perspective", C.C. Aggarwal (Ed.), *Managing and Mining Sensor Data*, Springer US, Boston, MA (2013), 383-428.

- Ali, M. Haseeb. "Radio Frequency Identification (RFID) Technology As a Strategic Tool Towards Higher Performance of Supply Chain Operations in Textile and Apparel Industry of Malaysia," *Uncertain Supply Chain Manag.*, 7 (2) 215-226. 2019.

- R. Angeles. "RFID Adoption In The Supply Chain: The Rational Expectations Hypothesis Alternative View," *Int. J. Integr. Supply Manag.*, 4 (3–4), 7-277. 2008.

- Murala, D.K., Panda, S.K., and Swain, S.K. "A Survey on Cloud Computing Security and Privacy Issues and Challenges," *J. Adv. Res. Dyn. Control Syst.*, 11, 1276–1290, 2019.

- Rao, K.V., Murala, D.K., and Panda, S.K. *Blockchain: A study of new business model, in Recent Advances in Blockchain Technology, Intelligent Systems Reference Library*, S.K. Panda, V. Mishra, S.P. Dash, A.K. Pani (Eds.), vol. 237, Springer, Cham, https://doi.org/10.1007/978-3-031-22835-3_9. 2023.

- L. Ardito, A.M. Petruzzelli, U. Panniello, and A.C. Garavelli. "Towards Industry 4.0: Mapping Digital Technologies for Supply Chain Management-Marketing Integration," *Bus. Process Manag. J.*, 25 (2), 323-346. 2019.

- M. Attaran. "Digital Technology Enablers and Their Implications for Supply Chain Management," *Supply Chain Forum*, Taylor and Francis Ltd., 10.1080/16258312.2020.1751568. 2010.

- S. Balamurugan, A. Ayyasamy, and K.S. Joseph "IoT-Based Supply Chain Traceability Using Enhanced Naive Bayes Approach for Scheming the Food Safety Issues" *Int. J. Sci. Technol. Res.*, 9 (3) 1184-1192. 2020.

- M. Ben-Daya, E. Hassini, and Z. Bahroun. "IoT and Supply Chain Management: A Literature Review," *Int. J. Prod. Res.*, 57 (15–16) 4719-4742. 2019.

- H.S. Birkel and E. Hartmann "IoT – The Future of Managing Supply Chain Risks," *Supply Chain Management*, 25, Emerald Group Publishing Ltd., 535-548. 2020.

- Murala, D.K., Panda, S.K., and Swain, S.K. "Secure Dynamic Groups Data Sharing with Modified Revocable Attribute-Based Encryption in the Cloud," *Int. J. Recent Technol. Eng.*, 8, 4, 2019.

- Murala, D.K., Panda, S.K., and Swain, S.K. "A Novel Hybrid Approach for Providing Data Security and Privacy from Malicious Attacks in the Cloud Environment," *J. Adv. Res. Dyn. Control Syst.*, 11, 1291 – 1300, 2019.

## REFERENCES

- F. Caro and R. Sadr. "The IoT in Retail: Bridging Supply and Demand," *Bus. Horiz.*, 62 (1), 47-54. 2019.

- S.A. Gawankar, A. Gunasekaran, and S. Kamble. "A Study on Investments in the Big Data-Driven Supply Chain, Performance Measures and Organisational Performance in Indian Retail 4.0 Context," *Int. J. Prod. Res.*, 58 (5), 1574-1593. 2020.

- Reece, E.M., Davis, M.J., Abu-Ghname, A., Castanon, J.M., Voris, M., Hoxworth, R., Winocour, S., and Buchanan, E.P. "Working Smarter, not Harder: Using Data-Driven Strategies to Generate Front-End Cost Savings Through Price Negotiation and Supply Chain Optimization," *Plast. Reconstr. Surg.* 149, 1488–1497. 2022.

- Aljabhan, B. A. "Comprehensive Analysis on the Adoption of IoT with Logistics and Supply Chain Management," In *Proceedings of the 2022 Second International Conference on Computer Science, Engineering and Applications (ICCSEA)*, Gunupur, India, 8 September 2022; IEEE: New York, NY, USA, 2022; 1–6.

- Wu, H., Shen, Y., Tömösközi, M., Nguyen, G.T., and Fitzek, F.H.P. "Demonstration of In-Network Audio Processing for Low-Latency Anomaly Detection in Smart Factories," In *Proceedings of the 2022 IEEE 19th Annual Consumer Communications and Networking Conference (CCNC)*, Las Vegas, NV, USA, 8–11 January 2022; IEEE: New York, NY, USA, 2022; 933–934.

- Belhadi, A., Kamble, S., Jabbour, C.J.C., Gunasekaran, A., Ndubisi, N.O., and Venkatesh, M. "Manufacturing and Service Supply Chain Resilience to the COVID-19 Outbreak: Lessons Learned from the Automobile and Airline Industries," *Technol. Forecast. Soc. Chang.* 163, 120447. 2020.

- Burgos, D. and Ivanov, D. "Food Retail Supply Chain Resilience and The COVID-19 Pandemic: A Digital Twin-Based Impact Analysis and Improvement Directions," *Transp. Res. Part E Logist. Transp. Rev.*, 152, 102412. 2021.

- De Vass, T., Shee, H., and Miah, S.J. "The Effect of 'Iot' on Supply Chain Integration and Performance: An Organisational Capability Perspective," *Australas. J. Inf. Syst.*, 22, 3–7. 2018.

- Murala, D.K., Panda, S.K., Sahoo, S.K., and Panda, S.K. "Securing Electronic Health Record System in Cloud Environment Using Blockchain Technology" In *Recent Advances in Blockchain Technology, Intelligent Systems Reference Library*, V. Mishra, S.P. Dash, A.K. Pani (Eds.), vol. 237, Springer, Cham, https://doi.org/10.1007/978-3-031-22835-3_4. 2023.

- Dileep Kumar Murala, and Sandeep Kumar Panda, "The IoT in Developing Metaverse," *Metaverse and Immersive Technologies: An Introduction to Industrial, Business and Social Applications*. October 20, 2023.

- Nozari, H. and Nahr, J.G. "The Impact of Blockchain Technology and the IoT on the Agile and Sustainable Supply Chain," *Int. J. Innov. Eng.*, 2, 33–41. 2022.

- Sun, Z.-H., Chen, Z., Cao, S., and Ming, X. "Potential Requirements and Opportunities of Blockchain-Based Industrial IoT in Supply Chain: A Survey," *IEEE Trans. Comput. Soc. Syst*, 9, 1469–1483. 2021.

- Xia, L. and Liu, S. "Intelligent IoT-Based Cross-Border E-Commerce Supply Chain Performance Optimization," *Wirel. Commun. Mob. Comput.*, 9961925. 2021.

- Nozari, H., Fallah, M., and Szmelter-Jarosz, A. "A Conceptual Framework of Green Smart IoT-Based Supply Chain Management," *Int. J. Res. Ind. Eng.*, 10, 22–34. 2021.

- Wei, X., Guo, H., Wang, X., Wang, X., and Qiu, M. "Reliable Data Collection Techniques in Underwater Wireless Sensor Networks: A Survey," *IEEE Commun. Surv. Tutor.* 24, 404–431. 2021.

- Singh, A., Sharma, S., and Singh, J. "Nature-Inspired Algorithms for Wireless Sensor Networks: A Comprehensive Survey," *Comput. Sci. Rev.* 39, 100342. 2020.

- Evans, V. and Horak, J. "Sustainable Urban Governance Networks, Data-Driven IoT Systems, and Wireless Sensor-Based Applications in Smart City Logistics," *Geopolit. Hist. Int. Relat.* 13, 65–78. 2021.

# Chapter 7

[1]  Khan, S.N., Loukil, F., Chedira-Guegan, C. et al. "Blockchain Smart Contracts: Applications, Challenges, and Future Trends," *Peer-to-Peer Netw. Appl.* 14, 2901–2925. https://doi.org/10.1007/s12083-021-01127-0. 2021.

[2]  Lambert, D.M., Cooper, M.C., and Pagh, J.D. "Supply Chain Management: Implementation Issues and Research Opportunities," *The International Journal of Logistics Management*, Vol. 9 No. 2, pp. 1-20. https://doi.org/10.1108/09574099810805807. 1998.

[3]  Erfan Babaee Tirkolaee, Saeid Sadeghi, Farzaneh Mansoori Mooseloo, Hadi Rezaei Vandchali, and Samira Aeini. "Application of Machine Learning in Supply Chain Management: A Comprehensive Overview of the Main Areas," *Mathematical Problems in Engineering*, vol. 2021, Article ID 1476043, 14 pages, https://doi.org/10.1155/2021/1476043. 2021.

[4]  Haifeng Lin, Ji Lin, and Fang Wang. "An Innovative Machine Learning Model for Supply Chain Management," *Journal of Innovation & Knowledge*, Volume 7, Issue 4, 100276, ISSN 2444-569X, https://doi.org/10.1016/j.jik.2022.100276. 2022.

[5] Mahmoud M. Bassiouni, Ripon K. Chakrabortty, Omar K. Hussain, and Humyun Fuad Rahman. "Advanced Deep Learning Approaches to Predict Supply Chain Risks Under COVID-19 Restrictions," *Expert Systems with Applications*, Volume 211, 118604, ISSN 0957-4174, https://doi.org/10.1016/j.eswa.2022.118604. 2023.

[6] Wenzel, Hannah, Smit, Daniel, and Sardesai, Saskia. "A literature review on machine learning in supply chain management," Chapters from the *Proceedings of the Hamburg International Conference of Logistics (HICL)*, in: Kersten, Wolfgang & Blecker, Thorsten & Ringle, Christian M. (ed.), *Artificial Intelligence and Digital Transformation in Supply Chain Management: Innovative Approaches for Supply Chains. Proceedings of the Hamburg Int*, volume 27, pages 413-441, Hamburg University of Technology (TUHH), Institute of Business Logistics and General Management. 2019.

[7] Hosseinnia Shavaki, F. and Ebrahimi Ghahnavieh, A. "Applications of Deep Learning into Supply Chain Management: A Systematic Literature Review and a Framework For Future Research," *Artif. Intell. Rev.* 56, 4447–4489. https://doi.org/10.1007/s10462-022-10289-z. 2023.

[8] A. E. Filali, E. H. Ben Lahmer, and S. E. Filali. "Exploring Applications of Machine Learning for Supply Chain Management," 2021 Third International Conference on Transportation and Smart Technologies (TST), Tangier, Morocco, 46-52, https://doi: 10.1109/TST52996.2021.00015. 2021.

[9] Violetta Giada Cannas, Maria Pia Ciano, Mattia Saltalamacchia, and Raffaele Secchi. "Artificial Intelligence in Supply Chain And Operations Management: A Multiple Case Study Research," *International Journal of Production Research*, https://doi: 10.1080/00207543.2023.2232050. 2023.

[10] Benjamin Rolf, Ilya Jackson, Marcel Müller, Sebastian Lang, Tobias Reggelin, and Dmitry Ivanov. "A Review on Reinforcement Learning Algorithms and Applications in Supply Chain Management," *International Journal of Production Research*, 61:20, 7151-7179, https://doi: 10.1080/00207543.2022.2140221. 2023.

[11] Mei Yang, Ming K. Lim, Yingchi Qu, Du Ni, and Zhi Xiao. "Supply Chain Risk Management with Machine Learning Technology: A Literature Review and Future Research Directions," *Computers & Industrial Engineering*, Volume 175, 108859, ISSN 0360-8352, https://doi.org/10.1016/j.cie.2022.108859. 2023.

[12] Luo, J. "Application of Machine Learning in Supply Chain Management," Proceedings of the 2022 3rd International Conference on Big Data Economy and Information Management (BDEIM 2022), pp. 489-498. doi:10.2991/978-94-6463-124-1_58. 2023.

[13] Dong, Z., Liang, W., Liang, Y. et al. "Blockchained Supply Chain Management Based on IoT Tracking and Machine Learning," *J Wireless Com. Network*, 127. https://doi.org/10.1186/s13638-022-02209-0. 2022.

[14] Reza Toorajipour, Vahid Sohrabpour, Ali Nazarpour, Pejvak Oghazi, and Maria Fischl. "Artificial Intelligence in Supply Chain Management: A Systematic Literature Review," *Journal of Business Research*, Volume 122, 502-517, ISSN 0148-2963, https://doi.org/10.1016/j.jbusres.2020.09.009. 2021.

[15] Ni, D., Xiao, Z. and Lim, M.K. "A systematic Review of the Research Trends of Machine Learning In Supply Chain Management," *Int. J. Mach. Learn. & Cyber.* 11, 1463–1482. https://doi.org/10.1007/s13042-019-01050-0. 2020.

[16] Md Abrar Jahin, Md Sakib Hossain Shovon, Jungpil Shin, Istiyaque Ahmed Ridoy, Yoichi Tomioka, and M. F. Mridha, "Big Data – Supply Chain Management Framework for Forecasting: Data Preprocessing and Machine Learning Techniques," *IEEE Access*, Vol 4, 1-26, 2016.

[17] Taherdoost H. "Smart Contracts in Blockchain Technology: A Critical Review," *Information.* 14(2):117. https://doi.org/10.3390/info14020117. 2023.

[18]  M. Alharby, A. Aldweesh and A. Moorsel. "Blockchain-Based Smart Contracts: A Systematic Mapping Study of Academic Research (2018)," in *2018 International Conference on Cloud Computing, Big Data and Blockchain (ICCBB)*, Fuzhou, China, 2018. pp. 1-6. doi: 10.1109/ ICCBB.2018.8756390. 2018.

[19]  Anna Vacca, Andrea Di Sorbo, Corrado A. Visaggio, and Gerardo Canfora. "A Systematic Literature Review of Blockchain and Smart Contract Development: Techniques, Tools, and Open Challenges," *Journal of Systems and Software*, Volume 174, 110891, ISSN 0164-1212, `https://doi.org/10.1016/j.jss.2020.110891`. 2021.

[20]  Alexander A. Varfolomeev, Liwa H. Alfarhani, and Zahraa Ch. Oleiwi. "Secure-Reliable Smart Contract Applications Based Blockchain Technology in Smart Cities Environment," *Procedia Computer Science*, Volume 186, 669-676, ISSN 1877-0509, `https://doi.org/10.1016/j.procs.2021.04.188`. 2021.

[21]  Zibin Zheng, Shaoan Xie, Hong-Ning Dai, Weili Chen, Xiangping Chen, Jian Weng, and Muhammad Imran. "An overview on smart contracts: Challenges, advances and platforms," *Future Gener. Comput. Syst.* 105, C (Apr 2020), 475–491. `https://doi.org/10.1016/j.future.2019.12.019`. 2020.

[22]  Haeok Lee, Mary Ellen Friedman, Peter Cukor, and David Ahern. "Interactive Voice Response System (IVRS) in Health Care Services," *Nursing Outlook*, Volume 51, Issue 6, 277-283, ISSN 0029-6554, https://doi.org/10.1016/S0029-6554(03)00161-1. 2003.

[23]  Kumari Ankita, Mohini Mehta, and Priti Puri. "Risk Assessment & Mitigation for Interactive Voice Response System," *Int. J. of Adv. Res.* Vol. 3 Issue. 8. pp.1280-1282. ISSN 2320-5407. 2015.

[24]  Ruikar V. "Interactive Voice/Web Response System in Clinical Research," *Perspect Clin. Res.* 7:15-20. 2016.

[25]  Ben Ismail, E., Jaana, M., Sherrard, H. et al. "IVR System Use by Patients with Heart Failure: Compliance and Services Utilization Patterns," *J. Med. Syst.* 46, 69. https://doi.org/10.1007/s10916-022-01847-7. 2022.

[26]  Wong, D.R., Bhattacharya, S. and Butte, A.J. "Prototype of Running Clinical Trials in an Untrustworthy Environment Using Blockchain," *Nat. Commun.* 10, 917. https://doi.org/10.1038/s41467-019-08874-y. 2019.

[27]  Alshammari, A. and Aldribi, A. "Apply Machine Learning Techniques to Detect Malicious Network Traffic in Cloud Computing," J. *Big Data* 8, 90. https://doi.org/10.1186/s40537-021-00475-1. 2021.

[28]    Aldribi, A., Traoré, I., Moa, B., and Nwamuo,
        O. "Hypervisor-Based Cloud Intrusion Detection
        Through Online Multivariate Statistical Change
        Tracking," *Comput Secur. 2020*;88:101646–101646.
        https:// doi. org/ 10. 1016/j.cose.
        101646. 2019.

[29]    Aldribi, A., Traore, I., and Moa, B.. "Data Sources
        and Datasets for Cloud Intrusion Detection
        Modeling and Evaluation, " In *Cloud Computing
        for Optimization: Foundations, Applications, and
        Challenges.* Cham: Springer. 333–66. 2018.

[30]    Zihao Wang, Kar Wai Fok, and Vrizlynn L.L. Thing,
        "Machine Learning for Encrypted Malicious
        Traffic Detection: Approaches, Datasets and
        Comparative Study," *Computers and Security,*
        Volume 113, 102542, ISSN 0167-4048, https://doi.
        org/10.1016/j.cose.2021.102542. 2022.

[31]    Liu, X. and Liu, J. "Malicious Traffic Detection
        Combined Deep Neural Network with Hierarchical
        Attention Mechanism." *Sci. Rep.* 11, 12363. https://
        doi.org/10.1038/s41598-021-91805-z. 2021.

[32]    Groschopf, W., Dobrovnik, M., and Herneth
        C. *Smart Contracts for Sustainable Supply Chain
        Management: Conceptual Frameworks for Supply
        Chain Maturity Evaluation and Smart Contract
        Sustainability Assessment.* Front. Blockchain
        4:506436. doi: 10.3389/fbloc.2021.506436. 2021.

[33] Terzi, S., Zacharaki, A., Nizamis, A., Votis, K., Ioannidis, D., Tzovaras, D., and Stamelos, I. "Transforming the Supply-Chain Management and Industry Logistics with Blockchain Smart Contracts," *Proceedings of the 23rd Pan-Hellenic Conference on Informatics - PCI '19.* doi:10.1145/3368640.3368655. 2019.

[34] Ethereum. https://ethereum.org/.

[35] Solidity. https://soliditylang.org/.

# Chapter 8

[1] Vailshery, L.S. "IoT Connected Devices Worldwide," Statista. www.statista.com/statistics/1183457/iot-connected-devices-worldwide/. 2023.

[2] Pesen, D. "IoT (Internet of Things): Everything You Need to Know in 2023," *Tech Business News.* www.techbusinessnews.com.au/blog/iot-internet-of-things-everything-you-need-to-know-in-2023/. 2023.

[3] Nakamoto, S. "Bitcoin: A Peer-to-Peer Electronic Cash System," https://bitcoin.org/bitcoin.pdf. 2008.

[4] Merkle, R. C. A Digital Signature Based on a Conventional Encryption Function," In: Pomerance, C. (eds) *Advances in Cryptology — CRYPTO '87. CRYPTO 1987. Lecture Notes in Computer Science,* vol 293. Springer, Berlin, Heidelberg. https://doi.org/10.1007/3-540-48184-2_32. 1988.

[5]  Porkodi, S. and Kesavaraja, D. "Blockchain for
     Green Smart Cities," In *Blockchain for Smart Cities*.
     211-231. Elsevier. 2021.

[6]  Buterin, V., Conner, E., Dudley,R., Slipper, M.,
     Norden, I. and Bakhta, A. "EIP-1559: Fee market
     change for ETH 1.0 chain, Ethereum Improvement
     Proposals, no. 1559." [Online serial]. Available at
     https://eips.ethereum.org/EIPS/eip-1559. 2019.

[7]  Szabo, N. "Formalizing and Securing Relationships
     on Public Networks." First Monday, 2(9). https://
     doi.org/10.5210/fm.v2i9.548. 1997.

[8]  Irei, A. and Scarfone, K. "Smart Contract Benefits
     and Best Practices for Security," *TechTarget*.
     www.techtarget.com/searchsecurity/tip/Smart-
     contract-benefits-and-best-practices-for-
     security. May 25, 2023.

[9]  Ramos, M. "What Is Supply Chain Sustainability?,"
     IBM. www.ibm.com/blog/what-is-supply-chain-
     sustainability/. 2022.

[10] Köhler, S. and Pizzol, M. "Technology Assessment
     of Blockchain-Based Technologies in the Food
     Supply Chain," *Journal of Cleaner Production*,
     269, 122193. https://doi.org/10.1016/j.
     jclepro.2020.122193. 2020.

[11] Tsai, F. M., Bui, T.-D., Tseng, M.-L., Ali, M. H., Lim,
     M. K., and Chiu, A. S. "Sustainable Supply Chain
     Management Trends in World Regions: A Data-
     Driven Analysis," *Resour. Conservation Recycl.* 167,
     105421. doi:10.1016/j. resconrec.2021.105421. 2021.

REFERENCES

[12] Oudani, M., Sebbar, A., Zkik, K., El Harraki, I., and Belhadi, A. "Green Blockchain Based IoT for Secured Supply Chain of Hazardous Materials," *Computers and Industrial Engineering*, 175, 108814. 2023.

[13] S. Jiang, K. Jakobsen, J. Bueie, J. Li, and P. H. Haro, "A Tertiary Review on Blockchain and Sustainability With Focus on Sustainable Development Goals," in *IEEE Access*, vol. 10, pp. 114975-115006, doi: 10.1109/ACCESS.2022.3217683. 2022.

[14] Mangla, S. K., Kazancoglu, Y., Ekinci, E., Liu, M., Özbiltekin, M., and Sezer, M. D. "Using System Dynamics to Analyze the Societal Impacts of Blockchain Technology in Milk Supply Chains," *Transportation Research Part E: Logistics and Transportation Review*, 149, 102289. 2021.

[15] Wang, Z-J., Chen, Z-S., Xiao, L., Su, Q., Govindan, K., and Skibniewski, M. J. "Blockchain Adoption in Sustainable Supply Chains for Industry 5.0: A Multistakeholder Perspective," *Journal of Innovation and Knowledge*, 8(4), 100425. 2023.

[16] Chen, Y. "How Blockchain Adoption Affects Supply Chain Sustainability in the Fashion Industry: A Systematic Review and Case Studies," *Information Technology and Operations Research*, Advance online publication. https://doi.org/10.1111/itor.13273. 2023.

[17]  Lotfi, R., Kargar, B., Rajabzadeh, M. et al. "Hybrid Fuzzy and Data-Driven Robust Optimization for Resilience and Sustainable Health Care Supply Chain with Vendor-Managed Inventory Approach," *Int. J. Fuzzy Syst.* 24, 1216–1231. https://doi.org/10.1007/s40815-021-01209-4. 2022.

[18]  Lotfi, R., Hazrati, H., Ali, S.S. et al. "Antifragile, Sustainable and Agile Healthcare Waste Chain Network Design by Considering Blockchain, Resiliency, Robustness and Risk," *Cent. Eur. J. Oper. Res.* https://dci.org/10.1007/s10100-023-00874-0. 2023.

[19]  Yakubu, B. M., Latif, R., Yakubu, A., Khan, M. I., and Magashi, A. I. "RiceChain: Secure and Traceable Rice Supply Chain Framework Using Blockchain Technology," *PeerJ Computer Science.* https://doi.org/10.7717/peerj-cs.804. 2022.

[20]  Tokkozhina, U., Martins, A.L., and Ferreira, J.C. "Multi-Tier Supply Chain Behavior with Blockchain Technology: Evidence from a Frozen Fish Supply Chain," *Oper. Manag. Res.* 16, 1562–1576. https://doi.org/10.1007/s12063-023-00377-w. 2023.

[21]  Abdallah, S. and Nizamuddin, N. "Blockchain-Based Solution for Pharma Supply Chain Industry," *Computers and Industrial Engineering,* 177, 108997. https://doi.org/10.1016/j.cie.2023.108997. 2023.

[22] Niu, B., Dong, J., and Liu, Y. "Incentive Alignment for Blockchain Adoption in Medicine Supply Chains," *Transportation Research Part E: Logistics and Transportation Review*, 152, 102276. https://doi.org/10.1016/j.tre.2021.102276. 2021.

[23] UNICEF. "Child labour. UNICEF Data." https://data.unicef.org/topic/child-protection/child-labour/. 2023.

[24] U.S. Department of Labor. "List of Goods Produced by Child Labor or Forced Labor." www.dol.gov/agencies/ilab/reports/child-labor/list-of-goods. 2022.

[25] Esmaeilian, B., Sarkis, J., Lewis, K., and Behdad, S. "Blockchain for the Future of Sustainable Supply Chain Management in Industry 4.0," *Resources, Conservation and Recycling*, 163, 105064. https://doi.org/10.1016/j.resconrec.2020.105064. 2020.

[26] M. Díaz, E. Soler, L. Llopis, and J. Trillo, "Integrating Blockchain in Safety-Critical Systems: An Application to the Nuclear Industry," in *IEEE Access*, vol. 8, 190605-190619, doi: 10.1109/ACCESS.2020.3032322. 2020.

[27] Oudani, M., Sebbar, A., Zkik, K., Harraki, I. E., and Belhadi, A. "Green Blockchain-Based IoT for Secured Supply Chain of Hazardous Materials," *Computers and Industrial Engineering*, 175, 108814. https://doi.org/10.1016/j.cie.2022.108814. 2023.

# Chapter 9

- Ahmad Tass, M. "Impact of Internet of Things (IoTs) on Inventory Management Systems and its Role in Industry 4.0-An Overview." In KVJ. Prof. Dr. Ganesan. R. (Ed.), *Holistic Research Perspectives,* 1st ed., Vol. 9, 1–13. NFED Publication. www.researchgate.net/publication/369559584. 2023.

- Ante, L. "A Place Next to Satoshi: Foundations of Blockchain and Cryptocurrency Research in Business and Economics," *Scientometrics, 124*(2), 1305–1333. https://doi.org/10.1007/s11192-020-03492-8. 2020.

- Atlam, H. F., Azad, M. A., Alzahrani, A. G., and Wills, G. "A Review of Blockchain in Internet of Things and AI," *Big Data and Cognitive Computing,* 4(4), 28. https://doi.org/10.3390/bdcc4040028. 2020.

- Bhat, S., Huang, N., Sofi, I., and Sultan, M. "Agriculture-Food Supply Chain Management Based on Blockchain and IoT: A Narrative on Enterprise Blockchain Interoperability," *MDPI, 12*(1), 1–25. https://doi.org/10.3390/agriculture12010040. 2022.

- Centobelli, P., Cerchione, R., Vecchio, P. Del, Oropallo, E., and Secundo, G. "Blockchain Technology for Bridging Trust, Traceability and Transparency in Circular Supply Chain," *Information and Management, 59*(7), 1–14. https://doi.org/10.1016/j.im.2021.103508. 2022.

- Chauhan, S., Singh, R., Gehlot, A., Akram, S. V., Twala, B., and Priyadarshi, N. "Digitalization of Supply Chain Management with Industry 4.0 Enabling Technologies: A Sustainable Perspective," *Processes, 11*(96), 1–22. https://doi.org/10.3390/pr11010096. 2023.

- Furneaux, N. *Investigating cryptocurrencies: understanding, extracting, and analyzing blockchain evidence.* John Wiley & Sons, Inc. https://books.google.com/books?hl=en&lr=&id=d4JaDwAAQBAJ&oi=fnd&pg=PP2&dq=forensic+accounting+blockchain+technology&ots=One33DLQ7K&sig=1O_RaBa6yYWuNVThHTHp-kAou1A. 2018.

- Gohil, D., and Thakker, S. V. "Blockchain-Integrated Technologies for Solving Supply Chain Challenges," *Modern Supply Chain Research and Applications, 3*(2), 78–97. https://doi.org/10.1108/MSCRA-10-2020-0028/FULL/HTML. 2021.

- Gromovs, G. and Lammi, M. "Blockchain And Internet Of Things Require Innovative Approach To Logistics Education," *Transport Problems, 12*(SE), 23–34. https://doi.org/10.20858/tp.2017.12.se.2. 2018.

- Grover, V., Anbarasi, A., Fuladi, S., and Nallakaruppan, M. K. "Decision Tree-Based Crowd Funding for Kickstarter Projects," *EAI Endorsed Transactions on Scalable Information Systems, 11*(2). https://doi.org/10.4108/eetsis.4639. 2023.

- Johri, I., Nallakaruppan, M.K., Balusamy, B., V, G., and Grover, V. "Application of Neural Networks and Genetic Algorithms in Establishing Logical Rules for Evaluating the Edibility of Mushroom Data," In Shaw, R.N., Paprzycki, M., Ghosh, A. (eds) *Advanced Communication and Intelligent Systems. ICACIS 2023. Communications in Computer and Information Science*, vol 1920. Springer, Cham. https://doi.org/10.1007/978-3-031-45121-8_18. 2023.

- Houshang Tajfar, A. and Gheysari, M. "Analysis the Effects of Internet of Things Technology in Managing Supply Chain," *International Journal of Information & Communication Technology Research*, 8(3), 15–25. 2016.

- Hrouga, M., Sbihi, A., and Chavallard, M. "The Potentials of Combining Blockchain Technology and Internet of Things for Digital Reverse Supply Chain: A Case Study," *Journal of Cleaner Production*, *337*, 130609. https://doi.org/10.1016/j.jclepro.2022.130609. 2022.

- Khan, Y., Su'ud, M. B. M., Alam, M. M., Ahmad, S. F., Ahmad (Ayassrah), A. Y. A. B., and Khan, N. "Application of Internet of Things (IoT) in Sustainable Supply Chain Management," *Sustainability*, 15(1), 1–14. https://doi.org/10.3390/su15010694. 2022.

- Kumar, S. and Pundir. "Blockchain—Internet of Things (IoT) Enabled Pharmaceutical Supply Chain for COVID-19," *International Conference on Industrial Engineering and Operations Management*, 1592–1599. www.ieomsociety.org/detroit2020/papers/375.pdf. 2020.

REFERENCES

- M. Bublitz, F., Oetomo, A., S. Sahu, K., Kuang, A., X. Fadrique, L., E. Velmovitsky, P., M. Nobrega, R., and P. Morita, P. "Disruptive Technologies for Environment and Health Research: An Overview of Artificial Intelligence, Blockchain, and Internet of Things," *International Journal of Environmental Research and Public Health, 16*(20), 3847. https://doi.org/10.3390/ijerph16203847. 2019.

- Madhogarhia, A. "Advancements in Supply Chain Management Using IoT," *International Research Journal of Engineering and Technology, 9*(1), 1690–1693. www.irjet.net. 2022.

- Martins, C. L. and Pato, M. V. "Supply Chain Sustainability: A Tertiary Literature Review," *Journal of Cleaner Production, 225*, 995–1016. https://doi.org/10.1016/j.jclepro.2019.03.250. 2019.

- Menon, S. and Shah, S. "An Overview of Digitalisation in Conventional Supply Chain Management," *MATEC Web of Conferences*, 1–5. https://doi.org/10.1051/matecconf/2019. 2019.

- Min, H. "Artificial Intelligence in Supply Chain Management: Theory and Applications," *International Journal of Logistics Research and Applications, 13*(1), 13–39. https://doi.org/10.1080/13675560902736537. 2010.

- Miraz, M. H. and Ali, M. "Applications of Blockchain Technology Beyond Cryptocurrency," *Annals of Emerging Technologies in Computing, 2*(1), 1–6. https://doi.org/10.33166/AETiC.2018.01.001. 2018.

- Nair, N. and Praveena T. "The Impact of Industry 4.0 on Supply Chain Management," In *International Journal of Supply Chain Management IJSCM* (Vol. 10, Issue 4). Online. http://excelingtech.co.uk/. 2021.

- P. Pal, V. Grover, M. Nandal, S. Gochhait, and H. V. Singh, "Artificial Intelligence Driven Intelligent Computational Model for Heart Disease Prediction: Leveraging Feature Selection," *2024 ASU International Conference in Emerging Technologies for Sustainability and Intelligent Systems (ICETSIS)*, Manama, Bahrain, 1422-1428, doi: 10.1109/ICETSIS61505.2024.10459563. 2024.

- Parker, B. and Bach, C. "Synthesis of Blockchain, Artificial Intelligence and Internet of Things," *European Journal of Engineering and Technology Research*, 5(5), 588–593. https://doi.org/10.24018/ejeng.2020.5.5.1912. 2020.

- Rejeb, A., Keogh, J. G., and Treiblmaier, H. "Leveraging the Internet of Things and Blockchain Technology in Supply Chain Management," *Future Internet*, 11(7), 161. https://doi.org/10.3390/fi11070161. 2019.

- Reyes, P. M., Visich, J. K., and Jaska, P. "Managing the Dynamics of New Technologies in the Global Supply Chain," *IEEE Engineering Management Review*, 48(1), 156–162. https://doi.org/10.1109/EMR.2020.2968889. 2020.

REFERENCES

- Sasikumar, A., Ravi, L., Kotecha, K., Saini, J. R.,
  Varadarajan, V., and Subramaniyaswamy,
  V. "Sustainable Smart Industry: A Secure and
  Energy Efficient Consensus Mechanism for Artificial
  Intelligence Enabled Industrial Internet of Things,"
  *Computational Intelligence and Neuroscience, 2022,*
  1–12. https://doi.org/10.1155/2022/1419360. 2022.

- Sharifpour, H., Ghaseminezhad, Y., Hashemi-
  Tabatabaei, M., and Amiri, M. "Investigating Cause-
  and-Effect Relationships Between Supply Chain 4.0
  Technologies," *Engineering Management in Production
  and Services, 14*(4), 22–46. https://doi.org/10.2478/
  emj-2022-0029. 2022.

- Sharma, M. and Kumar, P. "Adoption of Blockchain
  Technology," In R. Bansal, P. Malyadri, A. Singh, &
  A. Pervez (Eds.), *Adoption of Blockchain Technology:
  A Case Study of Walmart* (pp. 210–225). IGI Global.
  https://doi.org/10.4018/978-1-7998-8081-3.
  ch013. 2021.

- Sharma, S. K. and Singh Vinay. "Digitization of the Food
  Industry Enabled by Internet of Things, Blockchain,
  and Artificial Intelligence," In A. Tarfdar, A. Pandey,
  R. Sirohi, & C. Soccol (Eds.), *Current Developments
  in Biotechnology and Bioengineering Advances in
  Food Engineering* (Vol. 1, pp. 421–445). Elsevier Inc.
  https://doi.org/10.1016/C2020-0-04192-7. 2022.

- Shaw, S., Rowland, Z., and Machova, V. "Internet of Things Smart Devices, Sustainable Industrial Big Data, and Artificial Intelligence-based Decision-Making Algorithms in Cyber-Physical System-based Manufacturing," In *Economics, Management and Financial Markets* (2nd ed., Vol. 16, 106–116). Addleton Academic Publishers. www.ceeol.com/search/article-detail?id=963246. 2021.

- Singh, G. K. and Dadhich, M. "Supply Chain Management Growth With the Adoption of Blockchain Technology (BoT) and Internet of Things (IoT)," *2023 3rd International Conference on Advance Computing and Innovative Technologies in Engineering (ICACITE)*, 321–325. https://doi.org/10.1109/ICACITE57410.2023.10182619. 2023.

- Soori, M., Arezoo, B., and Dastres, R. "Internet of Things for Smart Factories in Industry 4.0, a Review," In *Internet of Things and Cyber-Physical Systems* (Vol. 3, 192–204). KeAi Communications Co. https://doi.org/10.1016/j.iotcps.2023.04.006. 2023.

- Tomar, P. and Grover, V. "Transforming the Energy Sector: Addressing Key Challenges Through Generative AI, Digital Twins, AI, Data Science and Analysis," *EAI Endorsed Transactions on Energy Web, 10*. https://doi.org/10.4108/ew.4825. 2024.

- Tsang, Y. P., Wu, C. H., Ip, W. H., and Shiau, W.-L. "Exploring the Intellectual Cores of the Blockchain–Internet of Things (BIoT)," *Journal of Enterprise Information Management, 34*(5), 1287–1317. https://doi.org/10.1108/JEIM-10-2020-0395. 2021.

- Tyagi, A. K., Dananjayan, S., Agarwal, D., and Thariq Ahmed, H. F. "Blockchain— Internet of Things Applications: Opportunities and Challenges for Industry 4.0 and Society 5.0," *Sensors*, *23*(2), 947. https://doi.org/10.3390/s23020947. 2023.

- Wamba, S. F. and Queiroz, M. M. "Blockchain in the Operations and Supply Chain Management: Benefits, Challenges and Future Research Opportunities," *International Journal of Information Management*, *52*(102064). www.sciencedirect.com/science/article/pii/S026840121931792X?casa_token=9ATT5yyp1FAAAAAA:KxX3bXPYCSjUa6Et X4NbfOfR8bTSdt2JPGSlKuw3AVMJ5h1 YD4jXYk7s9Dga2mSCbj4qYIiDh3yW. 2020.

- Wang, M., Wang, B., and Abareshi, A. "Blockchain Technology and Its Role in Enhancing Supply Chain Integration Capability and Reducing Carbon Emission: A Conceptual Framework," *Sustainability*, *12*(24), 1–17. https://doi.org/10.3390/su122410550. 2020.

- Yadav, S., Luthra, S., and Garg, D. "Modelling Internet of Things (IoT)-Driven Global Sustainability in Multi-Tier Agri-Food Supply Chain Under Natural Epidemic Outbreaks," *Environmental Science and Pollution Research*, *28*(13), 16633–16654. https://doi.org/10.1007/S11356-020-11676-1. 2021.

- Yadav, S. P., Agrawal, K. K., Bhati, B. S., Al-Turjman, F., and Mostarda, L. "Blockchain- Based Cryptocurrency Regulation: An Overview," *Computational Economics*, *59*(4), 1659–1675. https://doi.org/10.1007/s10614-020-10050-0. 2022.

- Zhao, J. L., Fan, S., and Yan, J. "Overview of Business Innovations and Research Opportunities in Blockchain and Introduction to the Special Issue," *Financial Innovation*, 2(1), 28. https://doi.org/10.1186/s40854-016-0049-2. 2016.

# Chapter 10

[1]  J T. Mentzer et al., "Defining Supply Chain Management," *Journal of Business Logistics*, vol. 22, no. 2, 1–25, doi: 10.1002/j.2158-1592.2001.tb00001.x. September 2001.

[2]  Raj A, Mukherjee A.A., de Sousa Jabbour Abl., and Srivastava S.K.. "Supply Chain Management During and Post-COVID-19 Pandemic: Mitigation Strategies and Practical Lessons Learned," *J. Bus. Res.* 2022 Mar;142:1125-1139. doi: 10.1016/j.jbusres.2022.01.037. Epub Jan 21, 2022. PMID: 35079190; PMCID: PMC8776498.

[3]  Wisner, Joel D., Keah-Choon Tan, and Keong Leong. *Principles of Supply Chain Management: A Balanced Approach.* South-Western, Cengage Learning, 2021.

[4]  Cho, Dong Won, Young Hae Lee, Sung Hwa Ahn, and Min Kyu Hwang. "A framework for Measuring the Performance of Service Supply Chain Management." *Computers and Industrial Engineering* 62, no. 3, 801-818. 2012.

[5] Cabral, Izunildo, Antonio Grilo, and Virgílio Cruz-Machado. "A Decision-Making Model for Lean, Agile, Resilient and Green Supply Chain Management." *International Journal of Production Research* 50, no. 17, 4830-4845. 2012.

[6] John Mangan and Chandra Lalwani. *Global Logistics and Supply Chain Management.* John Wiley & Sons, 2016.

[7] Amulya Gurtu and Jestin Johny. "Supply Chain Risk Management: Literature Review," *Risks* 9, no. 1, 16. 2021.

[8] Xu, Zhitao, Adel Elomri, Laoucine Kerbache, and Abdelfatteh El Omri. "Impacts of COVID-19 on Global Supply Chains: Facts and Perspectives," *IEEE Engineering Management Review* 48, no. 3, 153-166. 2020.

[9] Magableh, Ghazi M. "Supply Chains and The COVID-19 Pandemic: A Comprehensive Framework," *European Management Review* 18, no. 3, 363-382. 2021.

[10] Ozdemir, Dilek, Mahak Sharma, Amandeep Dhir, and Tugrul Daim. "Supply Chain Resilience During The COVID-19 Pandemic," *Technology in Society* 68, 101847. 2022.

[11] Sarkis, Joseph. "Supply Chain Sustainability: Learning from the COVID-19 Pandemic," *International Journal of Operations and Production Management* 41, no. 1, 63-73. 2020.

[12] Ivanov, Dmitry. "Predicting the Impacts of Epidemic Outbreaks On Global Supply Chains: A Simulation-Based Analysis on the Coronavirus Outbreak (COVID-19/SARS-Cov-2) Case." *Transportation Research Part E: Logistics and Transportation Review* 136, 101922. 2020.

[13] Zhitao Xu, Adel Elomri, Laoucine Kerbache, and Abdelfatteh El Omri. "Impacts of COVID-19 on Global Supply Chains: Facts and Perspectives." *IEEE Engineering Management Review* 48, no. 3, 153-166. 2020.

[14] Christopher Dirzka and Michele Acciaro. "Global Shipping Network Dynamics During the COVID-19 Pandemic's Initial Phases," *Journal of Transport Geography* 99, 103265. 2022.

[15] Luis Miguel Fonseca and Américo Lopes Azevedo. "COVID-19: Outcomes for Global Supply Chains." *Management and Marketing. Challenges for the Knowledge Society* 15, no. s1, 424-438. 2020.

[16] Alok Raj, Abheek Anjan Mukherjee, Ana Beatriz Lopes de Sousa Jabbour, and Samir K. Srivastava. "Supply Chain Management During and Post-COVID-19 Pandemic: Mitigation Strategies and Practical Lessons Learned," *Journal of Business Research* 142, 1125-1139. 2022.

[17] Luis Miguel Fonseca and Américo Lopes Azevedo. "COVID-19: Outcomes for Global Supply Chains." *Management ad Marketing. Challenges for the Knowledge Society* 15, no. s1, 424-438. 2020.

[18] Atif Saleem Butt. "Supply Chains and COVID-19: Impacts, Countermeasures, and Post-COVID-19 Era," *The International Journal of Logistics Management*. 2021.

[19] Ferdoush Saleheen and Mohammad Mamun Habib. "Global Supply Chain Disruption Management Post Covid 19." *American Journal of Industrial and Business Management* 12, no. 3, 376-389. 2022.

[20] Shuichi Ishida. "Perspectives on Supply Chain Management in a Pandemic and the Post-COVID-19 Era," *IEEE Engineering Management Review* 48, no. 3, 146-152. 2020.

[21] Fiona A. Miller, Steven B. Young, Mark Dobrow, and Kaveh G. Shojania. "Vulnerability of the Medical Product Supply Chain: The Wake-Up Call of COVID-19." *BMJ Quality and Safety*. 2020.

[22] Sharmine Akthe Liza, Naimur Rahman Chowdhury, Sanjoy Kumar Paul, Mohammad Morshed, Shah Murtoza Morshed, MA Tanvir Bhuiyan, and Md Abdur Rahim. "Barriers to Achieving Sustainability In Pharmaceutical Supply Chains In The Post-COVID-19 Era," *International Journal of Emerging Markets* 18, no. 12, 6037-6060. 2023.

[23] Michael Omotayo Alabi and Ojelanki Ngwenyama. "Food Security and Disruptions of the Global Food Supply Chains During COVID-19: Building Smarter Food Supply Chains for Post COVID-19 Era," *British Food Journal* 125, no. 1, 167-185. 2023.

[24]    Jill E. Hobbs "Food Supply Chains During the
        COVID-19 Pandemic," *Canadian Journal of
        Agricultural Economics/Revue Canadienne
        d'Agroeconomie* 68, no. 2, 171-176. 2020.

[25]    Zhitao Xu, Adel Elomri, Laoucine Kerbache, and
        Abdelfatteh El Omri. "Impacts of COVID-19 on
        Global Supply Chains: Facts and Perspectives."
        *IEEE Engineering Management Review* 48, no. 3,
        153-166. 2020.

[26]    Amine Belhadi, Sachin Kamble, Charbel Jose
        Chiappetta Jabbour, Angappa Gunasekaran, Nelson
        Oly Ndubisi, and Mani Venkatesh. "Manufacturing
        and Service Supply Chain Resilience to the
        COVID-19 Outbreak: Lessons Learned from the
        Automobile and Airline Industries." *Technological
        Forecasting and Social Change* 163, 120447. 2021.

[27]    Tapas Sudan and Rashi Taggar. "Recovering Supply
        Chain Disruptions in Post-COVID-19 Pandemic
        Through Transport Intelligence And Logistics
        Systems: India's Experiences and Policy Options."
        *Frontiers in Future Transportation* 2, 660116. 2021.

[28]    Louise Curran, Jappe Eckhardt, and Jaemin Lee.
        "The Trade Policy Response to COVID-19 and Its
        Implications for International Business," *Critical
        Perspectives on International Business* 17, no. 2,
        252-320. 2021.

[29] Parvaneh Tavakol, Bijan Nahavandi, and Mahdi Homayounfar. "A Dynamics Approach for Modeling Inventory Fluctuations of the Pharmaceutical Supply Chain in COVID 19 Pandemic," *Journal of Optimization in Industrial Engineering* 16, no. 1, 105-118. 2023.

[30] Daniel Joseph Finkenstadt and Robert Handfield. "Blurry vision: Supply chain Visibility for Personal Protective Equipment During COVID-19." *Journal of Purchasing and Supply Management* 27, no. 3, 100689. 2021.

[31] Roba Hasaneya, Khadija Mohammed, Swathi Shankar, Ignatius Fernando, Chaitanya Sonambekar, and Nikita Garg. "Assessing the Effects of the COVID-19 Pandemic on the Aviation Sector and Exploring Strategies for Industry Recovery," *International Journal of Tourism and Hospitality in Asia Pasific (IJTHAP)* 6, no. 3, 18-28. 2023.

[32] Sanjoy Kumar Paul, Priyabrata Chowdhury, Md Abdul Moktadir, and Kwok Hung Lau. "Supply Chain Recovery Challenges in the Wake of COVID-19 Pandemic," *Journal of Business Research* 136, 316-329. 2021.

[33] Mark Anner. "Power Relations in Global Supply Chains and the Unequal Distribution of Costs During Crises: Abandoning Garment Suppliers and Workers During The COVID-19 Pandemic." *International Labour Review* 161, no. 1, 59-82. 2022.

[34]   Patrick Brandtner, Farzaneh Darbanian, Taha
       Falatouri, and Chibuzor Udokwu. "Impact
       of COVID-19 on the Customer End of Retail
       Supply Chains: A Big Data Analysis of Consumer
       Satisfaction," *Sustainability* 13, no. 3,1464. 2021.

[35]   Mohsen Attaran. "Digital Technology Enablers and
       Their Implications For Supply Chain Management,"
       In *Supply Chain Forum: An International Journal*,
       vol. 21, no. 3, 158-172. Taylor & Francis, 2020.

[36]   Javaid Butt. "A Conceptual Framework to Support
       Digital Transformation in Manufacturing Using
       an Integrated Business Process Management
       Approach." *Designs 4, no. 3, 17.* 2020.

[37]   Imran Ali and Kannan Govindan. "Extenuating
       Operational Risks Through Digital Transformation
       of Agri-Food Supply Chains," *Production Planning
       and Control* 34, no. 12, 1165-1177. 2023.

[38]   Efpraxia D. Zamani, Conn Smyth, Samrat Gupta,
       and Denis Dennehy. "Artificial Intelligence and
       Big Data Analytics for Supply Chain Resilience: A
       Systematic Literature Review," *Annals of Operations
       Research* 327, no. 2, 605-632. 2023.

[39]   Efpraxia D. Zamani, Conn Smyth, Samrat Gupta,
       and Denis Dennehy. "Artificial Intelligence and
       Big Data Analytics for Supply Chain Resilience: A
       Systematic Literature Review," *Annals of Operations
       Research* 327, no. 2, 605-632. 2023.

[40] Harsh M. Shah, Bhaskar B. Gardas, Vaibhav S. Narwane, and Hitansh S. Mehta. "The Contemporary State of Big Data Analytics and Artificial Intelligence Towards Intelligent Supply Chain Risk Management: A Comprehensive Review," *Kybernetes* 52, no. 5, 1643-1697. 2023.

[41] Usama Awan, Narmeen Kanwal, Suha Alawi, Janne Huiskonen, and Ajantha Dahanayake. "Artificial Intelligence for Supply Chain Success in the Era of Data Analytics." *The Fourth Industrial Revolution: Implementation of Artificial Intelligence for Growing Business Success* 3-21. 2021.

[42] Sachin Modgil, Rohit Kumar Singh, and Claire Hannibal. "Artificial Intelligence for Supply Chain Resilience: Learning from Covid-19," *The International Journal of Logistics Management* 33, no. 4, 1246-1268. 2022.

[43] Aminu M. Jibrin "The Role of AI in Predicting and Mitigating Supply Chain Disruptions." PhD diss., University of Maryland University College, 2022.

[44] Raphael Preindl, Konstantinos Nikolopoulos, and Konstantia Litsiou. "Transformation Strategies for the Supply Chain: The Impact of Industry 4.0 and Digital Transformation." In *Supply Chain Forum: An International Journal*, vol. 21, no. 1, pp. 26-34. Taylor & Francis, 2020.

[45] Rana M. Amir Latif, Muhammad Farhan, Osama Rizwan, Majid Hussain, Sohail Jabbar, and Shahzad Khalid. "Retail Level Blockchain Transformation for Product Supply Chain Using Truffle Development Platform," *Cluster Computing* 24 1-16. 2021.

[46]  S. Rohan Chatterjee, Vinod Kumar Shukla, Leena Wanganoo, and Suchi Dubey. "Transforming Supply chain Management through Industry 4.0," In *2021 9th International Conference on Reliability, Infocom Technologies and Optimization (Trends and Future Directions)(ICRITO)*, 1-6. IEEE, 2021.

[47]  Mohamed Grida and Noha A. Mostafa. "Are Smart Contracts Too Smart for Supply Chain 4.0? A Blockchain Framework to Mitigate Challenges," *Journal of Manufacturing Technology Management* 34, no. 4, 644-665. 2023.

[48]  Xiaohong Chen, Caicai He, Yan Chen, and Zhiyuan Xie. "Internet of Things (IoT)—Blockchain-Enabled Pharmaceutical Supply Chain Resilience In The Post-Pandemic Era," *Frontiers of Engineering Management* 10, no. 1, 82-95. 2023.

[49]  Berty Argiyantari, Togar M. Simatupang, and Mursyid Hasan Basri. "Pharmaceutical Supply Chain Transformation Through Application of the Lean Principle: A Literature Review," *Journal of Industrial Engineering and Management (JIEM)* 13, no. 3, 475-494. 2020.

[50]  Haishang Wu, Hamid Mehrabi, Nida Naveed, and Panagiotis Karagiannidis. "Impact of Strategic Control and Supply Chain Management on Recycled Plastic Additive Manufacturing," *Journal of Cleaner Production* 364,132511. 2022.

[51]   Emily L. Tucker and Mark S. Daskin.
       "Pharmaceutical Supply Chain Reliability And
       Effects On Drug Shortages," *Computers and
       Industrial Engineering* 169, 108258. 2022.

[52]   Clinton Free and Angela Hecimovic. "Global Supply
       Chains After COVID-19: The End of the Road for
       Neoliberal Globalisation?," *Accounting, Auditing
       and Accountability Journal* 34, no. 1, 58-84. 2021.

[53]   Jamal El Baz, and Salomée Ruel. "Can Supply Chain
       Risk Management Practices Mitigate The Disruption
       Impacts on Supply Chains' Resilience And
       Robustness? Evidence From an Empirical Survey in
       a COVID-19 Outbreak Era," *International Journal of
       Production Economics* 233, 107972. 2021.

[54]   Ali Emrouznejad, Sina Abbasi, and Çiğdem
       Sıcakyüz. "Supply Chain Risk Management: A
       Content Analysis-Based Review of Existing and
       Emerging Topics," *Supply Chain Analytics* 3
       100031. 2023.

[55]   Dimitrios Bechtsis, Naoum Tsolakis, Eleftherios
       Iakovou, and Dimitrios Vlachos. "Data-Driven
       Secure, Resilient And Sustainable Supply Chains:
       Gaps, Opportunities, and a New Generalised
       Data Sharing and Data Monetisation Framework,"
       *International Journal of Production Research* 60, no.
       14, 4397-4417. 2022.

[56]   Waqar Ahmed and Sehrish Huma. "Impact of
       Lean And Agile Strategies on Supply Chain Risk
       Management," *Total Quality Management and
       Business Excellence* 32, no. 1-2, 33-56. 2021.

486

[57] Kaushal Rameshbhai Patel. "Enhancing Global Supply Chain Resilience: Effective Strategies for Mitigating Disruptions in an Interconnected World," *BULLET: Jurnal Multidisiplin Ilmu* 2, no. 1, 257-264. 2023.

[58] Daisy Valle Enrique, Laura Visintainer Lerman, Paulo Renato de Sousa, Guilherme Brittes Benitez, Fernando M. Bigares Charrua Santos, and Alejandro G. Frank. "Being Digital and Flexible to Navigate the Storm: How Digital Transformation Enhances Supply Chain Flexibility in Turbulent Environments," *International Journal of Production Economics* 250 108668. 2022.

[59] Sudhir Madhav Patil, Pune Baramati, Neelkanth Chandrakant Dhone, and Ravi Harendra Chourasiya. "Industry 4.0 Technologies in the Context of Supply Chain Management 4.0," *The Online Journal of Distance Education and e-Learning* 11, no. 2, 2048-2058. 2023.

[60] Cormac Bryce, Patrick Ring, Simon Ashby, and Jamie K. Wardman. "Resilience in the Face of Uncertainty: Early Lessons From the COVID-19 Pandemic," In *COVID-19*, 48-55. Routledge, 2022.

[61] Asha Albuquerque Pai, Amitabh Anand, Nikhil Pazhoothundathil, and Lena Ashok. "Leadership Perspectives on Resilience Capabilities for Navigating Disruption," *Journal of Asia Business Studies*. 2023.

[62]   Arriel Benis, Sofia Amador Nelke, and Michael
       Winokur. "Training the Next Industrial Engineers
       and Managers about Industry 4.0: A Case Study
       About Challenges and *Opportunities* in the
       COVID-19 Era," Sensors 21, no. 9, 2905. 2021.

[63]   Solomiia Fedushko and Taras Ustyianovych.
       "E-Commerce Customers Behavior Research
       Using Cohort Analysis: A Case Study of COVID-19,"
       *Journal of Open Innovation: Technology, Market,
       and Complexity* 8, no. 1, 12. 2022.

[64]   Kerstin Eriksson, Reidar Staupe-Delgado, and
       Jørgen Holst. "Drawing Lessons from the COVID-19
       Pandemic: Seven Obstacles to Learning from Public
       Inquiries in the Wake of the Crisis." *Risk, Hazards
       and Crisis in Public Policy* 13, no. 2, 165-175. 2022.

[65]   Mihoko Sakurai and Hameed Chughtai. "Resilience
       Against Crises: COVID-19 and Lessons from Natural
       Disasters." *European Journal of Information Systems*
       29, no. 5, 585-594. 2020.

[66]   Guilherme F. Frederico "Towards a Supply Chain
       4.0 on the Post-COVID-19 Pandemic: A Conceptual
       and Strategic Discussion for More Resilient Supply
       Chains," *Rajagiri Management Journal* 15, no. 2,
       94-104. 2021.

[67]   Md Abdul Moktadir, Sanjoy Kumar Paul, Anil
       Kumar, Sunil Luthra, Syed Mithun Ali, and Razia
       Sultana. "Strategic Drivers to Overcome the Impacts
       of the COVID-19 Pandemic: Implications for
       Ensuring Resilience in Supply Chains." *Operations
       Management Research* 16, no. 1, 466-488. 2023.

# Chapter 11

- Olaniyi, E.O. and Reidolf, M. "Organisational Innovation Strategies in the Context of Smart Specialisation." J. Secur. *Sustain*. Issue 5, 213–227. 2015.

- *Starship*. "Data Protection? We Need a Feasible Balance between Business and Privacy." `www.european-business.com/starship-technologies/interviews/data-protection-we-need-a-feasible-balance-between-business-and-privacy/`. Accessed May 19, 2018.

- *CBinsight*. "The Robotics Startup Funding Landscape Broken Down in One Infographic." `www.cbinsights.com/research/robotics-deals-consumer-enterprise-medical/`. Accessed May 19, 2018.

- *Worldwide Semiannual Robotics and Drones Spending Guide*; International Data Corporation: Framingham, MA, USA. 2017.

- Basu, S.; Omotubora, A.; Beeson, M.; and Fox, C. "Legal Framework for Small Autonomous Agricultural Robots." `https://link.springer.com/content/pdf/10.1007%2Fs00146-018-0846-4.pdf`. Accessed July 10, 2018.

- Zhu, B.; Li, C.; Song, L.; Song, Y.; and Li, Y. "A* Algorithm of Global Path Planning Based on the Grid Map and V-Graph Environmental Model for the Mobile Robot," In *Proceedings of the 2017 Chinese Automation Congress (CAC)*, Jinan, China, 4973–4977. October 20-22, 2017.

## REFERENCES

- Lin, M.; Yuan, K.; Shi, C.; and Wang, Y. "Path Planning Of Mobile Robot Based on Improved A* Algorithm," In *Proceedings of the 2017 29th Chinese Control And Decision Conference (CCDC)*, Chongqing, China. 3570–3576. May 28-30, 2017.

- Noreen, I.; Khan, A.; and Habib, Z. "Optimal Path Planning for Mobile Robots Using Memory E_cient A*," In *Proceedings of the 2016 International Conference on Frontiers of Information Technology (FIT)*, Islamabad, Pakistan, 142–146. December 19-21, 2016.

- Petavratzis, E.K.; Volos, C.K.; Stouboulos, I.N.; Kyprianidis, I.M.; Nistazakis, H.E.; and Tombras, G.S. "Robot's Path Planning Based on Emulated Finite Resistive Grids," In *Proceedings of the 2018 7th International Conference on Modern Circuits and Systems Technologies (MOCAST)*, Thessaloniki, Greece, 1–4. May 7-9, 2018.

- Samadi, M. and Othman, M.F. "Global Path Planning for Autonomous Mobile Robot Using Genetic Algorithm," In *Proceedings of the 2013 International Conference on Signal-Image Technology & Internet-Based Systems*, Kyoto, Japan, 726–730. December 2-5, 2013.

- Ajeil, F.H.; Ibraheem, I.K.; Sahib, M.A.; and Humaidi, A.J. "Multi-Objective Path Planning of an Autonomous Mobile Robot Using Hybrid PSO-MFB Optimization Algorithm," *Appl. Soft Comput.* 106076. 2020.

- Che, H.; Wu, Z.; Kang, R.; and Yun, C. "Global Path Planning for Explosion-Proof Robot Based on Improved Ant Colony Optimization," In *Proceedings of the 2016 Asia-Pacific Conference on Intelligent Robot Systems (ACIRS)*, Tokyo, Japan, 36–40. July 20-22, 2016.

- Akulovic´, M.; C˘ikeš, M.; and Petrovic´, I. "E_client Interpolated Path Planning Of Mobile Robots Based On Occupancy Grid Maps," *IFAC Proc.* 45, 349–354. 2012.

- Dewang, H.S.; Mohanty, P.K.; and Kundu, S. "A Robust Path Planning for Mobile Robot Using Smart Particle Swarm Optimization," *Procedia Comput. Sci.* 133, 290–297. 2018.

- Roman, R.C.; Precup, R.E.; Bojan-Dragos, C.A.; and Szedlak-Stinean, A.I. "Combined Model-Free Adaptive Control with Fuzzy Component by Virtual Reference Feedback Tuning for Tower Crane Systems," *Procedia Comput. Sci.* 162, 267–274. 2019.

# Chapter 12

[1] Agrawal, R., Nurmamatovna, I.S., Xudayarovich, T.S., Karimovich, S.J. and Khaldarova, G., "Sustainable Development with Industry 4.0: A Study with Design, Features and Challenges," *Journal of Integrated Science and Technology*, 12(2),737-737. 2024.

[2] Bibri, S.E., Krogstie, J., Kaboli, A. and Alahi, A. "Smarter Eco-Cities and Their Leading-Edge Artificial Intelligence of Things Solutions for Environmental Sustainability: A Comprehensive Systematic Review," *Environmental Science and Ecotechnology*, 19, 100330. 2024.

[3]   Dehshiri, S.J.H. and Amiri, M. *Evaluation of Blockchain Implementation Solutions in the Sustainable Supply Chain: A Novel Hybrid Decision Approach Based on Z-Numbers. Expert Systems with Applications,* 235,121-123. 2024.

[4]   Sharad Mangrulkar, R. and Vijay Chavan, P. "Case Studies Using Blockchain," In *Blockchain Essentials: Core Concepts and Implementations* Berkeley, CA: Apress. 203-227. 2024.

[5]   Fowdur, T.P., Hurbungs, V. and Babooram, L. "Leveraging the Power of Blockchain in Industry 4.0 and Intelligent Real-Time Systems for Achieving the SDGs," In *Artificial Intelligence, Engineering Systems and Sustainable Development.* Emerald Publishing Limited. 109-121. 2024.

[6]   Kusi-Sarpong, S., Gupta, H., Khan, S.A., Chiappetta Jabbour, C.J., Rehman, S.T., and Kusi-Sarpong, H. "Sustainable Supplier Selection Based on Industry 4.0 Initiatives within the Context Of Circular Economy Implementation in Supply Chain Operations," *Production Planning and Control,* 34(10), 999-1019. 2023.

[7]   Cahyono, Y., Purwoko, D., Koho, I., Setiani, A., Supendi, S., Setyoko, P., Sosiady, M. and Wijoyo, H. "The Role of Supply Chain Management Practices on Competitive Advantage and Performance of Halal Agroindustry SMEs," *Uncertain Supply Chain Management,* 11(1),153-160. 2023.

[8] Khan, M., Ajmal, M.M., Jabeen, F., Talwar, S., and Dhir, A. "Green Supply Chain Management in Manufacturing Firms: A Resource-Based Viewpoint," *Business Strategy and the Environment,* 32(4),1603-1618. 2023.

[9] Daghighi, A. and Shoushtari, F. "Toward Sustainability of Supply Chain by Applying Blockchain Technology," *International Journal of Industrial Engineering and Operational Research,* 5(2), 60-72. 2023.

[10] Radmanesh, S.A., Haji, A., and Fatahi Valilai, O. "Blockchain-Based Architecture for a Sustainable Supply Chain in Cloud Architecture," *Sustainability,* 15(11),9072. 2023.

[11] Hmouda, A.M., Orzes, G., and Sauer, P.C. "Sustainable Supply Chain Management in Energy Production: A Literature Review," *Renewable and Sustainable Energy Reviews,* 191, 114085. 2024.

[12] Gonçalves, H., Magalhães, V.S., Ferreira, L.M., and Arantes, A. "Overcoming Barriers to Sustainable Supply Chain Management in Small and Medium-Sized Enterprises: A Multi-Criteria Decision-Making Approach," *Sustainability,* 16(2), 506. 2024.

[13] Vashishth, T.K., Sharma, V., Sharma, K.K., Kumar, B., Chaudhary, S. and Panwar, R. "Intelligent Resource Allocation and Optimization for Industrial Robotics Using AI and Blockchain," *AI and Blockchain Applications in Industrial Robotics* IGI Global. 82-110. 2024.

REFERENCES

[14]  Kayikci, S. and Khoshgoftaar, T.M. "Blockchain Meets Machine Learning: A Survey," *Journal of Big Data*, 11(1), 1-29. 2024.

[15]  Kaur, A. and Tanwar, A. "Adoption Potential and Challenges of Artificial Intelligence in Banking," *Sustainable Investments in Green Finance.* IGI Global. 271-293. 2024

[16]  Agrawal, R., Nurmamatovna, I.S., Xudayarovich, T.S., Karimovich, S.J., and Khaldarova, G. "Sustainable Development with Industry 4.0: A Study with Design, Features and Challenges," *Journal of Integrated Science and Technology*, 12(2), 737-737. 2024.

[17]  Symons, J. and Abumusab, S. "Social Agency for Artifacts: Chatbots and the Ethics of Artificial Intelligence," *Digital Society*, 3(1), 2. 2024.

[18]  Sharma, W., Lim, W. M., Kumar, S., Verma, A. and Kumra, R., "Game on! A State-of-the-Art Overview of Doing Business with Gamification," *Technological Forecasting and Social Change*, *198*, 122988. 2024.

[19]  Abulibdeh, A., Zaidan, E. and Abulibdeh, R. "Navigating the Confluence of Artificial Intelligence and Education for Sustainable Development in the Era Of Industry 4.0: Challenges, Opportunities, and Ethical Dimensions," *Journal of Cleaner Production*, 140527. 2024.

[20]   Wang, Y., Han, J.H. and Beynon-Davies,
       P. Understanding Blockchain Technology for Future
       Supply Chains: A Systematic Literature Review and
       Research Agenda," *Supply Chain Management: An
       International Journal*, 24(1), 62-84. 2019.

[21]   Xiao, G., Samian, N., Faizal, M.F.M., As'ad, M.A.Z.M.,
       Fadzil, M.F.M., Abdullah, A., Seah, W.K.G., Ishak,
       M. and Hermadi, I. "A Framework for Blockchain
       and Internet of Things Integration in Improving
       Food Security in the Food Supply Chain," *Journal
       of Advanced Research in Applied Sciences and
       Engineering Technology*, 34(1), 24-37. 2024.

[22]   A'isy, Q., Mufaridah, F. and Nurkamilah, N. "The
       Challenges of Teaching Speaking to High School
       Students through Zoom Video Conference
       Application," *Pubmedia Jurnal Pendidikan Bahasa
       Inggris*, 1(2), 8. 2024.

# Chapter 13

- Zheng, Z., Xie, S., Dai, H. N., Chen, X., and Wang,
  H. "Blockchain Challenges and Opportunities:
  A survey," *International Journal of Web and Grid
  Assistance*, 14(4), 352-375. 2018.

- Aste, T., Tasca, P., and Di Matteo, T. "Blockchain
  Technologies: The Foreseeable Impact on Society and
  Industry," *Computer*, 50(9), 18-28. 2017.

- Crosby, M., Pattanayak, P., Verma, S., and
  Kalyanaraman, V. "Blockchain Technology: Beyond
  Bitcoin," *Applied Innovation*, 2(6-10), 71. 2016.

## REFERENCES

- Xie, S., Zheng, Z., Chen, W., Wu, J., Dai, H. N., and Imran, M. "Blockchain for Cloud Exchange: A Survey," *Computers and Electrical Engineering*, 81, 106526. 2020.

- Sanjay, S., Ananya, V., Prasat, S.K., Kishore, P., and Santhi, K. "Security and Privacy Trade-Off in Cryptocurrencies: An Implementation of Blockchain Technology," *Hybridization of Blockchain and Cloud Computing: Overcoming Security Issues in IoT*, 215–239. 2023.

- Shri, M.L., Gangadevi, E., Santhi, K., and Chowdhary, C.L. *Hybridization of Blockchain and Cloud Computing: Overcoming Security Issues in IoT*, 1–263. 2023.

- Gupta Paluri, C., Santhi, K. "Consensus Mechanism of Blockchain for Industrial Internet of Things (IIoT)," *Hybridization of Blockchain and Cloud Computing: Overcoming Security Issues in IoT*, 203–214. 2023.

- Lohia, G. and Santhi, K. *Hybridization of Blockchain and Cloud Computing: Overcoming Security Issues in IoT*, 187–202. 2023.

- Santhi, K. and Lawanyashri M. "Performance evaluation of transactions in blockchain based on workload using queueing model," *Journal of Green Engineering* Vol 10, Issue 5, 2446-2457. 2020.

- Santhi, K. and Saravanan, R. "Performance Analysis of Cloud Computing Using Series of Queues with Erlang Service," *International Journal Internet Technology and Secured Transactions* 9(1/2), 147-162. 2019.

- Santhi, K. and Saravanan, R. "Performance Analysis of Cloud Computing in Healthcare System Using Tandem Queues," *International Journal of Intelligent Engineering and Systems* 10(4), 256-264. 2017.

- Santhi, K. and Saravanan, R. "Performance Analysis of Cloud Computing Using Batch Queueing Models in Healthcare Systems," *Research Journal of Pharmacy and Technology* 10(10), 3331-3336. 2017.

- Santhi, K. and Saravanan, R. "Performance Analysis of Cloud Computing Bulk Service Using Queueing Models," *International Journal of Applied Engineering Research* 12(7), 6487-6492. 2017.

- Santhi, K. and Saravanan, R. "A Survey on Queueing Models for Cloud Computing," *International Journal of Pharmacy and Technology* 8(2), 3964 - 3977. 2016.

- Santhi K. and Patel R. "Sheds: A Simple and Secure Cost Efficient Data Storage in Heterogeneous Multiple Cloud," *International Journal of Pharmacy and Technology,* Vol 8, Issue 4, 26058 - 26065.

- Santhi, K. and Priyadarshini C. "Efficiently Allocating the Virtual Machines in Cloud Environment," *International Journal of Applied Engineering Research,* Vol 9, Issue 3, 887-392.

- Antidham, T. and Aung, Y. N. "Emergency Service for Smart Home System Using Ethereum Blockchain: System and Architecture," *2019 IEEE international conference on pervasive computing and communications workshops (PerCom Workshops).* 888-893. March 2019.

497

## REFERENCES

- Li, X., Zheng, Z., and Dai, H. N. "When Assistance Computing Meets Blockchain: Challenges and Opportunities," *Journal of Parallel and Distributed Computing*, 150, 1-14. 2021.

- Mohammadzadeh, N., Nogoorani, S. D., and Muñoz-Tapia, J. L. "Invoice Factoring Registration Based on a Public Blockchain," *IEEE Access*, 9, 24221 - 24233. 2021.

- Dai, H. N., Zheng, Z., and Zhang, Y. "Blockchain for Internet of Things: A survey," *IEEE Internet of Things Journal*, 6(5), 8076-8094. 2019.

- Yu, C., Zhang, L., Zhao, W., and Zhang, S. "A Blockchain-Based Service Composition Architecture in Cloud Manufacturing," *International Journal of Computer Integrated Manufacturing*, 33(7), 701-715. 2020.

- Park, J. H. and Park, J. H. "Blockchain Security in Cloud Computing: Use Cases, Challenges, and Solutions," *Symmetry*, 9(8), 164. 2017.

- Murthy, C. V. B. and Shri, M. L. "A Survey on Integrating Cloud Computing with Blockchain," *2020 International Conference on Emerging Trends in Information Technology and Engineering* (ic-ETITE) 1-6. February 2020.

- Lawanyashri, M., Balusamy, B., and Subha, S. "Energy-Aware Hybrid Fruitfly Optimization for Load Balancing in Cloud Environments for EHR Applications," *Informatics in Medicine Unlocked*, 8, 42-50. 2017.

- Lawanya Shri, M., Ganga Devi, E., Balusamy, B., Kadry, S., Misra, S., and Odusami, M. "A Fuzzy Based Hybrid Firefly Optimization Technique for Load Balancing in Cloud Datacenters," *Innovations in Bio-Inspired.* 2019.

- Shri, M. L., Devi, E. G., Balusamy, B., and Chatterjee, J. M. "Ontology-Based Information Retrieval and Matching in IoT Applications," *Natural Language Processing in Artificial Intelligence,* Apple Academic Press. 113-130. 2020.

- Shri, M. L. and Gangadevi, E. "Blockchain Technology-Based Industrial Internet of Things: Research Challenges," *Hybridization of Blockchain and Cloud Computing,* 61-74. 2023.

- Sujigarasharma, K., Shri, M. L., Gangadevi, E., Dhanaraj, R. K., Narmatha, C., and Balusamy, B. "Detection and Classification of Speech Disorder using FOA-SCNet," *2023 3rd International Conference on Computing and Information Technology (ICCIT)* IEEE. 391-395. September 2023.

- Hemalatha, T., Bhuvaneswari, A., Poornima, N., Shubha, B., Santhi, K., Lawanyashri, M., and Mara, G. C. "Secure and Private Data Sharing in CPS e-Health Systems Based on CB-SMO Techniques," *Measurement: Sensors,* 27, 100787. 2023.

- Hemalatha, T., Sangeetha, K., Rani, K. S. K., Kanimozhi, K. V., Lawanyashri, M., Santhi, K., and Deepalakshmi, R. "CPS in Block Chain Smart City Application Based on Distributed Ledger Based Decentralized Technique," *Measurement: Sensors,* 30, 100906. 2023.

- Radanović, I. and Likić, R. "Opportunities for Use of Blockchain Technology in Medicine." *Applied Health Economics and Health Policy*, 16(5), 583-590. 2018.

- Kraft, D. "Difficulty Control for Blockchain-Based Consensus Systems," *Peerto-Peer Networking and Applications*, 9(2), 397-413. 2016.

- Karamchandani, A., Srivastava, S. K., and Srivastava, R. K. "Perception Based Model for Analyzing the Impact Of Enterprise Blockchain Adoption on SCM in the Indian Service Industry," *International Journal of Information Controlment*, 52, 102019. 2020.

- Kernahan, A., Bernskov, U., and Beck, R. "Blockchain Out of the Box–Where is the Blockchain in Blockchain-as-a-Service." *Proceedings of the 54th Hawaii International Conference on System Sciences,* 4281. January 2021.

- Zhang, Y., Zhang, L., Liu, Y., and Luo, X. "Proof of Service Power: A Blockchain Consensus for Cloud Manufacturing. *Journal of Manufacturing Systems,* 59, 1-11. 2021.

- Tomar, P. and Grover, V. "Transforming the Energy Sector: Addressing Key Challenges through Generative AI, Digital Twins, AI, Data Science and Analysis," *EAI Endorsed Transactions on Energy Web, 10.* https://doi.org/10.4108/ew.4825. 2024.

- M. A. Ali, R. K. Dhanaraj, A. K. Sharma, B. Balusamy, G. V. and V. Grover, "Multi-Module Deep Learning and IoT-Based Pest Detection System Using Sound Analytics in Large Agricultural Field," *2023 International Conference on Electrical, Electronics, Communication and Computers (ELEXCOM)*, Roorkee, India. 1-6, doi: 10.1109/ELEXCOM58812.2023.10370552. 2023.

- T. Seetharaman, V. Sharma, B. B. V. Grover, and A. Agnihotri, "An Efficient and Robust Explainable Artificial Intelligence for Securing Smart Healthcare System," *2023 Second International Conference On Smart Technologies For Smart Nation (SmartTechCon)*, Singapore, Singapore. 1066-1071, doi: 10.1109/SmartTechCon57526.2023.10391664. 2023.

- Srivastava, S., Grover, V., Nallakaruppan, M.K., Krishwanth, B., and Saravanan, K, "Decentralization of Identities Using Blockchain", *2023 10th IEEE Uttar Pradesh Section International Conference on Electrical, Electronics and Computer Engineering*, UPCON 2023. 1304–1309. 2023.

- C. Sachdeva, V. P. Gangwar, V. Grover, and S. Gochhait, "Cognitive Dissonance in Banking Employees: Exploring Factors Amid the Artificial Intelligence Revolution," *2024 ASU International Conference in Emerging Technologies for Sustainability and Intelligent Systems (ICETSIS)*, Manama, Bahrain. 1731-1735, doi: 10.1109/ICETSIS61505.2024.10459558. 2024.

- M. G. Brahmam, V. Anand R, V. Grover, and S. Gochhait, "Optimizing Requirements Prioritization: Majority Voting Goal-Based Approach with Vertical Binary Search," *2024 ASU International Conference in Emerging Technologies for Sustainability and Intelligent Systems (ICETSIS)*, Manama, Bahrain.. 1283-1288, doi: 10.1109/ICETSIS61505.2024.10459533. 2024.

# Chapter 14

- Adivar, B., Hüseyinoğlu, I.Ö.Y., and Christopher, M. "A Quantitative Performance Management Framework for Assessing Omnichannel Retail Supply Chains," *Journal Of Retailing And Consumer Services*, Vol. 48 No. 3, 257-269. 2019.

- Agostini, L. and Filippini, R. "Organizational and Managerial Challenges in the Path Towards Industry 4 0", *European Journal of Innovation Management*, Vol. 29 No. 6, 910-936. 2019.

- Akbaripour, H., Houshmand, M. and Fatahi Valilai, O. "Cloud-Based Global Supply Chain: A Conceptual Model and Multilayer Architecture," *Journal of Manufacturing Science and Engineering*, Vol. 137 No. 4. 1-6, available at https://asmedigitalcollection. asme.org/manufacturingscience/article-abstract/137/4/040913/375206/Cloud-Based-Global-Supply-Chain-A-Conceptual-Model?redirect edFrom=fulltext. 2015.

- Albers, A., Gladysz, B., Pinner, T., Butenko, V., and Stürmlinger, T. "Procedure for Defining the System of Objectives in the Initial Phase of an Industry 4.0 Project Focusing on Intelligent Quality Control Systems." *Procedia CIRP*, Vol. 52 No. 1, 262-267. 2016.

- Alcácer, V. and Cruz-Machado, V. "Scanning the Industry 4.0: A Literature Review on Technologies for Manufacturing Systems," *Engineering Science and Technology, An International Journal*, Vol. 22 No. 3, 899-919. 2019.

- Almajali, D.A., Masa'deh, R., and Tarhini, A. "Antecedents of ERP Systems Implementation Success: A Study on Jordanian Healthcare Sector," *Journal of Enterprise Information Management*, Vol. 29 No. 4, 549-565. 2016.

- Ammirato, S., Sofo, F., Felicetti, A.M., and Raso, C. "A Methodology to Support the Adoption of IOT Innovation and its Application to the Italian Bank Branch Security Context," *European Journal of Innovation Management*, Vol. 22 No. 1, 146-174. 2019.

- Andoni, M., Robu, V., Flynn, D., Abram, S., Geach, D., Jenkins, D., McCallum, P. et al. "Blockchain Technology in the Energy Sector: A Systematic Review of Challenges and Opportunities," *Renewable and Sustainable Energy Reviews*, Vol. 100 No. 2, 143-174. 2019.

- Ang, J.H., Goh, C., Saldivar, A.A.F., and Li, Y. "Energy-Efficient Through-Life Smart Design, Manufacturing and Operation of Ships in an Industry 4.0 Environment", *Energies*, Vol. 10 No. 5, 1-14. 2017.

- Ardito, L., Petruzzelli, A.M., Panniello, U., and Garavelli, A.C. "Towards Industry 4.0: Mapping Digital Technologies for Supply Chain Management-Marketing Integration," *Business Process Management Journal*, Vol. 25 No. 2, 323-346. 2018.

- Bag, S., Telukdarie, A., Pretorius, J., and Gupta, S. "Industry 4.0 and Supply Chain Sustainability: Framework and Future Research Directions," *Benchmarking: An International Journal*, available at https://doi.org/10.1108/BIJ-03-2018-0056. 2018.

- Ballou, R.H. *Business Logistics Supply Chain Management: Planning, Organizing, and Controlling the Supply Chain*, 5th ed., Pearson Prentice Hall, Upper Saddle River, N.J. 2004.

- Bär, K., Herbert-Hansen, Z.N.L,. and Khalid, W. "Considering Industry 4.0 Aspects in the Supply Chain for an SME", *Production Engineering*, Vol. 12 No. 6, 747-758. 2018.

- Barata, J., Rupino Da Cunha, P., and Stal, J. "Mobile Supply Chain Management in the Industry 4.0 Era: An Annotated Bibliography and Guide for Future Research," *Journal of Enterprise Information Management*, Vol. 31 No. 1, 173-192. 2018.

- Bartnik, R. and Park, Y. "Technological Change, Information Processing and Supply Chain Integration: A Conceptual Model", *Benchmarking*, Vol. 25 No. 5, 1279-1301. 2018.

- Baruffaldi, G., Accorsi, R., and Manzini, R. "Warehouse Management System Customization and Information Availability in 3pl Companies: A Decision-Support Tool," *Industrial Management and Data Systems*, Vol. 119 No. 2, 251-273. 2019.

- Ben-Daya, M., Hassini, E., and Bahroun, Z. "Internet of Things and Supply Chain Management: A Literature Review," *International Journal of Production Research*, Vol. 7543 Nos 15-16, 1-24. 2017.

- Bibby, L. and Dehe, B. "Defining and Assessing Industry 4.0 Maturity Levels–Case of the Defence Sector," *Production Planning and Control*, Vol. 29 No. 12, 1030-1043. 2018.

- Bienhaus, F. and Haddud, A. "Procurement 4.0: Factors Influencing The Digitisation Of Procurement And Supply Chains," *Business Process Management Journal*, Vol. 24 No. 4, 965-984. 2018.

- Birkel, H.S. and Hartmann, E. "Impact of IoT Challenges and Risks for SCM," *Supply Chain Management*, Vol. 24 No. 1, 39-61. 2019.

- Borgia, E. "The Internet of Things Vision: Key Features, Applications and Open Issues," *Computer Communications*, Vol. 54 No. 18, 1-31. 2014.

- Buonafede, F., Felice, G., Lamperti, F. and Piscitello, L. "Additive Manufacturing and Global Value Chains: An Empirical Investigation at the Country Level", in van Tulder, R., Verbeke, A. and Piscitello, L. (Eds), *International Business in the Information and Digital Age* (Progress in International Business Research, Vol. 13), Emerald Publishing, 295-323, available at https://doi.org/10.1108/S1745-886220180000013013. 2018.

- Chan, H. K., Griffin, J., Lim, J. J., Zeng, F. and Chiu, A.S.F. "The Impact Of 3D Printing Technology on the Supply Chain: Manufacturing and Legal Perspectives," *International Journal of Production Economics*, Vol. 205 No. 11, 156-162. 2018.

- Chang, D.S. and Lai, S.T. "Develop a Novel Unified Interface Design on Automation Transportation System in LCD Industry," *International Journal of Advanced Manufacturing Technology*, Vol. 88 Nos 5-8, 2097-2108. 2017.

- Chen, I.J. and Paulraj, A. "Towards a Theory of Supply Chain Management: The Constructs and Measurements," *Journal of Operations Management*, Vol. 22 No. 2, 119-150. 2004.

- Chiarvesio, M. and Romanello, R. "Industry 4.0 Technologies And Internationalization: Insights From Italian Companies," in van Tulder, R., Verbeke, A. and Piscitello, L. (Eds), *International Business in the Information and Digital Age (Progress in International Business Research*, Vol. 13), Emerald Publishing, 357-378, available at https://doi.org/10.1108/S1745-886220180000013015. 2018.

- Choi, T.M. "A System of Systems Approach for Global Supply Chain Management in the Big Data Era," *IEEE Engineering Management Review*, Vol. 46 No. 1, 91-97. 2018.

- Chong, K.P. and Zhu, S. "Innovative Technologies in Manufacturing, Mechanics and Smart Civil Infrastructure," *International Journal of Smart and Nano Materials*, Vol. 9 No. 4, 261-278. 2018.

- Chopra, S., Meindl, P., and Kalra, D.V. *Supply ChainManagement: Strategy, Planning, and Operation*, 6th ed., Pearson/Prentice Hall, Upper Saddle River, N.J. 2016.

- Dalenogare, L.S., Benitez, G.B., Ayala, N.F., and Frank, A.G. "The Expected Contribution of Industry 4.0 Technologies for Industrial Performance," *International Journal of Production Economics*, Vol. 204 No. 10, 383-394. 2018.

- Dallasega, P., Rauch, E., and Linder, C. "Industry 4.0 As an Enabler of Proximity for Construction Supply Chains: A Systematic Literature Review," *Computers in Industry*, Vol. 99 No. 6, 205-225. 2018.

- Duclos, L.K., Vokurka, R.J., and Lummus, R.R. "A Conceptual Model of Supply Chain Flexibility," *Industrial Management and Data Systems*, Vol. 103 No. 6, 446-456. 2023.

- Eden, L. "The Fourth Industrial Revolution: Seven Lessons from the Past" in van Tulder, R., Verbeke, A. and Piscitello, L. (Eds), *International Business in the Information and Digital Age (Progress in International Business Research,* Vol. 13), Emerald Publishing Limited, 15-35, available at `https://doi.org/10.1108/S1745-886220180000013002`. 2018.

- Faheem, M., Shah, S.B.H., Butt, R.A., Raza, B., Anwar, M., Ashraf, M.W., Ngadi, M.A. et al. "Smart Grid Communication and Information Technologies in the Perspective Of Industry 4.0: Opportunities and Challenges," *Computer Science Review*, Vol. 30 No. 4, 1-30. 2018.

- Farooque, M., Zhang, A., Thürer, M., Qu, T. and Huisingh, D. "Circular Supply Chain Management: A Definition and Structured Literature Review," *Journal of Cleaner Production*, Vol. 228 No. 23, 882-900. 2019.

- Fosso Wamba, S. "Achieving Supply Chain Integration Using RFID Technology: The Case of Emerging Intelligent B-To-B E-Commerce Processes in a Living Laboratory," *Business Process Management Journal*, Vol. 18 No. 1, 58-81. 2012.

- Frank, A.G., Dalenogare, L.S., and Ayala, N.F. "Industry 4.0 Technologies: Implementation Patterns in Manufacturing Companies," *International Journal of Production Economics*, Vol. 210 No. 4, 15-26.5. 2019.

- Grover, V. and Nandal, M. "Education System Using Cloud Computing: A Proposed Model," In G. Prakasha, M. Lapina, D. Balakrishnan, & M. Sajid (Eds.), *Educational Perspectives on Digital Technologies in Modeling and Management* 178-194. IGI Global. https://doi.org/10.4018/979-8-3693-2314-4. ch009. 2024.

- Habraken, M. and Bondarouk, T. "Smart Industry Research in the Field of HRM: Resetting Job Design as an Example of Upcoming Challenges," in Bondarouk, T., Ruël, H. and Parry, E. (Eds), *Electronic HRM in the Smart Era (The Changing Context of Managing People)*, Emerald Publishing, 221-259, available at https://doi.org/10.1108/978-1-78714-315-920161009. 2017.

- Haddud, A., DeSouza, A., Khare, A., and Lee, H. "Examining Potential Benefits and Challenges Associated with the Internet of Things Integration in Supply Chains," *Journal of Manufacturing Technology Management*, Vol. 28 No. 8, 1055-1085. 2017.

- Jacobs, F.R., Chase, R.B., Aquilano and N.J. *Operations and Supply Management*, 12th ed., McGraw-Hill. 2008.

- Jiang, C., Ma, Y., Chen, H., Zheng, Y., Gao, S., and Cheng, S. "Cyber Physics System: A Review", *Library Hi Tech*, available at https://doi.org/10.1108/LHT-11-2017-0256. 2018.

- Kache, F. and Seuring, S. "Challenges and Opportunities of Digital Information at the Intersection of Big Data Analytics and Supply Chain Management," *International Journal of Operations and Production Management*, Vol. 37 No. 1, 10-36. 2017.

- Korpela, K., Hallikas, J., and Dahlberg, T. "Digital Supply Chain Transformation Toward Blockchain Integration," *Proceedings of the 50th Hawaii International Conference on System Sciences* 4182-4191. 2017.

- Lambert, D.M. *Supply Chain Management-Processes, Partnerships, Performance*, 2nd ed., Supply Chain Institute. 2014.

- Lambert, D.M. and Schwieterman, M.A. "Supplier Relationship Management As A Macro Business Process," *Supply Chain Management: An International Journal*, Vol. 17 No. 3, 337-352. 2012.

- Leminen, S., Rajahonka, M., Westerlund, M., and Wendelin, R. "The Future of the Internet of Things: Toward Heterarchical Ecosystems and Service Business Models," *Journal of Business and Industrial Marketing*, Vol. 33 No. 6, 749-767. 2018.

- Lin, D., Lee, C.K.M., Lau, H., and Yang, Y. "Strategic Response to Industry 4.0: An Empirical Investigation on the Chinese Automotive Industry," *Industrial Management and Data Systems*, Vol. 118 No. 3, 589-605. 2018.

- Liukkonen, M. and Tsai, T.N. "Toward Decentralized Intelligence in Manufacturing: Recent Trends in Automatic Identification of Things," *International Journal of Advanced Manufacturing Technology*, Vol. 87 Nos 9-12, 2509-2531. 2016.

- Lopes de Sousa Jabbour, A. "Going in Circles: New Business Models for Efficiency and Value," *Journal of Business Strategy*, Vol. 40 No. 4, 36-43, available at https://doi.org/10.1108/JBS-05-2018-0092. 2019.

- M. A. Ali, R. K. Dhanaraj, A. K. Sharma, B. Balusamy, G. V., and V. Grover, "Multi-Module Deep Learning and IoT-Based Pest Detection System Using Sound Analytics in Large Agricultural Field," *2023 International Conference on Electrical, Electronics, Communication and Computers (ELEXCOM)*, Roorkee, India. 1-6, doi: 10.1109/ELEXCOM58812.2023.10370552. 2023.

- MacCarthy, B.L., Blome, C., Olhager, J., Srai, J.S., and Zhao, X. "Supply Chain Evolution – Theory, Concepts and Science," *International Journal of Operations and Production Management*, Vol. 36 No. 12, 1696-1718. 2016.

- Majeed, M.A.A. and Rupasinghe, T.D. "Internet of Things (IoT) Embedded Future Supply Chains for Industry 4.0: An Assessment from an ERP-Based Fashion Apparel and Footwear Industry," *International Journal of Supply Chain Management*, Vol. 6 No. 1, 25-40. 2017.

- Martínez Sánchez, A. and Pérez Pérez, M. "Supply Chain Flexibility and Firm Performance: A Conceptual Model and Empirical Study in the Automotive Industry," *International Journal of Operations & Production Management*, Vol. 25 No. 7, 681-700, available at https://doi.org/10.1108/01443570510605090. 2005.

- Moher, D., Liberati, A., Tetzlaff, J., and Altman, D.G. "Preferred Reporting Items for Systematic Reviews and Meta-Analyses: The PRISMA Statement," *Journal of Clinical Epidemiology*, Vol. 62 No. 10, 1006-1012. 2009.

- Oh, J. and Jeong, B. "Tactical Supply Planning in Smart Manufacturing Supply Chain", *Robotics and Computer-Integrated Manufacturing*, Vol. 55, 217-233. April 2019.

- Oswald, G. and Kleinemeier, M. "Shaping the Digital Enterprise: Trends and Use Cases in Digital Innovation and Transformation," in Oswald, G. and Kleinemeier, M. (Eds), *Shaping the Digital Enterprise: Trends and Use Cases in Digital Innovation and Transformation*, Springer Nature, available at https://doi.org/10.1007/978-3-319-40967-2. 2017.

- Rachinger, M., Rauter, R., Müller, C., Vorraber, W., and Schirgi, E. "Digitalization nd Its Influence On Business Model Innovation," *Journal of Manufacturing Technology Management*, Vol. 30 No. 8, 1143-1160, available at https://doi.org/10.1108/JMTM-01-2018-0020. 2019.

- Ramadan, M., Al-Maimani, H., and Noche, B. "RFID-Enabled Smart Real-Time Manufacturing Cost Tracking System," *International Journal of Advanced Manufacturing Technology*, Vol. 89 Nos. 1-4, 969-985. 2017.

- Ranjan, S., Jha, V.K., and Pal, P. "Application of Emerging Technologies In ERP Implementation In Indian Manufacturing Enterprises: An Exploratory Analysis Of Strategic Benefits," *International Journal of Advanced Manufacturing Technology*, Vol. 88 Nos. 1-4, 369-380. 2017.

- Seuring, S. and Gold, S. "Conducting Content-Analysis Based Literature Reviews In Supply Chain Management," *Supply Chain Management*, Vol. 17 No. 5, 544-555. 2012.

- Sharma, A. and Foropon, C. "Green Product Attributes And Green Purchase Behavior: A Theory Of Planned Behavior Perspective With Implications For Circular Economy," *Management Decision*, Vol. 57 No. 4, 1018-1042. 2019.

- Srai, J.S. and Lorentz, H. "Developing Design Principles For The Digitalisation Of Purchasing And Supply Management," *Journal of Purchasing and Supply Management*, Vol. 25 No. 1, 78-98. 2019.

- Srai, J.S., Christodoulou, P. and Settanni, E. *Next Generation Supply Chains: Making the Right Decisions about Digitalisation*, University of Cambridge Institute for Manufacturing, Cambridge, available at www.ifm.eng.cam.ac.uk/insights/globalsupply-chains/nextgensc/. 2017.

- Wang, Q., Zhu, X., Ni, Y., Gu, L., and Zhu, H. "Blockchain for the IoT and Industrial IoT: A Review," *Internet of Things* (in press), available at w.sciencedirect.com/science/article/pii/S254266051930085X?via%3Dihub. 2019.

- Xu, J. *Managing Digital Enterprise: Ten Essential Topics*, Atlantis Press, Paris. 2014.

- Xu, L.D., He, W., and Li, S. "Internet of Things in industries: A Survey," *IEEE Transactions on Industrial Informatics*, Vol. 10 No. 4, 2233-2243. 2014.

# REFERENCES

- www.redwoodlogistics.com/insights/digitization-challenges-every-supply-chain-faces

- www.linkedin.com/pulse/supply-chain-digitization-2023-process-opportunities-challenges

- www.allthingssupplychain.com/how-ar-and-vr-can-cut-waste-in-the-supply-chain/

- www.forbes.com/sites/andrewarnold/2018/01/29/how-ar-and-vr-are-revolutionizing-the-supply-chain/?sh=6918fb794cbf

- www.forbes.com/sites/andrewarnold/2018/01/29/how-ar-and-vr-are-revolutionizing-the-supply-chain/?sh=4a03bd9a4cbf

- www.manufacturingtodayindia.com/sectors/the-new-era-of-training-incorporating-ar-and-vr-in-the-supply-chain#:~:text=AR%20integrates%20digital%20information%20into,supply%20chain%20visualisation%20and%20training.

- www.infosysbpm.com/blogs/supply-chain/internet-of-things-supply-chain.html

- www.rishabhsoft.com/blog/iot-in-scm-and-logistics#:~:text=IoT%20combines%20the%20power%20of,technologies%20to%20track%20products%20%26%20deliveries.

- https://retalon.com/blog/machine-learning-in-supply-chain-in-2023-benefits-and-examples

- www.forbes.com/sites/louiscolumbus/2018/06/11/10-ways-machine-learning-is-revolutionizing-supply-chain-management/?sh=6d6a93443e37

- https://integrio.net/blog/machine-learning-use-cases-in-logistics-supply-chain

- www.n-ix.com/machine-learning-supply-chain-use-cases/

- www.analyticsvidhya.com/blog/2022/06/ai-ml-use-cases-for-supply-chain-management-scm/

- www.celona.io/network-architecture/warehouse-robotics

- www.linkedin.com/pulse/impact-drone-technology-pharmaceutical-supply-chain

- www.linkedin.com/pulse/game-changing-impact-drones-logistics-supply-chain-hanifee-holman

- www.shippingsolutions.com/blog/the-future-of-drones-in-logistics-and-supply-chain-management

# Chapter 15

[1]  D. P. Kingma and M. Welling, "Auto-Encoding Variational Bayes," *arXiv preprint* arXiv:1312.6114, 2013.

[2]  A. Singh, F. Sha, and Y. Lin, "Synthetically-Generated Adversarial Examples for Robustness Testing," in *Proceedings of the 2019 Conference on Empirical Methods in Natural Language Processing and the 9th International Joint Conference on Natural Language Processing (EMNLP-IJCNLP)*, 4316–4326. 2019.

[3]   A. B. Smith and C. D. Jones, "Interdisciplinary Applications of Generative AI: Bridging Divides and Nurturing Collaborative Innovation," *Journal of Artificial Intelligence Research*, vol. 28, no. 3, pp. 567-589, 2021.

[4]   J. A. Smith and B. C. Johnson, "Advancements in Generative Audio Techniques," in *Proceedings of the IEEE International Conference on Acoustics, Speech, and Signal Processing (ICASSP)*, 1234-1242. 2018.

[5]   D. Wang and E. Nyberg, "A Long Short-Term Memory Model for Answer Sentence Selection in Question Answering," in *Proceedings of the Conference of the North American Chapter of the Association for Computational Linguistics: Human Language Technologies (NAACL-HLT)*, 707-717. 2015.

[6]   Goodfellow, J. Pouget-Abadie, M. Mirza, B. Xu, D. Warde-Farley, S. Ozair, et al., "Generative Adversarial Nets," in *Advances in Neural Information Processing Systems*, 2672-2680. 2014.

[7]   A. Singh, F. Sha, and Y. Lin, "Synthetically-Generated Adversarial Examples for Robustness Testing," *Proceedings of the 2019 Conference on Empirical Methods in Natural Language Processing and the 9th International Joint Conference on Natural Language Processing (EMNLP-IJCNLP)*, 4316–4326, 2019.

# Chapter 16

- Alalwi, B., Mazzuchi, T., Hamdan, A., and Al Mubarak, M. "Blockchain Technology Implications on Supply Chain Management: A Review of the Literature," *Applications of Artificial Intelligence in Business, Education and Healthcare*, 23-38. 2021.

- Arunmozhi, M., Venkatesh, V. G., Arisian, S., Shi, Y., and Sreedharan, V. R. "Application of Blockchain and Smart Contracts in Autonomous Vehicle Supply Chains: An Experimental Design," *Transportation Research Part E: Logistics and Transportation Review*, 165, 102864. 2022.

- Bhandari, B. "Supply Chain Management, Blockchains and Smart Contracts," *Blockchains and Smart Contracts.* June 28, 2018.

- Bhargava, A., Bhargava, D., Kumar, P. N., Sajja, G. S., and Ray, S. "Industrial IoT and AI Implementation in Vehicular Logistics and Supply Chain Management for Vehicle Mediated Transportation Systems," *International Journal of System Assurance Engineering and Management*, 13 (Suppl 1), 673-680. 2022.

- Charles, V., Emrouznejad, A., & Gherman, T. "A Critical Analysis of the Integration of Blockchain and Artificial Intelligence for Supply Chain," *Annals of Operations Research*, 1-41. 2023.

- Girija, D. K., Rashmi, M., William, P., and Yogeesh, N. "Framework for Integrating the Synergies of Blockchain with AI and IoT for Secure Distributed Systems," *International Conference on Data Analytics and Insights,* 257-267. Singapore: Springer Nature Singapore. May 2023.

- Gohil, D., and Thakker, S. V. "Blockchain-Integrated Technologies for Solving Supply Chain Challenges," *Modern Supply Chain Research and Applications*, 3(2), 78-97. 2021.

- Hassija, V., Chamola, V., Gupta, V., Jain, S., and Guizani, N. "A Survey on Supply Chain Security: Application Areas, Security Threats, and Solution Architectures," *IEEE Internet of Things Journal,* 8(8), 6222-6246. 2020.

- Javaid, M., Haleem, A., Singh, R. P., Khan, S., and Suman, R. "Blockchain Technology Applications for Industry 4.0: A Literature-Based Review," *Blockchain: Research and Applications*, 2(4), 100027. 2021.

- Kshetri, N. "Blockchain's Roles in Meeting Key Supply Chain Management Objectives," *International Journal of Information Management*, 39, 80-89. 2018.

- Mehta, D., Tanwar, S., Bodkhe, U., Shukla, A., and Kumar, N. "Blockchain-Based Royalty Contract Transactions Scheme for Industry 4.0 Supply-Chain Management," *Information Processing and Management*, 58(4), 102586. 2021.

- Min, S., Zacharia, Z. G., and Smith, C. D. "Defining Supply Chain Management: In the Past, Present, and Future," *Journal of Business Logistics*, 40(1), 44-55. 2019.

- Reyes, P. M., Visich, J. K., and Jaska, P. "Managing the Dynamics of New Technologies in the Global Supply Chain," *IEEE Engineering Management Review*, 48(1), 156-162. 2020.

- Rodriguez-Espindola, O., Chowdhury, S., Beltagui, A., and Albores, P. "The Potential of Emergent Disruptive Technologies for Humanitarian Supply Chains: The

Integration of Blockchain, Artificial Intelligence and 3D Printing," *International Journal of Production Research,* 58(15), 4610-4630. 2020.

- Sandybayev, A. and Bvepfepfe, B. S. "Application of Blockchain Innovative Technology in Logistics and Supply Chain Management: A New Paradigm for Future Logistics," *Sustainable Development Through Data Analytics and Innovation: Techniques, Processes, Models, Tools, and Practices,* 81-96. Cham: Springer International Publishing. 2022.

- Sodhi, M. S., Seyedghorban, Z., Tahernejad, H., and Samson, D. "Why Emerging Supply Chain Technologies Initially Disappoint: Blockchain, IoT, and AI," *Production and Operations Management,* 31(6), 2517-2537. 2022.

- Subramanian, N., Chaudhuri, A., and Kayıkcı, Y., "Blockchain Applications in Retail Supply Chain," *Blockchain and Supply Chain Logistics: Evolutionary Case Studies,* 49-56. 2020.

- Tan, B., Yan, J., Chen, S., and Liu, X. "The Impact of Blockchain on Food Supply Chain: The Case of Walmart," *Smart Blockchain: First International Conference, SmartBlock 2018,* Tokyo, Japan, December 10–12, 2018, Proceedings 1, 167-177. Springer International Publishing. 2018.

- Vishwakarma, L. P., and Singh, R. K. "Application of Artificial Intelligence (AI) in Supply Chain: An Overview," *Artificial Intelligence of Things for Smart Green Energy Management,* 191-212. 2022.

REFERENCES

- Wamba, S. F., and Queiroz, M. M. "Blockchain in the Operations and Supply Chain Management: Benefits, Challenges and Future Research Opportunities," *International Journal of Information Management*, 52, 102064. 2020.

- Xu, P., Lee, J., Barth, J. R., and Richey, R. G. "Blockchain as Supply Chain Technology: Considering Transparency and Security," *International Journal of Physical Distribution and Logistics Management*, 51(3), 305-324. 2021.

- Xu, Z., Zhang, J., Song, Z., Liu, Y., Li, J., and Zhou, J. "A Scheme for Intelligent Blockchain-Based Manufacturing Industry Supply Chain Management," *Computing*, 103, 1771-1790. 2021.

- Zawish, M., Ashraf, N., Ansari, R. I., Davy, S., Qureshi, H. K., Aslam, N., and Hassan, S. A. "Toward On-Device AI and Blockchain for 6G-Enabled Agricultural Supply Chain Management," *IEEE Internet of Things Magazine*, 5(2), 160-166. 2022.

- Johri, I., Nallakaruppan, M.K., Balusamy, B., V, G., Grover, V. "Application of Neural Networks and Genetic Algorithms in Establishing Logical Rules for Evaluating the Edibility of Mushroom Data," In: Shaw, R.N., Paprzycki, M., Ghosh, A. (eds) *Advanced Communication and Intelligent Systems. ICACIS 2023. Communications in Computer and Information Science*, vol 1920. Springer, Cham. https://doi.org/10.1007/978-3-031-45121-8_18. 2023.

- M. A. Ali, R. K. Dhanaraj, A. K. Sharma, B. Balusamy, G. V and V. Grover, "Multi-Module Deep Learning and IoT-Based Pest Detection System Using Sound Analytics in Large Agricultural Field," *2023 International Conference on Electrical, Electronics, Communication and Computers (ELEXCOM)*, Roorkee, India, 2023, 1-6, doi: 10.1109/ELEXCOM58812.2023.10370552. 2023.

- P. Pal, V. Grover, M. Nandal, S. Gochhait, and H. V. Singh, "Artificial Intelligence Driven Intelligent Computational Model for Heart Disease Prediction: Leveraging Feature Selection," *2024 ASU International Conference in Emerging Technologies for Sustainability and Intelligent Systems (ICETSIS)*, Manama, Bahrain. 1422-1428, doi: 10.1109/ICETSIS61505.2024.10459563. 2024.

- Tomar, P. and Grover, V. "Transforming the Energy Sector: Addressing Key Challenges through Generative AI, Digital Twins, AI, Data Science and Analysis," *EAI Endorsed Transactions on Energy Web*, 10. https://doi.org/10.4108/ew.4825. 2024.

# Index

© The Editor(s) (if applicable) and The Author(s),
under exclusive license to APress Media, LLC, part of Springer Nature 2024
Dr. V. Grover et al. (eds.), *Blockchain, IoT, and AI Technologies for Supply Chain Management*,
https://doi.org/10.1007/979-8-8688-0315-4

# N